# COMPLIMENT

**'If people aren't calling you crazy, you aren't thinking big enough.'**

These days taking chances isn't just for college dropouts in hoodies; everybody needs to think and act like an entrepreneur. We all need to be nimble, adaptive, daring – and maybe even a little crazy – or risk being left behind.

How do you take smart risks without risking it all? That's Linda Rottenberg's expertise. As the co-founder and CEO of Endeavor, the world's leading organization dedicated to supporting fast-growing entrepreneurs, she's spent the last two decades advising innovators.

Now Rottenberg shows you how to achieve your dreams: from overcoming fear to facing down critics, from stalking supporters to exploiting chaos.

*Crazy is a Compliment* combines inspiring stores, original research and practical advice to create a road map for getting started and going big- it brings to life iconic entrepreneurs such as Walt Disney and Estée Lauder, reveals how companies including GE and Burberry have broken the corporate mould, and introduces us to entrepreneurs such as Leila Velez, who started an $80 million hair-care company from her kitchen sink in Rio.

Linda Rottenberg, the co-founder and CEO of Endeavor, has been named one of 'America's Top Leaders' by *U.S. News*, one of 100 'Innovators for the 21st Century' by *Time* magazine, and the world's first 'mentor capitalist' by Tom Friedman. She lives in Brooklyn with her husband, author Bruce Feiler, and their twin daughters.

'Linda has tapped into something important – that we all need to be more entrepreneurial these days. With her impressive track record and inspiring story, she shows us all how to overcome our fears and take smart, achievable steps to improve our organizations'
SHERYL SANDBERG, COO of Facebook and
founder of LeanIn.Org

'Call me crazy, but I think Linda is on to something big here. She delivers powerful insights with her legendary wit and candour to show how everyone can think and act like an entrepreneur'
MICHAEL DELL, founder and CEO, Dell Inc.

'For nearly two decades, Linda has been teaching and learning from the boldest entrepreneurs around the world. In this terrific book, she shares what it takes to master the chaos of starting your own business – or simply to grow your own career in today's fast-changing world of work'
REID HOFFMAN, chairman of LinkedIn and co-author of
*The Start-Up of You*

'*Crazy is a Compliment* is a treasure trove. Linda Rottenberg is an extraordinary entrepreneur who has guided many of the world's greatest entrepreneurs and she offers invaluable insights – not only for start-ups, but also for companies, non-profits, governments and schools. If you have an idea or want to innovate, I highly recommend devouring this book'
ADAM GRANT, author of *Give and Take*

'Crazy is what they call people who don't fit in. And we need a lot more crazy like Linda is crazy. She is generous, curious, connected and driven to make a difference in the world. And this book captures all of that and more. Buy it, read it, live it'
SETH GODIN, author of *Linchpin*

# CRAZY

IS A

# COMPLIMENT

*The Power of Zigging*
*When Everyone Else Zags*

# LINDA ROTTENBERG

CO-FOUNDER AND CEO, ENDEAVOR

PORTFOLIO
PENGUIN

PORTFOLIO PENGUIN

UK | USA | Canada | Ireland | Australia
India | New Zealand | South Africa

Portfolio Penguin is part of the Penguin Random House group of companies
whose addresses can be found at global.penguinrandomhouse.com.

First published in the United States of America by Portfolio/Penguin,
a member of Penguin Group (USA) LLC 2014
First published in Great Britain by Portfolio Penguin 2014
This edition published 2016
001

Illustration credits
Page 44: courtesy of Rodrigo Jordan
Page 112: Endeavor

Printed in Great Britain by Clays Ltd, St Ives plc

A CIP catalogue record for this book is available from the British Library

ISBN: 978-0-670-92378-6

www.greenpenguin.co.uk

MIX
Paper from
responsible sources
FSC
www.fsc.org    FSC® C018179

Penguin Random House is committed to a
sustainable future for our business, our readers
and our planet. This book is made from Forest
Stewardship Council® certified paper.

*For Bruce*
*Who believes in all my crazy dreams*
*and*
*For Tybee and Eden*
*Who inspire me to go home*

# CONTENTS

# INTRODUCTION

# *Why Everybody Needs to Act Like an Entrepreneur*

*I* want to tell you about Leila.

Leila Velez grew up in the slums of Rio de Janeiro. Her mother was a maid; her father, a janitor. In the early 1990s Leila was serving hamburgers at McDonald's. But she had a dream.

Leila was frustrated by how few hair products there were for the curly locks of Afro-Brazilian women like her. "Poor people deserve to feel beautiful, too," she told her sister-in-law Zica, a hairdresser. In 1993 the two amateurs turned Leila's basement into a mad scientist's lab. They tested their first product on their husbands . . . and the men's hair promptly fell out.

Going back to the sink, Leila and Zica perfected their formula and opened a salon. It was an unimpressive place, down a dark corridor, a mere three hundred square feet. "How can you be successful in such a pitiful space?" their friends said. But the sisters pushed on. Soon women in Rio were waiting four to six hours for an appointment, and customers were crediting their products with not only improving their hair texture but also boosting their self-esteem.

When I tell this story to friends, they often say, "That must be one of those charming stories we keep hearing about women in microfinance." But there's nothing micro about Leila's story. Within a few years her company, Beleza Natural, was selling an array of hair products in a handful of "hair clinics." By 2013 Beleza Natural was serving 100,000 customers a month, employing 2,300 people, and earning $80 million a year.

So how did Leila do it? How did she go from being an hourly worker at McDonald's to the leader of a multimillion-dollar franchise? And more to the point: What can the rest of us learn from her story to be more daring in our own lives?

We can learn a lot.

First, we can be reminded of the value of looking at the world through fresh eyes. The legendary retailer Sam Walton once said, "If everybody else is doing it one way, there's a good chance you can find your niche by going in exactly the opposite direction." Leila saw that everybody else was just selling hair products; she would sell confidence. She called her niche lipstick psychology.

Many of the best ideas fulfill a need no one else knows exists. Earle Dickson was a twenty-eight-year-old cotton buyer for Johnson & Johnson in 1920, whose wife, Josephine, kept cutting herself while cooking. To stanch the bleeding, Josephine used the standard remedy, a piece of rag attached with string. The contraptions quickly fell off. Her husband began tinkering and soon presented his wife, then his bosses with an alternative: a self-adhesive bandage with the cotton built in. Band-Aids, as they were called, failed to take off until the company gave away free samples to butchers and Boy Scouts. More than a hundred billion of Earle's inventions have since been sold.

Next, we can learn that psychology plays an enormous role in tackling risk. The biggest barriers to success are not structural or cultural; they are mental and emotional. At every turn, someone (or, more likely, *everyone*) will call you and your idea crazy. The job of the innovator is to push past naysayers and find a way to drive forward. Leila was soft-spoken and shy. She wasn't used to bold action, confrontation, or speaking out. Before she could foster confidence in others, she first had to discover it in herself.

Finally, we can learn that risk takers rarely go it alone. Those seeking to disrupt the status quo need support. And support doesn't just mean financial, though that always helps. More often it means advice on handling fear, navigating tricky growth decisions, and breaking an intimidating task into manageable chunks. When Steve Jobs was just starting out, he sought the counsel of Robert Noyce, the coinventor of the microchip and the unofficial mayor of Silicon Valley. As with everything he did, Jobs took this relationship to an extreme. He would drop by Noyce's house uninvited on his motorcycle or telephone around midnight. An exasperated Noyce finally told his wife, "If he calls one more time I'm just not going to pick up the phone!"

But of course Noyce always picked up. Entrepreneurs always find a way.

So where did Leila go to get the backing she needed?

That's where my story intersects with hers. In 1997 I cofounded an organization called Endeavor to support dreamers like Leila. In nearly two decades, Endeavor has screened forty thousand candidates and selected roughly one thousand individuals from more than six hundred fast-growing companies to be part of our network. We discovered these innovators in the least likely places: cyber cafés in South Africa, sandwich shops in Mexico, women-only gyms in Turkey; gamer hangouts in Indonesia; ceviche stores in the United States. We've worked with founders in such crazily diverse fields as biometric eye scanning, snail farming, pharmacy franchising, and wind turbine manufacturing. We've helped daring individuals operate in such challenging environments as Athens in the midst of a currency crisis, Cairo in the throes of a revolution, and Miami as it emerged out of recession.

We call these business leaders high-impact entrepreneurs, a term Endeavor coined in 2004. High-impact means individuals with the biggest ideas, the likeliest potential to build businesses that matter, and the greatest ability to inspire others. Once we invite these leaders into our network we do whatever we can to help them succeed, from forming advisory boards to accessing capital, from hiring talent to honing leadership. And we encourage them to nurture and mentor the next generation.

Today Endeavor has offices in forty-five cities around the world, employs 350 people, and has a pool of 5,000 volunteer mentors. While some of our ventures lose steam, the vast majority have grown at an impressive rate. In 2013 the entrepreneurs we support generated close to $7 billion in revenues and provided more than 400,000 jobs.

My experience has taught me that the capacity to dream big is not confined to any country, age, or gender. The desire to take initiative, be your own boss, advance your life, and improve the world is universal.

But the roadblocks are universal, too.

I've spent the last two decades working to identify the common mistakes and specific stumbling blocks that innovators face as they attempt to turn their ideas into reality. I've sought to isolate the mix of concrete steps, strategic support, and emotional encouragement they need to bring their ideas to the next level. And I've learned when change makers need a shoulder to cry on and when they need a kick in the pants.

When I met Leila, for example, she was eager to expand yet scrambling to keep pace with demand. She was overwhelmed. To help, we introduced her to mentors who could support her growth. We encouraged her to create a shareholder agreement with her in-laws. When she got divorced, Leila even found a new husband through our network. (She got what I call the full-service treatment!)

But most important, we showed her that instead of being alone, she's part of the biggest movement in the world today, the unstoppable, unwavering trend toward individuals who seek to improve their own lives and, in the process, improve the world around them.

She's an entrepreneur.

## — *ENTREPRENEURSHIP ISN'T JUST FOR ENTREPRENEURS ANYMORE* —

I wrote this book because I believe that we all have a little Leila within us.

Every day I meet people with a dream. Those people are just like Leila—and just like you. Maybe you're serving coffee and fantasizing about launching a microbrewery; maybe you've skipped college and yearn to start your own design firm; maybe you're sitting in your cubicle and brainstorming a new idea that can improve your company; maybe you've got a plan to improve the environment; maybe you're a stay-at-home parent with an idea for a new mobile app; or maybe you're a retiree hoping to start a B&B.

You have a dream, but you don't know how to turn your dream into reality. Or you've already launched your dream, but you're unsure how to take it to the next level.

This book can show you the way.

I'm going to impart lessons I've learned from helping Leila and a thousand others like her. I'll disclose the results of intensive research conducted over several years by the Endeavor team and our partners at Bain & Company. I'll lay out the insights I've been taking to Fortune 500 companies the last few years because they, too, want to become more entrepreneurial. And I'll share my own up-and-down story of building (and occasionally rebuilding) a fast-growing organization that's a hybrid of nonprofit and for-profit.

Above all, I'm going to try to show you that no matter what you're doing right now, no matter what dream you're trying to get going or grow bigger, you need these lessons.

You need to think and act more like an entrepreneur.

When we started Endeavor in the late 1990s, the word "entrepreneur" was not very popular. It wasn't even used by most people who started companies. Adapted from the French word meaning "to undertake," entrepreneurship existed as an academic concept, but the expression—or any expression like it, for that matter—was barely used in most countries. Even most Americans viewed entrepreneurship as a rarefied notion that applied only to founders of the fastest-growing (or fastest-failing) enterprises. And at the risk of my pointing out the obvious, those leaders were mostly young, mostly in tech, and mostly male.

That stereotype no longer holds. Today entrepreneurship doesn't just mean starting a tech company. It means undertaking any bold venture—from improving your neighborhood to selling crafts out of your basement; from modernizing your family business to proposing a new initiative in your corporation. The techniques involved in sharpening your idea, facing down critics, recruiting boosters, and handling setbacks apply in almost every realm of work.

Entrepreneurship, defined as a nimble, creatively destructive, optimistic force, has become the go-to problem-solving technique of the twenty-first century. If some moments have been ripe for diplomats, financiers, soldiers, or politicians, today is ripe for entrepreneurs. Now, that may sound a little grand. But scroll through the Internet, flip through a corporate annual report, visit a college campus, listen to moms and dads at school drop-off: Everyone is talking about being a force of disruption, trying a fresh approach, becoming an agent of change. Alexis Ohanian, the founder of Reddit, put it well: "'I have a startup' is the new 'I'm in a band.'" Even the Boy Scouts now have an entrepreneurship merit badge and Mattel has Entrepreneur Barbie!

The reasons behind this shift are complex, but they come down to a simple reality: We live in a time of uncertainty. Our economies, our companies, our jobs are no longer stable and secure. Change is the only constant. To survive, we all need the skills required to continually reinvent ourselves. Everyone needs to take some risk or risk being left behind.

Here's the good news: Anybody can be a change agent today. There are no admission criteria. There is no wardrobe requirement. There is no secret vote.

Entrepreneurship is for everyone.

But here's the bad news: We don't really have a language to discuss this wide swath of workers who are becoming more entrepreneurial.

The word "entrepreneur," once underused, is now in jeopardy of being overused. As a result, lots of people (me included) began taking this clunky word and adding all sorts of qualifiers to it, making it even clunkier. Suddenly we had "social entrepreneur" to describe those building mission-driven organizations that focus on everything from human rights to the environment; "microentrepreneur" to describe individuals starting lifestyle businesses; "intrapreneur" to label change makers within large corporations; "copreneurs" to describe couples starting businesses; even "mompreneurs," "dadpreneurs," and "kidpreneurs." These terms became so unwieldy that on Twitter everyone just gave up and shortened "entrepreneurs" to #treps.

@*#&!

Trust me, as someone who's sat on a gazillion panels about the "future of entrepreneurship," I know we need a new lexicon.

In this book I want to try a different approach, one that I hope is clearer and certainly more fun. I've given each of these different groups a name. The names are simple, easy to understand, and reflective of the arenas in which people operate. They represent four different species, and they all need help in realizing their dreams. One of these species surely applies to you.

**GAZELLES**. This is the classic entrepreneur of myth and reality, someone who starts a new business venture and aims for it to explode into a white-hot phenomenon—Home Depot, Facebook, Jenny Craig, Under Armour, Instagram. High growth is the goal. The Endeavor entrepreneurs I work with fall into this category—or they aspire to, at least.

The term "gazelle" was coined by the economist David Birch in 1994. It describes high-growth businesses whose sales double every four years. Though only 2 to 4 percent of companies fit this model in the United States, this otherwise minuscule group accounts for nearly all private-sector job creation. When you hear politicians say, "Small businesses create most of the new jobs," they're really talking about the young and growing firms. They're talking about gazelles. Birch chose gazelles because they're fast moving and high jumping.

You would think gazelles already know how to be successful entrepreneurs, but in my experience, they don't. Sure, they know how to start something, but unfortunately they keep making the same mistakes over and over again: They expand too quickly; they lose focus; they tangle with their partners; they can't give up control. (And yup, I've made all those mistakes, too, which I'll discuss in detail.) After seeing these pitfalls repeatedly, I developed a list of the most common mistakes made by gazelles and a playbook for how to avoid them if you want your start-up to become a big enterprise.

**SKUNKS.** The term "intrapreneur," which first popped up in the 1970s and first appeared in the *American Heritage Dictionary* in 1992, is defined as a person within a large corporation who takes responsibility for "turning an idea into a profitable finished product through assertive risk-taking and innovation." While the word is no more pleasing today, the idea is a lot more popular: Encouraging people to be more independent and creative inside corporations has become an urgent cry.

In 2013 I was invited to speak at Dell World on a panel about disruption. The founder, Michael Dell, had just taken the company private after a long battle with shareholders. He declared his intention to restore the firm's entrepreneurial DNA, returning it to its roots in Room 2713 of the Dobie Center at the University of Texas. Michael opened the conference of six thousand people by saying, "Welcome to the world's largest start-up!"

But while encouraging employees to take more risks is simple, getting them to follow through is hard. "Some are afraid of change," Michael told me later. "This resistance is almost certainly a path of disaster in any fast-changing business." There are the quick, he said, or the dead.

Michael isn't the only corporate leader seeking to reclaim his company's entrepreneurial mojo. Most of the world's top CEOs realize they have to disrupt their own organizations before others beat them to it. Yet somehow this message is not getting through to many of their employees. If you work in a large corporation today, with a benefits package and retirement plan, you may think you're safe. You may think all this entrepreneurial undertaking is not for you. But you'd be wrong.

While starting something new involves peril, *not* starting something new today is just as perilous, if not more so. Pretending your job is safe and your company is stable leaves you dangerously exposed. If you think risk taking is risky, being risk averse is often riskier.

First of all, your company itself isn't safe. The topple rate of big companies, a metric that gauges how often they lose their leadership positions, more than doubled between 1965 and 2008. A new member of the S&P index in the 1920s could expect to remain on the list for sixty-five years. By 2012 that average had dropped to eighteen years. In the last five years alone, S&P 500 mainstays like Heinz, Sprint, Sara Lee, RadioShack, Kodak, Office Depot, and the New York Times Company all fell from the list.

Even if your company continues to thrive, your ability to survive in it depends on your capacity and willingness to innovate. Job security these days depends on the same qualities that make good entrepreneurs: agility, imagination, persistence, execution. To put it another way, adapt from within or you may be forced to adapt from without.

Become a skunk. I've adopted this term from the Lockheed Corporation, which during World War II set up a secret division to build fighter jets. It was called Skunk Works. Though rumor suggested the name came from the poor hygiene habits of the overworked employees, it actually came from the moonshine factory in the cartoon series *Li'l Abner.* (The moonshine was said to be created by grinding up dead skunks.) Either way, the message is clear: Entrepreneurs operating within large corporations go out of their way to stink up the joint.

**DOLPHINS.** For the last decade or so, there's been abundant lip service paid to the idea that the social sector must become more entrepreneurial. *Nonprofits need to employ more business techniques. Philanthropy needs to be more innovative and metrics driven.* I've been involved in this movement for twenty-five years and been lucky to have had the chance to work with two of its pioneers.

In 1989 I volunteered to help Wendy Kopp recruit college seniors to join her start-up, Teach For America. When she proposed creating a national teacher corps in her senior thesis at Princeton, her adviser responded, "My Dear Ms. Kopp, you are quite evidently deranged." But Wendy would not be deterred. Teach For America now receives more than fifty thousand applications each year and has an annual budget of $350 million.

I later went to work for Bill Drayton, the "godfather of social entrepreneurship." Bill was among the first to fund social entrepreneurs through his organization, Ashoka. Having supported more than three thousand nonprofit innovators across the globe, Bill champions the idea that anyone, anywhere can be a change maker. "Everyone gets to be a player," he said.

Despite these trendsetters, too many nonprofits, community groups, and social service organizations continue to lag behind the age of disruption. They lack leaders willing to deploy the full range of entrepreneurial skills needed to scale their ideas and maximize their impact. What they need are more dolphins.

Dolphins are my nickname for contrarians in the nonprofit or public sector who are willing to buck the conventions of their professions and agitate for real change. Why dolphins? Because they're smart and social (they live in cooperative groups, called pods) and are one of the few animals shown to be altruistic toward others. But they're not pushovers: Harm a dolphin's pod, and watch out! Today even causes for which there are no compelling private-sector solutions are ripe for entrepreneurial shake-up. It's dolphins making the waves.

**BUTTERFLIES.** There's a final collection of entrepreneurs who need these lessons, and they may be the fastest-growing group of all. These are small-scale or lifestyle entrepreneurs.

First among these are sole proprietors—plumbers, yoga instructors, freelance writers, organic farmers, artists. The U.S. Census Bureau estimates that a majority of U.S. businesses have no paid employees. Forty percent of American adults have now spent part of their careers working on their own, and 24 million more are expected to be self-employed by 2018. Globally the number of independent contractors will reach 1.3 billion by 2020. These fields are booming because they're open to anyone: moms, dads, grannies, twenty-somethings, even teens starting microventures in their basements, cars, or bathrooms. (Yes, bathtub brews are back!) As Jay-Z put it, "I'm not a businessman; I'm a business, man."

The second part of this group has just a handful of employees. There are seven million companies in America that employ workers; 90 percent of them have fewer than twenty. While some of these entrepreneurs aim to be fast-growing gazelles, most are content to stay small and local.

I'm dubbing this species butterflies because butterflies are varied (there are at least 17,500 different types of butterfly) and driven by freedom and individualism. In both Eastern and Western cultures, butterflies have long symbolized the soul, especially one reborn after a period of cocooning. Beyond personal transformation, butterflies are vital to their habitat and an indicator of its overall well-being. More butterflies equal a healthier ecosystem.

At first glance, this group would hardly seem a candidate for the skill set of groundbreaking entrepreneurs. Do you really need to be disruptive when you're selling homemade cheese at the farmers' market? The answer: You do, especially because your competitor probably has an in at Whole Foods, now accepts credit card payments with a Square reader, and has just launched a vibrant Web business. Etsy, the online arts, crafts, and food hub, now has more than a million "makers" selling goods directly to consumers. Even butterflies need to spread their wings.

Besides, butterflies are uniquely suited to this age of disruption. In chaos theory, "butterfly effect" is the term given to the idea that change can come from anywhere. The weather in Central Park can be affected by a butterfly's flapping its wings in South America.

I saw the sensitivity and fearlessness of butterflies firsthand on the eve of Superstorm Sandy, near my home in Brooklyn. I had stopped in to buy bread from my favorite local bakery, Bien Cuit. It was not long after the mayor announced evacuations. "I guess you'll be closing soon," I said to the man behind the counter.

"No way," he replied. "The neighborhood needs us. We're going to stay open all night."

Don't underestimate the tenacity of a butterfly.

Today, nearly two decades after I first started hunting down entrepreneurs, innovators of all types are popping up everywhere. They aren't waiting for changes to happen to them; they're making changes happen every day.

Whatever your passion, pick one of these species and start writing your story—or risk being an ostrich, with your head stuck in the sand.

## — *THE SECRET SAUCE OF ENTREPRENEURSHIP* —

But once you've embraced the life of a change maker, how do you know what to do next?

Again, that's where I come into the picture.

I'd like to invite you into my bedroom for a second. You'll find several things of interest there. An African bedspread I brought back from my travels. A poem my husband wrote for me when he proposed. And on the nightstand next to my side of the bed, a stack of half-read books. They're all about entrepreneurship.

I love entrepreneurship. I don't love its literature. When I sat down to work on this book, I made a list of everything I didn't want it to be. It wouldn't be a how-to manual for writing a business plan, developing a marketing strategy, or reading a venture capital (VC) term sheet. It wouldn't be an academic primer on the history of entrepreneurship. It wouldn't be an inspirational graduation speech filled with feel-good bromides. And it wouldn't be the story of one person's journey to success. If that's what you're looking for, go read Howard Schultz's *Pour Your Heart Into It*, Richard Branson's *Losing My Virginity*, Tony Hsieh's *Delivering Happiness*, or Walter Isaacson's *Steve Jobs*, all books I read and enjoyed.

Here's what this book is: It's the story of the entrepreneurial journeys of many people—gazelles, skunks, dolphins, and butterflies—and what the rest of us can learn from them. It's my attempt to break down a process that often seems overwhelming into a series of achievable steps. It's my shot at answering this question: Since everybody has to take risks these days, how do you make sure you're taking smart risks?

To answer that, I've divided the book into three sections: "Get Going," "Go Big," and "Go Home."

In "Get Going," I'll lay out the road map for becoming an entrepreneur: from battling inner fear to fending off skeptics, to stalking supporters, to exploiting chaos. The theme in this section is attitude: how to get yourself the right one and brush off the wrong one.

In "Go Big," I'll talk about how to take your idea to scale. To do that, I'll help you figure out your entrepreneur personality, avoid rookie mistakes, find the right mentors, and learn how to lead. "Leadership 3.0" is my term for the new skills required to attract and retain today's hyperconnected, hyperskilled, hypersensitive talent.

Finally, in "Go Home," I'll discuss what it means to live like an entrepreneur. This includes how to cultivate meaning in your workplace and how to integrate your work with your family. If the first two sections are the craft of entrepreneurship, I consider this the art. This part is also the most personal to me. I believe deeply that part of the mantle of entrepreneurship is to inspire and help others to follow this path. Also, as a mom who runs a large organization I've fought hard to maintain a harmony between my professional life and my family life, and I encourage my team to do the same.

Altogether, these topics capture what I've learned in two decades of experiencing the ups and downs of the entrepreneurial life. They are why I wanted to write this book. But there's one more reason that explains why I wanted to write it now.

## — YOU DON'T NEED A HOODIE TO BE AN ENTREPRENEUR —

In 2012 I visited Wilkes University, a vibrant campus tucked away in an old mining town in central Pennsylvania, to give a talk about entrepreneurship. Toward the end of the Q&A, a hand shot up in back. "I like your stories about entrepreneurs," he said, "but I'm wondering if they apply to me. I don't have an idea that's big enough. I don't have the right connections. And I don't live in Silicon Valley."

A little taken aback and somewhat distracted (I knew my seven-year-old daughters were waiting up for me at home), I said the first thing that came to mind: "Don't worry. You don't need a hoodie to be an entrepreneur. Anybody can be one." The answer worked fine enough, but all during my ride home, I was haunted by his question and increasingly disappointed by my glib response.

In the early years of Endeavor, whenever I bumped into anyone who didn't quite understand what we were doing (which is to say, most people I met), I would sum it up by saying, "We're taking the magic of Silicon Valley and sprinkling it in places with talent and big ideas, but no belief in the ability of individuals to turn those ideas into reality." I used to think that applied only to people like Leila.

Now everyone needs a bit of that magic.

We all need a little bit of Leila in our lives.

By the time I got home to Brooklyn that night, I had decided to write this book. I wanted to write it for those students in Pennsylvania. I wanted to write it for my twin daughters waiting up to say good night. I wanted to write it for all those who have a dream they don't know how to realize, who want to marry their passions with their everyday lives, who want to make an impact on their companies, their communities, or the larger world.

In her classic cookbook *Mastering the Art of French Cooking* Julia Child, herself a genre-making, ceiling-breaking entrepreneur, wrote, "Anyone can cook in the French manner anywhere, with the right instruction." This book takes a similar view toward dreaming big and making change.

I used to believe in the maxim that entrepreneurs are "born, not made." Now I believe that entrepreneurship, like great cooking, can be practiced and honed by anybody with a desire to learn. (Also, just like master chefs, even the most skilled entrepreneurs drop some pans and break a few eggs along the way.)

In the end, mastering the art of entrepreneurship is not simply about starting a business. It's about taking chances, overcoming doubts, managing risk, dealing with chaos, cultivating employees, coping with stumbles and successes, integrating work and family, and paying it forward to ensure that the next generation can dream big as well.

And it's realizing that all those people calling you crazy are giving you a huge compliment.

So let's get going.

# PART I

## Get Going

# CHAPTER 1

## Getting to Day One

*I*n the spring of 1998 I stepped into a small, unassuming office in a nondescript neighborhood of Buenos Aires. I went there to meet Wences Casares, a charismatic twentysomething with a crazy idea. When I walked out several hours later, I was carrying one of the more important lessons I ever learned about entrepreneurship: The most valuable backer you need to start any venture is not your mother, father, spouse, boss, banker, or friend. It's not anyone else at all. It's you.

And you're the hardest backer you'll ever have to win.

Before we talk about what it takes to get an initiative under way, we have to talk about what it means to get yourself in the proper frame of mind. You can't convince others until you first convince yourself. Few people I know have done this under more extreme circumstances than Wences.

Wences was born on a sheep farm in Patagonia—twenty miles from the nearest neighbor and one hundred miles from the closest town. His father was a rancher, but also a ham radio operator and DIYer. He gave each of his four children a computer in the bedroom and jerry-rigged a local network so they could communicate with one another.

"The biggest impact my father had on me was showing me how to be a doer," Wences said. "Living in the middle of nowhere, we constantly had to come up with creative ways of solving problems, like digging trenches or building bridges on the side of a mountain."

Being an entrepreneur is just a fancy way of saying you're a doer, he told me.

And did he ever do! In high school Wences started a T-shirt painting shop. He also downloaded a mismatched database of all the telephone numbers in Patagonia, corrected the mistakes, published a series of directories, and sold advertising. He earned $80,000. The first person in his family to attend college, Wences started yet another business while attending classes. It was the inaugural Internet service provider in Argentina. A year later he sold the firm in a deal he thought kept him as part of the team. After signing the contract, Wences showed up at his office and was locked out. He got virtually nothing.

In these early ventures, Wences was unbowed by fear, and no wonder, he had little at stake. But now the stakes were getting higher. While still enrolled at university, he set out to create a financial services portal for Latin America, a local E*Trade. But his studies were getting in the way, so he traveled one thousand miles back to Patagonia to inform his father he was dropping out of college. In what he described as the scariest moment of his life, Wences also told his dad he'd asked his two sisters to drop out of school, too, and join him.

His father considered the information for a few minutes, then said, "Do it right." His unspoken message: "Don't shame the family."

At this point things started to really get scary, and Wences, for the first time, began to question himself. He lived in a community where going it alone was not valued, family reputation was everything, and the ability of him or his sisters to build a career or find a spouse was now on the line. And worse, nobody liked his idea. Thirty-three investors turned him down. "We barely have a functioning stock market," he was told. "How can we possibly support an electronic trading platform?"

I listened to this story while sitting in Wences's grungy office in Buenos Aires, surrounded by a few broken-down computers and peeling wallpaper. "I want to keep going," he said. "But sometimes I look at my sisters sleeping in our tiny apartment, and I think, 'Am I crazy?'"

He turned to me. "Do you think I'm crazy?"

"Yes," I said. "But that's why you're going to succeed. Plus, I think I can help."

Wences's story shows that the first step to becoming an entrepreneur does not happen in a laboratory, a conference room, or even a pitch session. It happens in the mind. And not the part of the mind where the lightbulbs go off and the ahas are heard. It happens in the part where the darkness resides and the doubts cry out. It happens in that place where you start to get worried about your rent, your mortgage, your children, your debt building up on your credit card, your reputation in the cafeteria, your sisters sleeping on the couch.

It happens when you're exposed.

Jeff Bezos has a wonderful way of describing this heightened mind-set of being an entrepreneur. He calls the mix of anticipation, excitement, and uncertainty Day One. In Bezos's coinage, "Day One" is not a date on a calendar; it's a commitment to seeing every day as a fresh opportunity to create something new. Sixteen years after Amazon started, Bezos concluded a shareholder letter by saying his approach remains unchanged: "It's still Day One."

At Endeavor we adopted Bezos's concept and turned it into a rallying cry to help entrepreneurs acknowledge and overcome their moments of insecurity and fear. We even started a series of talks in which change makers described their Day One experiences. We tell speakers, "Don't focus on the idea; focus on the emotions, the challenges." When I gave one of these talks, my team rejected multiple drafts and pushed me to be more revealing.

In the next few chapters I'll talk about this process of overcoming emotional hurdles and getting an idea out of the shower, off the napkin, and into the world. While it may appear intimidating and others will surely call you nuts, there are actually a host of concrete ways to reduce your hazard and maximize your chances of success.

But first, I'm going to focus on what it means to give yourself permission to undertake such a challenge to begin with. To me this is the breakthrough step to thinking and acting like an entrepreneur. I'll even put it in a formula:

heart + mind - fear = entrepreneur

Or to put it another way, entrepreneurship begins with psyching yourself up instead of psyching yourself out.

## — THE DISTANCE BETWEEN YOUR EARS —

In the early 2000s green products were gaining popularity in the United States, but one industry was stubbornly resistant: home cleaning products. Eco-friendly offerings brought in only 1 percent of the industry's $12 billion in sales. Clorox, the market leader, was particularly slow to adapt. It took two corporate skunks to crack the formula, but first they had to crack an even trickier code: how to be entrepreneurial in a conservative company while also finding time to be moms.

Mary Jo Cook was in a bind. She was a new mother eager to spend time with her young daughter, but she was also an ambitious executive at Clorox. So she did something virtually unheard of at the century-old company: She made her job part-time. "People were pretty shocked," she told me. "There was only one professional working less than full-time." Initially Mary Jo went to four days, then to three and a half when her second child was born.

Part of negotiating her own schedule meant designing a new role. "There weren't typical jobs you could just drop into," she said. The job she eventually created was heading a new division focused on innovation. When the job became too big, a colleague and fellow parent, Suzanne Sengelmann, proposed that the two share the role— another breakthrough. Their arrangement perfectly embodies the flexibility required of these entrepreneurial times. Beyond dividing responsibilities, Mary Jo and Suzanne merged themselves into one entity. Each worked three days a week, overlapping on Wednesdays. They shared a title (vice president), a voice mail, and an e-mail account. They even went by a joint name, Sam, a combination of Suzanne and MJ.

Initially, Suzanne and Mary Jo were apprehensive. "Our biggest fear was failing at the job," Suzanne told me. "Because we were so high profile in the company, we were fearful that if we blew it, we would rob other women of the opportunity—both at Clorox and perhaps even broader."

To their relief, not only did the new arrangement work, but it had added benefits. The act of thinking more creatively about their responsibilities encouraged them to think more creatively about their work. Also, the fact that they weren't stuck in the office all day meant they were hanging out with their customers at the playground. "Sam" kept hearing from fellow moms in the Bay Area that they were concerned about the impact of cleaning products on their children. And it wasn't just others. "You know what?" Suzanne said. "I have concerns. I clean. I grocery shop. Just having the opportunity to live the life of our core consumer was a huge advantage."

"Sam" had found a new calling: Clorox should create environmentally sensitive products targeted to moms.

But MJ and Suzanne had a problem, too. They knew their plan could face resistance from colleagues. Any "nontoxic" product threatened to make Clorox's other products look "toxic." This was their true test: Would they talk themselves out of their project before it got started or risk alienating those around them by challenging the core identity of the company?

Their answer: They gave themselves a quiet, under-the-radar mandate. In Mary Jo's phrase, they took "smart risks." That included giving themselves permission to spend a fifth of their time dabbling with their idea. "We told our boss it was ten percent," Suzanne told me, "but really it was closer to twenty." They called it their skunk project.

"The beauty of a skunk project," Suzanne said, "is you don't have to go through the same processes and approvals and questions and all that; you can just do it."

And they did. First, they went to their local supermarket and bought every green product. None impressed them. Next, they reached out to target consumers, whom they dubbed chemical-avoiding naturalists. Then they discovered another underground group at Clorox—this one comprised of chemists. (It, too, was headed by a working mom.) This group was also tinkering with biodegradable formulas and had adopted the nickname Project Kermit to celebrate its interest in all things green. The two teams merged forces. They kept their bosses informed but didn't ask for explicit sign-off; they paid expenses out of existing budgets.

Project Kermit's early efforts failed. "The first time there wasn't enough of a market interest," Mary Jo said. "The second time the technology wasn't good enough. The third time all the pieces came together." In late 2007 Clorox released Green Works. Through a novel endorsement deal, products were packaged with the seal of the Sierra Club. Within six months the new line had captured 40 percent of the natural market. Within five years Green Works was a $60 million annual business. It may not be easy being green, but with a little ingenuity, two skunks named "Sam" found a way to make it profitable.

What's striking about this story is the willingness of two part-time executives to resist their own temptation to hold themselves back as they pursued an unconventional project. Time after time I've seen people considering doing something bold get stuck at this stage. They keep waiting for someone else to give them permission, but here's what I've learned: That someone doesn't exist.

The only person who can give you permission to take risk is you.

When I asked Suzanne how people inside more traditional corporations can give themselves that green light, she said, "I believe that in every company, no matter how traditional, there are entrepreneurial idea people. But ideas are fragile. Ideas require conviction. They require knowing something is right in your gut because there's no physics or data that supports the idea."

Egyptian-born Amr Shady also had an idea in his gut, but before he could pursue his entrepreneurial dream, he first had to get over his fear of disappointing his father. Growing up in Cairo, Amr was a talented math and physics student. He went to university at fifteen and after graduation went to work at a safe managerial job in his father's electrical engineering company with offices across the Middle East. By twenty-one he was running the company's Egypt operations. Soon, though, he grew bored. He didn't want to take over his father's company, he realized; he wanted to start his own. But it took him years to muster up the courage to confront his dad.

"I didn't want to let him down," Amr told me. "I was supposed to be helping him, and now I wanted to go out on my own. Facing my father was the biggest burden I had."

Amr's father surprised him by giving his blessing. "I was happy he had the entrepreneurial spirit," he said. Amr started a telecom company that provided apps and other services for mobile phones. In 2010 he became an Endeavor entrepreneur.

What he took away from this experience was the importance of confronting your demons. "When I started out," Amr told me, "I thought the biggest business challenges had to do with things like raising money, the cost of complying with tax regulations, and issues with the legal and regulatory environment. But these turned out to be minor issues." Even the revolutions that have swept the region proved relatively minor compared with the biggest challenge Amr faced.

The real problem was self-censorship, he said. When I asked him to explain, he reminded me of the story of how the under-four-minute mile came to be. Before 1954 everyone thought the four-minute mile was the physical limit of the human body. When Roger Bannister broke the world record, he also broke a psychological barrier. By the end of 1957 sixteen runners had accomplished the feat. "Too many aspiring entrepreneurs make the pre-Bannister mistake," Amr said. "We censor ourselves. We discount our potential and therefore don't make it big. I'm still guilty of that myself."

Amr's chief lesson: Don't look to others to validate your desires; look to yourself. Or as the legendary Bob Jones said about golf, it's "a game played on a five-inch course—the distance between your ears."

## — WHAT I'M SUPPOSED TO BE —

I relate to this idea of psychological tests because I faced one myself. I was raised in a traditional family in the suburbs of Boston. My parents were high school sweethearts in Rhode Island who met at a dance when they were fourteen and seventeen. My dad went on to become a lawyer; my mother, a homemaker. Throughout my childhood my parents were incredibly loving, intently focused on education, and almost genetically risk averse. Chance taking was for others; they valued steadiness and security above all else.

Some of this unease with risk rubbed off on me. I went to Harvard and then opted for the safe path and applied to law school. But once I got to Yale Law School, I quickly discovered that I didn't want to be a lawyer. This was hard for me to admit. I had spent my whole life playing it safe, trying to please others. Now I wanted to figure out who I was, and what I wanted to be.

I had a childhood pen pal in Uruguay and, on a whim, went to sleep on her couch. My parents said, "It's just a phase." (They also made sure I took the bar exam before I left.) Soon I moved to Buenos Aires and started dancing tango and cheering for local soccer teams. I paid my way by working at a local law school. But I was also looking over my shoulder and becoming enchanted with a new type of celebrity emerging back home: the start-up CEO.

This was the gilded age of Bill Gates, Michael Dell, and Howard Schultz. It was soon after the blockbuster initial public offerings (IPOs) of Netscape and Yahoo! sent Silicon Valley entrepreneurs scampering to start the "new new thing." It was when two computer science grad students named Sergey Brin and Larry Page were testing their idea to revolutionize Internet search; when Steven Spielberg, Jeffrey Katzenberg, and David Geffen were bucking the studio system to form DreamWorks; when Vera Wang left her mentor, Ralph Lauren, to revolutionize bridal wear; when Pierre Omidyar managed to auction a broken laser pointer on a new e-commerce site that would come to be called eBay; when Steve Jobs made his dramatic return to Apple; and when a Wall Street refugee named Jeff Bezos took a cross-country drive to Seattle during which he honed a plan to sell books online.

I became a convert to entrepreneurship. It seemed to fit the mood of rebellion and individualism I was experiencing. It seemed to offer the opportunity to remake the world in your image. It seemed daring.

Soon enough I tried out my newfound zeal in my newfound community. My friends were puzzled. "What do you mean start a business?" Once I told a group of students in Brazil the legendary story of Steve Jobs and Steve Wozniak's working on the first Apple computer in the Jobs family garage. "That's a nice story," one guy said, "but how does it relate to my life? No one will give me money to launch my idea . . . and I don't even have a garage!"

Then, one day, late for a meeting in Buenos Aires, I hopped in a taxi and struck up a conversation with the driver. He told me he had an engineering degree but couldn't find a job. The only employers hiring were government bureaucracies and old-school corporations, he said, neither of which had much use for someone with his skills.

"Forgive me," I said to the driver, "but wouldn't you rather be a—" I paused. I didn't know the Spanish equivalent for what I was trying to communicate. "An entrepreneur?" I asked, in English.

"A what?" he said.

"An entrepreneur," I repeated. "You know, someone who starts a business."

"Oh, you mean an *empresario*," he said dismissively, referring to the Spanish word for "big businessman," a term associated more with cronyism and greed than with innovation and growth.

"No, not *empresario*. What's the Spanish word for 'entrepreneur'?"

He shrugged. "I don't think there is a word like that here."

"Well, that explains it," I thought. No wonder I hadn't seen any high-flying, high-growth entrepreneurs in Latin America. Not only did these countries lack start-up capital, but they didn't even have a common word for such a person!

Suddenly I had a vision. What if there was an organization to help entrepreneurs around the world get started and go to scale? What if we harnessed the power of individual dreamers and high-growth businesses to transform local economies? What if we created a global movement around innovation?

I went back home to the United States and started talking up my idea. First, I went to my boss at my new job at Ashoka, the pioneering organization that works with social entrepreneurs. I suggested he branch out from nonprofit innovators (dolphins, in my lexicon) and start an arm to support for-profit entrepreneurs (gazelles). He told me he had his hands full. Next, I shared my idea with friends working in international development, on Wall Street, and even in Silicon Valley. Nothing.

I was beginning to learn an important lesson about starting anything new: Being misunderstood is part of the process. If contrarian thinking is the first step to becoming an entrepreneur, then you can't expect others—especially those following more traditional paths—to embrace your vision at the outset. Often your best hope is to find another outlier who's passionate about the same thing.

In my case that person was the twenty-seven-year-old American entrepreneur Peter Kellner. Peter's father is a Hungarian immigrant; his mother is from a suburb of Detroit. A JD-MBA student at the time, Peter had already started companies in Russia and Eastern Europe. When we met, he had just returned from China, where he, too, had the idea to support high-growth entrepreneurs. We quickly decided to team up.

In our first meeting we sat at my parents' kitchen table in Boston and, in cliché fashion, sketched out a plan to start an organization on the back of a napkin. Yes, an actual napkin. We chose our name from a quote Peter suggested by Henry David Thoreau: "I know of no more encouraging fact than the unquestionable ability of man to elevate his life by conscious endeavor." (I liked the word "endeavor" and ignored the whiff of sexism.)

My parents were listening from the other side of the room. They weren't pleased.

My mom interrupted. "Linda," she said, "you're not thinking of giving up your job for this, are you?" When I said yes, she glanced at my father with a look that said, "Alan, *you* talk her out of this!"

My dad calmly said, "You know we didn't send you to college and graduate school just to have you take early retirement." He reminded me I didn't have a trust fund and needed to be financially independent. He mentioned the promise I'd made after law school: I would take some "time off the treadmill" but would ultimately get a traditional job. If I wasn't interested in practicing law, then how about a consulting firm?

Sensing my father's approach wasn't working, my mom tried a different tack. "You know your eggs aren't getting any younger," she said. I was twenty-eight, and by that age my mom already had given birth to me and my brother and was about to become pregnant with my sister. Her message: I needed to think more about my ticking clock and less about my expanding dreams. She continued. "And you definitely need to stop getting on planes all the time if you ever want to get married."

So here I was, caught between what my parents wanted for me and what I wanted for myself. It's the same moment that Amr Shady experienced with his father, that Mary Jo and Suzanne faced when they first heard from moms on the playground, that Wences sensed when he looked at his sisters sleeping on the other side of the room, that almost every entrepreneur I've ever met confronted at one time or another. It's that juncture between doing what's safe and expected and doing what's uncertain and unknown. It's the crux between fear and hope.

I chose hope. "I can't turn back," I told my mother, tearing up. "I've been thinking about this too long. This is what I need to do. This is who I'm supposed to be."

My mother looked stunned; my dad was speechless. Peter immediately jumped in to support me. "Debbie," he said, "I understand Linda needs to have some stability. We've agreed that she'll move to New York, set up our operations, and try to raise money." Then he turned to my dad. "And I've decided to take a semester off from grad school and move to Latin America. I'll be sharing the risk." My parents nodded silently. To this day I assume they thought our dream would fizzle, and I would be back applying for a "real" job.

In the years that followed, I've thought often of that scene at my parents' kitchen table. In many ways, my passion to help entrepreneurs is fueled by my desire to help them push through similar inflection points in their lives: when few others believe; when they feel anxious and alone; when they're on the verge of figuring out who they want to be.

As it happens, the figure that best captures that moment is Kermit the Frog. In the opening of *The Muppet Movie* (1979), Kermit sings a hymn to becoming something more than what you are. "Why are there so many songs about rainbows?" he asks. Rainbows are about visions, illusions, and dreams. Rainbows are about hearing voices and people calling your name. The "rainbow connection" is what you feel when you finally discover what you're supposed to be.

To me, getting to Day One is finally embracing what you're supposed to be.

## — FAN THE FOOLISH FIRE —

Thomas Edison was being stubborn. Though he would later be known as the Wizard of Menlo Park, Edison in the late 1870s was considered the fool of New Jersey. Having already invented the telegraph, he had moved on to one of the more elusive goals of modern science, the incandescent lightbulb. One critic called the pursuit "sheer nonsense"; another predicted "final, necessary, and ignominious failure."

A chief problem Edison and other inventors faced was that electricity was considered extremely dangerous—*ignis fatuus*, "foolish fire." Health experts warned that too much exposure to light would cause eye ailments, nervous breakdowns, and—horrors—freckles! Even defenders admitted it made the interiors of houses look wan, gave food an unappetizing paleness, and exposed the wrinkles on the faces of ladies.

In 1879 Edison threw open the doors of his Menlo Park workshop to introduce the prototype of his incandescent light— the "little globe of sunshine" that promised a softer glow. Skeptics were unmoved. They called Edison a con man and taunted him to prove his bulb could light up a larger stage.

That soon happened, but not by him. On a cold December night in 1880, an inventor named Charles Brush strung twenty-three arc lamps on fifty-foot poles along a short stretch of Broadway from Union Square to Madison Square in New York City. Endeavor's headquarters are on this stretch today. The daughter of the city's treasurer was supposed to flip the switch, but she feared electrocution and backed out. When the lights finally came on, they filled the air with intense brightness and stark shadows. A *New York Times* reporter captured the scene: "The great white outlines of the marble stores, the mess of wires overhead, the throng of moving vehicles, were all brought out with an accuracy and exactness that left little to be desired." (This account earned Broadway its enduring nickname, the Great White Way.)

The arrival of electric light into public places was greeted with all the warmth of the plague. Pedestrians used umbrellas to shield themselves; people complained they looked like ghosts.

Despite the naysayers, Edison pushed on. Brush pushed on, too, though unlike Edison, a gazelle who employed hundreds of engineers and dreamed of building a big business, Brush was a butterfly, preferring solitary nights of tinkering away in his one-man lab. Edison would be the one to assuage critics and make the lightbulb a household item. More important, he owned the key patent and formed the Edison Electric Light Company, with backing from J. P. Morgan and the Vanderbilts.

What Edison and Brush both demonstrate is the importance of sticking with your vision, knowing what you want out of your entrepreneurial venture, and being strong enough to accept criticism for your choices.

In my experience, almost all entrepreneurs at one point or another have been accused of being out of their minds. You can't rock the boat without being told you're off your rocker. Consider just a few examples:

*Gazelles*

- When Sam Walton had the idea to create a discount store at age forty-four, his brother dismissed it as "just another of Sam Walton's crazy ideas." Walton himself said everybody he met "really did think I'd completely lost my mind."

*Skunks*

- In 1999 four Microsoft employees met over a bowl of jelly beans to concoct a game console that could take on the Sony PlayStation. They called it Xbox; their skeptical colleagues dubbed it coffin box. Even their partners at Intel scoffed. "We laughed at the idea they would blow a few billion dollars," one executive said. But the jelly bean club kept scheming and recruiting allies, until they wooed the biggest ally of all, Bill Gates. Xbox went on to become Microsoft's largest "internal start-up."

*Dolphins*

- When Raymond Damadian, a little-known professor in New York, first had the idea that he could detect cancerous tumors in the body using nuclear magnetic resonance, his academic colleagues called him a crackpot, a charlatan, and a screaming lunatic. Worse, they denied him tenure. "It's a totally harebrained theory," one colleague said. Undeterred, Damadian filed for patents and raised just enough money to build a device. In 1977 he conducted the first full-body MRI.

### Butterflies

• Twenty-two-year-old Jeffrey Braverman was earning six figures on Wall Street when he left in 2002 to join the struggling family business started by his grandfather. The Newark Nut Company, which had once employed thirty people, was now down to two. "My dad and my uncle both thought I was crazy," Jeffrey said. He took the business online and relaunched it as Nuts.com. In under a decade the company employed eighty people and generated more than $20 million in annual revenues.

Why is it that so many entrepreneurs, in so many divergent fields, are all called, well, nuts?

The short answer is that seeing things in an unconventional way is threatening: It's threatening to those who benefit from the status quo, and it's equally threatening to those outside the establishment who might have had that idea or taken those steps, if only . . . Niccolò Machiavelli made that point in *The Prince*: "There is nothing more difficult to carry out, nor more doubtful of success, nor more dangerous to handle, than to initiate a new order of things." Machiavelli's explanation: The reformer has fierce enemies in all those who profit from the old order and only fair-weather supporters among those who would profit from the new one.

So given that you're going to be criticized for your crazy idea, how should you respond?

Own it.

I learned this in one of the defining moments of my career. A few months after the showdown with my parents, I got a call from Peter, who was living in South America searching for entrepreneurs, while I was in New York searching for funders (and, yes, Mom, a husband, too).

"Linda, pack your bags," Peter said. "I've gotten you a meeting with a real estate tycoon here in Argentina. His name is Eduardo Elsztain." In a legendary story, Eduardo, a college dropout, had talked his way into George Soros's office in 1990 and pitched his unlikely vision that Argentina was emerging from decades of debt crisis and was ripe with opportunity. Eduardo walked out of the meeting with a $10 million check, which he proceeded to turn into the nation's largest real estate empire.

Eduardo had given me ten minutes. Five minutes into our meeting he looked at his watch and explained he would do his best to secure an appointment for me with Soros. "Thank you very much," I said. "But I'm not looking for a meeting with George Soros." Puzzled, he motioned for me to continue. "Look, Eduardo, you're an entrepreneur. I'm an entrepreneur. Endeavor is all about supporting entrepreneurs. Here's what I do want: your time, your passion, and two hundred thousand dollars."

Our meeting had been in English, but after my direct request, Eduardo turned to his right-hand man, Oscar, and started speaking in Spanish. "*Esta chica está loca!*" he said. He went on, telling Oscar that meeting with me was like being in a bad horror movie in which the protagonist at first appears charming, but then you find yourself in the shower, and she's coming at you with a knife.

This bad-movie character, however, understands Spanish. When he finished, I smiled and said, "Eduardo, *estoy muy decepcionada*. ["I'm very disappointed".] I didn't expect to hear this from the man who walked into a billionaire's office and walked out with a $10 million check. You're lucky I asked you for only two hundred thousand!"

Eduardo gaped at me, looked back at Oscar, and took out his check-book. He handed me $200,000 on the spot and, along with his dona-tion, agreed to become the founding chairman of Endeavor Argentina.

That experience led to one of my guiding principles of entrepre-neurship: Crazy is a compliment!

I also propose this corollary: If you're *not* called crazy when you launch something new, it means you're *not thinking big enough*.

The point is: Given that you're going to be called bonkers when-ever you threaten the status quo, you might as well accept the term as a source of pride. I did this myself. For years, many in Latin America referred to me as *la chica loca*, and the nickname later spread to the Middle East. Instead of taking offense, I wore it as a badge of honor.

If you're going to agitate for change, you're going to generate push-back. Don't be surprised; don't be hurt; don't give up. Press on.

Fan the foolish fire.

## — STOP PLANNING, START DOING —

In 2013 I appeared on the *Today* show in a segment about helping peo-ple start their own businesses. My fellow guest was an MBA-trained Internet entrepreneur who explained that she had written a seventy-five-page business plan before starting her business. She recom-mended that viewers do the same. I almost fell off my stool. "On that we can agree to disagree," I said.

Wait! Everybody knows that the one thing you need to execute an idea is a step-by-step plan. Everybody agrees that once you have your crazy idea, you should put it on the page to make it seem more real. You should add numbers, buzzwords, projections, graphs. You should create a PowerPoint to impress your bosses, your friends, your lover. You should draft a business plan.

Well, let me tell you: "Everybody" is wrong. There's another way to approach this phase of entrepreneurship. Stop planning. Start doing.

Vinny Lingham grew up in the Eastern Cape Province of South

Africa during apartheid and was raised in a segregated area desig-
nated for Indians. He remembers watching the movie *Wall Street* as a
boy and thinking, "I want to be something more." Vinny developed a
passion for starting enterprises, from selling stickers in grade school to
managing rock bands in college. In 2003 he left his first corporate job,
sold his house, and convinced his fiancée and two friends to join him
in launching an online marketing company. He was finally living the
self-made life he'd dreamed of.

But Vinny wasn't satisfied. He'd identified a new problem: Many
small businesses lacked the capital or know-how to create Web sites.
So he left his own start-up and launched another one. Soon Google
chose his new firm, Yola, for a major initiative, and HP offered to preinstall its product on its computers. In 2009 *Businessweek* declared
Yola one of "Fifty Startups You Should Know." Several years later
Vinny launched yet another new company, Gyft—a mobile gift card
wallet—that was nurtured by Google Ventures.

Vinny is a serial gazelle, and he soon became a mainstay of Silicon
Valley. Along the way he developed strong opinions about most entrepreneurs he met: They overthink, they overplan, they overanalyze. I
once moderated a panel involving Vinny, Leila, and other entrepreneurs before a roomful of finance types. "You guys think too much,"
Vinny told the audience. "You spend all your time talking about ideas,
learning theory, and writing business plans, and not enough time trying stuff out." He added this kicker: "By the time you've perfected your
plan on paper, guys like me will have signed up loads of real-life customers for our businesses."

Vinny is not alone. Research we did of the nearly one thousand
Endeavor entrepreneurs found that two-thirds did not write formal
business plans when starting their ventures, more than 80 percent
launched their first product within six months, and nearly half
changed their business model at least once. Wences didn't have a business plan when he started his company, and neither did Leila.

Our gazelles are in good company. A 2002 survey of the founders of Inc. 500 companies revealed that only 12 percent conducted formal market research before launch and only 40 percent wrote formal business plans. Of those who wrote plans, two-thirds admitted they ditched them later. The founders of Microsoft, Pixar, and Starbucks didn't follow business plans; Intel's business plan was a mere 161 words, with a number of those words, including "and," being misspelled.

Corporate skunks, too, can use this stop-planning, start-doing approach. When I asked Mary Jo Cook, of Clorox, what advice she would give to those in big companies who were thinking of becoming more entrepreneurial, she said, "Instead of analyzing and analyzing and analyzing and trying to predict the perfect case in an imperfect, messy, constantly changing world, just try something." The key to entrepreneurship, she said, is to "learn by doing." What's valuable about this approach within corporations is that instead of trying to impress your boss with a PowerPoint, you can make your case with proof points.

Consider what happened at Pfizer, one of the world's largest pharmaceutical companies, with more than ninety thousand employees. In 2005 Jordan Cohen, a mid-level human resources officer, noticed that a new father on his team was staying late to create spreadsheets and do research online. Cohen didn't think this was a valuable use of time and wondered if individual employees could outsource grunt work to India.

Instead of crafting an elaborate proposal, Cohen tested the idea using a handful of workers and his own limited budget. He dubbed his initiative Office of the Future and kept it secret from his superiors for an entire year to gain evidence, traction, and allies. The first test failed miserably. Assignments came back filled with typos; data were riddled with errors. Cohen discovered his colleagues weren't being specific enough with their outsourced assistants about what they needed, so he spent months breaking down projects into four usable tasks: creating documents, manipulating spreadsheets, scheduling meetings, and conducting research.

At this point he recruited a senior manager from a different department, who offered to pilot the program and pay for it out of his budget, giving Cohen both resources and cover. Pfizer's top brass was still kept in the dark. Word of the program began to spread, and two hundred employees eventually joined the initiative. Armed with a trove of data showing thousands of employee hours saved, Cohen and his adviser finally pitched top execs, who green-lighted a company-wide program. Today the renamed pfizerWorks serves ten thousand managers, including the chairman and CEO. In internal surveys, employees rated it the company's most popular service, even though they have to pay for it out of their own department budgets.

Butterfly entrepreneurs often dive into their enterprises without a plan. They see something that needs fixing, and they go about fixing it. In their case, it's often not a choice because many don't even realize they're starting something when they do. That was the case of Margaret Rudkin.

The oldest of five children in an Irish American family, Rudkin (née Fogarty) was born in 1897 in New York. With the reputation of being a fiery redhead, she was her high school valedictorian and went to work at a Wall Street brokerage firm, where she met her husband. The two had three sons and moved to a lovely piece of property in Fairfield, Connecticut. The year was 1929. When the stock market crashed, the family suffered, selling apples and pigs to pay their bills. But Rudkin's bigger challenge was the severe allergies and asthma of her youngest son, Mark, who was unable to eat processed foods.

When a doctor ordered Mark to go on a diet of natural foods, Rudkin decided to try baking him some stone-ground whole wheat bread. "My first loaf should have been sent to the Smithsonian Institution as a sample of Stone Age bread," Rudkin said. "It was hard as a rock and about one inch high." After a few tries she finally had an edible loaf. Mark loved it, and so did his doctor, who started "prescribing" it to his patients. Rudkin promptly marched to her local grocer and asked if he was interested in selling her bread. "No way," the grocer said. Rudkin had no experience in the baking business; besides, she wanted twenty-five cents a loaf instead of the going rate of ten cents.

So she cut him a slice. The grocer tasted it and bought every loaf on the spot; then he called her later and ordered some more. Rudkin named her bread after her beloved home in Connecticut, Pepperidge Farm, which itself was named for an old pepperidge, or tupelo, tree. "Although I knew nothing of manufacturing, of marketing, of pricing, or of making bread in quantities," she said, "with that phone call, Pepperidge Farm bread was born."

Margaret Rudkin had become an accidental entrepreneur. All she had was a motive, a kitchen, and a recipe, as well as a husband who was willing to tote her loaves to Grand Central Station to sell. Within a few years she had moved her operation to her garage. After *Reader's Digest* touted her bread in 1939, demand exploded. As one reporter noted, "In response to this growing demand, Margaret Rudkin pushed her vivid red hair back from a perspiring brow and said she had always known the people of the United States wanted homemade bread—but did they have to have it all at once?"

Lots of butterfly entrepreneurs begin like this, often after someone loses a job or when their kids no longer need them full-time. They don't write business plans because they don't have the knowledge or resources—and wouldn't know what to do with such a plan if they had it.

Still uneasy about forgoing that plan? Bill Sahlman, the guru of entrepreneurial finance at Harvard Business School, wrote a piece for *Harvard Business Review* titled "How to Write a Great Business Plan." His surprising conclusion: "In my experience with hundreds of entrepreneurial startups, business plans rank no higher than 2—on a scale of 1 to 10—as a predictor of a new venture's success." Sometimes, he continued, "the more elaborately crafted the document, the more likely the venture is to, well, flop."

Bill's explanation was that most business plans spend too much time on padded numbers and inflated language that fail to acknowledge that smart businesses adapt and change. Early ventures bear little resemblance to what they ultimately become. Bill even included a handy key explaining what business plan–speak really means.

| What They Say . . . | What They Really Mean . . . |
|---|---|
| We conservatively project . . . | We read a book that said we had to be a $50 million company in five years, and we reverse-engineered the numbers. |
| The project is 98 percent complete. | To complete the remaining 2 percent will take twice as long as it took to create the initial 98 percent and cost twice as much. |
| Customers are clamoring for our product. | We have not yet asked them to pay for it. |

To be clear, I'm not saying that business plans themselves are bad. Nor is Bill Sahlman saying that. Vinny, for example, eventually did write a plan for his various ventures when the time came to raise money from VCs. (Actually, he hired an MBA to do it for him.) Jordan Cohen ultimately did write a proposal to expand his outsourcing initiative across Pfizer. It's when you make your plan that's important. Do it too early, and it's likely to stifle your momentum and bury your enthusiasm under a deluge of doubt and made-up numbers.

Instead, the lesson of this early stage of becoming an entrepreneur is that the most important things you can do relate to mind-set: (1) First, give yourself permission to be a contrarian, to flout convention, to follow the unsafe path, to zig when everyone else zags; then (2) take some action to get going. Allow yourself to try; then try. As Wences would say, be a doer.

Keep moving toward Day One.

Be warned, you will be called crazy for having a big dream, for taking a career-threatening chance, for plunging in without knowing exactly where you're going. That is an undeniable side effect of being an entrepreneur. There is no reward without some risk.

But if I could stress one thing, the smartest entrepreneurs don't take blind risks; they take smart risks. They don't risk it all; they risk just enough to get going, then hedge those risks at every step along the way.

It's how to pull off that delicate balance that I want to turn to next.

# CHAPTER 2

# *Derisking Risk*

Sara Blakely felt like a failure. She tried to become a stand-up comedian but fell short. She planned to go to law school but bombed the LSAT. She became a cast member at Disney World but quit after three months. Finally she found work selling fax machines.

One day, suffering in the heat and humidity of Florida, Sara needed panty hose to wear with white pants and sandals, so she cut the feet off a regular pair. They rode up her leg, annoyingly. "I needed an undergarment that didn't exist," she said. She started researching fabrics at night and eventually designed a product she liked. She even taught herself patent law to save money. Her total investment: $5,000. She called her product Spanks.

"I knew that Kodak and Coca-Cola were the two most recognized names," Sara said, "and they both have 'K' sounds in them." As a comedian she also knew that *K* sounds make people laugh. At the last minute she changed the *KS* to an *X* after learning that made-up words make better brands and are easier to trademark. "Spanx is edgy, fun, extremely catchy, and for a moment it makes your mind wander (admit it)," she said. Her slogan: "Don't worry, we've got your butt covered."

I love this story for a lot reasons: It's fun, impressive, inspiring. In 2012, at age forty-one, Sara became the youngest self-made woman to make the *Forbes* billionaire list. (And well, I like the product, too. I'm happy Sara has my butt covered!) But I especially like that it encompasses a number of key lessons I've learned about becoming an entrepreneur—namely, how to take big, unmanageable dreams and slice them into small, manageable tasks.

It's what Sara did after committing to her dream that's so illustrative. Although she knew nothing about the hosiery business, Sara didn't bog down in some meta-analysis. Instead, she hopped into her car and drove door to door in North Carolina, trying to talk mill owners into manufacturing her product. They always asked the same three questions: "And you are?" "And you are representing?" "And you are backed by?"

"When I answered 'Sara Blakely' to all three," she said, "most of them sent me away."

But faced with multiple rejections, she didn't cave. She pushed on. Finally one mill owner who had sent her away called back. "I've decided to help make your crazy idea," he said. Why? she asked. "I have two daughters," he replied.

Sara's experience embodies the second key step of becoming an entrepreneur: deciding how much to put on the line, developing a prototype, finding users, and (my favorite) stalking supporters. If the first step to becoming an entrepreneur is about managing mind-set, this one's about managing risk. Specifically, it's about derisking risk.

When Sara first had the idea for butt-flattering panty hose, for example, she didn't quit her day job selling fax machines. For *two years*, Sara hawked office products nine to five on weekdays and sold panty hose on nights and weekends. She didn't resign until she was fairly confident her entrepreneurial venture would take off. What gave her that confidence? Oprah had picked Spanx as one of her "favorite things."

While the popular impression of entrepreneurs is that they're reckless cowboys, the reality is quite different. Dig below the surface and what smart entrepreneurs actually know is how to get an idea going with minimal expense, nominal exposure, and limited liability.

So how do you do that? How do you differentiate smart risks from foolish ones? The four strategies in this chapter can help. Contrary to what those inspirational posters say, the first step is not always the hardest.

This one is.

## *– DON'T BET THE FARM –*

One of the trickiest questions entrepreneurs face early on is: Once you have your idea and are convinced it will fly, how far should you go? The popular myth goes something like this: Go all in. Sell the baseball card collection. Mortgage the house. Max out your credit cards. Dip into your IRA.

Bet the farm.

The legendary CEO of McDonald's, Ray Kroc, captured this sentiment well: "If you're not a risk taker, you should get the hell out of business." Like a lot of the lore around entrepreneurship—and business in general—this myth appeals to a kind of macho bravado. In fact, the phrase "bet the farm" comes from poker tables in the Wild West, where betting the farm in a game of five-card draw proved you had cojones.

Well, boys will be boys, but entrepreneurs will be savvy. Talk to actual entrepreneurs, and the story around risk is often quite different.

Richard Branson is certainly no wimp. Yet as he wrote in *Losing My Virginity*, "If you are a risk-taker, the art is to protect the downside." When we honored him at one of our annual Endeavor galas, he told the story of his ill-fated foray into soft drinks, Virgin Cola. "I thought we could take on Coca-Cola," he said. In Branson's telling, Virgin Cola was a disaster, but it was a "contained disaster." It was the result of a calculated entrepreneurial risk that didn't threaten the

Virgin brand. His lesson to our entrepreneurs: "Make sure a single failure won't ruin everything."

Many entrepreneurs I've worked with echo this idea. Rodrigo Jordan is one of the biggest adventure junkies I know. The Chilean-born CEO loves extreme sports, including rock and ice climbing. In 1992 he became the first South American to scale Everest, a feat he has repeated many times. (In 2012 he texted me a fun photo of the Endeavor flag staked on the summit.)

Rodrigo leveraged his mountaineering techniques to form a corporate leadership training company, so I was surprised when he told me this: "The common wisdom is all wrong: Entrepreneurs don't like to take risks. I hate risks. I'm always trying to avoid and minimize risks. An entrepreneur should never be a daredevil who puts it all on the line."

Endeavor's research backs this up. When we asked our entrepreneurs to rate their attitude toward risk, the overwhelming majority veered toward the middle, not the extreme. Ninety-five percent said they did not risk their ability to provide food and shelter for their families when starting their businesses. More than 80 percent had enough savings or other resources set aside to cover basic expenses for at least one year. This doesn't mean they were rich—most lived on very tight budgets at the outset—but it does speak to their attitude toward limiting liability and continuing to provide for their families while they pursued their crazy dreams.

Still, some risk is necessary. So how much? If you're not supposed to bet the farm, what amount should you bet?

Just enough to get you into the game. Sixty-one percent of the 2013 Inc. 500 entrepreneurs originally wagered less than $10,000 on their businesses. For most start-ups, the number is significantly less. In *The Lean Startup*, Eric Ries advocates investing just enough for a starter product—nothing too fancy, nothing too expensive. The goal is to create what he calls a minimum viable product. "This is a hard truth for many entrepreneurs to accept," Ries wrote. You may be wishing for a mind-blowing prototype that will change the world or one that will impress that snarky cousin at Thanksgiving.

The smarter approach is to take incremental steps, get feedback, and adjust. Ries labels this the "build-measure-learn" feedback loop. It's the same reason you shouldn't fuss over a business plan: You'll quickly outgrow your prototype. As Reid Hoffman, cofounder of LinkedIn and an Endeavor board member, says, "If you're not embarrassed by your first product, you've waited too long."

One advantage of not betting the farm is that you're not laying out a lot of cash. In 1999 a former ticket seller for the San Diego Padres, Nick Swinmurn, had the provocative idea that people might be willing to buy footwear from a grand online emporium. It's fairly easy to see the appeal: infinite selection, year-round. Also, $2 billion of shoes were annually purchased at that time through a catalog. But it's also easy to see the downside: I, for one, have problematic feet and have to try on multiple pairs before I find one that fits.

Swinmurn could have spent years studying the market, analyzing consumers' buying habits. Or he could've invested in a warehouse and stuffed it with shoeboxes from floor to ceiling. He might have racked up debt only to discover that people were no more likely to buy shoes online than martinis. Instead, Swinmurn tried an experiment. He walked into a shoe store in Sunnyvale, California, one day and asked if he could take pictures of its products and put them online. If people bought the shoes, he would return to the store and buy them at full price.

This obviously was not a viable business model, but here's the thing: Swinmurn's experiment wasn't designed to *be* a business; it was designed to *test the idea* for a business. And it worked: He quickly proved that people would be willing to buy shoes online. Even more important, he garnered key information about his customers: who they were, what products they liked, how many samples they wanted to try on before making a purchase, etc. In June 1999 Swinmurn opened ShoeSite.com, which he soon rechristened Zappos.com.

Using low-risk tactics to launch high-risk ventures is especially valuable in larger corporations, where failures can potentially derail your career. Two skunks at MTV understood this. In the mid-1990s the Internet was just catching on, and two mid-level employees at MTV Europe wanted to find a way to incorporate e-mails and user-generated content into a show. But instead of marching into the CEO's office to get a sign-off, Henrik Werdelin and Eric Kearley began stealthily developing a pilot. Werdelin borrowed equipment from technicians he hung out with after work; Kearley paid for a camera out of his own pocket. They built a prototype studio inside an unused tiny room near Kearley's office. They even managed to recruit a well-known MTV anchor, using only a bottle of scotch.

Still, a prototype was not enough. The two skunks needed to air their show live to prove the technology would work. But how could they convince their superiors to cede valuable airtime to their cobbled-together idea? The answer: They didn't. They persuaded some technicians in the control room to air their pilot in the middle of the night, when the network normally ran taped programs. The risk was minimal, they argued. If the show went horribly wrong, the technicians could simply switch back to the canned programs.

That didn't happen. The show was a hit. "When I approached our CEO," Kearley said, "I was able to tell him that we had a new idea, that we had made it work technically, that we had already broadcast it successfully." The concept became the award-winning *Top Selection*, and the technology they pioneered went on to form the backbone of *Total Request Live*, MTV's groundbreaking show hosted by Carson Daly, that propelled the careers of Britney Spears, Christina Aguilera, and Justin Timberlake.

This incremental approach to developing an idea is also valuable for butterfly entrepreneurs, who often don't have the cash to build expensive prototypes or the freedom to quit their jobs and ignore the kids. Cleveland-born Warren Brown had an undergraduate degree from Brown University and a JD and master's degree in public health from George Washington University. He was working as a litigator for the Department of Health and Human Services when he hit a wall of frustration. A lifelong tinkerer in the kitchen, Brown made a New Year's resolution in 1999 to learn to bake. He worked during the day, baked cakes every night, and stopped in on bakeries during business trips.

Before visiting relatives in New York one weekend, he prepared a simple chocolate cake, put it on a white plate, and carried it on the plane. "Walking through the airport and onto the plane, security guards, flight attendants, passengers, and other travelers came up to me. *Did you make that cake? Is it your birthday? Are you a baker?*" It was like a focus group, he said: cake = love. "Waiting by the curb that night for my aunt Yvette, I realized I was staring at my future."

In the mythic version of this story Brown quits his job, borrows money from friends and family, and opens a bakery. But in the actual version of this story he worries, is afraid to tell his friends and family, and works himself into a state of agitation. Six months after that flight, in a whirl of working, baking, and running errands for his sideline business, Brown collapsed at his home, unable to move or breathe. "I was confused, tired, and desperate," he said. "I wanted to bake, but I didn't know how I could pull it off. How do I tell my parents, who sent me to law school?" A friend drove him to a hospital, where doctors instructed him to slow down.

Brown went to his boss and asked for a three-month unpaid leave of absence. He didn't quit outright, but he did think he could write a business plan (sigh), raise some money, and open a store. He rented a kitchen, baked fifteen showcase cakes, and invited seventy-five friends to a tasting. And yes, he also invited his parents. His mother said, in a small voice, "Well, if that's what you really want to do . . ." His father said his passion had better come with a real salary.

Three months later he hadn't written a word of the business plan and hadn't raised a nickel. He got some orders—birthday parties, weddings, a few restaurants—and decided to extend his leave. The *Washington Post* caught wind and wrote an article—not about his store but about his decision whether or not to open one. The headline: WILL WARREN BROWN GIVE UP A PROMISING LEGAL CAREER TO MAKE CAKES? The *Today* show called. *People* magazine labeled this handsome thirty-year-old African American one of "50 Most Eligible Bachelors in America."

But still no store! "The process is long and tough," he said. "Starting a business is not easy." Another year passed. Finally he got a small business loan, and in 2002, almost four years after his resolution, Brown opened CakeLove in Washington, D.C. The next year he started a café; a cookbook followed, as did six other stores and a Food Network series. But as Brown said, his fast growth would not have been possible without his slow start.

"You listen to entrepreneurs talk about their experience," he said, "and you often don't hear all the difficult things that happened along the way." Brown added, "You have to be a little unhinged" to do what he did, but you also have to push forward without throwing everything you've built out the door.

In my experience, most entrepreneurs are not risk maximizers; they are *risk minimizers*. They don't focus on optimal returns; they focus on acceptable loss.

Leave the high-ante games for the poker table. When it comes to your ideas, don't bet the actual farm. Wager a few chickens at a time.

## — FRIENDS DON'T LET FRIENDS TEST-DRIVE THEIR IDEAS —

But how do you know if betting even a few chickens is a good idea? Your inclination may be to go to the people you trust the most: your friends, your family, your jogging partner, the neighbor across the street, the smart guy in the cubicle around the corner. So you build up the confidence, you practice your pitch, you slide on the Spanx (yes, they have them for men, too), and you ask: "So tell me, is my crazy idea brilliant or is it just crazy?"

Please ignore whatever they say.

As the old saying goes, love is blind, and what you need at the moment is to see your idea more clearly. Sara Blakely, when she started dabbling with nylons, didn't tell her friends and family. The only people who knew, apart from patent lawyers she consulted, were her roommate and her boyfriend. "My family knew that 'Sara's working on some idea,'" she said, "but I never told them what it was." Her reason: "Ideas are fragile in their infancy, and I sensed that if I talked about it with friends, I might be discouraged."

Your loved ones are likely to greet your idea in one of two ways, neither of which is all that helpful to you. For some, it will be mindless flattery: "OMG, that's the greatest idea I've ever heard! You're a genius. You'll make millions!" It's the equivalent of taking a bridesmaid to the final fitting of your wedding dress and expecting anything other than "You look perfect!" These responses may boost your mood, but they don't help you test the quality of your idea.

For others, it will always be negative: "You're thinking of quitting your job to do WHAT?" "Somebody else is bound to do it first—and better." "How will you ever send your kids to college?" This is what Warren Brown's parents effectively said to him.

In both cases, the people you're talking to are usually responding out of emotion—either trying to make you feel good or trying to make themselves feel good (or at least justify their own risk aversion). Neither does you much good at all.

Consider these two cautionary tales, both involving butterflies, but with very different endings.

Mel and Patricia Ziegler were weary of their high-stress, low-wage jobs. He worked as a reporter; she, a courtroom sketch artist. They were young, newly in love, and unbeknownst to each other, both quit their jobs on the same day in hopes of building a life of freedom and travel. First they downsized; then they read a book on how to start a business; then, out of nowhere, Mel got a freelance writing gig in Australia. Looking for cheap clothing in Sydney one day, Mel happened on a secondhand British Burma jacket. "Made of thick but soft khaki cotton twill, it looked like a safari jacket," he recalled. "It had the tailored feeling of a fine garment." He topped it off with an olive green Australian bush hat.

Patricia almost didn't recognize her clothes-averse boyfriend when he walked through customs two weeks later. "Something was different," she said. "Had he acquired this new worldliness, this rather heroic nonchalance from his adventures Down Under, or was it the jacket?" Impressed with its "perfect color" and "slightly worn collar and cuffs," she set about doctoring the jacket, adding suede elbow patches, leather trim, and wooden buttons. Mel wore it almost every day, and everywhere he went, people stopped him. "Where did you get that fabulous jacket?"

"The jacket had a message for me," he said, "and it didn't take me long to get it: here was the business we'd been looking for." Patricia got the same message, too.

They invested $750 into a line of used, short-armed Spanish paratrooper shirts (the British Burma jackets were impossible to find and, even used, too pricey). Mel and Patricia described the move as their stop-planning, start-doing moment: "Therein lay the full and complete business plan of a writer and artist who had quit their jobs to make it on their own."

After a few hot afternoons hawking their wares at a flea market, the couple decided to spend their remaining cash on a homemade catalog filled with Patricia's hand-drawn illustrations and Mel's quirky, conversational dialogue. (Mel dubbed himself minister of propaganda.) The pair eagerly took their pride and joy, fresh off the printer, to two friends. After flipping through the pages, one friend said, "You don't expect this to sell anything, do you?" The other added, "You sure you want to mail this?" Shaken, Patricia turned to Mel after they left and asked if they should quit. "We can't turn back now," he said.

Patricia and Mel's quirky idea, Banana Republic, has grown to more than six hundred stores across the globe. Five years after Mel first bought that used jacket, the couple sold their company to the Gap and left to pursue their dreams of freedom and artistry. A key reason Gap took an interest in Banana Republic: Its eccentric, chatty, hand-illustrated catalogs had taken off. Had the Zieglers listened to their friends, they never would have taken it off the drawing board.

One problem with listening to those closest to you is that they might rain on your safari. But the opposite problem is equally bad: Your friends might butter you up. And if your dream is to make jam, that butter might be awfully tempting.

Alison Roman and Eva Scofield were coworkers at Brooklyn's trendy Momofuku Milk Bar who longed to join the artisanal food movement sweeping through their neighborhood. Offered the chance to sell something at Brooklyn Flea, the trendy market at the pinnacle of the farm-to-table trend, they jumped. They started testing recipes in off-hours; each put in a couple of hundred dollars for ingredients.

Finally they came up with a winner: fresh organic fruit jams with unusual flavors—vanilla-lemon, grapefruit-hibiscus. One particular jar caught Roman's eye: It was well-made, gorgeous, but, at $1.85 a pop, costly. Things went smoothly at first. The jams tasted great. Friends cheered them on, even pushing them to raise their prices, from the already expensive $7 to downright outrageous $9 per jar. "Handmade in Brooklyn with local fruit" drew a crowd. People raved about the jars. Maiden Preserves appeared to be another dishrags-to-riches success story.

But the reality was more bitter. The company never broke even. "Friends would say, 'You guys are doing so well,'" Roman said. "I'd say, 'No, we're not.' There's this fantasy, but it's not as simple as putting fruit in a jar and selling it." Soon the partners were bickering over strategy. Roman wanted to go more nichey, selling to baby and bridal showers and cute boutiques. Scofield wanted to spin off a line with cheaper jars. "It was becoming clear we didn't have the same vision," Roman said. Soon they stopped making jam together.

For most entrepreneurs, the surprising truth is that the people you trust most are usually the least trustworthy when it comes to your ideas. A team of researchers from Babson College and IPADE Business School surveyed 120 founders in Hong Kong, Kenya, Mexico, Nigeria, the United Kingdom, and the United States, asking for the biggest mistakes they had made. One conclusion: selling early to family and friends.

This problem was particularly pronounced in the clothing, food, and financial services industries, the researchers found. (The founders of Banana Republic and Maiden Preserves were not alone.) "You never know why relatives are buying from you," the researchers said. "Often their motivation is love, pity, or a sense of obligation, not compelling product quality." Founders, in retrospect, wished they had ignored what family had to say and instead pursued "arm's-length transactions with customers who would have given them candid feedback."

The appeal of turning to loved ones for early input is obvious: They're close; they're cheap; they often share your tastes. But the downsides are equally great. Smart entrepreneurs move as quickly as possible from finding their true passions to finding their true customers, and they often skip the troublesome step of asking what those around them think.

Next time you consider phoning a friend and sharing your crazy concept before it's ready for prime time, remember: Friends don't let friends test-drive their ideas.

## — FOLLOW THE CROWD —

So once you have a minimum viable product in hand, how do you test its appeal? Specifically, how do you test it in a cost-effective way that doesn't imperil your idea, your life savings, or your ability to pay the electric bill?

Like so many other areas of contemporary life, the Internet has opened previously unimaginable paths. Crazy dreamers now have a new way to stop planning and start doing, avoid betting the farm, and sidestep letting their friends test-drive their ideas. This way was not available to Edison or Branson or to the founders of Banana Republic or even Spanx.

That new way is the crowd.

In 2002 Perry Chen was an electronic musician and busboy living in New Orleans, experimenting with what he calls dropping out of society. He tried to bring a pair of Austrian DJs to town for JazzFest. The duo asked for $15,000 plus five business-class tickets, an insurmountable sum for the barely employed Chen, who would be left to foot the bill if no one bought tickets for the show. But he "had a feeling that this was a problem that should be solvable," he said. What if he could ask those who might enjoy the show to precommit to buying tickets?

Though it took him seven years to flesh out his idea, in 2009 Chen and two cofounders launched Kickstarter. A missionary dolphin at heart, Chen insisted he was building an ecosystem to help creative people, not a business. Three weeks in, a twenty-two-year-old singer-songwriter from Athens, Georgia, tried to raise funds to release an album titled *Allison Weiss Was Right All Along*. She reached her goal in ten hours. "That's when we knew a movement had been launched," Chen said.

It took Kickstarter four months to fund one hundred projects and a year to reach a thousand. By year two it was funding a thousand projects a month; five years in, Kickstarter had enabled fifty thousand projects to raise $850 million from over five million contributors. Today more than five hundred crowdfunding sites have joined the revolution, and the field continues to double every year.

Crowdfunding has proven especially powerful for butterflies because the medium thrives on helping underdogs. Movie directors can bypass Hollywood studios; musicians can avoid record companies; authors can sidestep publishers. The same is happening with comic books, video games, and theater productions. In 2013 alone Kickstarter helped *Moby-Dick* get translated into Emojis and the documentary *Inocente* win an Oscar.

Yet it's not just butterflies. Dolphins, too, are taking advantage of the crowd. A number of Kickstarter-like platforms have popped up to help cause-driven organizations. Do Good Bus, the brainchild of a team of Los Angeles musicians, embarked on a bus tour of twenty-two cities promising "altruistic adventurism." They played music and promoted programs for at-risk youth. Their appeal attracted 680 backers and $101,000.

Crowdfunding is not foolproof, and it's not easy street. Only 44 percent of Kickstarter projects ever get funded. Also, while persistent creators find ways to build word of mouth, many projects start off with a built-in base of friends, family, and fans. As one aspiring creator said, "You have to bring your own crowd." (And to be clear, just because you don't ask friends for their opinion before you get going, once you're under way, there's no reason not to ask them to help spread the word and rustle up customers.)

Still, crowdfunding has already altered the start-up landscape. First, it's democratized access to capital, especially for people in out-of-the-way places. Second, it provides valuable market feedback.

Instead of spending precious time and money on prototypes or store-fronts, entrepreneurs can ask potential customers to give input, vote on features, and place preorders. Imagine if Warren Brown had launched a Kickstarter campaign after he appeared on the *Today* show and in *People*. He might not have had to wait an entire year to get a loan for his first CakeLove store.

Third, crowdfunding sites offer publicity in case you're one of the millions of entrepreneurs who aren't Sara Blakely or Warren Brown and don't find yourself on national television. A leading scholar of crowdfunding, Anindya Ghose of New York University, said the expo sure is often more valuable than the money. "Crowdfunding helps to create a lot of buzz, word-of-mouth, and awareness of a project." Finally, crowdfunding has made looking scruffy desirable. While start-ups long wanted to appear polished and professional, now they often want to appear scrappy and grassroots.

Even corporations want some of that scrappiness. IBM launched an internal crowdfunding platform where skunks pitch projects to one another (instead of their bosses) for $2,000 in seed money. Coca-Cola announced it was "crowdsourcing happiness" through a "smile-back" video campaign; Sam Adams produced the first "collaborative ale." And in 2013 GE formed a partnership with Quirky, a platform on which "citizen inventors" submit ideas that the crowd can vote on, improve, and bring to market.

Using customers to help design products is another way the crowd is helping entrepreneurs cut down on risk. Two entrepreneurs in our network did just that. Jo Bedu is a Jordanian apparel company that selects designs for its edgy products through crowdsourcing. Michael Makdah and Tamer Al-Masri were high school friends who reunited in their twenties and discovered a way to merge their passions in art and marketing. They withdrew $4,200 from savings and created six hundred T-shirts from Tamer's witty designs. They stored inventory at Tamer's house and sold the shirts at Souk Jara, a local street market. The products were well received; they hired their first employee. But sales soon stalled.

Then the two had an idea. Why not outsource designs to the eventual buyers? They launched a Facebook campaign inviting their followers to submit design ideas. Jo Bedu then bought the best designs and printed them. The resulting T-shirts sold forty thousand units. With proof in hand, the company opened its first store; within two years it was selling Jo Bedu clothing and accessories at the Virgin megastore in Amman. Today the company still solicits customer designs and receives two thousand submissions for every request.

These days the best way to stand out from the crowd is to follow it.

## — THE LOST ART OF STALKING —

All these techniques are legitimate ways of testing your idea and getting it going without assuming unnecessary risk. But there's one more strategy I want to mention. It's part of what we might call the dark arts of entrepreneurship, the kind of thing that's not taught in business school but that every entrepreneur I know uses at one time or another.

Several years after my meeting with Eduardo Elsztain, where I earned my *la chica loca* moniker, I was invited to address the first-year class at Harvard Business School. On that day the school was unveiling a new case study about Endeavor. It had been commissioned by Bill Sahlman, the same guru of entrepreneurship who mocked business plan doublespeak. Bill introduced me by explaining how I had built Endeavor by using a nonconventional technique to recruit boosters: I trapped them in confined spaces from which they had little chance to escape. I loitered outside airplane bathrooms; I lurked in fancy restaurants; I hovered around gym treadmills.

"Linda was a stalker," Bill announced to his class.

I chuckled. "And from what I've seen, stalking is an underrated start-up strategy!"

Bill himself had been among my victims. Six months into the life of Endeavor I began to realize we needed some "cred." By then Peter and I had recruited two friends, Gary Mueller and Jason Green, to join our board. Gary was a successful Internet entrepreneur; Jason, an up-and-coming venture capitalist. Still, everywhere I went, people kept asking who our backers were. They would say something to the effect of "We've never heard of you. This is an outlandish idea. Prove to us you can attract big names."

So when I heard that Peter Brooke, the legendary pioneer of international VC and private equity, was slated to speak on a panel at Harvard Business School, I pounced. Literally. I attended the event, eyed the sixty-eight-year-old Brooke walking offstage and into the men's bathroom, and waited.

When he emerged, I stepped in front of him. "Hi, my name is Linda, and I've started an organization to support entrepreneurs around the world. I'd love to come by your office for a few minutes to tell you more about it." Brooke did not miss a beat. I clearly was not the first person to accost him like this.

"Who else is backing you?" he said.

"Um, well, Bill Sahlman is a supporter," I said, improvising.

"Really? Sahlman is backing this? In that case, here's my card. Give me a call."

Minutes later I marched up to Bill's office and said, "Guess what? I'm pretty sure Peter Brooke is going to cochair our global advisory board. And he's asked for you to be the other cochair."

Not until three years later, at the third annual gathering of Endeavor's global advisory board, did the two cochairs realize that neither had ever officially agreed to play any role in our organization.

A crazy lady coming at you with a knife, indeed. Only it's a butter knife. The better way to butter you up.

There's a common misperception in the world of entrepreneurship that in order to be successful, you must start with personal wealth, a fancy degree, a golden Rolodex, or some combination of the three. The reality is often the opposite. Most of the entrepreneurs I encounter on a daily basis lack connections to elite networks and don't have trust funds as a safety net. What they do possess is chutzpah.

Still, learning to deploy that audacity is tricky. There are a number of ways you can perfect the art.

*Stalk the competition.* You can never learn too much about the field you're trying to disrupt. If a major consulting group is working on a case for a cruise line, it pays its junior employees to dress as tourists, go on rivals' cruises, and take lots of pictures. When Sam Walton was getting started, he loved to sneak around rival stores on family trips. His wife would wait in the car with the kids, who always complained, "Oh, no, Daddy, not another store." Once Walton was slinking around a Price Club in San Diego, making notes on a tape recorder, when an employee caught him. Forced to hand over the incriminating evidence, Walton wrote a note to Robert Price, the owner's son. "Robert, your guy is just too good. Here's the tape. If you want to listen to it, you certainly have that privilege, but I have some other material on here I would very much like back." Four days later the tape recorder was returned, with all of Walton's notes still on it.

The Internet has made this kind of sleuthing a lot easier. You can set a Google alert for your competition or track its personnel moves on LinkedIn. A LinkedIn career adviser told *Forbes* that not stalking competitors was one of the biggest mistakes novices make. "If you're a game developing startup," she said, "you should absolutely be following Electronic Arts," which allows you to know who's left the company. "Maybe you want to hire them, maybe they've got some dirt they can share, but either way, keeping track of the industry players can give you a competitive advantage."

*Stalk customers.* Sometimes, if you're new to a field, you have to try unconventional ways to attract customers. If that field is protection from cybercriminals, well . . .

Marcelo Romcy and João Mendes were teenage hackers from rural Brazil. After meeting in college, they decided to go straight and set up a cybersecurity business, Proteus. When I met them, Marcelo and João had achieved regional penetration and were eager to expand overseas. But there was a problem: They had built their business using a hazardous technique. They would pick a bank or financial firm they wanted as a client, breach its firewall, and temporarily "borrow" $10,000. Then they would knock on the CEO's door with the money in hand, explain how they'd got it, and pitch themselves to fix the problem. Their strategy paid off: Proteus soon became one of South America's leading IT auditing firms.

My first suggestion was that they not try this strategy in the United States, where this technique would likely get them a visit from the SEC! Instead, I encouraged them to fly to Jordan, where I was hosting an event. There they zeroed in on one of the region's top CEOs, with six thousand employees and lots of contacts around the world. After Marcelo made his pitch, the CEO turned cocky. "We have the best IT security in the region," he said. "Why do we need you?"

Marcelo offered to hack into his system to show how much he needed Proteus.

"Go ahead," the CEO said. "You won't find a hole."

Three days later Marcelo called the CEO. "Would you like for me to tell you the password to your e-mail?" he asked. "I'm looking through your messages right now." The company became a client and soon recommended Proteus to others.

*Stalk allies.* If you're a skunk trying to drum up an entrepreneurial idea in a large corporation, stalking often means finding subtle ways to beat your own drum. Instead of badgering higher-ups, you're often better off subtly pestering your colleagues, reminding them that you're working on a new idea, gently leaving the door open if they want to walk through it. One of the most ubiquitous products in American cubicles came from this approach.

In 1968 a chemist at 3M named Spencer Silver invented the first superadhesive that could be peeled off surfaces without ruining them. It seemed like a blockbuster product, but the company couldn't figure out what to do with it. Silver became known as Mr. Persistent because he wouldn't give up, always knocking on people's doors, forever slipping his product into presentations. Silver kept at it for five years; still, the invention sat unused.

Then in 1974, another 3M scientist, Art Fry, who had heard one of

Silver's countless talks, was fiddling with his hymnal at church one day when he had a revelation. During Wednesday night choir practice, Fry would bookmark his hymnal with pieces of paper, but by Sunday morning they would have fallen out. "What I need is a bookmark that would stick to the paper without falling off and not damage the sheets," Fry thought. The next day, recalling Mr. Persistent, Fry requested a sample of Silver's adhesive. It took several more years to hone the product, and Fry's supervisors initially balked, fearing the product would seem "wasteful." But 3M executives began noticing more and more employees using the new sticky notes to remind them of their to-do lists. The executives got on board. Today 3M sells 50 billion Post-it notes a year.

*Stalk gatekeepers.* There's an undercurrent that runs through many stalking stories. Entrepreneurs are often outsiders. They're usually not from the best families, the best schools, or the best neighborhoods. That's a key reason you find guerrilla tactics in so many stories of women entrepreneurs. We're not part of the old boys club; we don't tend to hang out in smoke-filled rooms; we're not likely to be sitting at the poker table.

When Sara Blakely was struggling to get Spanx into stores, she cold-called the buyer from Neiman Marcus, who offered her "five minutes" if she flew to Dallas. The two met in a conference room, but after a few minutes Sara realized she wasn't connecting. So she took the woman to the ladies' room, pulled a sample out of her "lucky red backpack," and performed a live demonstration. Three weeks later the product was on Neiman Marcus shelves. "I became notorious for lifting up my pant leg to every woman walking by," Sara said.

One of the most iconic female business leaders of the twentieth century used a similar technique. Josephine Esther "Estelle" Mentzer was the embodiment of an outsider. Born to Hungarian Jewish immigrants in an Italian neighborhood of Queens, Estelle lived over her father's modest hardware store, where she longed for a life of affluence and glamour. When she asked a woman at the beauty salon where she had bought her lovely blouse, the woman coolly replied, "What difference could it possibly make? You could never afford it."

Estelle walked away, heart pounding, face burning. She vowed she would someday have whatever she wanted—"jewels, exquisite art, gracious homes, everything."

Estelle's uncle was a struggling chemist with a line of skin creams he couldn't sell. Estelle tried a new approach: stalking. She stopped women on trains, in elevators, at the market, on the way to a Salvation Army meeting. She whipped out her jar of Super-Rich All-Purpose Cream, pointed out wrinkles on her unsuspecting victims, and insisted she could make them glow. When the ladies demurred, saying they really had somewhere to be, Estelle cut them off mid-sentence. "Just give me five minutes," she implored.

She stalked retailers, too. Because luxury was what Estelle wanted, luxury was what she presented. She changed her first name to Estée and, coupled with her married surname, sold her creams under the brand Estée Lauder—but only in salons and boutiques, never in drugstores. She also kept her sights focused on the grand prize, Saks Fifth Avenue. She hounded the store's cosmetics buyer, Robert Fiske, who made it clear that Saks was not interested in an unproven product by an unknown brand.

So Estée waited for an opening. At a charity luncheon in 1948 at the Waldorf Astoria, she gave away lipstick in metallic sheaths, a significant step up from the more commonly used plastic. When women asked where they could buy the product, Estée smiled and told them to go across the street to Saks.

As Fiske recalled, "There formed a line of people across Park Avenue and across 50th Street into Saks asking for these lipsticks, one after another." The next day Fiske placed an order for $800.

Altogether, the techniques of stalking, following the crowd, building prototypes, and betting just a few chickens at a time highlight a broader theme of getting started as an entrepreneur: What seems like a daunting process from the outside can actually be broken down into less daunting steps. You don't need to risk everything to be an entrepreneur, but you do need to take smart risks. And the key word here is "take." None of these strategies will work if you don't muster the courage to try them.

A few years ago the fashion designer Tory Burch invited me to an event hosted by her foundation. It was a speed dating session between mentors and butterflies. Mentors were stationed at long tables; mentees sat down for ten minutes and at the sound of a bell moved to the next person. I met a woman who ran a catering company and another who sold flower arrangements. Then a young clothing designer sat across from me.

"I'm so happy to be here!" she began. "I know this is cheesy, but Tory's like my role model. She has had an amazing career, and her designs—"

At this point I stopped listening and started looking around the room. Spotting Tory, who was leaning against a wall, I turned back to the young designer and said, "You should say all of that to her. She's right there."

"But—what?" the young designer stammered. "Am I supposed to, like, go up to Tory Burch?"

"Yes!" I said.

"Oh, no, I couldn't do that," she said, shaking her head.

"Look, Tory *invited* you here," I said. "She's an entrepreneur. Go talk to her."

At that point the bell rang, and the woman moved on to the next table. But as the evening was drawing to a close, I saw the young designer chatting with Tory, proudly handing her business card to her role model.

Entrepreneurs know how to hedge their bets, but they also know when to play their cards.

# CHAPTER 3

## *Chaos Is Your Friend*

**W**alt Disney was on top of the world. At twenty-six the fiercely determined, relentlessly optimistic movie director, who still looked so young he wore a mustache and carried a pipe to appear sophisticated, had come to New York to celebrate his new movie series featuring the character Oswald the Lucky Rabbit. He even brought along his wife, Lillian.

Walt was finally ready to cash in on the success he had been seeking his entire life, but unbeknownst to him, he was about to receive the biggest blow of his career. The way he responded led to a defining moment in American popular culture and created a signature lesson for entrepreneurs: How you handle defeat is even more important than how you handle success. What you do in the face of fear will ultimately determine whether you surmount that fear. Succumb, you'll always stay small. Overcome, you give yourself the chance to go big.

Walter Elias Disney was a classic entrepreneur. His father, an itinerant carpenter and cabinetmaker, was a teetotaling disciplinarian. He staunchly disapproved when his fourth child showed an interest in drawing. "Walter, you're going to make a career of that, are you?" he said. Walter certainly tried. After a stint in France during World War I,

Walt was repeatedly rebuffed as a newspaper illustrator and went to work at an ad company, where he met a fellow illustrator, Ub Iwerks. The neophytes quickly left to form their own art studio. It failed in a month. They turned to animation, making cartoons in a backyard shed. That company went broke in a year.

During those years Walt learned resilience, what it meant "to take advantage of opportunity." When his brother Roy moved to Los Angeles, Walt followed. He had just forty dollars in his pocket. He sent a proposal to Margaret Winkler, a film distributor in New York, to make a series of short films about Alice in Wonderland and a new creation, Oswald the Lucky Rabbit. Winkler gave him funding, and Walt naively gave her control of the rights. Walt, his brother, and Iwerks hired a team of animators.

When "Ozzie" scored with audiences, Walt traveled to New York to meet Winkler's new husband, Charles Mintz. Walt intended to ask for higher profits; instead he got a nasty surprise. Mintz had secretly hired away Disney's team of animators. Mintz offered Walt a pay cut and demanded full ownership of Oswald. This was Walt's equivalent of Wences's sisters-on-the-couch moment. Lillian was terrified; Roy urged him to settle. But Walt marched into Mintz's office, shoved the new contract in his face, and said, "Here. You can have the little bastard!"

On the long train ride home, Walt brooded. "He was like a raging lion on that train," Lillian said. He had no contract, no income, no employees. Worse, he had no cartoon character. With cats, dogs, bears, rabbits, and every other lovable animal taken, there was nothing left. "About the only thing that hadn't been featured," he thought, "was the mouse."

So he began sketching on train stationery, and by the time they reached Kansas City, he had created a mouse with red velvet pants and two pearly buttons. Walt reportedly wanted to call it Mortimer, but Lillian hated the name. "Too sissy," she said. What did she think of Mickey, an Irish name, an outsider's name? "It's better than Mortimer," she said.

One of the most epic creations in the history of popular culture grew out of a combination of fear and desperation. Mickey Mouse was conceived in a moment of chaos. As Walt summed up his own personality, "I function better when things are going badly than when they're smooth as whipped cream."

Which is why he was such a great entrepreneur.

Setbacks. All dreamers face them. No matter what kind of risk taker you are, eventually you . . . will . . . hit . . . a . . . wall. And if you don't slam into the wall yourself, some external force will send you hurtling toward it.

How you respond represents the third big challenge of getting going: handling moments of instability. One thing I learned working in unstable economies over the years is that stability is the friend of the status quo; chaos is the friend of the entrepreneur. When Endeavor surveyed two hundred entrepreneurs to identify their strengths and weaknesses, the most commonly selected strength was "I see opportunities where others see obstacles."

So how should you react to disorder? Instead of fearing it, embrace it.

Make chaos your friend.

To help you remember, I've organized this chapter into an acronym: CHAOS.

## — CHAMPAGNE FOR YOUR ENEMIES —

The first thing to know about chaos is that it happens to everybody. Turbulence is the official climate of entrepreneurship. Sometimes the source of unrest is external: a natural disaster, a revolution, a war, or, as happened to me, a high-risk pregnancy. Whatever the situation, the key is not to flee from the situation but to run into it.

Like many, I had little choice but to confront my chaotic test. After six years in Latin America, we began to explore taking Endeavor to new continents. Edgar Bronfman, Jr., the CEO of Warner Music, became chairman during this time and vowed, "I don't want us to be charming; I want us to be important." Our first target was South Africa, and I began traveling back and forth to meet potential board members. Over the course of a year I made nine trips.

And then, I got pregnant. With twins. Fulfilling the promise I had made to my parents at their kitchen table, I had managed to find a husband, the author and *New York Times* columnist Bruce Feiler, who was also a dreamer, with just enough "crazy" in him. (He had once been a circus clown.) Suddenly, though, our lives were upside down.

During the most pivotal moment in Endeavor's existence, I was put on bed rest for three months, gave birth to two beautiful daughters, and learned to breastfeed using the "double football" technique, a baby tucked Heisman Trophy–like in each arm. Once, one of my girls slipped off the armrest and tumbled to the ground. My sister-in-law comforted me with a quote from Dr. Spock: "If you haven't dropped your child before age two, you're an overprotective parent."

It was chaos, indeed.

But that disruption forced me to change as an entrepreneur. When I returned from maternity leave, I had no choice but to restructure our organization so it was less reliant on me, a common mistake I had seen other entrepreneurs make yet still repeated myself. I recruited some senior management. I built an international expansion team. I enlarged our board.

By acknowledging the challenging situation, we were forced to become creative, and in the process became stronger. Over the next three years, Endeavor launched offices in five countries in Africa and the Middle East, some that I didn't even visit until they were open. And I never dropped a football again.

The act of turning hardship into change is especially true for dolphin entrepreneurs in the nonprofit sector. Some of the highest-profile social entrepreneurs have turned personal tragedy into groundbreaking initiatives that transformed debates, changed public policy, and saved lives.

• In 1980 thirteen-year-old Cari Lightner of Fair Oaks, California, was walking along a quiet road on her way to a church carnival when a driver swerved out of control and killed her. When Cari's mother, Candace, learned the driver had a record of arrests for intoxication (including a hit-and-run and drunk-driving charge booked only a few days earlier), she decided to fight back. She founded Mothers Against Drunk Driving, which became one of the country's leading organizations pushing for stricter alcohol policy.

• In 1990 Michael J. Fox, already a three-time Emmy Award–winning actor at age thirty, woke up one morning to find a tremble in his left pinky. It was the first sign of Fox's early on-set Parkinson's. He kept the disease secret for eight years. When he finally went public, he vowed to turn his plight into medical breakthroughs. In 2000 he quit his role on *Spin City* and launched the Michael J. Fox Foundation for Parkinson's Research, which has raised more than $400 million.

• The supermodel Petra Nemcova and her fiancé, the photographer Simon Atlee, were vacationing in a beachfront bungalow in Thailand in December 2004, when the Indian Ocean tsunami ripped through their resort and swept them away. Nemcova's pelvis was shattered, and her arm crushed; Atlee was killed. When Nemcova returned the following year, she discovered that emergency relief efforts had stalled and many children had no schools. She founded the Happy Hearts Fund, which has built more than seventy schools in countries affected by natural disasters.

These individuals stumbled into awful situations for which there were no existing solutions. The only solution was to take the initiative themselves to help others prevent, or handle, similar misfortunes. External chaos often affects for-profit entrepreneurs differently.

You're a gazelle; you're going along quite nicely when you suddenly find yourself in the middle of a turmoil you did nothing to create. That's when your entrepreneurial IQ gets tested. In my experience, the flat-footed grow conservative; the nimble-footed get imaginative.

Cairo today has 20 million people and 14 million vehicles, making it one of the world's most crowded and clogged metropolitan areas. Getting stuck in traffic is inevitable. People schedule workdays, weddings, even walks outside around traffic patterns. A recent World Bank study found that Cairo congestion costs the economy $8 billion a year. A presidential debate in 2012, hailed as a sign of burgeoning democracy, was delayed when one of the candidates got stuck in traffic. A CNN reporter tweeted: "No matter who is running [for president], #cairotraffic always wins."

Five cousins set out to create a mobile solution. In 2010 they created an app to crowdsource traffic reports in real time. They named it Bey2ollak (yes, that's a 2, but the name is pronounced bay-oh-lek), Arabic for "it is being said." The name evokes an expression used by frustrated drivers when they roll down their windows and shout traffic warnings to others. Hoping to inject fun into an annoying situation, Bey2ollak invites users to report road conditions using cheeky options like "sweet" (no traffic) and "no hope" (avoid this road at all costs).

While the Israeli crowdsourced traffic app Waze was soaring at the time, the Bey2ollak founders set their sights low. "We didn't really expect that much success," one cousin said. "At the beginning we just wanted to create it because we all got stuck in traffic." But the Egyptian app gained instant traction, amassing five thousand users in its first day. One week after launch Vodafone reached out for an exclusive sponsorship.

Then came the Egyptian revolution. Weeks of instability became months, became years. The stock market plummeted; investment dried up. Did the founders give up and go home? Nope. They adapted. They found a new niche, adding options they never would have imagined, one that gave protesters a list of emergency numbers; a second that marked areas too dangerous because of vandalism. When fuel shortages caused a panic, the Bey2ollak team added a feature displaying the location of gas stations. By 2013 Bey2ollak, which became an Endeavor company, had enlisted more than six hundred thousand subscribers and had expanded into Europe.

The lesson from this story is that events that kick up dust and topple regimes favor the quick and nimble. Because disruption is the essence of entrepreneurship, the more disruptive the world becomes, the more you should look for openings—and keep looking. This strategy can be especially effective for skunks. In the face of sudden change, sometimes even the most plodding companies can drop their normal tendency to drag their feet.

In August 2005 Hurricane Katrina stormed ashore on the Gulf Coast. Marian Croak, a researcher at AT&T's Bell Laboratories, watched the weak relief efforts with dismay. "If people needed clothes, if they needed money, it wasn't clear how to get it to them quickly," she said. Croak had spent her career studying breakthroughs in data communications; she was the first woman in the history of AT&T to receive one hundred patents. She recalled that AT&T had set up a text message voting system for *American Idol* in 2003. If viewers could use their mobile phones to cast votes for Carrie Underwood and Jennifer Hudson, why not have them do the same to donate money to those in need? The contribution would be charged to the customer's cell phone bill, and AT&T would pass the funds quickly to organizations like the Red Cross.

Croak had the idea in late August; she filed for a patent that September. Now that's a skunk who can sprint! When a magnitude 7 earthquake hit Haiti in 2010, relief organizations collected more than $30 million through Croak's text-to-donate invention.

These stories have one thing in common: flashes of entrepreneurship emerging from flashes of instability. My favorite story of this kind occurred two hundred years earlier in an entirely different sort of upheaval.

In 1813, during the Napoleonic Wars, Russia had just invaded France. When Russian troops occupied Reims, in the Champagne region, soldiers were given free rein to loot and pillage local vineyards, including one run by Barbe-Nicole Ponsardin, the young widow of François Clicquot.

But Veuve Clicquot, as she was widely known (*veuve* is French for "widow"), was a cunning adversary, who also happened to have a sharp business mind. Born to prominent parents, Barbe-Nicole Ponsardin had married the heir to the House of Clicquot. He died six years later, leaving the twenty-seven-year-old novice in charge of the family businesses, including banking, wool, and sparkling wine. At the time champagne was a small-time enterprise. Veuve Clicquot revolutionized the industry by storing the bottles upside down in special racks, turning them, then freezing off the excess yeast. The new technique resulted in a sharper taste, less sweet, with smaller bubbles. Her 1811 vintage is said to have been the first truly modern champagne.

Yet no sooner had she perfected it than swarms of Russian soldiers were at her cellar door. Her more experienced rivals chose to go underground. They shuttered their businesses and protected their vineyards against marauding soldiers. At first, Widow Clicquot considered this approach. "Everything is going badly," she wrote a friend. "I have been occupied for many days with walling up my cellars, but I know full well that this will not prevent them from being robbed and pillaged. If so, I am ruined."

Then Clicquot did what all good entrepreneurs do. She pivoted to seize a marketing opportunity. She resolved to get the Russian Army wasted. Her bet was that when the soldiers returned to Russia, they would have an insatiable taste for her champagne. "Today they drink," she said. "Tomorrow they will pay!" She drowned them in wine but smartly held back the vintage of 1811. When French soldiers arrived a few months later to push out the Russians, she repeated her stunt. She gave Napoleon's officers free champagne and glasses, but because they couldn't hold the flutes while riding on their horses, they took their military sabres and lopped off the necks of the bottles. The ceremonial custom of *sabrage* was born.

Veuve Clicquot's biggest gambit came in 1814. When it became clear that the war would soon end, she took several thousand bottles of that 1811 vintage and decided to risk them all, running the blockade, shipping them to Russia, beating her competitors to a lucrative market. The plan worked. Russians had already been clamoring for the Widow by name. The moment a cease-fire was announced, her bottles arrived in Moscow and St. Petersburg, a drinking frenzy ensued, and Czar Alexander soon declared he would drink nothing else. Veuve Clicquot became a leading international luxury brand and the Grande Dame of Champagne is often credited with becoming the first woman to lead a multinational business.

There is a kicker to this story. In recognition of the Widow's achievement, Veuve Clicquot today gives annual awards to female business leaders. In 2008 I won one of these awards. The prize was having a grapevine in Reims named after me. The Rottenberg grape may be coming to a vintage near you someday soon!

In case after case, entrepreneurs who succeed in times of turmoil manage to contain their fear or anxiety. They don't succumb to the agitation around them; they stay calm, recognize the opportunities that the disruption around them creates, then seek to exploit them. They respond to chaos not with panic but with strategic precision. If anything, they use the disruption to outflank their competitors.

So next time adversity approaches or you face down a foe, don't rush for shelter. Instead, channel the Widow, pop some bubbly, and clink with the enemy.

## — HUG THE BEAR —

Bubbles don't only burst in war, of course. Sometimes the chaos that hits an entrepreneur is economic: recession, downturn, credit crunch, market collapse. Through no fault of your own, suddenly expenses mount, business dries up, donations wither. Then what?

Whet your appetite.

Warren Buffett says his approach to investing is: "Be fearful when others are greedy and be greedy when others are fearful." Entrepreneurs can learn a lot from that attitude. When markets collapse, the temptation is to retrench, harbor assets, wait out the storm. To be sure, sometimes you do need to step back and conserve resources to prepare for growth later, but whenever possible, resist that temptation.

Downturns are often the best time to strike big. The history of entrepreneurship shows that moments of distress—the ones that are most miserable for entrenched players—are precisely the ones that are most favorable for outsiders. A study by the Kauffman Foundation found that over half of today's Fortune 500 companies were started during recessions or bear markets. The list includes IBM, General Motors, and Microsoft. Some of the country's most storied brands were launched in troubled times: Hyatt, Revlon, IHOP, Burger King, *Sports Illustrated*, CNN, and MTV. FedEx was started during the oil crisis of 1973, HP during the Great Depression, and Procter & Gamble as far back as the Panic of 1837.

The same dynamic occurred in the Great Recession of 2008. Kauffman has tracked the number of new firms started in the United States ever since 1996. Before the recession the number stood at 470,000 a month; afterward it reached 565,000 a month. The rate of start-ups surged 15 percent between 2007 and 2009.

How can instability be good for business? Two ways.

First, it's a good time to hire. Jim Collins, the author of the management classics *Good to Great* and *Great by Choice*, said, "In rapid-growth times it's hard to get the right people—you're more likely to compromise on who you get." In periods of uncertainty, that logjam opens. Many talented people get laid off, leaving them more willing to consider nontraditional careers, even take pay cuts. Many workers who still have jobs meanwhile start to realize their positions are not safe, opening them up to new opportunities with more flexibility and freedom.

This freeing up of talent clearly benefits dolphins. At first blush, nonprofit entrepreneurs would seem to be in for rough times when the economy gets tough. And it's true that government grants and philanthropic dollars often shrivel up during recessions. But hiring gets easier. When making money gets more challenging for people, having more meaning becomes more important. A report from Johns Hopkins University chronicling employment for the first decade of the twenty-first century, a period that included two recessions, found that nonprofit employment grew at an average annual rate of 2.1 percent while for-profit employment declined 0.6 percent.

I saw this firsthand at Endeavor. Starting in 2009 we were able to bring on a suite of senior managers—executives with twenty years of experience in top-flight companies like Dell and Bloomberg. We became a magnet for college and business school grads seeking jobs with impact and meaning. And we weren't alone. Applications at Teach For America grew by a third; at AmeriCorps, they tripled. Diana Aviv, head of a nonprofit trade group, said it became common to hear of more than one hundred applications for a single position. "Some of these people haven't been employed for a while and are happy to have something," she said. "But once they're there, they've recalibrated and reoriented themselves toward public service."

Second, periods of instability provide a good opportunity for taking chances.

A great case study is Greece in the wake of its 2009 economic meltdown. Entrepreneurship boomed. Forty-one thousand new businesses were formed in 2012. Ninety percent of these newcomers were small-scale enterprises—restaurants, cafés, clothing stores. But the biggest gains came from the minority of high-growth businesses. A 2013 study by Endeavor Greece found that this group, which included energy, technology, and food-processing companies, grew by 40 percent a year for three consecutive years. Most of these founders were not people who were forced into starting businesses. They were young people between twenty-five and forty-five, with high education and at least three years' experience in the private sector. They had options. Still, the destabilized economy had turned them into entrepreneurs—gazelles—by choice.

Nikos Kakavoulis and Phaedra Chrousos are good examples. They met at Columbia Business School in 2006 and bonded over their love of Athens. Nikos returned to Greece to launch digital editions of *Vogue, Glamour,* and *Men's Health.* Phaedra worked as a consultant. When the economy spiraled downward, the two grew frustrated by all the negative press. Nikos began sending friends daily e-mails listing one unique local discovery in Athens, a "best-kept secret," from a hidden bakery to a hush-hush event.

The e-mails went viral. From a few dozen friends, Daily Secret grew to more than thirty thousand members in just three months. The curated notices attracted users with their upbeat tone and stunning visuals. "It wasn't too long before we realized that cities all over the world were starving for a daily dose of positive energy," Nikos said. Daily Secret soon launched in Istanbul and has rolled out a new city nearly every month since. By early 2014 the company was covering thirty cities worldwide and had grown to over a million and a half subscribers.

I met Nikos and Phaedra in 2012, just as Endeavor publicly launched in Athens. They were among our first entrepreneurs in Greece. That September I appeared on CNBC's *Squawk Box* to announce our first country operation in Europe. The host, Andrew Ross Sorkin, was skeptical. "If you were going to start doing business in Europe," he said, "why in God's name would you choose Greece?"

"Because when economies turn down, entrepreneurs look up!" I said.

Now I'm not Pollyanna. I know that entrepreneurship is hard and that recession can make it harder. Most firms will not survive. But working with gazelles in places where the environment is brutal even in the best of times has convinced me that periods of decline are when entrepreneurs show their grit. If anything, entrepreneurs feel more at home during these times because it reminds them of their earliest days, when their families wouldn't support them, banks wouldn't lend to them, and industry bigwigs wouldn't respond to them. They had no choice but to be scrappy.

Even people who've never done anything entrepreneurial but then suddenly lose their jobs have reason to feel optimistic about their new-found willingness to take risk: They're in good company. Bernie Marcus (forty-nine years old) and Arthur Blank (thirty-six) started Home Depot after being booted from Handy Dan. Michael Bloomberg (thirty-nine) used his severance check from Salomon Brothers to launch his firm. Maybe the most famous of these inadvertent entrepreneurs is the twenty-six-year-old woman who was sacked from her secretary job in London.

In the late 1980s Joanne Rowling was working at Amnesty International, supposedly researching human rights violations but secretly writing stories on her work computer. She was fired. Next, she took a secretarial job at the Manchester Chamber of Commerce but was, in her own words, "the worst secretary ever." Again she spent her days inventing characters. Again her employers got fed up and gave her the boot. Not long after, Rowling was on a long train ride from Manchester to London when a thought popped into her head: What if a little boy embarked on a train that enabled him to escape the boring adult world and enter a place where he was literally and metaphorically powerful? She had outlined several books of the young wizard's adventures by the time her train pulled into the station.

Rowling's butterfly path was hardly direct. She had briefly married, had a child, divorced, and was forced to live on the dole with her young daughter before she finished her manuscript. It was rejected by a dozen publishers. The chairman of Bloomsbury, however, brought it home for his eight-year-old daughter to read. The little girl loved it. Rowling received an advance of £1,500 for *Harry Potter and the Philosopher's*

*Stone*. Fearing that boys would not want to read a book by a woman, the publisher insisted she adopt a gender-neutral pen name. With no middle name, Rowling added the *K* in honor of her grandmother Kathleen. (The comedian in Sara Blakely would approve.)

Part of acting like an entrepreneur is learning to turn around bleak situations. I'm not suggesting it's easy. It's not *supposed* to be easy. But if you want to overturn the old order, what you need is a little disorder. Embrace it. If you can't run with the bulls, you might as well hug the bear.

## — ADMIT YOU SCREWED UP —

Sometimes the chaos you face as an entrepreneur is not outside your control. It's a crisis of your own doing: You picked the wrong strategy; you made the wrong bet; you executed poorly; you lost your way. In short, you screwed up. Your instinct may be to pretend it didn't happen and hope the problem goes away. You're not alone. Lots of entrepreneurs have chosen this path, but it's the wrong one. The truth is, there's only one way out.

Own it.

Leon Leonwood Bean was managing his brother Ervin's dry goods store in Freeport, Maine, in 1911, when he decided to address a pressing problem: his constantly rain-soaked feet. He hit upon the idea of sewing lightweight leather uppers to the rubber soles of galoshes and convinced a local cobbler to make him a pair. Eureka! Bean became so convinced these boots were his ticket to financial success that he had one hundred pairs made and set out to sell them through the mail. He obtained the addresses of out-of-state Maine hunting license holders and sent each a flyer, in which he proclaimed: "You cannot expect success hunting deer or moose if your feet are not properly dressed. The Maine Hunting Shoe is designed by a hunter who has tramped the Maine woods for the last 18 years. We guarantee them to give perfect satisfaction in every way."

His marketing worked: All one hundred pairs of shoes were sold. Ninety were promptly returned. The stitching that held the leather tops in place had come undone as soon as the shoes were out of the box. Bean lived up to his word: He refunded everyone's money. But he also went a step further. He borrowed money and convinced the U.S. Rubber Company to mold a heavier bottom that would support the stitching. Then he sent every unsatisfied customer a new pair of shoes, free of charge. Word of mouth about his honesty and quality service spread; more orders poured in; Maine had its first retailing superstar, L. L. Bean.

Bean's near-fatal mistake formed the bedrock of his business philosophy. He would field-test every new product the company sold, sneaking out of the office for afternoons of camping, hunting, and fishing. Reminiscent of the Banana Republic founders, Bean also wrote his own advertising copy and personally responded to customer letters. As one observer wrote, "It's as if Bean were family, some sort of mildly eccentric but amiable uncle who lives up in Maine and sends us packages." And it wasn't just hype. Customers could return any L. L. Bean product for a replacement or full refund, and he never even charged for shipping. Bean's brand became known for its 100 percent satisfaction guarantee.

A century later the founders of another clothing company learned a similar lesson, though in their case it was more than a pair of boots that needed repairing. Bonobos is an online men's clothing retailer founded in 2007, but a mistake in 2011 almost brought down the company. It happened on Cyber Monday. Bonobos was offering discounts as large as 60 percent, and executives knew that traffic would be hefty. CEO Andy Dunn had hired a new head of technology, and the two had spent weeks bracing for orders. Still, they were unprepared for the volume. Internet sales exploded that year, and Bonobos was swamped. The site crashed.

Dunn took ownership of the problem. He took the site down and announced he was leaving it dark for as long as it took to fix the glitches. More important, he fessed up. In place of the cleanly designed Bonobos home page, he put a "fail whale" page that showed a guy with his pants at his ankles and the line "Caught us with our pants down." He told *Inc.* magazine later, "We were saying, 'We screwed up.'" Using the hashtag #SaveBonobos, the company also took to Twitter with witty self-deprecating remarks. On Quora, a question-and-answer Web site, Bonobos's design team began a dialogue with customers.

The Web site remained off-line for another two days. When it went back live, customers who had missed out on the sale were offered discounted prices. The company had an awful month, "because we deserved it," Dunn said. "It felt insurmountable, but it brought people together. I remember seeing everybody jamming on a Saturday and seeing the good energy and thinking, 'We'll be OK.'" Customers agreed. On social media, shoppers praised the company's honesty. One Facebook user wrote: "You guys have always topped my Best Customer Service list and have handled this outage beautifully. Keep up the great service and great communication! Signed, Customer for life."

One of the more dramatic business turnaround stories of recent years hinged not on one apology but two. In July 2011 Reed Hastings, the CEO of Netflix and *Fortune*'s "Businessperson of the Year," announced he was splitting his company into two services, one to ship discs, the other to stream video. Eight hundred thousand customers immediately bolted. Hastings issued an apology on the company's blog. "I messed up," he wrote. "It is clear from the feedback that many members felt we lacked respect and humility in the way we announced the separation." He went on: "In hindsight, I slid into arrogance based upon past success." He even issued a video confession. But he continued to move forward with the unpopular strategy, and the stock continued to plunge.

Media critics swarmed. Even *Saturday Night Live* mocked Hastings and his Hawaiian shirts. Three weeks later Hastings posted another entry on his blog. The company would stay as one. "It is clear that for many of our members two websites would make things more difficult, so we are going to keep Netflix as one place to go for streaming and DVDs." The stock kept falling, from a high $298 to $53.

At that point Hastings stopped talking and went back to work. He rebuilt his business; he invested $100 million in *House of Cards*; he even changed how he dressed (less beachwear, more business attire). The turnabout worked. The company added millions of streaming subscribers; *House of Cards* was a critical and commercial hit. Netflix ended 2013 as the single best-performing stock in the S&P 500, rising 298 percent. By early 2014 the stock was trading near $400.

So what did Hastings learn from the debacle and recovery? "I realized, if our business is about making people happy, which it is, then I had made a mistake," he told the columnist James Stewart. "The hardest part was my own sense of guilt. I love the company. I worked really hard to make it successful, and I screwed up. The public shame didn't bother me. It was the private shame of having made a big mistake." Hastings said he didn't expect the apology alone to turn things around. "I wasn't naïve enough to think most customers care if the C.E.O. apologizes, but I thought it was honest and appropriate." His new focus: "pleasing and growing our membership."

Apologies need to be real and meaningful to make a difference. Dov Seidman, the founder of LRN, a firm that advises companies on their cultures, dismissed most CEO mea culpas as "apology theater." In 2014 Seidman, along with the *New York Times* journalist Andrew Ross Sorkin, established an "apology watch" to call out fakers. The one CEO Seidman cited whose genuine apology and subsequent actions succeeded: Netflix's Reed Hastings.

Entrepreneurs face enough setbacks that you can't control. If you're the source of your problems, be honest, be forthright, be contrite. Then get back to work.

## — *ONCE UPON A TIME* —

The easiest thing to do when your company hits rocky waters is to abandon your core principles and do anything to survive. That's understandable. It's also misguided.

One consistent theme of entrepreneurs who deftly navigate chaos is they don't just look forward; they also look back. They don't just seize opportunities, own their mistakes, and move on. In the midst of whatever mess they're in, they also return to their core values. They reconnect with their origin stories. As the great business historian Alfred Chandler, Jr., liked to put it, "How can you know where you're going if you don't know where you've been?"

One stunning example of this strategy is Howard Schultz. In January 2008 Schultz, the chairman and retired CEO of Starbucks, called an emergency meeting of the board. With the stock down 50 percent, Schultz announced that he had fired his handpicked successor and was returning to run the company. Executives had "watered down" the Starbucks experience, he said, crowding counters with stuffed animals, eliminating aromas by pregrinding coffee, and, worst of all, installing automated espresso machines that removed the "romance and theater" of the barista's work. "It is not going to be good enough to 'go back to the future,'" he said. "There is a piece of the past that we need; we have to find and bring the soul of our company back."

Those are just words, of course, but Schultz took unheard-of actions. First he closed all 7,100 stores in the United States for three and a half hours on a Tuesday afternoon to retrain the baristas in the "art of espresso." Wall Street was furious. Analysts were more upset when he spent $30 million taking ten thousand store managers to New Orleans for a retreat. Schultz said he wanted to be "vulnerable and transparent with them about what is really at stake here, how desperate the situation is." He also batted away personal pleas from big investors to cut back on health care costs and dial back on quality, a potential savings of hundreds of millions of dollars.

From its all-time low a few months after Schultz retook control, Starbucks stock rose nearly tenfold in the next five years. Asked why, Schultz credited the company's return to its bedrock: "The equity of the brand is defined by the quality of the coffee, but most importantly, the relationship that the barista has with the customer."

Founders aren't the only ones who can return to their entrepreneurial origins in times of turmoil. Consider Angela Ahrendts, whom I think of as the skunk in a trench coat. In 2006 Ahrendts, who grew up in New Palestine, Indiana (population 2,053), was not a likely candidate to take over the iconic British fashion brand Burberry. One of six siblings growing up in a modest house, Ahrendts had slept in a coat closet underneath a stairwell and sewn her own clothing. The London press mocked her midwestern style and unglamorous roots.

But the six-foot-three-inch-tall Ahrendts, who went on to work at Donna Karan and Henri Bendel, had a formidable business sense. She loved strong, consistent brands that hewed to their traditions. Burberry was far from that. The 150-year-old company was faltering. At a time of rapid expansion in luxury brands, Burberry was flat. The company had twenty-three licensees around the world, each selling something different, from dog leashes to kilts. "In luxury, ubiquity will kill you," Ahrendts said. "It means you're not really luxury anymore."

The turning point came in her first strategic planning meeting. Her top sixty managers had flown to London from around the world. The weather was quintessentially British—chilly, gray, and damp. But not one of the managers was wearing a Burberry trench coat. Ahrendts thought, "If our top people weren't buying our products, despite the great discount they could get, how could we expect customers to pay full price for them?"

Ahrendts turned to a young designer from her Donna Karan years, Christopher Bailey, to help her return Burberry to its roots. The process was messy. She dubbed Bailey the brand czar and declared all designs would go through his office, no exceptions. She then fired the entire Hong Kong–based design team and brought designers from around the world to the U.K. to be retrained by Bailey. At one point, Ahrendts was called to testify before Parliament about her controversial decision to shutter a Welsh factory. But she never deviated. Burberry must return to its heritage: rainwear.

In the 1880s young Thomas Burberry, a former draper's apprentice, had invented gabardine, a waterproof fabric that he used to make raincoats. He was asked to design a durable coat to be worn by British soldiers in the trenches of World War I. After the war the Burberry "trench coat" became synonymous with British culture, eventually earning a royal warrant that entitled the company to supply the royal family. The explorer Ernest Shackleton wore his Burberry across Antarctica; George Mallory wore his on his failed attempt to scale Everest. Hollywood stars, from Humphrey Bogart to Greta Garbo, donned them in movie stills.

Ahrendts wanted to return the company to that glittering past. "I always remind employees that we didn't found the company, Thomas Burberry did—at the age of 21. He was young. He was innovative. We say that his spirit lives on, and that it's this generation's job to keep his legacy going."

Being nonconventional skunks, she and Bailey weren't content with the familiar beige and plaid. They added metallic purple and alligator epaulets. While her brand czar pushed the designs, Ahrendts focused on expansion. In six years she opened 132 stores, all focused on selling outerwear. She reeducated the staff to sell the Burberry craftsmanship and reoriented the marketing around a new generation of customers: millennials.

In 2011 Burberry was named the fastest-growing luxury brand on the Interbrand index and the fourth fastest-growing brand overall, behind Apple, Google, and Amazon. The next year the company reached $3 billion in revenues, double the amount of five years earlier. In 2013 Ahrendts announced she was leaving Burberry to join Apple—not as CEO but as the skunk in charge of retail. Score one for trench coat warfare!

Score another for one of the key lessons for entrepreneurs in chaos: If you're feeling lost in the woods, go back to "once upon a time."

## — SHIFT HAPPENS —

A year after my children were born, I took one of my trips abroad, to São Paulo. While there, I went to see Jorge Paulo Lemann and Beto Sicupira, who now run 3G Capital, one of the most influential global investment firms in the world, owners of Anheuser-Busch and large chunks of Burger King and Heinz. Both men were founding board members of Endeavor Brazil. I was still tender from all the turmoil Endeavor had been going through and expressed my frustration and fear.

I wanted to understand from Beto and Jorge Paulo what I was doing wrong. Weren't things supposed to get easier? Beto, who is the scrappier, more tactical of the two, gave me a brisk pep talk. "You're a pioneer. It's supposed to be hard. If it were easy, someone else would have done your idea before you." He patted me on the shoulder and walked out of the room.

Then Jorge Paulo said something that has stuck with me ever since. A graduate of Harvard and onetime tennis prodigy who played in Wimbledon, Jorge Paulo has a smooth, avuncular manner that masks a steely will. He told me to imagine the hard times he and his partners had faced: currency devaluations, triple-digit inflation, stock market crashes, coups, general strikes. "Every day in our world is another existential threat," he said.

But that's what made them strong, he continued. "Our main advantage is that we've been tested in an environment of great economic turmoil and major transformations. The ups and downs of the economy prepared us to deal with adverse situations."

His point was clear: Entrepreneurs have to be masters of chaos.

Research backs him up. A major study of business leaders in emerging markets, conducted by professors at the University of Pennsylvania and the University of Oviedo in Spain, found that because they came of age in turbulent environments, they're less crippled by fear than their U.S.-bred counterparts and better positioned to exploit opportunities. The study concluded: "All companies need to be able to function in chaotic, unpredictable business environments."

I heard the same point as well from two Endeavor entrepreneurs I met on that trip to Brazil. Mario Chady and Eduardo Ourivio were running several quick-dining restaurants when the country's monetary system collapsed. Inflation spiked 70 percent a month. "We changed the menu pricing once a week," Mario said. "Life was crazy. I raced back and forth among my restaurants on my motorcycle." Unable to withstand the pressure, the entrepreneurs declared bankruptcy.

Then they set out to rebuild. Mario went to work full-time at his worst-performing store. Each corner of the restaurant had a different food station, and Mario and Eduardo soon noticed that the most popular was the pasta station, where the chef prepared meals in front of the customers. Seizing on that insight, they created the concept of Spoleto, where the customer can choose the ingredients of a meal— the pasta, the sauce, the toppings—then watch it being prepared.

Next, Mario and Eduardo turned to culture. With so much turmoil, employees felt anxious about their future. While few emerging market firms offer profit sharing or stock options, Spoleto offered both. "We wanted everyone, from the CEO down to the dishwashers, to share our dream," Mario said. Even fewer companies go public, meaning that the stock options were not likely to amount to much. So Mario and Eduardo infused every aspect of Spoleto with their own natural enthusiasm and fun. They hired a former actor to train the waitstaff on presentation and a circus performer to teach chefs how to juggle. Allowing the team to make meal preparation more theatrical empowered the staff to feel like ambassadors for the company.

The bet paid off. In an industry racked with high turnover, Spoleto's turnover is a third of the national average. In 2013 Spoleto generated annual revenues of $340 million, employed 7,000 people, and managed 470 restaurants. They were also preparing to open the first Spoleto outlet in the United States.

Reflecting on his journey, Mario told me, "Even when it's hard, even on those days when you want to crawl back into bed, you have to keep remembering the big dream. Don't let outside chaos, like the economy, deter you. Use it to your advantage."

Eduardo added, "In businesses like ours, *shift* happens!"

When I first started out, I believed that rough patches were just that, rough patches. Now I know better. I tell our entrepreneurs not to make the same naïve mistake I did. After the hard spells things don't "go back to normal." Hard *is* normal. Status quo is Sturm und Drang.

Or as Eduardo put it, shift happens.

So be prepared. When chaos is the everyday, you'd better make chaos your friend. If not, while you're busy complaining about your misfortune, somebody else will board a train somewhere and conjure up Harry Potter, Mickey Mouse, or some other crazy invention.

And you'll be stuck holding Oswald the rabbit.

# PART II

# Go Big

# CHAPTER 4

# *Your Entrepreneur Personality*

K atherine Briggs didn't dislike the man her daughter, Isabel, brought home for Christmas in 1915. But she did think their personalities were incompatible. Isabel was spontaneous, imaginative, and whimsical. Her boyfriend, Clarence "Chief" Myers, was logical, deliberate, and meticulous. Yet the two appeared happy. How could that be?

Inspired by her daughter's unusual taste in men, Katherine began scouring biographies and identified four personality types: meditative, spontaneous, sociable, and executive. When she hit upon Carl Jung's book *Psychological Types*, she told Isabel, "This is it!" and integrated his research into her typology. Both mother and daughter, now married to Chief, continued observing people and labeling their "types" for the next two decades. (Actually, Isabel continued for sixty-one years, the length of her marriage to her "incompatible" boyfriend.)

After the start of World War II Isabel read an article in *Reader's Digest* about how women flooding into the workplace were having trouble finding the right job. She realized her mother's research might be able to help women secure work that fitted their personalities. Isabel began testing everyone she could find—friends, students, office workers. The test she created, the Myers-Briggs Type Indicator, became the most popular workplace diagnostic ever, taken by over 50 million people.

I'm a big fan of Myers-Briggs and other tests like it. (I'm an ENTP in Myers-Briggs, an ID in DISC, and a Type 7 in Enneagram.) I know from experience they help me understand myself better. And as someone who's occasionally accused of being impatient, I also know they've helped me at work to realize that not everybody is motivated in the same way. Perhaps that's why, a few years into running Endeavor, after realizing that almost every entrepreneur I met kept tripping on familiar hurdles in his or her quest to go big, I decided to do something similar. I set out to create a personality test that could help entrepreneurs identify their best and worst traits.

The process took several years. First, my team and I analyzed the thousands of entrepreneurs we screened over the years and the fifty international selection panel events, during which we debated the merits of candidates at their inflection points. Then we brought in from Bain & Company a top team that sent a detailed questionnaire to two hundred of our entrepreneurs. Bain followed up with in-depth interviews; we crunched the data; we debated. In the end we settled on four entrepreneur personality types:

**Diamond:** *Visionary dreamers leading disruptive ventures*

**Star:** *Charismatic individuals building personality brands*

**Transformer:** *Change makers reenergizing traditional industries*

**Rocketship:** *Analytical thinkers making strategic improvements*

These types are different from the species I've been talking about so far—gazelle, skunk, dolphin, and butterfly—which have to do with the field you work in. The profile types are more focused on your personality: your strengths and pitfalls as a leader; your good tendencies as a change maker and your bad ones. The more you know about your instincts as an entrepreneur, the more effective you'll be.

That's especially true at the stage I want to turn to in this section: going big.

Many books about entrepreneurship play the same trick, and it's the same one they pull in romantic comedies in Hollywood. They show the meet-cute moment between the founders, the amusing hurdles they face on the way to the altar, and the drive they make into the sunset, after they have their first big win. From there on it's happily ever after.

If only.

"Starting a company is like getting married," said Georges Doriot, the father of venture capital. "Most of the problems are discovered after the honeymoon is over."

In this section I'm going to help you tackle those post-honeymoon problems. Over the next few chapters, I'll focus on the raucous day-to-day challenges of managing a fast-moving enterprise, especially honing your leadership skills, finding and keeping talent, and getting the most out of your mentors.

But I want to begin with what I believe is the first critical step to going big: knowing who you are. Just as all the new workers flooding into the workplace in the 1940s needed to understand who they were, so all the entrepreneurs flooding into the workplace today need to know who they are. Every entrepreneur has a personality type. What type are you?

## — DIAMONDS —

Steve Jobs. Mark Zuckerberg. Sergey Brin and Larry Page. Ted Turner. George Lucas. Elon Musk. Diamond entrepreneurs are brilliant dreamers who start bold, disruptive organizations. They are charismatic evangelists who capture the imagination of everyone they meet as they talk about revolutionizing people's lives. Diamonds envision a more exciting world, then inspire others to help them achieve it. But diamonds often lack a clear road map for growth; they tend to have highly unstable and unpredictable futures. When diamonds succeed, they can be game changers. But when they fail, it's often quick and messy.

Endeavor entrepreneur Brahms Chouity grew up in Lebanon and Saudi Arabia, studied hospitality in Switzerland, and started a number of companies in the Middle East that ranged from interior design to finance. He even opened the Saudi office for a line of British sports cars. He moved fast, acted quickly, and took ninety trips a year. Then, in 2010, when his wife announced she was pregnant, Brahms declared he was taking a sabbatical. His wife was thrilled. Yet when he stationed himself on the couple's couch in Beirut and proceeded to indulge himself in his favorite pastime, playing video games, her patience ebbed. Three days into Brahms's sabbatical, she gave him an ultimatum: "Find some way of making money or no more consoles in the house."

He needed a new scheme, quick. Late one night, after a daylong binge of gaming, he watched *The Social Network*, about the early days of Facebook. This was his level-up moment: There was no social network to connect gamers across different platforms—Xbox, PlayStation, PC. "If Mark Zuckerberg can do it, why can't I?" he said. "That little kid is younger than me." So he did. With the help of a designer, Brahms created At7addak (pronounced at-ha-dak), Arabic for "I challenge you." Gamers flocked to the site, EA and Activision offered sponsorship, but revenues were modest. So Brahms pivoted to a more user-generated model. He invited contributors to submit reviews and videos, offering to split the advertising with them. Within two years he had 600,000 active users and 8 million monthly page views.

Brahms's strengths as an entrepreneur are apparent to anyone who meets him. He's driven; he's confident; he's an idea machine. But his weaknesses are also clear. He's impulsive. One minute he's studying hotel management, the next he's selling sports cars, soon he's building a social network. Can he stick to anything? Does he have the patience to build a sustainable business, or will he jump at the new, new thing the second he has the chance?

Brahms, in my classification, is a diamond. Entrepreneurs like him either go big or fail fast.

With each profile type, we've identified key questions the entrepreneurs should be asking, along with their backers, team members, mentors, even friends and family. With diamonds, these questions are:

- Is there a big enough idea, product, or service that gives the enterprise an edge?

- Is the entrepreneur likely to stick with this venture or will s/he cut and run the minute a shiny, new opportunity presents itself?

- Is the entrepreneur open to feedback and criticism?

- Does the entrepreneur share credit?

These last points are particularly critical for diamonds. Consider Elon Musk, the South African entrepreneur behind PayPal and the groundbreaking mind who created SpaceX and Tesla. Musk is frequently described as a genius, a tech wunderkind. When Musk started Tesla Motors, the electric car company, in 2003, he declared, "We're going to be the next GM," and vowed to put 100,000 cars on the road by 2009. Though he missed his initial goal by 99,400 cars, eventually Musk's relentless vision won out: *Consumer Reports* named the Tesla Model S its overall top pick for 2014 and that year the electric car maker reached a valuation of $30 billion, or just over half of GM.

But this gazelle-diamond is equally often described as autocratic and stubborn. His first CEO sued him, saying Musk had slandered him and taken undue credit for founding the company. When the *New York Times* criticized the Model S, Musk called the story a "fake" and an "ethics violation" and launched a month-long personal attack on the reporter.

Diamonds are brilliant, but it's often all about them.

The ultimate diamond was Steve Jobs. On the upside, at every stage of his storied career, Jobs succeeded in bending reality to fit his vision. A member of his Macintosh design team likened Jobs's mixture of stubbornness and creativity to the reality distortion field in *Star Trek*. "In his presence, reality is malleable," the designer said. But that conviction meant he tuned out others (including customers) and was unwilling to share the spotlight. Apple's design guru Jony Ive described what it was like to bring Jobs fresh ideas. "He will go through a process of looking at my ideas and say, 'That's no good. That's not very good. I like that one.'" Later Ive said, "I will be sitting in the audience and he will be talking about it as if it was his idea. I pay maniacal attention to where an idea comes from, and I even keep notebooks filled with my ideas. So it hurts when he takes credit for one of my designs."

A diamond is not always an employee's best friend.

Not all diamonds are fast-growing, profit-seeking gazelles. Some, like me, are dolphins. When Peter and I founded Endeavor, we believed we had a revolutionary idea. We vowed to build something unique on the basis of a future only we could see. That confidence was our positive. Our negatives were that we both are stubborn, I'm easily distracted and was slow to prove I could work with others, and Peter generates lots of ideas and left the daily operations of Endeavor after a year to pursue another one. That left me to prove I could focus, hire the right people, and give them the freedom to succeed.

Each entrepreneur type has risks. Knowing your potentially fatal flaws—or what I call "red flags"—can help you avoid disaster. For diamonds, this is my advice:

**Listen to learn.** *Diamonds often say they want to be their own bosses, but no one can do it alone. You need a robust team of* *mentors, partners, and employees. If you're too stubborn to take criticism, you'll be too slow to uncover problems.*

**Share your success.** *Hiring a team is not enough; you need to reward your team. And remember, everyone is not like you. Some people like praise; others like perks; others prefer a challenge they can master or time off. Find out what motivates and inspires your team members and give it to them. Remind yourself to share the credit and spread the spoils.*

**The customer is sometimes right.** *Your personal drive and vision may be your greatest assets, but sorry, you're not Steve Jobs. Don't dismiss your customers. Your organization might be offering something totally groundbreaking, but that doesn't mean users will unconditionally like it. Design the right feedback system and act on what you hear.*

## — STARS —

Oprah Winfrey. Martha Stewart. Richard Branson. Estée Lauder. Giorgio Armani. Jay-Z. Star entrepreneurs are dynamic trendsetters with big personalities who inspire deep loyalty among diverse audiences. Stars instinctively know what's coming in the culture; they're two steps ahead of everyone else. Stars become a source of pride for their communities, their cultures, and their countries. When they become big, they can go global. But they're often one-person shows, change their minds frequently, and can be undisciplined with time and money.

The Endeavor entrepreneur Anton Wirjono wanted to be more than just the best DJ in Jakarta. While studying business in California, the Indonesia native had spun records to earn extra cash. Returning home, he put aside his accounting books and pursued his passion for dance music. He quickly became the godfather of Indonesia's hip-hop scene. MTV Indonesia named him one of "10 People with a Midas Touch."

Inspired by Jakarta's overnight markets, Anton and four partners organized a series of four-day pop-up fashion markets. They attracted seventy-five thousand people. The group opened a department store called The Goods Dept that sold carefully curated products. A Goods Café followed, along with two more stores and an e-commerce site. With Indonesia's creative class booming, the Goods Group was becoming the go-to destination of a new class of urban sophisticates. Anton was its icon or, as he billed himself, the "universal provider of everything cool."

When I met Anton, his strengths as an entrepreneur were clear: He's charismatic; he's hip; he has an eye for trends. Also, he attracts loyal followers and gives them a satisfying experience. He's a taste-maker. But Anton's weaknesses were equally clear. Would his artistic sensibilities take precedence over his business instincts? Knowing the latest trends is great, but sooner or later you're going to need those accounting books under the bed. Was he willing to sully himself with day-to-day management? If not, maybe he'd be better as the chief curation officer instead of chief executive officer. Finally, would he lose his touch for taste making?

Anton, in my classification, is a star. Some stars continue to burn bright, while others ignite quickly then fade.

Stars face steep challenges to going big:

- Can the idea grow beyond the entrepreneur's charisma? Is it a cult of personality, a one man/woman show?

- Because many stars charge premiums, is the reputation of the entrepreneur's brand strong enough that consumers will pay extra for the product or experience?

- Is the entrepreneur comfortable using data and analysis and not just marketing, creativity, and artistic vision?

• Does the entrepreneur have what it takes to build a great organization in addition to a great brand?

The trouble with many stars is they are constantly told how charismatic and appealing they are. They're "rock stars." But in order to
grow, they need collaborators. When this type of entrepreneur asks
my advice on how to go big, I say, "Be a rock band, not a rock star."

Consider one of the biggest rock stars in the food world. Wolfgang
Puck was raised by a coal miner father and pastry chef mother in
Austria. He started working in restaurants when he was fourteen and
came to America at twenty-four. After serving as chef at Ma Maison
in Los Angeles in the mid-seventies, Puck decided it was time to open
his own restaurant. In his vision, it would have red-checkered table-
cloths and a poster of Mount Vesuvius on the wall. But in the mind of
his soon-to-be wife, Barbara, Spago had spacious windows, white ta-
blecloths, and the first-ever open kitchen where patrons could watch
Puck prepare California cuisine. Barbara's vision prevailed, and Spago
was an instant hit. Soon Puck became a fixture on talk shows, red carpets, bookshelves, and supermarket shelves. He was America's first celebrity chef with a food empire worth $400 million.

Puck was always honest about knowing little about business. He
had no financial skills, fell asleep at the accountant's, and dealt with
money pressures by putting on weight. "A good chef has to be a manager, a businessman, and a great cook," he said. "To marry all three together is sometimes difficult." To get around this problem, he hired a
Harvard MBA to help run his businesses, but the MBA ran up too
much overhead, and Puck fired him. Barbara was a good businesswoman, so for a time she managed the restaurants and negotiated the
endorsement deals. But when the two divorced, Puck was on his own.
Today Puck focuses on being the public face of the brand and partners
with firms like Campbell Soup to run the businesses with his name.
His lesson for star entrepreneurs: "The brand has to be bigger than the
person."

Collaborate or be content to remain small.

Stars also face another minefield. When an initiative is based largely on the personality of the founder, what happens if that personality is tarnished? When Donald Trump goes in and out of the gossip pages (or the political arena), it jeopardizes his brand as a luxury icon. When Tiger Woods gets caught in a sex scandal, it causes headaches with his corporate sponsors. When Martha Stewart gets sent to prison, it flatlines her billion-dollar lifestyle empire.

Nonprofits built around stars are especially vulnerable. The Lance Armstrong Foundation was one of the most recognizable brands in the nonprofit world. The ubiquitous yellow wristbands representing strength in the face of cancer were a case study of the power of entrepreneurial ingenuity. But when doping allegations against the star became too big to ignore, donations plummeted—down 45 percent in three years. After Armstrong admitted the allegations were true, the foundation's board asked him to resign from the organization and took his name off the door. The Lance Armstrong Foundation became Livestrong. The head of external affairs said, "When you have a famous face as the head of your organization, the urgency to explain what you do isn't that great—but now the urgency is really great."

Live by the star, die by the star.

To avoid that plight, heed these red flags:

**Follow the full recipe.** *Cooking a complete meal requires more than one ingredient. The same goes for creating an enduring brand. Your organization has to deliver on the promise of your personality. Make sure someone is keeping an eye on all aspects, from operations to customer service.*

**Build up promoters inside and out.** *Strong personalities need other strong personalities around them. When building your team, don't be tempted by flattery. Rather than people who*

*compliment the boss, you need people whose skills comple-
ment your own.*

**Find a "left brain."** *Stars are often right-brained individuals,
meaning you think more intuitively, imaginatively, and creatively. Terrific, but your venture also needs someone who's
more left-brained—analytical, rigorous, and happy to wade
knee-deep into the data.*

## — TRANSFORMERS —

Howard Schultz. Ray Kroc. Ingvar Kamprad, the founder of Ikea.
Anita Roddick, the founder of The Body Shop. Blake Mycoskie, the
founder of Toms Shoes. Transformer entrepreneurs are catalysts for
change. They typically operate in old-line industries yet aspire to
transform their firms or causes through innovation and moderniza-
tion. Ray Kroc brought franchising to the ho-hum hamburger drive-
through; Ingvar Kamprad replaced the staid furniture showrooms
with sleek Swedish designs in trendy warehouse settings. Change can
be good, but can it be enough to restore growth to a sector that's lost
its luster?

Consider the case of the Endeavor entrepreneur René Freuden-
berg. In 2006 he took over his father's industrial grease company in
Guadalajara, Mexico. On the surface, what can be less glamorous than
grease! Yet this lowly niche, which includes everything from machine
oils to rust preventatives, brings in $8 billion a year worldwide. René's
father had started the first grease producer in Latin America, but his
son wanted to shake things up. "I shared my dad's philosophy, but at a
certain point I no longer admired him because he kept repeating the
same things," he said. When René took over, he shifted focus to the
high-end market and green technology. Interlub became an industry
leader in eco-friendly, custom-made products that increased efficiency
but cost more. He set an ambitious goal of 20 percent annual growth.

To achieve that, René rebranded the company. He tried to make lubrication, well, sexy. He began referring to Interlub as a "world leader in the field of tribology," a fancy word for "friction." He put jazzy music on the company's Web site and changed the tagline to "X-treme lubrication." The moves worked. Interlub captured half of the Mexican market and sold its products in thirty countries. In 2013 Interlub's annual revenues reached $27 million; its profits doubled.

René clearly showed entrepreneurial prowess. He took a decades-old business that made a boring product and turned it into a cutting-edge producer of a hot commodity that people paid top dollar for. He even added an environmental twist, biodegradability. But he and his company also had shortcomings. For all the company's sizzle, Interlub was still making grease for factories, a decidedly nineteenth-century product. Also, would bigger and better-financed competitors eventually steal back the market share Interlub had poached? Finally, René wasn't the best manager. He was "not cold enough," he told us. He "cared too much about protecting people" and "needed to make decisions faster." Could he sustain major growth?

René, in my classification, is a transformer. Like him, many transformers are socially oriented with a strong desire to improve the world. Think of Toms Shoes' giving away a pair of shoes to the poor with every pair sold to a customer or The Body Shop's denouncing animal testing. Transformers take the old and make it seem new again, often by adding a cause.

They also face questions:

- Is the "transformation" they're focused on truly meaningful or just window dressing?

- Is the "change-the-world" mission backed up by a solid business model?

- Will the entrepreneur be able to overcome the traditional obstacles that have hamstrung its industry?

• Will the mission have to be scuttled in order to take the initiative big? Will selling more require selling out?

A good example of the dramatic impact—and potential downsides—of transformers can be seen in one of the more colorful entrepreneurs of the last generation. The Texas lawyer Herb Kelleher and a partner created the concept for Southwest Airlines in 1967 on, yup, the back of a cocktail napkin. They battled lawsuits for four years before flying their first plane. Nearly everything about their business model threatened the traditional carriers. While other airlines flew many types of planes, Southwest flew only one, the Boeing 737, minimizing maintenance costs. While other airlines touted their inflight services, Southwest touted their absence—better to keep prices down. While most airlines operated in a hub-and-spoke model, Southwest flew point to point, often landing in secondary airports. The company made a profit every year beginning in 1973.

Central to the company's image was that of its founder. Kelleher was a Stetson-wearing, bourbon-drinking, chain-smoking renegade. He told the truth about the crappy service of most airlines and in doing so advanced the message that Southwest would be different. The company ran an ad that taunted other carriers: "We'd like to match their new fares, but we'd have to raise ours." When other carriers started raising service fees, Southwest placed inserts in newspapers that read, "Don't #$*!% Me Over," accompanied by "Southwest is the only airline that accepts this coupon." It elaborated: no checked bag fees, no change fees, no fuel surcharges, no snack fees, no phone reservation fees.

*Money* magazine named Kelleher one of the top ten entrepreneurs of his generation.

Inevitably, when Kelleher stepped down in 2008, he took his reputation as a transformer with him. The new CEO, Gary Kelly, was a numbers guy. Soon enough, he stopped touting the company's low frills and ran ads declaring Southwest "America's largest domestic airline." Instead of tweaking the big guys, Southwest had become a big guy. Plus, Southwest's prices were no longer the cheapest in most markets, and Kelly even hinted the airline would drop its long-standing policy of free bags. Transformers can be forward-thinking iconoclasts, but in the end, the organizations they build often revert to the means of their industries.

A vivid example of this paradox is the quixotic story of one butterfly transformer, an original farm-to-sink entrepreneur. In 1984 Roxanne Quimby was a thirty-three-year-old, down-on-her-luck, single mom having difficulty finding a job. One day, while hitchhiking to a post office in Dexter, Maine, she was picked up by Burt Shavitz, a beekeeper in his late forties who lived in a turkey coop and made $3,000 a year selling jarred honey out of the back of his pickup truck. Locals called him the bee guy. The two became lovers.

One day, looking at all the unused beeswax he had accumulated, Shavitz recommended that Quimby make some candles and sell them at the local crafts fair. She started tinkering—first with candles, then with furniture polish, eventually with lip balm. "It was clear, very early, that people bought lip balm ten times faster than they bought beeswax furniture polish," Quimby said. "Next was a moisturizing cream. It sold better than the polish too." A onetime graphic designer, Quimby crafted a logo featuring a man drawn in Shavitz's likeness with a well-worn face, beaming eyes, a faint smile, and a hefty beard. She labeled the products "Burt's Bees." Her timing was impeccable. The interest in eco-friendly products was just taking off, and Burt's Bees's homespun packaging and all-natural ingredients were a perfect fit. By 1993 the company was earning $3 million a year; by 2000 the amount was $23 million.

Quimby and Shavitz were the ultimate transformers. They had taken a staid industry, with low-margin products like lip balm and skin salve, and revitalized it with a cutting-edge, organic brand that made people feel good about paying more for items that would rattle around in their pockets for a few weeks, then get lost before they got finished. Their story was a landmark success. But then trouble.

First, their relationship failed. After the couple moved to North Carolina to save on taxes, the two split. Shavitz moved back to Maine, and Quimby bought out his one-third share of the company by purchasing him a house for $130,000. A few years later she sold 80 percent of the company to private investors for $175 million; Shavitz's share would have been worth $59 million. (He complained, and Quimby gave him $4 million in a settlement.) A few years after that, Clorox bought Burt's Bees for $913 million, netting Quimby an additional $183 million.

That's when the real problems for the brand began. Like many transformers, Quimby had built her company's reputation as being socially conscious, natural, and homespun. Those were not exactly ideas associated with Clorox. (The sale took place a few months before the company released its Green Works line.) Executives at Clorox said they hoped to learn about natural practices from their new acquisition, but consumers were skeptical. They accused Quimby of selling out. Loyalists even created a petition on Change.org accusing Clorox of tampering with the recipe for Burt's Bees products.

Burt's is not alone, of course. Tom's of Maine, the makers of natural toothpaste, sold a majority stake to Colgate-Palmolive for $100 million. The Body Shop sold to L'Oréal for more than $1 billion. Ben & Jerry's sold to Unilever for $326 million. Four years later Ben & Jerry's own audit of its social practices said, "We are beginning to look like the rest of corporate America."

And that's the point: Transformers can be transformational, but their success is often built around temporary advantages or the founders' direct touch. When those go away, the changes often recede.

With that in mind, transformers should watch out for these red flags:

**Make sure your business model is as compelling as your mission.**
*Transformers want to prove that those in traditional fields can still innovate. But innovation isn't enough. You also need a strong strategy to sustain your change over time.*

**Get real.** *Sometimes transformers propose changes, but they're more cosmetic than real. Be prepared to defend your innovations as worth the costs and risks involved, and align your team to push back against critics.*

**Don't shy away from data.** *Entrepreneurs who focus on social goals often downplay finances and dismiss pesky data. While your sense of purpose is important, try to balance it with objective analysis. It's hard to change the world if your numbers don't add up.*

## – ROCKETSHIPS –

Jeff Bezos. Bill Gates. Fred Smith. Michael Dell. Mike Bloomberg. Rocketship entrepreneurs are penetrating thinkers who apply a laser focus on metrics to accelerate growth and change. They are tinkerers and fixers, with a relentless drive toward efficiency, who aim to improve every element of their endeavors, making them cheaper, faster, better. Rocketships often have a background in mathematics, science, systems, or management and use their analytical minds to set clear goals and formulas for success. They are the rocket scientists of the entrepreneurial world. In an increasingly data-driven universe, they are uniquely poised to soar. But their obsession with numbers comes with clear risks.

The Endeavor entrepreneurs Nicolás Loaiza and Gigliola Aycardi like to crunch numbers. As MBA students in Bogotá, Colombia, the sports-loving friends complained about the lack of high-quality gyms in their country. They undertook a market analysis of Colombia's personal fitness industry and determined that a private gym offering individual exercise regimens would have huge potential. They started a company, Bodytech, which positioned itself as a medical sports center instead of a gym. Bodytech's highly qualified medical experts offered personalized health services, educating members about how to avoid chronic illnesses and how to identify personal exercise goals. They set a target of one thousand new members in six months; in the first thirty days they signed up eighteen hundred. In surveys, half the members said they had not exercised regularly before joining Bodytech.

Buoyed by their success, Nicolás and Gigliola expanded Bodytech rapidly. Over the next decade they opened twenty-six branches in six Colombian cities and signed up fifty thousand members. They merged with another chain and increased their membership by 34 percent. They did an exhaustive analysis of neighboring countries and concluded that the penetration rate of gyms in Latin America was a fraction of that in North America. Then Nicolás and Gigliola went out to raise enough capital to realize their aggressive expansion targets. By 2012 Bodytech had become the largest chain of gyms in South America.

When I met the founders, I was impressed with their strengths. They're analytical, data oriented, and laser focused on growth. They're doers—superefficient and effective. They set milestones, achieve them, then calculate new ones. They embody drive and success. But they showed some weaknesses, too. They came across as somewhat cocky. They're quick talkers, who have an answer for everything and bombard naysayers with a blizzard of statistics. We weren't sure they would listen. Also, they move so fast they might overlook the needs of their employees. Were they all in their head? we wondered. Where's the heart?

Gigliola and Nicolás, in my classification, are rocketships. They reflect the current vogue in business toward metrics, but they raise issues about the tendency to value numbers above all else. Rocketships should mind these flags:

- Confidence is one thing, but overconfidence is another. Will the entrepreneur be open to critical feedback?

- Tinkering around the edges is fine, but is there real differentiation here from what's currently available?

- In the entrepreneur's relentless push for efficiency, is there sufficient room for creativity, passion, and occasionally a new idea based on intuition, not spreadsheets?

- Does an uncompromising focus on customer satisfaction come at the cost of employee satisfaction? Can these entrepreneurs rally their own troops?

Jeff Bezos is the quintessential rocketship. In 1994 he was a senior vice president at a New York financial firm studying the Internet. He realized he wanted to be part of that movement. But instead of leaping into his passion, Bezos followed a methodology. First, he systematically analyzed business activities that could be enhanced by the Web. He concluded he should be a middleman between manufacturers and customers, selling nearly everything all over the world. Since starting with everything was impractical, he next made a list of twenty possible categories. He chose books. Then he approached his boss. "You know, I'm going to do this crazy thing," he said. "I'm going to start this company selling books online." The boss's response: "This actually sounds like a really good idea to me, but it sounds like it would be a better idea for somebody who didn't already have a good job."

This gave Bezos pause. So he did the most rocketship-like thing imaginable: He created a "regret minimization framework" to reduce the chances that he would regret his decision. Here's how he explained it: "I wanted to project myself forward to age 80 and say, 'Okay, now I'm looking back on my life. I want to have minimized the number of regrets I have.'" He wouldn't regret participating in the Internet, he concluded, and he wouldn't regret failing. "But I knew the one thing I might regret is not ever having tried."

Once under way, Bezos continued his focus on data, analysis, and efficiency. He sweated the small stuff. He crossed out every word on press releases that distracted from the company's core message: Amazon is the cheapest, friendliest place to buy books. (Later "books" changed to "everything.") He insisted that every Tuesday every department hold metrics meetings, in which employees were asked to justify every decision based on numbers. And he openly distributed his e-mail address, so customers could send complaints directly to him. He then forwarded those complaints to relevant employees with just one addition, a question mark. Nothing was said to elicit more fear than one of Bezos's voiceless queries: "?" When one worker asked at a company retreat why entire teams were required to drop everything on a dime to respond to a "question mark escalation," his savvier colleagues explained: They were jeff@amazon.com's way of making sure the customer's voice trumped all.

So what's the downside? Well, while Amazon's efficiency was a boon to consumers, sometimes it chafed employees. Bezos thrives on conflict. He prefers an adversarial work atmosphere to one based on cohesion. Also, one of his leadership principles is frugality: He refuses to spend money on anything not directly related to customer happiness. Even at the height of the Internet boom in the late 1990s, Amazon employees never had perks like other tech firms: no free massages, no free food, not even free parking. The only thing workers received free was aspirin. But when the tech boom went bust, Bezos had to convince investors he was cutting costs. Out went the aspirin.

Rocketships have formidable minds, but sometimes they give those around them headaches.

The same applies to rocketships in the nonprofit sector. Bill Gates is the rare entrepreneur who has been a pioneer in both the for-profit and nonprofit worlds. And in both arenas his entrepreneurial profile—data driven, efficiency focused, metrics obsessed—has been key to his successes and shortcomings.

Gates is often credited with spearheading the personal computer revolution, but he was less of an inventor and more of a curator. Others created the first operating system. Gates's brilliance was creating a business that bundled that operating system with a suite of services (spreadsheets, word processing, e-mail, etc.), then requiring hardware makers to preinstall it. Also, Gates was a tireless competitor. One of his early backers said, "This guy knows more about his competitors' products than his competitors do." Finally, Gates was relentlessly focused on the bottom line. An e-mail once warned employees, "If you find yourself relaxed and with your mind wandering, you are probably having a detrimental effect on the stock price."

Over time these attributes proved costly. Gates dismissed the Internet, which soon passed him by, and he missed what Steve Jobs understood: that creativity and passion also drive people's attachments to their technology. Sure enough, Apple's products were described as art; Microsoft's, as artless. It's hard to build brand loyalty on that.

But what's even more telling is that when Gates stopped running Microsoft and turned his attention to his philanthropy, he brought the same single-minded commitment to metrics and results. In the often squishy and subjective world of nonprofits, the impact has been profound. Every grant of the more than $3 billion the Gates Foundation gives out each year comes with a framework to measure performance quantitatively. As the foundation explains, these evaluations "can help depersonalize decision making and provide objective data that can inform action."

I know of few stories that better capture the ability of these profile types to transcend fields of activity than how Bill Gates, the gazelle-rocketship who had been running Microsoft, became Bill Gates, the dolphin-rocketship who took over the Bill and Melinda Gates Foundation. The arena was different, but the man was the same. And so was his entrepreneurial personality.

I tell rocketships to keep these issues in mind:

**Look beyond the numbers.** *Rocketships love analytics, but you won't always have the data you need to feel 100 percent confident. Learn to be comfortable with ambiguity and taking educated risks. Anecdotal feedback from users may feel "soft" and unreliable, but it can reveal insights that the data may miss.*

**Let your creative juices flow.** *Rocketships approach change differently from other entrepreneur types. They look to bridge a* *market gap or solve a customer need rather than embrace innovation for its own sake. Many rocketships prefer tinkering with already proven models rather than discovering untested ones. While this can cut down risk, it can hold you back. Mix in some novelty.*

**Heart matters.** *Emotions might not be quantifiable, but they matter. Some of the most successful brands get that way because they appeal to the hearts and minds of both customers and employees. If you aren't comfortable getting outside your head every now and then, surround yourself with some people who are.*

## — YOUR ENTREPRENEURSHIP PERSONALITY —

The idea of identifying different personality types goes back to antiquity. The ancient Greeks analyzed body fluids (blood, bile, and phlegm) and linked them to moods. Two hundred years ago scientists measured bumps on people's heads to ascertain certain personality characteristics. The idea of actually *asking people about themselves* didn't take hold until a century ago, first in the military. Personality tests have been a fact of life ever since—and a pretty good business, too, half a billion dollars a year in the United States alone.

It's time we bring that rigor to the fastest growing groups of workers today, entrepreneurs.

The main lesson of these four profile types is this: Just as there is no singular path to being an entrepreneur today, so there is also no set entrepreneur personality. There are multiple paths and multiple personalities. Each has its strengths and weaknesses.

So instead of peering outward, picking a hero to emulate, then struggling to model yourself on that ideal, look inward. Figure out what you're good at—and what you're not—then play up your strengths. The first step to going big is to know thyself.

# CHAPTER 5

# *The Whiteboard*

*B*y the time Henry Ford had his do-or-die moment as an entrepreneur, he was already something of a success. Yet he was still unprepared for the magnitude of the pressure. Moments like these happen to all entrepreneurs. They occur at unexpected times, when you're about to release a transformational product, land a massive client, move into a fresh space, or secure the long-awaited OK to take your idea to the world. You're about to go big when suddenly you're caught short. Now what do you do?

For years I've been studying these moments and how entrepreneurs react to them. I've tried to identify patterns to help people get through them more easily. My nickname for them comes from the man who was called Crazy Henry.

Ford faced his test in 1908, when he was forty-four years old. The Michigan native had built his first automobile in a backyard shed in 1896 at age thirty-three. Soon after, he quit his job at the Edison electric plant to start the Detroit Automobile Company. It failed without producing a car. Next he turned to building race cars. When one of his creations won a race, he secured funding to start the Ford Motor Company. Within two years the company was producing 1,700 cars a year in three different models.

Still, something nagged at Ford. A stop-planning, start-doing entrepreneur, he despised business plans and ran his company on instinct. The smart business move was to sell expensive cars to the elite, but Ford wanted to build a car for the masses. "It will be so low in price that no man making a good salary will be unable to own one," Ford declared. He would create a four-cylinder five-passenger touring car that would retail for the shockingly low price of $825.

He picked a room on the third floor of his factory at 461 Piquette Avenue in Detroit and staffed it with his smartest designers. He called it his experimental department. The tiny space was filled with a blackboard, milling machines, and drill presses. Ford sat in the middle in his "lucky" rocking chair that once belonged to his mother. He was a gazelle who was skunking himself.

But his plan enraged his backers. Investors were furious that his new car would undermine profits. Banks were concerned about the costs and refused to loan him money. Suppliers pushed back on his exacting timelines. The only people enthusiastic were his competitors. "How soon will Ford blow up?" they asked.

Finally, in early 1908, forty members of his secret team and many of his harshest critics gathered for the ceremonial assembling of the first prototype. Workers wrapped the engine in fifty feet of rope, hoisted it into the air, and began lowering it into the chassis. But as the future of the company slowly descended, the engine started spinning faster and faster and eventually broke free of the ropes, crashed to the ground, and smashed into pieces.

This was Ford's test: Go big or go home?

He quietly stepped forward and announced he would personally build a replacement. Six months later the Model T went on sale. Ford's populist dream, derided as foolhardy and dismissed as socialist, went on to sell 15 million cars over the next twenty years, making it the most successful invention of the automotive age and what many consider the most influential consumer product ever created.

To me, the image of that first Model T engine lying in pieces on the

concrete floor perfectly captures a turning point that all risk takers encounter. All entrepreneurs I know have confronted at least one of these
engine-on-the-floor moments, a crucial juncture where everything
they've worked for up until that point is at stake, and they have to make
what seems like *the one decision* that will determine whether their ideas
go huge or fall flat. I've seen the fear in entrepreneurs' eyes in these moments. I've watched them break down in tears. And I've learned what
they need most in that instant is the reassurance that they're not alone.

Well, you're not alone. Even better, solutions do exist. When I first
started noticing similarities in these moments, I kept a running tally
in my head. Later I started scribbling notes in the middle of the night.
Eventually I decided to do something with this list other than leave it
by the side of my bed (and bug my husband with it in the morning). So
I bought a whiteboard.

I leaned it behind my desk, and when entrepreneurs came in and
shared their problems, I would grab the board, point to an entry, and we'd
start brainstorming solutions. Entrepreneurs liked it because it gave them
relief that there was a path forward. I liked it because it gave me a way to
help someone who was feeling desperate. Here's what it looks like today:

1. Close Doors
2. Fire Your Mother-in-Law
3. Minnovate
4. Drop the Pens
5. Dream Big but Execute Small
6. Eat the Elephant One Bite at a Time

This list is by no means exhaustive. Some of these items might apply to you; others might not. We've done research at Endeavor to back up most of them. In effect, this list is the product of my own experimental department. It's my attempt to put into one place solutions to the make-or-break problems entrepreneurs confront in their attempt to go big.

The next time you drop an engine on the floor, perhaps one of these lessons might help you pick it up and move on.

## *— 1. CLOSE DOORS —*

Two Endeavor entrepreneurs from Jordan came to my office one afternoon. Ramzi Halaby and Zafer Younis were at a breaking point. Their company, The Online Project, helped businesses manage their social media strategies. The firm had secured a number of top clients and employed over seventy people. But most clients wanted to deal directly with one of the founders, not their highly trained staff. Ramzi and Zafer outlined the situation, we discussed possible solutions, but they still seemed tense. Feeling more like their mom than their adviser at this point, I asked if anything else might be contributing to their stress.

"Well, we still own the radio station back in Amman," Ramzi said. "That takes about twenty percent of our time. We have an offer to sell it, but we're not sure we're ready to let go."

I grabbed my whiteboard. "You guys need to close doors," I said.

In the early stages of being an entrepreneur a little foot-dragging is understandable. Sara Blakely kept selling fax machines until she got booked on *Oprah*; Henry Ford kept working at the power plant while he was building his first car. In the year that it took to get Endeavor off the napkin, I wrote grant applications for other organizations on the side to earn extra money.

But at some point the hedging has to stop. This issue comes up at Endeavor selection panels. The executives and VCs we bring in to screen gazelles at their scale-up moments say it's a deal breaker if a founder isn't willing to give up outside projects and go all in.

The same applies to mission-driven dolphins aiming to go big. Bill Drayton, my former employer at Ashoka, insists that social entrepreneurs' willingness to leave everything else behind is a precondition for support. "It usually takes about three years," he said. "They have to test and refine their idea. They have to build an organization and start a movement." Only after the founders agree to quit their day jobs does Ashoka give them funding.

Often the reluctance to cut the cord is financial. You need the money. This is understandable at the outset. I'm all for not betting the farm on Day One. But once you're up and running, and there's some money coming in, your unwillingness to commit full-time becomes a hindrance. You can't expect to go big without accepting some added risk.

Bette Graham is a good example of how it can take years to reach that point. In 1951 Graham was a divorced single mom living in North Dallas. She wanted to be an artist but took a job as a bank secretary. Unfortunately, she was an awful typist, and the only way to fix her many mistakes was to retype the entire page, a Sisyphean torture. One day she watched some painters make a slipup on the bank's Christmas windows and cover over their blunder with white paint. "Why can't I do that with my bad typing?" she thought.

She mixed up some tempera at home, brought it into work, and used a watercolor brush to neaten up her errors. She called her concoction Mistake Out. For five years she kept her elixir secret from everyone, including her boss. Eventually her colleagues caught on and wanted some for themselves. She sold her first bottle in 1956.

Unable to afford employees, Graham recruited a high school chemistry teacher to make the product dry faster and roped in her son to fill bottles in their garage. (That son, by the way, went on to become a founding band member of The Monkees.) By 1957 Graham was selling around one hundred bottles a month and renamed her product

Liquid Paper. But she kept her secretarial job—until she used her own letterhead in lieu of the bank's one day and was fired.

This was her first close doors decision: Would she find new employment or attempt the life of a solo entrepreneur? Graham chose the freedom of a butterfly. She would brew her concoction without a safety net. Three years later she faced another juncture: Should she stay a mom-and-son operation or aim bigger? Again she chose the more daring path. She hired her first employee, moved into a shed in her backyard, and later bought a factory. By 1969 Graham's Liquid Paper Company was selling a million bottles a year; a decade later she sold it to Gillette for $47.5 million plus royalties.

The calendar here is instructive. For five years Graham kept her avocation a secret; for the next two she sold her product but kept doors open by keeping her job; finally she closed that door but stayed small for another three years. Not until a decade after her initial inspiration did she finally take maximum risk and try to go as big as she could.

An even better example of this measured pace—and the one I told Ramzi and Zafer that morning—is all the more startling because it involves somebody who's often thought of as a go-for-broke entrepreneur.

Phil Knight was a teenage runner in his home state of Oregon who hated clunky American athletic shoes, which were mostly made by tire companies. After a stint in the army, Knight attended Stanford's business school, where he wrote a paper on the high quality and low cost of Japanese sports shoes. In 1962 the newly minted MBA traveled to Japan, where he struck a deal to distribute Onitsuka Tiger shoes in the United States. Along with his former track coach, Knight sold Tiger shoes out of the back of his green Plymouth Valiant. But he was still under the influence of his father, who insisted he get a "real job" as an accountant. So Knight had someone else sell the shoes while he did other people's books.

Not until 1971, when a colleague conjured up the name Nike and Knight paid $35 for the "swoosh" ("I don't love it," he said, "but I think it will grow on me"), did Knight finally hang up his wingtips. The next year he sold $3.2 million worth of shoes. The "just do it!" moment for Phil Knight came nearly a decade after he'd first had the idea.

To be sure, not everyone wants to go big. Some entrepreneurs aspire to have lifestyle enterprises. Remember those Brooklyn jam makers: one wanted to stay local; the other wanted to scale. Both paths can be meaningful.

But as I told Ramzi and Zafer, many entrepreneurs cling to their conventional work out of fear rather than necessity. They continue typing other people's letters or doing other people's taxes even after their ventures produce sufficient income. My advice: Cut the umbilical cord.

When we're young, we're often told to keep as many doors open as possible. But for an entrepreneur seeking to scale, the better path forward is to close doors.

## — 2. FIRE YOUR MOTHER-IN-LAW —

Gabriel and Guillermo Oropeza had a vision. The two brothers from Mexico City would reinvent the traditional document storage companies of Latin America. They started by taking over their father's firm and introducing a more sophisticated information platform. When they showed up at an Endeavor selection panel, the two boasted impressive technology, traction in their home market, and stellar résumés. Guillermo had studied at MIT and worked at the Boston Consulting Group; Gabriel had an MBA and experience at Coca-Cola and Johnson & Johnson.

But they faced a potential calamity. It may be the biggest single problem I've seen in all my years working with entrepreneurs. Yet like most who face it, the Oropezas weren't even aware of it.

They were precariously mixing their personal and professional lives.

Gabriel and Guillermo, both in their early thirties, held the titles of commercial director and director of planning; each owned 16.67 percent equity in the company, called Doc Solutions. The father, meanwhile, still held the title of CEO and controlled 50 percent of the equity. Although Guillermo senior was largely disengaged from the day-to-day business and had little understanding of the new IT platform, he still controlled the company.

We turned the Oropeza brothers down. One panelist said: "Tell your father to become nonexecutive chairman and then come back." To my surprise, a year later the pair showed up at another panel—with dad in tow. "Hola, Linda," Guillermo senior said, shaking my hand. "I'm here now as chairman." He promised to sit in the back and say nothing to prove his sons were in control. He did, and the brothers became Endeavor entrepreneurs. Since then Doc Solutions has grown to $12 million in revenues and nearly one thousand employees.

A few years ago I asked our in-house research group at Endeavor to examine the best- and worst-performing entrepreneurs in our network. The goal was to see if we could detect any commonalities linking those in the top quartile and those in the bottom.

Here's what we found: Three-quarters had launched their business with a partner, and 70 percent of these partners were people close to them—a best friend, a family member, a spouse, an in-law. Things start off swimmingly. "We know each other so well!" the cofounders effuse when we meet them. "Our skills are complementary!" "We practically finish each other's sentences!"

Then trouble brews. Cash problems arise, and cuts need to be made. Or business booms, and one partner wants to expand while the other prefers to stay small. Or it becomes clear that one partner lacks the skills to take the venture to the next level.

Yet the founders have no mechanism in place to handle these routine disputes. Familiarity breeds informality.

Half the entrepreneurs in the bottom quartile of our network shared one thing in common: They lacked a shareholder agreement among partners.

In many firms we work with, it's a founder's sibling who's in charge of business development, an in-law who controls the finances, or the father who claims to be "letting go" while still retaining power and majority ownership. Wences used that approach; he hired his sisters. So did I; my sister, Rebecca, was head of marketing at Endeavor for a few years. While that familial structure may work early on, it often presents challenges as the company matures. Suddenly the interests of different family members start to diverge. In Rebecca's case, she left to pursue an independent career. But in many cases family members hang on past a healthy point.

That's why the second item on my whiteboard is: Fire your mother-in-law. That may sound harsh, but there are ways to do this gracefully.

Endeavor entrepreneurs aren't alone in this struggle. More than 80 percent of American business is family owned; outside the United States the number is 90 percent. Also, look around. Gossip pages are filled with tales of business family feuds gone bad. From the sons of the IKEA founder Ingvar Kamprad to the wives of Rupert Murdoch, from Beyoncé's dad to Usher's mom ("I never fired my mother," Usher told Oprah. "I relieved her of her duties"), families that work together often stop playing together. The celebrity chef and reality TV star Gordon Ramsay had to split with his father-in-law, business partner, and best friend, Chris Hutcheson, after discovering that Hutcheson had been funneling money to a mistress and their secret family for thirty years. Talk about a kitchen nightmare!

The way to keep these issues out of the boardroom is to create what I call a start-up prenup, a document that puts the rights and responsibilities of each partner on paper. Just as it can seem inconceivable for a young couple in love to plan in case of divorce, so it can seem awkward and insulting to draft a formal contract between a parent and a child or two best friends from childhood. But too often I've seen the dreadful alternative. Even Leila had to tiptoe through the minefield of divorcing her partner-husband (who left the company) and renegotiating with her other partner, now her ex-sister-in-law Zica (Leila officially became CEO while Zica remained the face of the Beleza Natural brand).

These agreements work. John Davis, a family business expert at Harvard, told me that his research confirms what I've seen on the ground. "One of the basic rules of families is that structure is your friend," Davis said. The best way to avoid problems is to write down in advance what happens if someone wants to leave, cash out, or spend more time at the beach. "If you have a plan in place," John said, "then you still can show up at family occasions together."

A vivid illustration of how shareholder agreements work, whenever they're created, is Lucille Ball and Desi Arnaz. The redheaded comedian and the hotheaded Cuban met in 1940 on a movie set. Though she was six years his senior, the two soon eloped. A decade into their tempestuous marriage, they decided to make a sitcom. When the network balked at the awkward pairing, the two formed Desilu Productions, the first independent television production company, and spent $5,000 of their own money on the pilot of I Love Lucy.

Lucy and Desi were savvy pioneers. They insisted their shows be shot on film, which allowed the first-ever reruns; they cut their salaries in order to own the shows; and they sold syndication rights for $5 million, then plowed the money back into their studio, acquiring thirty-three sound stages—more than MGM or Twentieth Century Fox. The Dick Van Dyke Show, The Andy Griffith Show, and My Three Sons were all shot on their lot.

Yet the king and queen of television never improved their relationship. They divorced in 1960 but continued to work together. When that partnership finally soured, they took a coolly rational approach. "Instead of divorce lawyers profiting from our mistakes, we thought we'd profit from them," Lucy said. In what we might call a start-up postnup, the pair drafted an agreement: Lucy bought Desi's shares for $2.5 million and became the first female CEO of a major production company. Five years later Lucy sold the company to Paramount for $17 million. Her final act was green-lighting Star Trek and Mission: Impossible.

Whether you're a comedian, technologist, or hair colorist, avoid the single most common mistake we see in entrepreneurs: absence of a shareholder agreement. Put the terms of your partnership on paper. It's okay to love Lucy, but make sure you know what to do if the love goes away.

## – 3. MINNOVATE –

As entrepreneurship has gotten sexier in recent years, a few flashy stories have dominated the discussion: Apple, Facebook, Twitter. These businesses have one thing in common: They were based on big, breakthrough ideas that created new markets where none existed.

As influential as those stories have been in encouraging others, they've also had the opposite effect: They've discouraged even more people from chasing their dreams or taking their initiative to the next level. Why? Because they leave a false impression. They lead people to believe that the *only way to be a successful entrepreneur is to have a big, breakthrough idea.* In fact, the opposite is true. Most entrepreneurs don't have a big idea at all; they have lots of small ones.

The Babson College professor Dan Isenberg nailed the term for this phenomenon. Successful entrepreneurs don't innovate; they minnovate. They don't create Google; they create a more targeted search engine that serves a market or location that was overlooked. Two-thirds of Endeavor entrepreneurs started out by minnovating. The technique has multiple benefits: It mitigates risk by starting with a proven business model; it saves costs by making small adaptations instead of massive ones; it works.

In 1999 two Argentinean Stanford graduates, Marcos Galperin and Hernán Kazah, launched MercadoLibre ("free market" in Spanish), an online auction company modeled on eBay. Some said they were creating a copycat. Actually they minnovated. When the company started, only 2 to 3 percent of Latin Americans had Internet access. Also, neither buyers nor sellers trusted the notoriously inept and corrupt local postal system. So MercadoLibre tweaked the model. First, it focused on selling new goods, not used, so buyers could trust the quality. Second, when consumers balked at online auctions, the company moved to fixed prices. Finally, it encouraged buyers and sellers to meet in cafés and other public places to exchange goods instead of putting them in the mail.

The founders became Endeavor entrepreneurs, and the site became Latin America's number one e-commerce platform, serving 100 million users in twelve countries. In 2007 MercadoLibre went public on NASDAQ at a valuation of $400 million. Six years later it was worth $6 billion.

While minnovation is valuable in the start-up phase, it can be even more valuable in the scale-up phase, particularly when one of those engines comes crashing to the floor. When your product isn't selling, your market isn't growing, or your idea isn't taking hold around the water cooler, there's a temptation to scrap the playbook and throw a Hail Mary in a desperate attempt to score a game-changing touchdown. Yet a massive move may not be what's called for. Sometimes a small pivot is all you need.

In 1957 Wilbert "Bill" Gore, a chemical engineer at DuPont, was part of a skunk team that discovered a new application for the synthetic polymer PTFE, the basis of Teflon. But DuPont wasn't interested in pursuing new applications, so Bill left the company. At age forty-five, with five children to support, he and his wife, Genevieve "Vieve," started a business in their Delaware basement. They incorporated on their twenty-third wedding anniversary. "All of our friends told us not to do it," Vieve said. "It's hard to describe what it's like to bring your husband home and turn him loose." Bill did the math and figured they had two years to make it, or he'd have to slink back to DuPont.

Everything Gore did was a minnovation from the original PTFE, starting with a ribbonlike cable that could be used to insulate wires and pipes. For two years the Gores tried selling the product, but nobody was buying. Their self-imposed deadline was nearing. "We came very close to calling it quits," Vieve said. One day, while Bill was running an errand, the telephone rang in the basement. Vieve, who was alone sifting PTFE powder, answered the call. It was a man from the Denver water department. He asked for the product manager. Vieve said he was out. How about the sales manager? Not here either. The president? Vieve said he couldn't be reached. "What kind of company is this anyway?" the caller hollered.

One with a pipe dream that would soon come true. The man ultimately ordered $100,000 worth of ribbon. The Gores had a viable business, but it was still a modest one. The company grew sluggishly over the next decade. It took Bill and Vieve's son Bob, who joined the company in the mid-sixties, to come up with the minnovation that changed everything.

In 1969, fearing that the wire and cable business was slowing, Bob began trying to stretch PTFE to the breaking point to see how malleable it was. An even more flexible product would reduce costs and increase profits. Each attempt failed. Fed up one day, Bob, dressed in a white lab coat and asbestos gloves, grabbed a rod from the oven and angrily yanked it. The footlong rod stretched to almost five feet. "I couldn't believe it," he said. Fearing it might be a fluke, he didn't tell anybody. The next day he re-created the experiment, then gathered his dad and colleagues and performed it publicly. "We were all very quiet," Bill Gore said. "We were all trained scientists, so we recognized the importance of what Bob had done."

What he had done was invent Gore-Tex. This minnovation, which grew out of a moment of desperation, allowed the company to pivot in an entirely new direction, breathable fabric. Gore moved quickly to exploit the new discovery but didn't abandon its legacy clients. The company had supplied cables to NASA for the first moon landing in 1969, for example; now it sold NASA the fabric that would be used in the spacesuits of the first space shuttle astronauts. Gore went on to capture 70 percent of the waterproof outerwear market (including my daughters' snow boots) and became one of the two hundred largest privately held companies in the United States. The company's string of successes, stretching across seven decades, all stemmed from a series of minnovations from a single core product.

This story shows how entrepreneurs need to be stubborn enough to keep pounding away at their initial ideas, yet open minded enough to pivot to more attractive products or markets if they present themselves. That approach perfectly captures the case of the "snail sisters."

The Endeavor entrepreneurs Maria and Penny Vlachou grew up in Corinth, Greece. In 2007, while traveling in Switzerland, Maria was chatting with Penny on the phone and complaining about the high cost of escargot—thirty-seven euros for a dozen. Looking out her bedroom window, Penny joked she could grow snails in her backyard. "I'd buy them!" Maria said. Within months the sisters had opened a snail farm and started selling escargot to shops and restaurants. But they couldn't keep too many snails on hand because they easily spoiled, so they pivoted and recruited a network of farmers from whom they could buy on demand.

When we first met the snail sisters, I was skeptical. "Aren't we about *high-impact* entrepreneurs?" I asked. Then Adrian Gore, Endeavor South Africa's chairman and one of the toughest number crunchers I know, told me, "Linda, I've been trying to poke holes in their business model, but I can't." A top auditor from EY said, "That's it, I'm quitting my job and starting a snail farm!"

What everyone most admired was how Penny and Maria had tweaked their strategy to survive do-or-die moments. When the sisters realized that consumers didn't have time to prepare live snails, they began selling canned escargot. When the Greek financial crisis wiped out the domestic market for luxury molluscs, the sisters looked abroad. "Our sales in Greece wouldn't increase," Maria said, "so we turned to other countries. Every problem has a solution." Today 70 percent of the sisters' revenue comes from exports to Spain, Italy, and France. Impressing a South African executive is one thing, but Penny and Maria managed to sell Greek escargot to the French: *Vive la minnovation!*

Finding new uses for old products is another way to demonstrate flexibility in the face of crises. Executives from Kimberly-Clark were touring Europe in 1914 when they discovered a cotton substitute called creped cellulose wadding. They sold it to the U.S. military to use as filters in gas masks in World War I. Stuck with a huge surplus after the war, they could have shut down that line. Instead they marketed the product to women as a sanitary cold cream remover. Women wrote back that while the product worked fine, they were annoyed that their husbands and kids kept swiping the cold cream removers to blow their noses. The intraprenuerial skunks inside Kimberly-Clark took note. The company repositioned the product as a tossable hankie and rebranded it as Kleenex.

Yet another way to minnovate involves how you market your product. In 1959 the Mattel cofounders Ruth and Elliot Handler introduced a new doll at New York's annual toy fair. The doll was modeled on a German adult entertainment toy named Lilli, known for her large breasts and sexy clothing. The Handlers toned down the makeup but kept the bosom. If she was going to be a role model for little girls, Ruth said, "it was a little stupid to play with a doll that had a flat chest." The Handlers named the doll after their daughter, Barbara. They called it Barbie Millicent Roberts.

The Handlers' plan had been to do what toy companies had always done: market Barbie to moms. But when moms took one look at the "shapely teenage model," they revolted. Her body was unrealistic, they said. (And they didn't want their husbands gawking at the doll.) This was the Handlers' engine-on-the-floor moment. Instead of panicking, they pivoted and did something previously unheard of in American business: They advertised the product directly to children. Barbie's first appearance was in a televised ad on *The Mickey Mouse Club* in 1959. The company sold 351,000 Barbie dolls that year.

The twentieth century's ultimate minnovator in chief will always be Henry Ford. With the Model T, he upgraded the transmission of existing cars, improved the engine, and elevated the suspension. He also developed a new kind of steel that was significantly lighter and three times as strong. As he said, "I invented nothing new. I simply assembled into a car the discoveries of other men behind whom were centuries of work." (The most significant of Ford's minnovations was his decision to relocate the steering wheel from the right side of the car to the left. Before, drivers worried about steering into a ditch, so they wanted to eye their outer wheels. Ford correctly anticipated that in the future drivers would be more anxious about oncoming traffic and would prefer to sit closer to the middle of the road.)

I tell my entrepreneurs: "Stop trying to shoot the moon all the time." In make-or-break situations sometimes the smarter move is to make an incremental adjustment. Innovation may capture more headlines; minnovation captures more markets.

## — 4. DROP THE PENS —

But don't minnovate to the point of distraction. Resist the urge to launch dozens of different products and scores of niggling side projects. Focus.

In 2011 a business accelerator in California set out to understand which start-ups went big, which fell flat, and why. One question it examined: Is there a right or wrong amount to pivot? To get at that dilemma, researchers looked at the number of adaptations a company made to its product line. Researchers compared start-ups that made no changes, start-ups that made one or two changes, and start-ups that made more than two.

Their discovery: Start-ups that *pivoted once or twice* raised two and a half times more money, had almost four times more user growth, and were 50 percent less likely to scale prematurely than start-ups that pivoted either more than twice or not at all. The takeaway: Be open to change, but not *too* open.

In 2010 Sugianto Tandio took over his wife's family's plastics company in Indonesia. For four decades the firm, Tirta Marta, had sold flexible packaging products, but Sugianto had other ideas. Trained at 3M, he immediately took the company in a new direction. He refocused Tirta Marta on "eco-friendly" innovation. His most daring was a plastic polymer made from tapioca—yes, tapioca—that became the first "Fair for Life" certified bioplastic in the world. It had the dual benefit of improving the environment and giving local farmers a livelihood. Retailers pounced, and the company's plastic goods gained 90 percent of the local market. By the time Sugianto applied to become an Endeavor entrepreneur, he was building a strong green company.

But our business experts uncovered a flaw. "He's a great promoter for Indonesia, and he can solve a world problem," one said, "but he has too many business models and too many products." Joanna Rees, an Endeavor board member, said, "He spends a lot of time talking about making branded pens, which is a completely different business. He needs to focus."

The deliberations lasted over an hour, but the panel ultimately decided he deserved to be supported. When the judges were asked if they had any advice, Joanna didn't hesitate: "Drop the pens!"

A year later Tirta Marta was focusing on expanding abroad and developing an eco-friendly home shopping bag. Not on its horizon: a biodegradable pen.

Joyful exuberance can be an entrepreneur's greatest strength, but it can also lead to crippling distraction. Many entrepreneurs make the mistake of expanding to a new region before their brands have momentum in their own neighborhoods. Or they'll start new product lines when their initial business is just taking off.

Compare two iconic companies. The first is Apple. Steve Jobs was a strict proponent of discipline and focus. He first learned this philosophy while working the night shift at Atari as a college dropout. Atari's games came with no manual and needed to be uncomplicated enough that a stoned college freshman could figure them out. The only instructions for its Star Trek game were: (1) Insert quarter. (2) Avoid Klingons.

When Jobs returned to Apple in 1997, after a decade away, the company was producing a random array of computers and peripherals, including a dozen different versions of the Macintosh. "Which ones do I tell my friends to buy?" Jobs asked. After a few weeks of review, he'd finally had enough. "Stop!" he shouted during a strategy session. He grabbed a Magic Marker, padded in stocking feet up to the whiteboard (yes, a whiteboard; he thought they promoted focus), and drew a two-by-two grid. He labeled the two columns "Consumer" and "Pro" and the two rows "Desktop" and "Portable." Your task, he told his team, is to focus on four great products, one for each quadrant. All other products should be canceled. There was a stunned silence.

But Jobs did not stop there. Next he asked his top managers, "What are the 10 things we should be doing next?" After much jockeying, the group identified a list. Jobs then slashed the bottom seven and announced, "We can do only three."

As Jobs said, "Deciding what not to do is as important as deciding what to do. That's true for companies, and it's true for products."

Contrast this approach with Sony. As the *New York Times* pointed out in 2012, Sony, once a beacon of innovation, had not turned a profit in four years. A former Sony executive acknowledged this, saying, "Sony makes too many models, and for none of them can they say, 'This contains our best, most cutting-edge technology.'"

The lesson for entrepreneurs: Don't muddy up your brand with too many peripheral products or services. Focus on what you do well, and exploit it fully.

Consider one of the most iconic toy companies of all time. In 1932 a struggling Danish carpenter named Ole Kirk Christiansen started making wooden toys: piggy banks, yo-yos, pull toys, cars. He held a contest among his staff to name the company, offering a bottle of homemade wine as a prize. Two finalists emerged; Christiansen chose his own entry, Lego, a variant of the Danish expression "play well." (Presumably he also kept the bottle of wine!)

During World War II Danish parents bought up Lego toys as a

distraction for their children, but the war also created a wood short-age. So in 1947 Christiansen bought a plastic injection molding machine and came up with a line of interlocking, stackable blocks. Customers hated them, preferring the wooden toys. Over the years the company improved the quality, and the firm grew modestly. In the 1970s, when busy baby boomers became parents and saw the blocks as educational, demand surged, and Lego's profits doubled every five years.

But by the 1990s Chinese knockoffs were flooding the market, crippling sales. In response, Lego went on an innovation spree. Designers dreamed up blocks in every color, tie-ins with *Star Wars* and *Harry Potter*, even Lego jewelry. The number of Lego pieces ballooned from 7,000 to 12,400. And it nearly killed the company. By 2003 Lego, like one of those Frankenstein-like creatures a four-year-old makes that can't stand up, was on the edge of bankruptcy. "We almost did innovation suicide," a senior executive said. So the Christiansen family brought in a former McKinsey consultant to be CEO. He sold a chunk of the company, slashed jobs, and outsourced production. He also issued strict orders to go back to the brick. Every Lego had to go up for a vote among designers. The selection shrank back to seven thousand.

Lego's sales soared, growing by almost 25 percent a year. In 2012 the firm reached a valuation of $15 billion, passing Mattel (and Barbie!) to become the world's most valuable toy company.

Experimenting, exploring, expanding are all part of entrepreneurship, but sometimes you have to do the opposite. Sometimes the best thing is to turn away from the shiny new thing. Ignore the distraction. Stop creating more trouble for yourself. Your engine didn't just fall on the floor; you let it fall by not keeping your eye on what really mattered. Don't worry, you'll have plenty of time to expand later on. For now drop the pens and go back to the core ideas that got you here in the first place.

## – 5. DREAM BIG BUT EXECUTE SMALL –

It was the kind of out-of-the-blue gift from the PR gods of which entrepreneurs dream. In December 2012 the *Slate* columnist Farhad Manjoo wrote a piece in which he called the hooded sweatshirt sold by San Francisco–based start-up American Giant the greatest hoodie ever made. "There is really no comparison between American Giant's hoodie and the competition," Manjoo wrote. "When you wear this hoodie, you'll wonder why all other clothes aren't made this well."

The story went viral. ABC News, NPR, and the BBC did follow-ups. Within thirty-six hours, the company had sold out of hoodies. "We were down to the bare shelves," Bayard Winthrop, the company's founder, said.

What an inspiring story of well-deserved success, right?

Hardly. The company could not cope with the demand. Those shelves remained bare for nearly *six months*. As one disgruntled customer commented on *Slate*, "The company may in fact make the world's best hoodie (I'll judge for myself if mine ever comes), but they obviously completely suck at scaling up to meet the demand created by this article."

The flub was even more painful because Winthrop, before starting the company, had been an expert in scaling. He was the guy companies called when they needed to grow but couldn't. Now he was facing the opposite problem. "Inventory planning, your systems, your ability to scale . . . that's all great in theory," Winthrop said. But when your execution doesn't meet your planning, you have what one reporter deemed a catastrophic success, a business whose overnight fame propels it to overnight doom.

Dreaming big is admirable, but if you can't execute small, don't expect your vision to come true.

In 2011 a group of entrepreneurs, VCs, and academics in Silicon Valley, who called themselves Blackbox, set out to identify what they called the genome of tech start-ups. "More than 90 percent of startups fail," the group wrote in a document titled "The Startup Genome Report," "due primarily to self-destruction rather than competition." Even those that do succeed, they said, experience several near death experiences along the way.

Blackbox created a database of 3,200 high-growth Internet start-ups and received in-depth feedback from 650 companies. Their number one conclusion: Premature scaling is the most common reason for start-ups to fail. Three-quarters of start-ups fail for this reason, they said. Think about that: The gravest threat to success is not bad products, poor design, or lack of funds. The biggest hindrance to going big is trying to go big too early. Or as the report put it, entrepreneurs "tend to lose the battle early on by getting ahead of themselves."

Some of the most common reasons these companies failed:

- Building a product that didn't solve a problem

- Spending too much on acquiring customers and not enough on perfecting the product

- Plowing forward without getting feedback from the users

The common theme here: Don't get ahead of yourself. As one interviewee said, "Scaling comes down to making sure the machine is ready to handle the speed before hitting the accelerator." The genome report even put a number on it. Firms that approach going big in a step-by-step way grow twenty times faster than the norm.

I've seen that in our network. When Mark Chang opened Job Street.com in Malaysia in 1997, he assumed his company, a recruitment site akin to Monster.com, would bring him a steady paycheck, but not much more. "I really thought it would be a mom-and-pop thing," he said. But as soon as he gained traction, everyone asked, "*Why aren't you expanding across Asia? What about listing on the NASDAQ?*" "People were just handing out cash in those days," Mark said. "Ignoring their advice was exhausting."

Innately conservative, Chang instead focused on writing software, including custom tools for Shell and Dell. He also hired a seasoned CEO to complement his engineering skills. He avoided rapid expansion. The result of all this plodding? Chang survived the dot-com bust of 2000, which wiped out many of his competitors. He also weathered the 2008 downturn. Today Chang sits on the board of Endeavor Malaysia and JobStreet is considered among the most successful Internet companies in Southeast Asia. In 2014 it was acquired for $524 million. Chang greeted the news with characteristic understatedness. "We only know the 'kerbau way,'" he said, referring to the Indonesian water buffalo. "Work hard and wait for the rain."

Now there's a mascot for the execution-oriented entrepreneur: Be a water buffalo. Work hard and wait for the rain.

The Mexican entrepreneur Miguel Angel Dávila knows how hard it is to actually do this, especially when everyone is out to squash you. A Harvard-trained MBA, Dávila felt Mexico was ready for an alternative to the "brick and stick" model of going to the movies, meaning "You bring a brick to sit on and a stick to beat away the rats." So he and some friends opened Cinemex, a chain of comfortable movie houses with cutting-edge projection, surround sound, and stadium seating. His biggest asset, he told me, was a minnovation: putting lime juice and chili sauce on the popcorn instead of butter.

His biggest challenge, though, was something far less glitzy than Hollywood: Mexican unions had a seventy-year lock on the theater business with arcane rules, such as one that said anyone who sold soft drinks could not sell food. When the unions boycotted his opening day, Dávila fought back at the labor board, which ultimately sided with Cinemex. The union was replaced with a modern workforce. Dávila worked hard to satisfy both employees and customers, and a decade later came the rain: Cinemex sold for $300 million.

Dávila, who serves on Endeavor Mexico's board, counsels entrepreneurs not to try to compete with stories of lightning-fast, hockey-stick growth. "Those things are Halley's comet," he said. "They come around once every hundred years." Instead, "figure out something people need and find a way to execute it better than everyone else."

The lesson: Don't go from zero to sixty too fast. Dream big, but execute small.

## — 6. EAT THE ELEPHANT ONE BITE AT A TIME —

One day I was leaning my whiteboard against the wall when I realized something: These ideas, which had sprung from a hundred different conversations and a dozen different scenarios, all had one theme in common. It's the same theme that united my advice in the start-up phase.

We think of entrepreneurship as being a big, scary thing, involving terrifying leaps of faith and sweeping acts of disruption. In fact, it's something quite different. It's about building up your emotions to take on the status quo, then tamping down your emotions once the problems start to hit. It's about taking courageous actions to destabilize the world but doing so through a series of judicious moves that won't destabilize you. It's about both embracing risk and mitigating risk.

It's about achieving daring dreams through prudent steps.

The lesson here is to act in the opposite way of everyone around you—and perhaps counter to your own instinct. When your path seems smooth and secure, unsettle it. Push yourself to imagine something fresh, to drum up a dangerous idea, to startle the everyday. As I've said, zig when everyone else zags.

But when your path is rough and unsure, I urge you not to cut and run. Stay calm; narrow your options; get the right people on board (and get rid of the wrong); make targeted changes; fulfill your promises.

Keep going.

The journalist Ben Sherwood spent years talking to people who survived extraordinary circumstances, from plane crashes to lion maulings. In his bestseller *The Survivors Club*, he says that many survivors share a mind-set. "In a crisis, they're alert, engaged, and aware. They think—they plan—and they take action." What they don't do is panic, freeze, or feel overwhelmed.

In air force survival school, Sherwood explained, people are taught to conquer moments of confusion with a memorable axiom: *You eat an elephant one bite at a time.* Survival is a big, ornery animal. If you try to eat a fifteen-thousand-pound pachyderm in one sitting, you'll either give up or get sick. Instead, the key to survival is to take it slow, Sherwood concluded. "Take one small bite. Chew. Swallow. Then take another."

The same applies to entrepreneurs. Reid Hoffman delivered a similar message to our founders at an Endeavor summit. Lots of gurus compare entrepreneurship with running a marathon or riding a roller coaster, he said, but he rejected those analogies. Instead, Reid compared the challenges of starting and scaling a venture with what pioneers faced in settling the American West. "In charting the new frontier," he said, "they didn't scale the plains in a day. They broke up the trip into many legs. Step by step, day by day, they got closer to their dream."

Going big doesn't always mean going fast. Surviving the onslaught of tests during the scale-up phase often requires slowing down at points. As Henry Ford put it, "Nothing is particularly hard if you divide it into small jobs."

From his experimental department to mine: The next time a piece of your dream comes crashing to the floor, take a breath, pick it up, go back to work. And chalk it up as your Model T moment.

# CHAPTER 6

# *Leadership 3.0*

A bout four years after cofounding Endeavor, I was fired by my assistant. I was on a trip to Cambridge, Massachusetts, where I was addressing the first-year class of Harvard Business School. The occasion was the unveiling of the first business case study about Endeavor. (It was the same day I was introduced as the stalker.) Afterward I was feeling pretty high. The day felt like a milestone in my own entrepreneurial journey, and I was pumped. Then my assistant, Belle, called.

"Linda, did you remember to authorize this month's payroll?" she asked.

"No, but I'm sure someone else did," I said. "Now can I tell you what happened today?"

"Someone else!" she said. "You're the CEO. No one else is authorized to pay everybody." Belle paused. "That's it." She continued. "You're fired. You're no longer in control of payroll. You may not realize this, but your employees need to pay rent."

*"Employees?"* I thought. *"I don't have employees."* In my mind, the eight people who then worked in Endeavor's New York office were my teammates. I wasn't their boss; I was their partner. There were no

hierarchies, no bureaucracies, no processes. We were a start-up, and we were all in this together.

It took Belle, one of the youngest employees in my organization, to teach me one of my most grown-up lessons. I wasn't just a founder, a teammate, and an entrepreneur. I was a leader, too. And I had better start learning to lead or I wasn't going to have a team to rely on.

In the years since that blunt awakening, I've seen many entrepreneurs falter on the same terrain in the course of going big. Having gotten their start-ups up and running, founders sometimes forget they actually have to run them. Whereas once they worked in their pajamas, tinkered in their garages, or sent e-mails in the middle of the night, now they have proper offices, proper employees, and proper meetings, and they continue to operate in crazed start-up mode because they don't know how else to lead.

But while seat-of-the-pants is no way to lead, high-and-mighty doesn't work either. Most leadership books bulge with research drawn from august generals, Olympic champions, and corporate titans, most of which is incompatible with running a lightning-fast, hyperwired organization. Jack Welch has about as much in common with the modern everyday entrepreneur as an aircraft carrier has with a surfboard.

I wanted to identify the "Goldilocks rules" for leading like an entrepreneur—not so "hard" that they apply only to button-downed organizations; not so "soft" that they apply only to T-shirted start-ups. Leadership 3.0 is what I call these new skills. They're a blueprint for remaining nimble in the midst of growth, navigating the rush of social media, and taking the measured risk of exposing yourself to your team.

Everyone I meet is searching for these rules. High-jumping gazelles certainly need them. Leadership development comes up constantly when we ask the Endeavor entrepreneurs what they need most in order to take their businesses to scale. Mission-driven dolphins and lifestyle-focused butterflies are equally baffled. At school drop-off I talked to a mom who had been running a design shop from her living room and was about to hire her first employee. "What if they don't do what I say?" she asked.

But to my surprise, even intrapreneurial skunks and top corporate executives—the ones I would have thought had leadership figured out—are seeking guidance. In recent years I've been invited to a number of Fortune 100 companies to run Leadership 3.0 workshops. At first I wondered what veterans of big business, with their five-year plans, could learn from quicksilver start-ups, whose plans change every five minutes. Turns out these captains of industry view their elaborate infrastructure and grinding deliberations as more detriment than asset nowadays.

For corporate leaders, the greatest risk is not being nimble enough.

With so many start-ups eating the lunch of big corporations, these executives find themselves borrowing the famous line from the deli scene in the film *When Harry Met Sally*: "I'll have what she's having."

So what are successful entrepreneurial leaders doing right? In my view, they have four attributes in common. They are:

**Agile**

**Accessible**

**Aware**

**Authentic**

The Three R's might be fine for the classroom; for the office it's the Four A's. I'd like to go through them one at a time.

## — AGILE —

One night a few years ago my husband came into our bedroom and announced he wanted to turn us into an agile family. I'd never heard the word "agile" used in this way before. With the passion of a convert, he launched into an explanation.

In 1983 Jeff Sutherland, the chief technologist at a financial firm, was appalled by the dysfunction of software development. Companies followed the waterfall model, in which executives issue from above orders that trickle down to frustrated engineers. Eighty-three percent of projects failed. Sutherland became a skunk entrepreneur. He designed a new system in which ideas don't flow from the top; they percolate from the bottom. In his model, which came to be known as agile, workers are divided into small teams, meet daily to review progress, experiment liberally, and succeed or fail quickly.

Today agile is standard practice in a hundred countries, and its techniques also have flooded into management suites, from Google to Facebook to TED. Many Endeavor entrepreneurs rely on it. Wences Casares, the onetime Patagonian sheep farmer, told me using agile was the best leadership decision he ever made. It reminded him that he wasn't always right and that good ideas can come from anywhere in his organization. (Meanwhile, ask Wences his best *life* decision, and he'll tell you it was marrying Belle, the fiery assistant who fired me!)

As it happens, my family did adopt some agile techniques, including a new way to reduce chaos in the mornings and a weekly family meeting to review progress, from eating more vegetables to less screaming. (And yes, that includes the parents.) The team at TED became so enamored of the idea that they asked my husband, Bruce, to deliver a TED talk, "Agile Programming—for your family."

More important, I began to see why agile is so relevant for entrepreneurs. While the approach has many tools, three in particular apply to leaders: (1) constant experimentation, (2) small, self-governed teams, and (3) embracing failure.

First, agile leaders don't issue rigid five-year plans. They encourage their teams to adjust and experiment constantly. Consider the Chinese appliance manufacturer Haier. In 1993, when Zhang Ruimin took over as CEO, the stodgy refrigerator company had barely averted bankruptcy and had little chance of competing against the global brands GE and Whirlpool. Zhang divided the company into four thousand teams and encouraged them to become more autonomous and customer focused. The team at the struggling call center took note. They vowed to answer calls within three rings and dispatch technicians within three hours.

Not long after, a technician took a call about a clogged washing machine in rural Sichuan and quickly discovered that the owner had been using the machine to clean mud off his newly harvested potatoes. Instead of blaming the farmer, the response team sent the story back to Haier's engineers, along with research showing that millions of other Chinese had been clogging their washing machines with dirty produce. The engineers responded by inventing a machine that could not only wash potatoes but also peel them. They also developed a model for Mongolian herders to help churn yak milk into butter. All this experimentation led to the holy grail of laundry, a washing machine able to wash clothes without detergent. In 2013 Haier ranked as the number one global appliance brand in the world for the fourth year in a row.

Second, agile leaders organize their workers into small, self-managed teams. Bountiful evidence shows that the tighter the working group, the better the work. The legendary advertising executive George Lois, the image guru behind Xerox, Tommy Hilfiger, and MTV and the inspiration for *Mad Men's* Don Draper, insisted that team size is a key to success. "If you had ten incredibly bright people—nothing could come out of it," Lois said. "You could have Nobel laureates in the room, and you'd have big trouble." How large should teams be? "Nothing great can come of more than three people in a room," he said. "*Nothing.*"

Jeff Bezos agrees. He instituted a two-pizza rule at Amazon: If a team can't be fed with two pizzas, it's too big. At a company retreat where someone suggested that employees start communicating better, Bezos stood up and declared, "No, communication is terrible!" He preferred a decentralized, even disorganized company where independent ideas flourished over groupthink. Today 90 percent of Amazon is run with agile.

Third, agile leaders are not afraid of the *F* word: failure. Being willing to tolerate failure has always been critical to the start-up phase of being an entrepreneur. Thomas Edison famously said of his iterative lightbulb experiments, "I have not failed 10,000 times. I have not failed once. I have succeeded in proving that those 10,000 ways will not work. When I have eliminated the ways that will not work, I will find the way that will work."

But as important as failure is to leaders getting started, it's even more important to leaders going big. Many of the most innovative ideas in larger organizations never come to the surface because the skunks behind them are too afraid of losing out on promotions, making their bosses look bad, or getting shown the door. A 2013 survey of five hundred U.S. companies found that nearly 40 percent of the executives surveyed cited anxiety about being held responsible for mistakes or failures as their greatest impediment to taking initiative. Better to just keep quiet and continue doing your job.

These days more and more companies are pushing back and finding ways to create a free-to-fail zone. For one such business, failure is inherent to the brand. In 1953 Norm Larsen, the head of the fledgling Rocket Chemical Company in San Diego, was trying to solve a long-standing problem of the aerospace industry, rust. General Dynamics, a leading defense firm, was working on America's first intercontinental ballistic missile, but the weapon's outer shell kept corroding. Larsen thought a water displacement solution could keep moisture away from the steel skin.

His first formula didn't work. Neither did his second. His third, fourth, and fifth iterations were equally ineffective. On thirty-nine tries, Larsen kept coming up short. But on his fortieth attempt, he hit on a cocktail of oil and hydrocarbon that could repel water.

General Dynamics bought the first batch, and it worked so well employees began sneaking the solution home in their lunch pails to fix rusty car parts and squeaky doors. This gave Larson an idea: Why not sell directly to the public? He packaged his secret formula into aerosol canisters, and soon the blue and yellow cans popped up across the United States. Larsen called the product WD-40, his abbreviation for what he had recorded in his lab book: "Water Displacement, 40th formula."

Today the WD-40 Company is still based in California. In deference to its origins, the CEO, Garry Ridge, has made failure central to the company's daily operations. All of the firm's three hundred employees are encouraged to share both the positive and negative outcomes of every situation. "There is no penalizing for lack of success," he said, no whack-a-mole culture where the minute someone tries something new and comes up short, he or she is beaten down by others. "At WD-40 Company, we don't make mistakes," Ridge said. "We have learning moments. We give people permission to have a conversation about things that go wrong."

One thing going wrong was that customers complained for years they were losing the red straw that came with the WD-40 can. A team was established to solve the problem but couldn't. The group reached out to an external design firm, which came up with a "smart straw" built directly into the cap. The new device added $1.25 per can, but customers were thrilled. One wrote: "It's about damned time." From a base of $130 million in revenue when Ridge took over the company in 1997, revenues topped $300 million a decade later, while employee retention grew to three times the national average.

One fierce advocate for this new style of mistake-tolerant leadership is Scott Cook, the cofounder and executive committee chairman of Intuit. He told an *Economist* conference in 2011 that in thirty-five years in business, he had completely altered his view of leadership. "My father learned leadership in the U.S. military in the Second World War," he said. "In his time, leaders were those who framed the options, made the decisions, and told people what to do. Very much like Eisenhower planning D-Day." In our day, Cook continued, leaders must be more like Thomas Edison. "The new skill in leadership is leadership by experiment."

Cook cited a five-skunk team from TurboTax as an example.

Their hypothesis: If people could fill out tax forms on their cell phones, they wouldn't have to pay tax consultants to do it. The group's first experiments failed, but its second ones surprised them. When customers snapped photos of their W-2s, accuracy improved. Snap-Tax was released nationally in January 2011; within two weeks it was the number one finance app on both Android and iOS with over 350,000 downloads.

"When the bosses make the decisions," Cook said, they're made by "politics, persuasion, and PowerPoint." When leaders empower self-directed teams, the best idea wins.

And it's never too late to embrace failure. India's iconic business leader Ratan Tata became a convert in the twilight of his career. The seventy-five-year-old executive ran a conglomerate of over a hundred companies, from software to steel to tea that generated $100 billion annually. In his last year as chairman, Tata instituted an unconventional competition: a prize for the *best failed idea*. "Failure is a gold mine," he said. It's the only way to foster innovation, keep the company fresh, and reward employees for trying new things.

Take it from one of the most iconic names in global business: Don't fear the *F* word.

Instead, go agile. Drop the long-range planning in favor of constant adaptation; slash bureaucracies in favor of two-pizza teams; and create a culture that prizes experimentation and occasional disappointment over mindless repetition.

And every now and then go out of your way to give someone an A for getting an F.

## – *ACCESSIBLE* –

It was a four-star panel. Marc Benioff, the founder and CEO of Salesforce.com, was hosting a discussion with the retired general Colin Powell and the GE chief executive Jeffrey Immelt. The setting was the 2012 Dreamforce conference; the subject was leadership.

Powell went first. "I was born analog," he said, "and I've been desperately trying to keep up with the digital world." (Benioff pointed out that he was doing pretty well. The former secretary of state had nearly three million followers on Facebook.) Powell said that with so much technology, leaders risked being disconnected from their teams. "Young people are digitally wired, so you have to keep up with them," he said. Leaders can no longer sit back and wait for problems to come to them. They have to reach out and engage people at all levels.

Immelt agreed. "In my world, I'm always fighting size and bureaucracy," he said. Immelt had initiated a major effort to return GE to its entrepreneurial roots. Quoting "the great philosopher" Mike Tyson, Immelt suggested that large companies like GE ought to be more nimble: "Everybody has a plan until they get punched in the mouth." A big part of that change fell on executives like him, who needed to become more responsive to employees. Technology helped.

"What social media does for me is it gives me access to customers and employees," Immelt said. Through digital platforms, he now got raw data from his sales force in the field. He'd use this to press managers up the corporate chain, saying, "What's going on here, guys?" Also, social media obliged him to be more open as a leader, he said. "You have to be willing to share more, and you better just deal with it." In Immelt's case, that meant keeping an internal blog for GE employees. "I've been doing it for two years. It's just my voice. It's my message, my way." He added dryly that he doesn't let his general counsel see it.

Immelt isn't alone. A 2012 Weber Shandwick survey of executives in ten countries found that "sociability" among CEOs had doubled in the prior two years. Two-thirds of CEOs post to a company Web site; half post to a company intranet. Like the heads of Marriott and Zappos, some corporate leaders blog; like Rupert Murdoch, Marissa Mayer, and Richard Branson, others tweet; like the founders of Google, still more hold in-person Q&As with employees. Garry Ridge, of WD-40, sends his employees a daily inspirational quote and promises to address each grievance within twenty-four hours.

However you choose to interact, your team will eat it up. Half the employees in the Weber Shandwick survey said they felt more inspired when their CEOs engaged social media.

I had to learn this reluctantly. In the early years of leading Endeavor, I had the reputation of a bad delegator. I was deemed mercurial, meddling, and reluctant to give up control. Worse, I had no clue how to manage a growing team. If I was serious about going big, I had to follow the same advice I give to entrepreneurs and bring in experienced senior managers.

So I hired a chief operating officer. After less than a year she complained that everyone was going around her and coming directly to me. She quit. A year later I hired a second COO. It quickly became clear that the team didn't respond to him. "He's too corporate for our culture," they said. I had to ask him to leave. By this point I had made a bad situation worse. The whispers that I was a prima donna became more like a loud din. Even when I hired several impressive senior VPs from Dell, Bloomberg, and Silicon Valley the clamor continued.

By this point we were reaching a crisis. Whereas once our whole office could survive on one pizza, now we needed a delivery truck to feed us all. Endeavor was nearing three hundred full-time team members worldwide. I needed a partner. So I called up Fernando Fabre, an economist and for six years the managing director of Endeavor Mexico. He was adored by our entrepreneurs and respected across our network. He'd also become the point person for anyone worldwide who had an issue to pick with me. (This kept him quite busy!)

"Hey, Fer, how are you?" I said.

"Good, and you?"

"Excellent. How would you like to become the COO of Endeavor?"

There was silence on the other end of the phone.

I went on. "You know we're scaling the organization. I'll need to focus externally. So we need someone strong to take over day-to-day management. I thought you—"

He cut me off. "Linda, I get it," he said. "But I won't take the job with that failed COO title. If you're willing to bring me on as Endeavor's president, then I accept."

I was, and he did. Fernando moved to New York, and our new era began. At which point I promptly blew it again. Not with Fernando, but with everybody else. I thought that with a new president and other senior executives we were beginning to feel like a mature organization, so I did what I thought mature organizations did: I convened senior management meetings.

They backfired. First, Fernando was forced to hold countless planning sessions before these meetings and numerous debriefs afterward. "My calendar was filled with meetings about meetings," he said. Second, the meetings were chipping away at our culture. Before, Endeavor had been a communal organization; now the "cabinet" was meeting in a conference room with glass walls, so that everyone else could see they hadn't been invited. I clearly needed a new way to lead.

The solution was social media. At the suggestion of several younger members of our team, Endeavor had recently installed Salesforce Chatter, a social network for the workplace that enables employees to post questions, comments, and concerns. Fernando launched an all-out effort to get everyone hooked. He offered various incentives for team members to post a weekly wrap-up (including, in a nod to his Mexican roots, a bottle of tequila). Fernando himself started commenting on soccer matches; I challenged him to a "Chatter throwdown" over who could accrue more "likes."

The plan worked. Our entire global team gravitated to Chatter, sometimes preferring it to e-mail. Ideas got stoked; new connections bloomed. Endeavor had returned to its start-up roots as a collaborative company. As for the cabinet meetings, they're done.

Perhaps the ultimate example of how leaders have to step outside their bubbles is the one who lives in the biggest bubble of all, the president of the United States. When Barack Obama was elected, he fretted, like all his predecessors, about disappearing behind the oval curtain. He fought to keep his BlackBerry, for example, to let friends and aides reach him directly. (He was denied an iPhone for security reasons.)

During the 2008 campaign, one of those aides, a twenty-five-year-old Pentecostal pastor named Joshua DuBois, sent an unsolicited e-mail directly to Obama's BlackBerry during a particularly difficult time. The e-mail contained a meditation on the Twenty-third Psalm. Now that's a skunk move: pushing preaching on your boss. "I didn't know how he would respond," said DuBois, the faith outreach director. "But in just a few minutes, he got back to me and said the message helped him, and he'd like me to continue each day." The e-mails wove together Scripture, history, jazz, and current events, and Obama enjoyed them so much he asked DuBois to keep writing them once he moved to the White House. "Every morning I get something to reflect on," the president said.

Presidents, like all leaders, don't communicate with just their teams but with the larger world as well. Here, too, Obama has experimented with accessibility. He held the first Twitter town hall and an online chat about housing on Zillow. He even went open kimono on a Reddit "Ask Me Anything" session. In 2012, while Republicans were holding their convention in Florida, Obama stepped into a nondescript back room in a Charlottesville, Virginia, arena furnished with a desk, a floor lamp, and a MacBook Pro.

Obama typed out, "Hi, I'm Barack Obama, President of the United States. Ask me anything." Two hundred questions flooded in during the first nine minutes. They ranged from the serious—"Are you considering increasing funds to the space program?"—to the silly—"What color is your toothbrush?" Obama's digital chief was supposed to filter the questions, and a speechwriter was there to transcribe the president's answers, but the plan didn't last. Obama refused to abandon the keyboard. "I'll just keep going," he said.

So off he went. On work-family balance: "The big advantage I have is that I live above the store—so I have no commute!" On the White House beer: "I can tell from firsthand experience, it is tasty." On the toughest decision of his term: "The decision to surge our forces in afghanistan." (Little details, like forgetting to capitalize "Afghanistan," actually increased the president's credibility.) Nearly three million people visited the Web page during the forty-five minute session; over the next twenty-four hours, another two million stopped by.

No matter what kind of organization you're in, all leaders today must make themselves accessible—to their closest partners, their lowest employees, their far-flung constituents. They must act, in other words, like entrepreneurs. And guess what? Most leaders who leave the bubble enjoy the fresh air. As the president typed at the end of his first AMA, "By the way, if you want to know what I think about this whole reddit experience—NOT BAD!"

## – AWARE –

A few years ago I was giving a speech about the state of Endeavor to around five hundred of our supporters, mentors, and entrepreneurs. I showed a draft to my husband, Bruce. His response: "Too much Superman, not enough Clark Kent." He went on to explain (lovingly, but *still*) that he thought I was spending too much time touting our successes and accomplishments and not enough time discussing our challenges and needs. "When you make yourself sound invincible, you don't sound real," he said. "Plus, you're not inviting the listener in." His insight got me thinking. Now that we're in an age when leaders have to come down off the summit, what posture should they adopt with their employees, clients, and customers?

One answer emerging from a new generation of scholars and thinkers is that leaders need to be much more open about their own shortcomings and assertive about taking responsibility. They need to be aware.

Two stars in organizational behavior, Alison Fragale of the University of North Carolina and Adam Grant of the Wharton School, both found overwhelming evidence of the perils of being omnipotent in how you present yourself. In his bestseller *Give and Take*, Grant lays out the case for what he calls powerless communicators, those who "are more inclined toward asking questions than offering answers, talking tentatively than boldly, admitting their weaknesses than displaying their strengths, and seeking advice than imposing their view on others." Whereas powerful communicators put people off with their seemingly superhuman qualities, powerless ones draw others in with their imperfections and self-awareness.

Effective leaders, in other words, are less super, more human.

I heard a term that encapsulates this idea perfectly: "flawsome." A combination of "flawed" and "awesome," "flawsome" is a way to say something is great but imperfect. In business the term has come to mean an awareness of, and a willingness to admit, your shortcomings. This includes your products, your workers, and your organization.

In April 2009 two employees at Domino's made a video of themselves sticking cheese up their noses and waving meat under their rear ends (subtle!) before adding it to food being delivered to customers. The video went viral, garnering a million views on YouTube. Though the offending employees were fired and arrested, the company still had a PR nightmare. Domino's took forty-eight hours to respond—forever in social media time—then issued a perfunctory video apology from the company head, Patrick Doyle.

But to his credit, Doyle didn't let the story end there. The crisis revealed that Domino's had an image problem that went far beyond rogue pizza makers. The company spent months soliciting feedback. One survey ranked its pizza the worst in flavor, tied with Chuck E. Cheese. Doyle made the unusual decision to embrace the critics. Nine months after the initial crisis, Domino's released a brutally honest video entitled *The Pizza Turnaround* to announce that it was scrapping its old recipe. The video featured Domino's employees talking about how much people hated their product. Doyle appeared first, wincing at a consumer's saying, "How hard can it be? There doesn't feel like there's much love in Domino's pizza." Doyle responded, "You can either use negative comments to get you down, or you can use them to excite and energize your process." One employee added, "It hits you right in the heart. This is what I've done for twenty-five years now." Another started crying.

When the new recipe appeared in stores, Domino's added a Twitter feed to its Web site (#newpizza), showing both positive and negative responses. It also introduced an online pizza tracker, which asked consumers for feedback. Responses were delivered in real time to employees and broadcast on a billboard in Times Square. Word of mouth exploded, and sales soared. Even more important, the effort boosted company morale. With Domino's back in the news for positive reasons, employees were "proud to come to work every day," one executive said. CNBC named Doyle the best chief executive of 2011.

Two Endeavor entrepreneurs went even further in embracing their critics and restoring employee goodwill. Mario Chady and Eduardo Ourivio were the Brazilian childhood friends who built the line of pasta bars featuring juggling chefs. Their focus on fun-loving service brought the company back from bankruptcy; within a few years Spoleto was running three hundred restaurants. Then one day in 2012 a wildly popular Brazilian comedy troupe called Porta dos Fundos ("Back Door") released a YouTube video that spoofed the chain's fast-talking chefs.

"Good morning," said the customer.

"Good morning," said the chef.

"I'd like the penne with—"

*"Penne!"* the chef shouted into the kitchen. "What sauce?"

"I'd like the tomato sauce."

"What toppings?"

"I'll have some corn."

"Corn. What else?"

"H—"

"Ham. What else?"

"Ummm . . ."

"Speak up."

"Give me a second."

"WHAT ELSE DO YOU WANT?"

At the end of the video the chef tosses hearts of palm at the customer, the customer pleads, "I just want to eat lunch," and the chef explodes, "Nobody told you to come eat lunch in hell!"

The video scored, topping nine million views. Though it was titled only *Fast Food*, everyone knew its target was Spoleto. The comedians braced for a call from the company's lawyers. Instead, when the phone rang, it was one of the company's founders. "We want to take you out for a beer," Eduardo said.

Over the objection of Spoleto's PR and legal teams, Mario and Eduardo went forward with the rendezvous. Beers were drunk, jokes were exchanged, then Mario and Eduardo came clean about their real intention: First, they wanted to sponsor the troupe's YouTube channel; second, they wanted the comedians to change the title of the video to *Spoleto*; and third, they wanted to pay the troupe to make a sequel.

Why would the company's founders go out of their way to make fun of themselves?

"We were simply acting according to our culture," Eduardo told me, "not taking ourselves too seriously, always searching for the silver lining."

In the second video, the ill-tempered chef is fired and finds himself working at a call center. He returns to Spoleto and appears wearing an apron that reads, "In Training!" When he insults another customer, he's finally let go for good. The screen reads: "This should never happen, but sometimes it's beyond our control. If you receive bad service at Spoleto, tell us and help us improve." An e-mail address appears.

The spoof of the spoof racked up four million views, but even more valuable, it pumped up employees. "The chefs loved it," Eduardo said. The exposure helped attract new talent. "When we recruited, forty percent of candidates listed the two videos as one of their primary reasons for applying," Eduardo told me.

These days it's awesome to work for a company that's flawsome.

The lesson for leaders is that in an age when social media magnifies and leaves a permanent digital trail of your flaws, how you respond to them becomes even more critical. One entrepreneur I know has made how he responds to mistakes the signature of his entire brand.

Danny Meyer is the celebrated New York restaurateur behind Union Square Café, Gramercy Tavern, and Shake Shack. He and his restaurants have won an unprecedented twenty-five James Beard awards. Born in St. Louis, Danny visited Europe as a teenager and later worked as a tour guide in Rome. It was during those trips that he first became enamored with the culture of gracious hospitality. "The hug that came with the food made it taste even better," he said. That realization led to what he calls his core business strategy, enlightened hospitality. As he describes it in his leadership manifesto, *Setting the Table*, "Hospitality exists when you believe the other person is on your side."

Danny's test as a leader was to take his vision for service (which he honed in his first restaurant, where he could be present around the clock) and figure out how to translate it across a growing collection of establishments spread throughout the country. Even as he went big, he still wanted to feel small. And he wanted his customers to feel cared for.

I've gotten to know Danny a little over the years, and his answer to this challenge is to accept that everyone will not be happy with every meal and prepare his team to react appropriately. He starts at the hiring stage, with an idiosyncratic job application that includes questions like "How has your sense of humor been useful to your service career?" "What was so wrong with your last job?" and "Do you prefer Hellmann's or Miracle Whip?" His explanation: In hospitality there must be a certain amount of fun involved, and those questions give him an idea of whether applicants can join in.

Second, he trains all employees on what he considers the difference between hospitality and service. Service, he says, is mindlessly giving customers more choices and empty chitchat. He cites the

Ritz-Carlton, whose workers say a rote "my pleasure" in response to everything. "Hearing 'my pleasure' over and over again can get rather creepy after a while," Danny said. "It's like hearing a flight attendant chirp 'Bye now!' and 'Bye-bye!' two hundred times as passengers disembark from an airplane." Service is the mechanical act of delivering a product, Danny said. "Hospitality is how the delivery makes the recipient feel."

Finally, Danny put his views on paper. He wrote a step-by-step manual for how employees should treat mishaps. Some of his tips:

- Spill a bowl of soup on a customer? Offer to pay for dry cleaning and send out a dish for the customer to enjoy while others are dining.

- Make a mistake? Never make an excuse. Say, "I am sorry this happened to you," not "We are short-staffed tonight."

- Something goes wrong during a meal? Have the kitchen send out a complimentary dessert or beverage as an additional generosity.

Above all, he said, employees must write a "great last chapter" to every incident. When Bob Kerrey, the former senator and a regular customer, cheerily informed Danny over lunch at Eleven Madison Park that one of his tablemates at Gramercy Tavern the previous night had found a beetle in his salad and the staff had handled it perfectly, Danny felt embarrassed. He was also determined not to let a near-eaten bug be the end of the story. So he sent a complimentary salad to the senator's table adorned with a piece of paper that said, "RINGO." The server said, "Danny wanted to make sure you knew that Gramercy Tavern wasn't the only one of his restaurants that's willing to garnish your salad with a Beatle."

Leadership today is not simply about making yourself look good; it's also about how you respond when you look bad. Even Superman isn't Superman around the clock. To be an effective leader, be aware of how others perceive you and cop to your flaws every now and then. Embrace your inner Clark Kent.

## — AUTHENTIC —

The final lesson of entrepreneurial leadership may be the most challenging and most important of all. Expose yourself. Allow yourself to be vulnerable.

Be authentic.

In late 2005 the Indianapolis Colts were undefeated through thirteen games. If the Colts kept up their streak, the head coach, Tony Dungy, would become the first African American to lead his team to a Super Bowl title. Dungy had always been a different sort of leader. A deeply spiritual man, he was open about his faith.

Dungy translated his values into a compassionate leadership style, something rare in his profession. While he was coaching in Tampa, his place kicker started missing crucial field goals. Instead of cutting him, as most coaches would have done, Dungy asked if something was wrong. He was told the player's mother had recently died of cancer. Dungy reassured him: "You're a part of our team." The next week, the kicker nailed the game-winning score. He said of Dungy, "What he did was relieve the pressure from me. A lot of other coaches would have just let me go."

As the 2005 season neared its climax, Dungy gave his team off for Thanksgiving, a rare treat. The eldest of Dungy's five sons, Jamie, who was attending college in Tampa, flew in to visit his father. At the end of his short stay, Jamie hurried to catch a plane. There was no time for a good-bye hug. "I knew I'd see Jamie again at Christmas and get my hug then," Dungy wrote in his memoir, *Quiet Strength*.

The next month the Colts finally lost their first game. Three days later Dungy's phone rang at 1:45 A.M. "I hope one of our players isn't hurt," Dungy thought. But it wasn't one of his players. Jamie had been found in his apartment in Tampa after hanging himself. "As the nurse was speaking to me, I frantically began to pray for Jamie," Dungy wrote. "But as her words sank in, it became increasingly clear that we were beyond that point. Jamie was gone."

Beyond the pain he faced as a father, Dungy also faced a leadership challenge. The entire Colts organization flew to Tampa for the funeral. Dungy addressed the team in his eulogy. "Continue being who you are," he said. "If anything, be bolder in who you are, because our boys are getting a lot of wrong messages today about what it means to be a man in this world."

The owner of the Colts told Dungy he could take the rest of the season off. Dungy discussed it with his family and decided to return to the sideline. With the Colts assured of a play off spot, the last game didn't matter, but it mattered to the team. The game came down to the final play, a quarterback sneak from the opposing team. When the Colts held, the hometown crowd erupted. "Even though we hadn't needed to win the game," Dungy said, "the players had wanted to win it for me and my family."

The Colts lost in the opening round of the play-offs that year. The next season Dungy became the first African American coach to win the Super Bowl.

There was a time when leaders could keep personal tragedies like this away from the teams they led. That time is gone. The same forces that are obliging leaders to be more agile, accessible, and aware— social media, a younger workforce, a greater need for employees to feel invested in their work—also require today's leaders to be more open about their own lives. Vulnerability, once the antithesis of the strong leader, has become almost a requirement.

The leading voice of vulnerability these days is Brené Brown, a professor at the University of Houston and the author of *Daring Greatly*. Even though "soft" topics are usually considered the provenance of Oprah, Dr. Phil, and the like, Brown's message has been embraced by the business community. Speaking at an *Inc.* magazine leadership forum, Brown said entrepreneurship is all about the courage to open yourself up. "To be an entrepreneur is to be vulnerable every day," she said. It's a mix of uncertainty, risk, and emotional exposure. But while people often seek vulnerability in others, she said, they tend to conceal it in themselves. The challenge is to accept that vulnerability is not a weakness but the "absolute heartbeat of innovation and creativity."

Of all the qualities of Leadership 3.0, this one, being vulnerable, raw, authentic, has been the hardest one for me to learn. But it's also the one I learned most viscerally.

In 2008 my husband was diagnosed with a rare, aggressive form of bone cancer. Doctors found a ten-inch osteosarcoma in his left femur. Our daughters were three at the time. For six months Bruce endured more than a dozen rounds of brutal chemotherapy, during which he was hospitalized on multiple occasions. He then had a seventeen-hour surgery in which doctors removed his femur and replaced it with titanium, relocated his fibula from his calf to his thigh, then cut out half his quadriceps. Only two people had survived this surgery before him. Afterward he returned for four more months of chemo. For more than a year Bruce was in and out of the hospital, walking on crutches, losing his hair and body weight, and fighting for his life.

Bruce's cancer arrived in our lives at the exact moment when Endeavor had decided to rapidly expand, doubling the number of continents and countries we served and aggressively spreading our model. I was initially paralyzed about how to handle this situation. I was determined to go to every chemotherapy session and doctor's appointment, and I needed to provide stability for our daughters. But my demands were also increasing at work. My instinct as a leader, especially a female one, was to do what I had been trained to do: hold it together, compartmentalize, put on a brave face. Never let anyone see you sweat or, especially, cry.

But the truth is I had no choice. No poker face could hide the struggle. So I did the opposite. First I told my board. I telephoned our chairman, Edgar Bronfman, Jr., the one who'd pushed hardest for our expansion plan, and described my situation. The board would step into the breach, he said. Edgar's continuous displays of emotional intelligence and grace had helped me through many stressful situations, so in one sense I wasn't surprised by his reaction. Nor did it surprise me when the Endeavor team blossomed in my absence, with everyone adjusting and taking on slightly different roles. The expansion continued.

But what happened next did surprise me. By mid-2009 Bruce had been declared cancer-free and I returned to work full-time. But the experience had changed me. And so I let down my guard, dismantling the wall I'd built to separate Endeavor issues from personal ones. I kept the team informed of Bruce's progress. I shared how the twins were responding. I even broke down on occasion. Rather than freak teammates out and distance me from them—Would they know what to say? Would they consider me weak?—my vulnerability drew us closer.

And it changed me as a leader. By showing my true self, by revealing that I needed other people, by communicating through every meeting, e-mail, and, yes, the occasional tear that I wasn't invincible, I allowed people—especially employees—to relate to me as they never had before. By indicating that I needed help, I received it in ways I never would have otherwise.

And our organization's culture was transformed. Several younger team members came up to me and admitted that before my family crisis, while they'd admired my passion and entrepreneurial pluck, they hadn't found me, well, relatable. Now that they thought they knew who I was *as a person*, they said they were more willing to follow me anywhere.

I had always thought I needed to be invincible as a leader, that we must mimic the stone-faced expressions of the marbled leaders we grew up admiring. But those unfeeling faces are exactly what's become outmoded. Because a core tendency of entrepreneurs is to be forces of creative destruction, entrepreneurial leaders need to creatively destroy old-fashioned leadership styles. The risk is that you may make yourself a little more exposed; the reward is a deeper bond with your team.

Leave the marble and bronze for the Caesars, Lincolns, and Pattons. Today's leaders must display a much wider emotional breadth. You can begin by embracing the four A's of Leadership 3.0: Be agile, accessible, aware, and authentic.

And in so doing, kick some A.

# CHAPTER 7

# *A Circle of Mentors*

They call him the Nerd Whisperer. The Gipper. The Coach. He's one of the most influential people in Silicon Valley, yet few people outside a small circle have ever heard his name. He likes to hug. He likes to tease. He likes to curse. And he's quietly amassed a reputation as the most effective, behind-the-scenes adviser in American business.

Bill Campbell is the ultimate example of an entrepreneur's best friend. He's a mentor. Eric Schmidt said of him: "His contribution to Google—it is literally not possible to overstate." Danny Shader, the CEO of PayNearMe, said: "Outside of my father, he's the most important male figure in my life." Steve Jobs, who used to take weekly walks with Campbell and who put him on Apple's board, said: "There's something deeply human about him."

Born and raised in Pennsylvania steel country, Bill Campbell was a failure at his first major job. As the coach of the Columbia University football team he was 12-41-1. His fatal flaw, he said, was that he wasn't tough enough to ask players to put football first. He went to work in advertising and became vice president of sales at Apple, where he helped get the company's famous "1984" ad past naysayers and onto the air during Super Bowl XVIII. Later he ran a failed start-up and served as the chief executive of Claris and Intuit.

But it's Campbell's role as an informal adviser that generated his greatest impact. With a style that *Fortune* likened to a mash-up of Oprah, Yoda, and the college football coach Joe Paterno, Campbell became the man top entrepreneurs in Silicon Valley called when they got into a jam.

His first client was Jeff Bezos. Amazon's board brought Campbell in to ensure that the former Wall Streeter had the "operational chops" to run a business. At Google, Campbell was recruited when Schmidt joined as CEO to smooth the transition with the company's cofounders. Schmidt's initial reaction: "I don't need any help." But soon Campbell was helping him tweak everything from how he hired senior executives to how he ran board meetings. As Schmidt put it, "I'll say, 'What should we talk about at the meeting?' and he'll say the three most interesting things and the tone." When Google acquired YouTube, Campbell was dispatched to offer the same guidance to the CEO Chad Hurley.

What does Campbell believe he's offering? "Since I've been around a little bit, I give a little advice here and there," he said. "How fast they should grow, how fast they should hire, how they should raise money, how they should use the money, and when they should bring in financial people." And what does he charge for his services? "My fees are well known," he told the *New York Times*. "Zero. Nobody has to negotiate with me." At Google he did get a coveted parking space.

Few ideas in business conjure up more vivid images of bold individualism than the do-it-yourself entrepreneur. Entrepreneurs go it alone, the mythology insists. Even when working in pairs or small groups, entrepreneurs are considered swashbuckling mavericks, bucking the establishment, tilting at windmills. The philosopher Ayn Rand captured this ideal in her novels *The Fountainhead* and *Atlas Shrugged*, and today she's often celebrated in entrepreneurial circles for glorifying the morality of individual achievement. The economist Friedrich

Hayek championed the idea that societal changes are wrought by creative lone wolves.

That image of self-reliance is irresistibly romantic, deeply entrenched, and completely misleading. Far more than others in business, entrepreneurs need help. Lots of it. A survey we did of Endeavor entrepreneurs showed that the most valuable contribution to their success—outside of their team—came not from those who provided financing but from those who gave good advice. As one entrepreneur put it, "There's lots of money out there, and it's all worth the same. But there's not a lot of good advice."

In this chapter I'll tell you the best way to get that advice. From the beginning, mentorship has been a big part of our model at Endeavor. In our first fifteen years, our volunteer mentors provided over a million hours of counseling to our entrepreneurs. Tom Friedman, in *The World Is Flat*, called us "mentor capitalists." What I've learned is that nearly everything people think about mentors is wrong. For starters, forget that notion that you have to spend years finding and wooing the "right person" to settle down into a lifelong relationship with. A mentor as your soulmate?

Not anymore. These days, you need one set of mentors early in your career and a different set later. You need mentors for leadership, mentors for brand building, and mentors for dealing with that pain-in-the-butt colleague who's holding you back. You even need mentors who are *younger* than you to help you see what's coming.

In our hyperfast age, mentoring relationships are no longer marriages that go on for a half century. If you want to go big, you need a team of mentors. As Kathy Kram, the leading expert in the field, said, "The advice used to be, 'Go find yourself a mentor.' Now the advice is to build a small network of five to six individuals who take an active interest in your professional development." Save monogamy for your private life; in your work life, you want to be polymentor-ish.

So what does that configuration look like? To me, the right model is a 360-degree approach: a circle of advisers who can give you a rotating mixture of tough love, specialized advice, fresh insights, and clear direction. This circle of mentors is as disruptive to the traditional workplace as entrepreneurship is to the traditional economy. And not surprisingly, entrepreneurs are leading the revolution. Here's what you need to do to join.

## — GET YOURSELF A SIMON COWELL —

The first myth I want to explode about mentors is that they're your protectors whose chief job is to shield you from harm and make you feel good. They're not. They're bearers of the truth—or at least should be. But that raises the undeniable question: Can you handle the truth?

The English word "mentor" is derived from Homer's *Odyssey*. In the classic epic poem, when Odysseus goes off to fight in the Trojan War, he puts his young son, Telemachus, under the care of his friend Mentor. The surrogate father figure is supposed to be wise and encouraging. In actuality, Mentor does his job poorly (he robs the boy), and Telemachus grows up to be too timid to stand up to the unwanted suitors courting his mother. The goddess Athena, disguised as Mentor, steps in. "Forget the pastimes of a child," she tells Telemachus. "You are a boy no longer." Athena urges Telemachus to man up, confront the suitors, and go abroad to find his father. This is the tough love he needs. Telemachus heeds the advice, kills the suitors, reunites with his father, and becomes the epitome of perseverance.

This tradition of tough love is still alive in the land where the Trojan War was fought.

The döner is to Turkey what the hot dog is to the United States. A popular street food made from sliced meat and served on the go, the döner is a symbol of Turkey's deep roots as a hub of travel and trading. But as the country became more prosperous, a new generation of Turkish families was turned off by eating food from street vendors. The entrepreneurs Levent Yilmaz and Feridun Tunçer saw an opening. They would create a casual restaurant chain specializing in Iskender döners, those drenched in tomato sauce and yogurt but served in a clean, sit-down environment. They called their company Baydöner ("Mr. Döner") and focused on the new wave of shopping mall food courts, vowing to make their restaurants meet international standards.

Levent and Feridun were ambitious. As soon as they opened their first restaurant, they registered the Baydöner brand in twenty other countries. They believed they could quickly open two hundred stores across Turkey and would soon have a Baydöner in every food court in the Middle East and Europe. And they got off to a promising start: Their flagship restaurant broke even within a year, and over the next five years they opened forty stores across Turkey.

Still, when the fast-moving founders joined Endeavor, our mentors quickly offered sobering advice: Go slow. First, the entrepreneurs faced real estate challenges because mall construction was slowing. Second, wages were already beginning to creep up, pressuring their bottom line. Finally, expanding to new markets would be hard. Customers might have different tastes and workers different skills. A Saudi mentor said expansion would require more training because local employees wouldn't know how to make a döner. Sami Khouri, the head of a Lebanese conglomerate, was blunter: "You should go big in Turkey before going abroad."

For the empire-minded entrepreneurs, the advice was hard to hear. But a year later Levent told me it was the best advice he ever received. "Sami was right. We were not even at seventy stores in Turkey, and our aim was two hundred and fifty. Before we expand internationally, we have to finish our national expansion. Then we can try for the world."

In my experience, what entrepreneurs think they want from a mentor is wrong. They believe they're looking for a wise elder statesman who will eagerly open doors and gingerly offer encouragement; instead, what they need is a tough-talking truth teller. In lieu of a warm bath, most entrepreneurs need a cold shower.

The best mentor-mentee relationships I've seen follow this path. They thrive on painful honesty. The Internet pioneer Kevin Ryan is a frequent Endeavor mentor. Kevin is a serial entrepreneur whose ventures include Gilt Groupe, Business Insider, and 10gen. His natural instinct is to encourage entrepreneurs. Yet he's learned he's most effective when he's delivering his harshest advice. In 2009 Kevin met Amin Amin, a young Jordanian who was attempting to improve education in the Middle East. Amin formed a company to train teachers. Kevin, who serves on the board of Yale, loved the concept. "I'm more passionate about education than anything else," he said.

But a year later the company was stalling, and Amin was feuding with his investors. Kevin was the one to deliver the harsh assessment. "I love the field you're in," he told Amin, "but this company is not worth your time." As Kevin told me later, "For many people, tough love is hard to hear. That's why it's called tough love! But in Amin's case"— Kevin continued—"it was not a difficult message to give because in many ways it was an inspirational message. Because he is so good, I thought he should and could launch a company from scratch."

A year later Amin formed another educational reform company, ASK, for Attitude, Skills, and Knowledge. Within two years the company employed over ninety-five people and generated revenues of $4 million. More important, its programs were showing results. Amin told me, "I was stuck in the details of my conflict with the investors. Kevin made me understand that we are stuck only when we make ourselves stuck."

Finding the right mentors and getting the right advice are hard enough. But the even bigger challenge is following the advice once you receive it. My experience has led me to a simple maxim: Listen especially closely to suggestions that you initially most disagree with.

This is particularly true for people who are already flying high. The bigger entrepreneurs get, the more closed their ears become. In 2009 Twitter was a rapidly growing start-up with what seemed like an unlimited upside, but its organizational structure was a mess. The cofounder Evan "Ev" Williams was the CEO, but there was no CFO, CTO, or COO. The board kept pressuring Williams to fill those positions, but he couldn't make up his mind. The founder of several start-ups and coiner of the term "blogger," Williams liked to surround himself with friends—people he trusted and who would not question him. But by inviting only yes-men into his inner circle, Williams had no one willing to speak truth to power.

So the board intervened. It decided to bring in—you guessed it—the Nerd Whisperer, Bill Campbell. As Nick Bilton reported in *Hatching Twitter*, Williams asked in their first meeting, "What is the worst thing I can do as CEO to screw the company up?" Campbell's response: "Hire your friends." The coach then launched into a ten-minute rant about the perils of mixing friendship and business. (Fire your mother-in-law!) The founders of Twitter had never drawn such a distinction. Office meetings were social occasions, and nights out often morphed into brainstorming sessions. Campbell called this approach a recipe for disaster. Williams took notes.

And then the CEO proceeded to do exactly what the mentor had warned him against. Williams put his sister in charge of procurement for the company kitchen and hired his wife to redesign the company's office. He also brought in vanloads of friends from Google, including Dick Costolo, who had recently sold his start-up to the search giant. Williams ran into his old pal at a party and asked him on the spot if he would become COO. Costolo later tweeted, "First full day as Twitter COO tomorrow. Task #1: undermine CEO, consolidate power."

A former professional improv comedian, Costolo was joking, though his tweet proved prescient. Williams and Campbell had begun meeting weekly by then, and though @ev was always willing to listen to Campbell's advice, he seemed loath to execute it. This made Twitter's board members unhappy. They believed Williams's indecision was creating an organizational pileup. Costolo, meanwhile, was excelling as COO, including brokering $25 million in deals with Microsoft and Google. Faced with a CEO who would not take advice from either his formal board or the best mentor in the industry, the board stepped in. Williams was asked to step down. His replacement: his old friend @dickc.

Just because you have the vision and moxie to get an initiative going doesn't mean you can make the tough decisions to help it go big. The skills are quite different, and knowing the moment to pivot is almost impossible to detect. You need someone to provide honest advice, and then you need to act on it.

A colorful example of why truth telling can be more effective than sweet talking is Simon Cowell, the acerbic music executive who skyrocketed to infamy in the early 2000s by dispensing withering critiques on *American Idol*. Among his most notorious zingers:

"You sound like a cat jumping off the Empire State Building."

"It was a little bit like a chihuahua trying to be a tiger."

"Whoever your voice coach is, fire her!"

Cowell's antics inevitably produced a backlash. When Maroon 5 lead singer Adam Levine was recruited to mentor young singers on a rival show, *The Voice*, he told producers, "We're not going to make fun of these people. We're not going to sit there and criticize them in a mean way." But while *The Voice* is a fun show and a ratings success (OK, I admit it: I watch), it has yet to produce a breakout star. Cowell, meanwhile, helped launch at least a half dozen multiplatinum acts, including Kelly Clarkson, Carrie Underwood, Susan Boyle, and One Direction. "It's not about winning a silly trophy," Cowell said. "It's about mentoring someone to become a star."

If you want someone to make you feel good (or even someone who's good to look at), find yourself an Adam Levine. But if you want to go big, get yourself a Simon Cowell.

## — CUT THE CORD —

The second big myth about mentors is that you find them when you're getting started and keep them for the rest of your career. Wrong. For starters, you need a different set of mentors with each successive set of challenges you face. But even more important, the mentors you acquire early in your career may give bad advice, grow bored with you, become your rival, or otherwise outlive their usefulness. You have to find a way to move on and get the help you need.

There comes a time when you have to cut the cord.

As a boy growing up in Jordan, Ala' Alsallal loved books. He loved them so much he couldn't wait to read the latest Harry Potter volume in Arabic. But the lag time was usually eight months, so Ala' translated the books himself and posted them online. His lag time: three months. While his pluck was admirable, his business was unlawful, as he learned soon enough, when the books' publisher shut him down.

But Ala' would not be squelched. While doing graduate work in computer science, he crafted a plan to open the first online bookseller in the Middle East. This idea was foolhardy in a number of regards: (1) Internet access was still a luxury in the Arab world, (2) fearing fraud, customers were reluctant to enter their credit cards, and (3) Amazon had a twenty-five-year head start and was known for crushing competitors. Ala' didn't care. He registered the domain name Jamalon.com ("top of the pyramid") and wrote a business plan. Then he stalked potential mentors.

His initial target was the perfect early-stage mentor, Fadi Ghandour, the founder of the global logistics company Aramex, the first Arabic company to go public on NASDAQ. Fadi, also an Endeavor board member, loves entrepreneurs. And he's a truth teller. "Ala' was kind of a pain in the ass, in a good way," Fadi said. "I knew the first time I met him that he was special." But his business model wasn't ready. "I told him to finish his degree, go back, and work on it," Fadi said.

Two years later, degree in hand, Ala' launched Jamalon.com out of his family's home with a $2,000 investment. When an order would come in, Ala' would buy the book from the publisher and ship it to the customer. To promote his brand, he painted the family van purple and drove it around town. After two months Ala' scored a $15,000 seed investment from Fadi and the same from another backer. Everyone else turned him down. "Amazon will slaughter you," people said.

Ala' entered the Endeavor network two years later, and while his growth had been steady, we had the same concerns. So we did something radical. We telephoned Diego Piacentini, the head of international business at Amazon. If Amazon were going to swallow up Jamalon, Diego would be doing the swallowing. But Diego was also Endeavor Mentor of the Year in 2011. "I envy entrepreneurs," Diego told me. "Early in my career I became a company executive. I'm inspired by people who start their own ventures."

At first the two were allies. Diego advised Ala' to change his business model. Instead of ordering books on demand, Jamalon started warehousing its fifteen thousand most popular titles, allowing for quick delivery. Diego also brokered a deal between Jamalon and Amazon that would fulfill Jamalon orders outside the Middle East. For Ala', working with Diego was helpful—and tactical. "I like maintaining a good relationship with competitors," he said. But then Jamalon started growing, and Diego realized that Ala's model overlapped too much with Amazon's; he could no longer give impartial advice. "I can't wear two hats in this situation," Diego said.

Ala' wanted to maintain the lifeline, but I told him it was time to cut the cord. Diego and Ala' maintained a personal relationship but parted ways professionally.

Another way you might outgrow your mentor is if you enter a new profession. After you cut the cord with your old life, you need a midwife to your new one. This is especially true for butterflies who choose to become entrepeneurs after pursuing more traditional paths. This need has become so widespread a novel solution has emerged.

Gerry Owen was a fiftysomething assistant pastor at a megachurch in Garland, Texas, when he retrieved the prayer box from the sanctuary one Sunday afternoon. Inside, he found a card: "Pray for me. I need to sell my coffee shop." Owen turned to his wife: "Can we do this?" Gerry and Melissa had been married several months before (in a coffee shop!), and Melissa had been dreaming of opening a similar place for years. But they had no experience. Melissa was an operating room nurse; Gerry had been an executive at Frito-Lay before entering the ministry. They needed a mentor, and they found him through the Internet.

In the early 2000s Duncan Goodall was a Yale grad and management consultant who hated his life. He was working one hundred plus hours a week and traveling all the time. "I was a virtual stranger to my wife," he said. So he quit and bought a coffee shop in New Haven, changed its name to Koffee on Audubon, and started a catering operation. He became known as Yale's "professor of coffee shops."

Eventually Goodall enlisted to become a mentor on PivotPlanet, one of a handful of new Web sites designed to hook up those dreaming of opening a business with experienced entrepreneurs. "The money is nice, but that's not the real reason I do this," he said. "On a deep philosophical level, I believe people are more happy and free if they have their own business."

The Owens found Goodall's profile on the site. For $2,000, they got to tail him for two days and get tutorials on everything from pouring espresso to arranging a pastry shelf. Goodall gave them some tips for going big:

- Employees are your greatest source of joy and frustration.

- Money is made by attention to the smallest of details (and the "right" details).

- If you try to be everything to everyone, you become nothing to everyone. Choose a specific customer niche and be everything to them.

Two years after reading the prayer request, Gerry and Melissa opened the Fourteen Eighteen Coffeehouse in downtown Plano. (The first thing Goodall had said to them: "Don't buy the shop for sale; start your own.") The new shop was shabby chic, with comfy couches, games, and live music. Inspired by Goodall, Owen distributed a manual that urged employees to "ADJUST," to keep tweaking what they did until they got it right.

The main lesson from these examples is that mentorship is like a revolving door. Whether you're starting the climb to go big or starting to climb a new ladder, get the advisers you need at each new phase of your career. And if your old mentors are no longer helping, continue to show your gratitude, but otherwise cut the cord.

## — PHONE A FRENEMY —

The third myth about mentors I'd like to shatter is that they have to be more experienced than you. Sometimes the sharpest tips come not from someone who went through what you're experiencing in a different era but from someone who's going through it right now.

I've gotten to know a group of Turkish tech entrepreneurs who are bonded by equal parts friendship, business, and mentorship. They play poker together, go clubbing together, vacation together. At thirty-six and forty-five, Nevzat Aydin and Sina Afra are the senior members of the group. They met in the 2000s, when Sina was starting a flash sale Web site similar to Gilt and Nevzat was running an online food delivery business similar to Seamless. Their Turkish elders had no idea what they were doing. "We both had Internet businesses, which no one else understood, so we coached each other," Sina said. "As a young entrepreneur you can get information everywhere. The most valuable guidance comes from people who are dealing with the same challenges and pushing for the same transformational change."

One advantage of sideways mentors is that the relationships are often less formal and more frequent, allowing your peer to see through the more polished image you present to others. That's what happened to this group. Nevzat brought along another young entrepreneur,

Hakan Baş, who ran an online jewelry store. He easily fitted in. The buddies partied together and followed one another on Twitter. One day Hakan tweeted about attending a panel at a university, one of several speaking commitments he had accepted. Nevzat tweeted back, saying Hakan should stay in his office and do his day job. "He made the tweet sound so funny," Hakan said, "but it was also good guidance."

The next year Hakan made headlines when he became romantically involved with a model. Nevzat called him up. "People now know you as someone dating a model rather than the CEO of your company. Your personal life is overshadowing your professional life." Hakan was jolted but grateful. "Nevzat explained that he was not telling me to do anything in particular, but he just wanted to let me know what was happening. He cares about my image. Lots of people give me advice about business; he's more focused on coaching me as a leader."

Contrary to the conventional wisdom, sometimes the best mentoring advice comes not from the wizened sage sitting in his armchair but from the guy swaying next to you on the dance floor. New research backs this up. Kathy Kram, the mentorship scholar, and University of Virginia professor Lynn Isabella compared peer-mentor pairs with more traditional relationships and found greater reciprocity when the two were at the same stage in their careers. Peers "can coach and counsel," they wrote. "They can provide critical information; and they can provide support in handling personal problems and attaining professional growth."

This is the philosophy behind groups like YPO, Entrepreneurs' Organization, and peer support networks like the one British Telecom started. "We found that 78 percent of our employees preferred to learn from their peers," a BT executive explained. "But little money or attention was focused on this." So the company launched Dare 2 Share, a podcasting platform that allows employees to share knowledge and advice.

But what happens if the peers are competitors? That actually may enhance the advice. Kathryn Mayer, an executive leadership coach and the author of *Collaborative Competition*, argues that mentoring relationships can be even more fruitful if there's a touch of rivalry between them. "Frenemies" can also be your friends.

Consider two of the most high-profile rivals in modern technology. In 2001, when Google was just a few years old, its cofounders, Larry Page and Sergey Brin, met Steve Jobs. The trio went for long walks, and Jobs gave them advice. He even recommended his personal life coach, Bill Campbell, as a mentor.

But in 2008 Page and Brin were the recipients of one of Jobs's legendary tirades, which quickly led to one of Apple's equally legendary lawsuits. The subject: Google's foray into iPhone's turf with Android. And while I would like my young daughters to read this book, I think it's worth quoting in full what Jobs told Walter Isaacson about the incident: "Our lawsuit is saying, 'Google, you fucking ripped off the iPhone, wholesale ripped us off.' Grand theft. I will spend my last dying breath if I need to, and I will spend every penny of Apple's $40 billion in the bank, to right this wrong. I'm going to destroy Android, because it's a stolen product. I'm willing to go to thermonuclear war on this. They are scared to death, because they know they are guilty. Outside of Search, Google's products—Android, Google Docs—are shit."

Okay, Mr. Potty Mouth, you made your point. But get this: Only three years later, with Page set to return as the CEO of Google, he went to see the one figure in Silicon Valley who had made a similar move back to the helm of a company he'd founded. Page said Jobs requested the meeting. "He was quite sick," Page said. "I took it as an honor that he wanted to spend some time with me." But in Isaacson's recounting, it was Page who asked Jobs if he could drop by. Jobs wasn't thrilled. "My first thought was, 'Fuck you,'" he told his biographer. But then Jobs remembered that the HP cofounder Bill Hewlett had once guided him and thought it best to pay it forward. "So I called Larry back and said sure."

Page dropped by Jobs's Palo Alto home. The two lived fewer than three blocks apart. They spent their time discussing Google's future.

"The main thing I stressed was focus," Jobs said. "Google is now all over the map. What are the five products you want to focus on? Get rid of the rest, because they're dragging you down. They're turning you into Microsoft. They're causing you to turn out products that are adequate but not great."

A short time later Page gathered employees and told them to focus on just a few priorities, such as Google+ and Android, and to make them "beautiful," the way Jobs would have done. The following year Page announced that Google would discontinue some products and that he intended to focus on unifying customers' experience, the strategy that made Apple the largest company in the world. This time, though, there would be no accusation that Page had "ripped off" the playbook from Apple; Google's strategy had come straight from Steve Jobs.

## — NOT ALL MENTORS HAVE GRAY HAIR —

Why would John Donahoe need any help? The tall, tastefully gray-haired, conventionally handsome fifty-four-year-old carries himself with the élan of someone who's been at the head of his class his whole life. And he has! He was an econ major at Dartmouth, earned an MBA from Stanford, and worked at Bain for nearly twenty years, including six as CEO. When we sat down to have dinner, he was the chief executive of eBay, credited with rejuvenating the e-commerce giant. John struck me as one of the few people in Silicon Valley who didn't need Bill Campbell's advice (though the two are friends). Surely he didn't need to learn anything at this stage of his career.

But I was wrong.

That night John told me a story that perfectly captures the way mentorship is being disrupted in the age of entrepreneurship. In 2012, when eBay had a market value of around $40 billion, John called the influential VC Marc Andreessen and asked for an introduction to the best young founder in Silicon Valley. John believed eBay's site was stodgy, and he wanted some advice on how to spruce up its design. Andreessen introduced him to Brian Chesky, the thirty-year-old founder and CEO of Airbnb, the white-hot online platform that allows individuals to rent anything from an extra bedroom to an entire house.

John drove over to Airbnb's offices and grilled his much younger "colleague" about how he satisfied customers' need for change, how he tweaked his design, how he updated his products. "I was furiously taking notes," John said. After two hours John got up to leave. "Oh, no!" Chesky said. "You don't get to do that. Now I get to pick your brain." The graduate of the Rhode Island School of Design then started quizzing the management guru on how to reorganize his team, how to centralize operations, how to lead. The two have been meeting regularly ever since. John said, "I got to tutor him on the timeless principles of leadership. He's been my mentor on how to run a more nimble entrepreneurial company."

These days it's not enough to have seasoned advisers to give you tough love and peers who are willing to give you direct feedback. You also need to have mentors who are younger than you. The reasons are not hard to fathom. First, younger people have access to the tastes, habits, and customs of their generation. If you're over forty, did you see twerking coming? Would you have guessed that an app that deletes images from a recipient's phone within ten seconds would be worth billions? Second, younger people know technology; they're digital natives, not digital trespassers. Finally, they're eager to help. Unlike trying to get on the calendar of an esteemed elder stateswoman, snagging a meeting with the social media whiz kids is a breeze. Just send them a Snapchat.

Some people call these relationships reverse mentoring, but I prefer upside-down mentoring. Jack Welch is often given credit for legitimizing the idea. In the late 1990s he ordered five hundred top-level executives to reach out to people below them to learn about the Internet. The concept has been gaining momentum ever since, picked up in places like GM, Unilever, and the Wharton School. In a rare academic study of the idea, Sanghamitra Chaudhuri and Rajarshi Ghosh found that upside-down mentoring was particularly effective in today's entrepreneurial economy because it forces companies to abandon their hierarchies and take the best ideas from wherever they come.

The biggest upside to these programs, Chaudhuri and Ghosh found, is that they keep boomers engaged and millennials committed. Merrill Lynch started a program to teach executives how to lead diverse employees; Lockheed Martin used one to boost morale among young people. One of the oldest companies in America, 176-year-old Procter & Gamble, used upside-down mentorship to tackle an especially dogged problem: the absence of women in top management. In 1992 only 5 percent of vice presidents and general managers were women. "There have been meetings where you look around at thirty people in the room, and they're all men," said CEO John Pepper. "This is screwy," he added, especially when the topic being discussed was feminine hygiene products.

So P&G launched a Female Retention Task Force and named the Tide executive Deborah Henretta its skunkette in chief. The first thing she did: changed the name of the group to the Advancement of Women Task Force. (Um, memo to anyone who's never been pregnant: "Retention" means something totally different to women. . . .) Next Henretta did market research to find out why two-thirds of employees who were leaving the company were women. What she discovered is that they weren't leaving to have children, as the company had expected. Forty-eight out of fifty were leaving for other high-stress jobs where they worked even more hours. They didn't mind working; they just minded working at P&G.

Henretta's solution? A program called Mentor Up in which senior managers would become the protégés of younger, female employees. The idea was greeted with skepticism on both sides. When the twenty-nine-year-old brand manager Lisa Gevelber was paired with the forty-three-year-old vice president Rob Steele, she thought, "What could I say to Rob that would teach him something new?" Steele was even harsher. "Do I really want this?" he thought. But over time their mentor relationship thrived. Gevelber explained that women felt passed over for promotions and looked down on for being moms. Mothers even felt that taking a sick child to the doctor in the middle of the day was frowned upon at P&G.

In the program's first five years the number of female VPs and general managers increased sixfold; by 2012, 43 percent of managers worldwide were women. As for Henretta, *Fortune* magazine included her on its Most Powerful Women list for six years in a row, and in 2013 she was named president of P&G's global beauty group. It took a skunk to put lipstick on a dinosaur.

In her bestseller *Lean In*, Sheryl Sandberg credits *Fortune* magazine's Pattie Sellers with conceiving a new metaphor for modern-day professional paths: "Careers are a jungle gym, not a ladder." The same may be said for mentoring: Instead of simply looking upward a few rungs for someone to pull you along, try looking above, alongside, below, anywhere you can to find someone to give you the gentle push you need.

## – FEED THE LITTLE FISH –

Once you've gotten yourself a circle of mentors, there's one more step to make the circle complete: Become a mentor yourself.

In 2001 I was invited to visit a group of wealthy Mexican businessmen in one of the country's most exclusive clubs. As I was walking through the halls, I asked if I was the only businesswoman in the building. "No," said my escort. "There is one other."

I had been brought here by Pedro Aspe, Mexico's former finance minister, who was interested in encouraging entrepreneurship in Mexico. He offered to introduce me to some "key businessmen." When I walked in the room, I realized he had undersold the group: Ten percent of the country's GDP was represented, including Carlos Slim, who for a time was the "world's richest man."

Slim started off. "Linda, we don't understand. We're starting to see young entrepreneurs in Brazil, Argentina, and Chile. Why not in Mexico?"

"With all due respect," I said, "you are the big fish. Here in Mexico you tend to *eat* the little fish."

The men stared at me with blank faces. There was silence, which I promptly filled with anxious laughter. I glanced at Pedro, who nodded at me to continue. "If you want entrepreneurship to thrive here," I said, "why don't you think of building an aquarium, where the big fish— that's you—learn to *feed* the little fish?"

A year later we launched Endeavor Mexico, with Pedro as our founding chairman and four others in the room on the board. Over the next decade we set up offices in nine Mexican states and supported more than eighty high-growth companies. In 2012 Mexico's leading business magazine published an article about the country's thriving entrepreneurial ecosystem. The headline: BIG FISH FEEDING THE LITTLE FISH. The source: one of the men in that room.

Over a number of years Endeavor has done extensive research that demonstrates the ripple effect of mentoring. When entrepreneurs mentor other entrepreneurs the spirit of entrepreneurship spreads. Wences Casares, for example, the Patagonian sheep farmer turned Internet entrepreneur I met in the early days of Endeavor, sold his e-trading platform in March 2000 to Banco Santander for $750 million. The news electrified young entrepreneurs across the region. "If Wences can do it, I can do it too," they said. Even more important, Wences turned his attention to helping others. He became an angel investor, he joined Endeavor's board, and today he still devotes an hour a day to mentoring the next generation.

If Wences can do it, *you* can do it, too.

Scholars who've studied how phenomena like happiness and divorce spread have identified what they call social contagion theory. The idea is that when one person embraces a life-changing philosophy, he or she eagerly passes it on to others. The spirit of chance taking, change making, and dream chasing belongs on that list. Entrepreneurship is contagious. The chief way it spreads is mentoring.

When I first started helping entrepreneurs, I would not have placed mentorship that high on a list of things they needed most. Surely money would be number one. But two decades later I realize I was wrong. I've heard the same thing from so many different entrepreneurs that I now believe it's true: Mentor capital is even more valuable to them than financial capital.

Why? Part of it comes down to what I experienced when I was trying to take Endeavor to the next level. We had a growing organization and a wonderful idea. I had passion and desire. But I kept hitting walls. I would reach a tricky place and feel isolated, scared, and exposed.

At every juncture, the way I escaped was to turn to someone for help: colleagues in the nonprofit world, veterans of fast-growing companies, the first generation of working moms. I especially turned to my board. When Edgar became chairman, he unwittingly became *my* mentor, both guarding my back and pushing me forward. And he did it without any recognition. One reason mentorship has become so central to who I am is that I'm forever trying to help others who find themselves in situations similar to those moments when I felt most alone and someone stepped into the breach to help me.

Which brings me back to what I said at the outset of this book: The biggest barriers to success in the entrepreneurial age are not physical, financial, educational, or national. They are psychological. The keys to unlocking success are believing in yourself and finding others who believe in you. That last one may be the hardest of all, which is where mentorship comes in.

Everything in the life of the entrepreneur is conditional. If the work isn't interesting or fun enough, the employees leave. If the profit or impact isn't great enough, the funders leave. If the product or service isn't effective enough, the customers leave. Even your family's support is often conditional. The entrepreneur is always dangling on the precipice, at the risk of feeling abandoned, on the cusp of falling over.

That's why you need such a large circle of mentors. Mentors keep you balanced.

But how do you find them? That may be the most surprising lesson of all: Chances are you already know them—or someone who does. In my experience, the real problem in getting the right support is that nobody knows you're looking. It's been a common theme in all these discussions about going big. Sometimes the most important thing you can do is to admit you're vulnerable and need help in the first place.

It's like the old Taoist saying "When the student is ready, the master appears." Want to find the right mentor? Reach out. Tell those around you what you need.

Open the door, and the mentors will walk through.

# PART III

## Go Home

# CHAPTER 8

# The Purpose-Driven Workplace

Early one evening when my daughters were in third grade, Tybee and I were walking to school to see Eden's class perform *The Tempest*. Tybee started excitedly telling me about a book she was reading, a girls' self-esteem manual I had somewhat heavy-handedly placed in their bedroom. She was particularly animated about a spread on fashion and body image through history.

"Mommy, can you believe all the things women used to do to look fashionable?" she said. "Some removed their ribs so they could pull their corsets tighter!"

"Oh, really?" I said.

"And did you know that in the 1920s, women started bandaging their breasts so they would have more boyish figures?"

"Actually, I didn't know that until recently," I said. "But I was just reading a book about how entrepreneurs don't just try to make money, they also try to make the world a better place. And I learned about the woman who undid those bandages!"

Then I told Tybee this story.

Ida Kaganovich was born in Belarus in 1886. Her father was a Talmudic scholar, so her mother supported the family by running a small grocery store. Ida moved to Poland as a teenager to study math and Russian, as well as to apprentice as a seamstress. While there, she became a socialist, dedicated to the idea that capitalism could not provide justice for women. Back at home, she met a fellow revolutionary, William Rosenthal.

In 1905 Ida and William, facing persecution, fled to Hoboken, New Jersey. Unwilling to take a factory job, Ida bought a Singer sewing machine and launched her own dressmaking business. "Why risk it?" friends said. "Because I don't want to work for anyone else," she answered. The dyed-in-the-wool socialist had become cotton-and-crinoline capitalist.

But Ida's figure-flattering dresses clashed with the undergarments of the times. By the 1920s, the bodice-squeezing corset of the Victorian era had fallen out of favor, replaced with a strip of fabric that flattened breasts against the rib cage. The bandeau, as it was called, was said to be necessary because it allowed women to dance the Charleston without their breasts falling out. For the fashion conscious, the goal was to look boyish.

Ida didn't have a boyish figure. She was buxom, and she designed dresses for "real women" like herself. "Companies used to advertise, 'Look like your brother.'" she said. "Well, that's not possible. Nature made women with a bosom, so why fight nature?"

Ida and William started designing an alternative—dresses with fitted brassiere cups. At first, these mesh cups were built into the dresses, but the cups proved so popular that Ida and William began selling them as add-ins for a dollar. To contrast with "boyish form," they sold them under the name "Maidenform."

From their shop on 57th Street, the accidental entrepreneurs launched a revolution. They took advantage of another hallmark of the new era: advertising. Their signature "I dreamed" campaign showed women, topless except for a Maidenform bra, working in an office or throwing a baseball, with the line, "I dreamed I went to work in my Maidenform bra" or "I dreamed I opened the World Series in my

Maidenform bra." One showed a woman in a red skirt and white bra, surrounded by ballot boxes and fireworks, with the slogan, "I dreamed I won the election in my Maidenform bra."

A Maidenform in the Oval Office: Now that's dreaming big!

By the 1930s, Maidenform was selling half a million bras a year; by the 1970s, it was selling 100 million a year. Ida's comfortable, affordable products liberated millions of women. But what interests me about this story, I told Tybee, is that it shows how not just fashion but entrepreneurship, too, has changed over time. In the old days it was enough for entrepreneurs to say they were benefiting society by offering innovative products, generating profits, and handing out steady paychecks. By these measures, Ida Rosenthal was a barrier-smashing success.

But times have changed. Products, profits, and paychecks are not enough anymore. These days, society cares how you treat your own workers. Customers want to know you promote the same values inside your walls as you do outside; job hunters want to know you care about them before they send in an application. Your culture is your brand.

And on that score, Ida fell short. A devotee of modern management techniques, the chain-smoking CEO sped up her assembly lines, browbeat her union workers, and argued that her seamstresses should be able to work longer since they got less fatigued because their breasts were "uplifted." The only place women didn't dream of working, it seems, was Maidenform itself!

In the first two sections of this book I've talked about what it means for entrepreneurs to get going and go big. But there's a third component to living like an entrepreneur. It begins when you focus on a series of larger questions: What purpose am I trying to achieve? What's the meaning behind what I'm doing? What type of life do I want to live?

I'll spend the next two chapters addressing those questions. Everything up to now might be thought of as the nuts and bolts of entrepreneurship. Now it's time for the spit and polish. I sometimes think of this part as the *art* of entrepreneurship. I call it "going home."

The first topic is how to build an organization that doesn't just maximize efficiency but is infused with values. Today, entrepreneurs are at the forefront of a new era in which organizations put talent at the heart of their business models. And they have no choice. Having grown up surrounded by entrepreneurial freedoms, workers expect flexibility. They insist on collaboration. They demand meaning.

I've watched leaders struggle with these issues for years (and struggled with them myself). Here's what I've learned: If you want to build a cohesive organization, it's no longer enough to think about your own leadership style; you need to spend an equal, if not greater, amount of time thinking about how to satisfy and nurture talent.

Leadership, as hard as it is, may be the easier side of that equation. At least you can control your own behavior. Creating an environment that brings out the entrepreneurial instincts in your workforce—a worldview we might call "employeeship"—now that's tricky.

Here are some ideas that can help.

## – PSYCHIC EQUITY –

Look around any major city and you'll see the names of the biggest corporations plastered on the grandest buildings. Scores of companies from Dubai to Dallas have made their glimmering headquarters the public face of their economic might. The bigger the building, the more clout the brand.

But look around Buenos Aires and there's one name you won't see on a skyscraper.

Globant is a technology company started by four friends in a bar in 2003. From their base in Argentina, the scrappy founders set their ambitions high. "Our goal is to be the world leader in creating innovative software products," they said. Boosted by A-list clients like Disney, American Express, and Coca-Cola, Globant quickly spread to eight countries, its annual revenues topped $150 million; its workforce swelled to three thousand people.

As Globant's reach grew, the founders faced a familiar decision. They needed to expand their operation and rally their workforce for a new phase of growth. The easiest way to do that would be to consolidate everyone in a flashy, state-of-the-art headquarters. The press would write about it; competitors would take heed; the world would be on notice that a Major New Player had arrived. In short, everyone would love it.

Everyone, that is, except their employees.

Globant had made workplace culture the heart of its identity. It promoted team-building initiatives like Stellar, a peer recognition program in which workers, called Globers, could award gold stars to colleagues for promoting core values. It allowed employees to compete for new projects. When Nike invited Globant to bid for an ad campaign, the company didn't turn to its marketing team. It hosted a crowdsourcing session in which everyone in the company had a shot. One hundred Globers submitted ideas; Globant won the account, and the Glober behind the winning submission got an iPod.

Nothing tested Globant's employee focus more than the question of where they would work. The founders' instinct was to assemble everyone in a downtown tower. But when they plotted employees' addresses on a map, they quickly discovered that almost no one lived downtown. Forcing employees to waste time in long commutes would rob them of personal time and violate one of the company's core values: Globers set their own schedules. So the founders took the opposite tack: They built three smaller offices whose locations were chosen to minimize travel times.

The story of Globant's invisible headquarters perfectly captures the first major issue I feel you need to consider when focusing on today's workers: You have to know what motivates them. If you think it's primarily money, think again. The biggest single change in the workforce of the entrepreneurial age is the list of priorities workers bring to the job. Paycheck is on the list, but it's increasingly crowded out by a host of new considerations: impact, freedom, quality of life.

There are benefits to this new reality—organizations with fewer financial resources can compete for talent—but there are risks as well. Fail to give workers what they want, they'll walk.

One Monday morning in 1965 Bill Gore, the former DuPont engineer who founded W. L. Gore & Associates, was taking his usual stroll through his Delaware plant. But that morning he noticed something unusual: He couldn't name everyone. Instead of making him happy (business was booming!), the discovery made him upset. He quickly dashed off a memo: No Gore facility would have more than two hundred employees. Also, each facility must be interdisciplinary—no isolating the PR department or "siloing" the engineers. Everyone must be able to know everyone else's name and be in position to work with everyone on the team.

More memos followed, as Gore developed a philosophy he called the Lattice Organization. He wrote: "Most of us delight in going around the formal procedures and doing things the straightforward and easy way." Gore introduced an informal, nonhierarchical approach that unleashed individual creativity. His company had no titles and no job descriptions. There were also no "employees" or "bosses." Instead all workers were "associates" who were guided by "sponsors" and who organized themselves into self-managed teams. Gore's approach became known as unmanagement, and it helped turn his company into one of the most innovative in the last fifty years, succeeding in such wildly varying fields as medicine (heart patches), clean energy (air pollution filters), dentistry (Glide dental floss), and music (Elixir guitar strings).

Unmanagement did not work for everyone. Gore once said that for those who can't adapt to the amorphous structure, "it's an unhappy situation." The current "un-CEO," Terri Kelly, admitted that many workers still need more external direction. "Some people want to see a road map," she said. But the vast majority of Gore associates relish the freedom. They become designers of their own work lives, entrepreneurs within a collective of entrepreneurs. As one said, "This company

trusts you as soon as you walk in the door to make good decisions."
Today turnover at Gore is 8 percent, less than half the industry average. And it is one of the few companies to have been included on the
*Forbes* Best Places to Work list every year since the magazine started
the ranking in 1984. In 2004 *Fast Company* named Gore "pound for
pound the most innovative company in America."

In an economy where companies compete on service as much as
they do on quality and price, finding ways to unleash creativity is becoming increasingly crucial. Research from the Hay Group found that
companies with highly engaged people have 50 percent higher employee retention, 89 percent higher customer satisfaction, and 400
percent higher revenue growth. Retail stores that scored higher on
employee satisfaction generated $21 more in earnings per square foot.
Still, most companies do a poor job at engaging their teams. A Gallup
survey of companies worldwide found that only 13 percent of employees are engaged at work.

So what can you do to invigorate your team members? It turns out
what you might think is the most obvious answer—give them more
money—is not the complete answer. When Endeavor surveyed entrepreneurs and employees at our sixty fastest-growing companies in
2013, we discovered that they all used a number of strategies with employees that were similar to Gore's lattice. These include nonhierarchical structures, open and frequent communication, ways for employees
to submit and implement ideas, and creative reward systems. As Nemr
Badine, a digital marketing entrepreneur from Lebanon, said, "At the
end of the day, monetary incentive is nice, but you have to cater to
people's emotional needs. Make them feel like they are a part of something bigger."

It's what I like to call psychic equity.

A growing body of research shows that employees need more than
the carrots that have long been dangled before them. Duke University
economist Dan Ariely, a pioneer in this field, has done a number of
studies to test the effectiveness of financial incentives. This research is

tricky, he admits, because academics don't have the resources to do these tests on Wall Street. He did his first test in India. He asked eighty-seven participants to perform simple tasks, then offered them rewards ranging from fifty cents (a day's labor) to five dollars (a month's labor) to fifty dollars (five months' labor).

Conventional economics would hold that the participants' performance should improve commensurately with the size of the bonus. Ariely found the opposite. The lowest bonus group performed no better than the middle bonus group. Even more surprising, the highest bonus group performed worst of all. When Ariely replicated the study at MIT, offering sixty-dollar and six-hundred-dollar rewards to students, he found the same thing. In eight of nine times that Ariely did similar experiments around the world, he found that higher financial incentives led to worse performance. His conclusion: Human beings are naturally happy to do things but not when they're paid to do things.

Ariely is not saying that people should not be paid to work; nor am I. What he's saying is that thinking your employees need only a paycheck is out of date. Entrepreneurs understand this better than most because they're often cash squeezed at the outset. Without the ability to fall back on money, they're forced to find innovative ways to motivate employees. One technique: Rethink job titles.

The Endeavor entrepreneurs René Lankenau and Luis Garza realized that Mexico had a problem. There were too many babies and not enough day care. To address this pain point, René and Luis started their company, Advenio, to provide on-site child care at corporations, beginning in Mexico City. As Advenio expanded to new cities, the founders grew concerned they'd lose quality control, so they took an unusual step for a start-up. They hired a dedicated person to monitor company culture. Her title: chief mom. She in turn hired a dream manager to help workers achieve their goals. Not only were these job titles fun and empowering, but they also sent a message that each employee's success was key to the company's success.

Dolphins, because they work in nonprofits, have long understood the need for nonfinancial incentives. Nancy Lublin runs Do Something, a nonprofit that encourages young people to take action through social change. Each year it recruits more than two million volunteers. Nancy is the CEO, though she lists her job title as chief old person. One of her ideas: Give out job titles that make people proud. "People aspire to the higher title, so why not give it to them?" Nancy wrote in her book *Zilch*. "Better yet, you can make up a new title that makes employees feel valued."

Plenty of for-profit businesses are following suit. Pinterest designers are called pixel pushers. The owner of a candy store chain styles himself chief gummy bear. One ad agency calls its administrative assistants first-impressions officers.

Make a good impression with your employees: Let them have a say in picking their titles.

Another step is to follow Globant's playbook and give workers more autonomy. For years companies have been giving employees chunks of time to work on pet projects. At 3M, it was 15 percent of their time; at Google, it was 20 percent. LinkedIn has an initiative to let employees pursue an approved project for up to three months; that's 25 percent of the year.

But forget the arms race of percentages for a second. Quicken Loans has a program called Bullet Time that allows independent projects every Monday afternoon after one. Facebook runs a programming marathon called Prototype Forum that encourages employees to develop experimental products. One winning idea was Facebook Wi-Fi, which offers people free Wi-Fi at cafés anywhere in the world if they log in and give the company their coordinates.

Butterflies operating small businesses are also finding creative ways to grant employees more self-expression. At Artists Frame Service in Chicago, framers are assigned their own color screws. Jay Goltz, the founder of Artists Frame, explained the impact of the signature screws this way: "It creates pride of ownership." Also, the frames' quality significantly improved once autonomy replaced anonymity.

"When the wire on a frame falls off and it comes back, we know who did it," Goltz said.

The days when entrepreneurs could rely on their natural charisma and brilliant ideas to compensate for creating brutal places to work are over. Employees today have higher expectations. As Dan Pink pointed out in *Drive*, the best way to tap into people's intrinsic motivations is to give them freedom, mastery, and purpose. In my frame, these are components of psychic equity. They're especially crucial for the book-end generations—older workers and younger workers. Neither generation rates money as the most important form of compensation. Instead, Pink wrote, "they choose a range of nonmonetary factors, from a 'great team' to 'the ability to give back to society through work.'" And if they can't find that package, they'll leave. In other words, make your workplace more entrepreneurial or find your workers fleeing to launch enterprises of their own.

## — CULTURE CLUB —

Every other year Endeavor holds a summit at which our founders meet high-profile business leaders to discuss strategy, trends, and how to make their organizations thrive. In 2013 one of the speakers was Jenn Lim, the CEO and chief happiness officer of Delivering Happiness, the company she cofounded with Zappos CEO Tony Hsieh. Jenn's mission is to inspire others to follow the example of the online retailer and make joy a core business strategy. At Zappos, workers are called "Zapponians" and they take "zolidays." Every year the company publishes a *Zappos Culture Book* with entries from employees.

Jenn's message to our entrepreneurs was that since your culture is your brand, your employees are your chief asset, so you'd better make sure you have the right assets on board. About halfway through her talk, Jenn said something that jumped out at me, because it captured what I and many of our entrepreneurs have learned: Successful leaders "hire slow and fire fast."

The first half of that equation involves your taking the time up front to not cost you time and money later. Zappos holds two sets of interviews. First, the team hiring asks candidates questions about experience and skills. Then the HR department grills them to gauge cultural fit. Zappos is so serious about culture that it offers $4,000 for new hires to quit after their first week, so as not to waste resources training someone who doesn't gel with the group. Think about that: Zappos will pay you to walk away after five days if you don't fit in with its culture!

What resonated with me about Zappos is that workers today aren't just recipients of your culture; they are ambassadors for it. They can't project your values if they don't embody your values. That's why you have to screen them carefully.

No one understood that better than Debra Jane Sivyer. Debbi was a high school graduate who found work as a foul ball girl for a baseball team and as a water ski performer. At eighteen, she met the economist Randy Fields; the two were married the following year. As a housewife Debbi baked cookies for her husband's office. Everyone liked them, so she thought of opening a store. "I knew my disadvantages," she said. "I was young, had no college credentials, came from little means. I was blond and people figured I had no brains." Her husband said her idea was "loony"; her father balked. "The thing that really got me going," she said, "was when my mom said I would fail."

The first Mrs. Fields Chocolate Chippery opened in August 1977. At three o'clock she had not sold a single cookie, so Debbi loaded up a tray with cookies and walked down the street, giving them away. By day's end she had lured enough people back to the store to make seventy-five dollars. By 1980 she had 15 stores; by 1986, 350 stores. (By then she was also buying 10 percent of the world's supply of macadamia nuts.) But she had a problem: how to hire people who embodied her upbeat personality and could re-create the "Mrs. Fields experience." Debbi remembered all of her customers' birthdays, for example, and expected her employees to do the same. So she devised a creative hiring strategy.

First, she brought out a tray of cookies and asked applicants to taste them, so she could gauge their enthusiasm for the product. Next, she asked candidates to take trays of cookies out onto the street and give the samples away, to test how outgoing they were. Finally, she asked them to sing "Happy Birthday" in the store, as they would be required to do if they were hired. "I wasn't trying to see how well they sang," she said. "I was looking to see would they be willing to do what I asked them to do to make the customer happy. When you're trying to build a business and make customers happy, you have to do anything it takes." Debbi called the process the three S's: sampling, selling, and singing.

As important as it is to hire slowly, it's even more important to fire fast. In *Good to Great*, the management expert Jim Collins talks about the dual importance of getting the right people on the bus and moving the wrong people off the bus. Collins says great bus drivers (read: great leaders) begin not with "where" but with "who." "They start by getting the right people on the bus, the wrong people off the bus, and the right people in the right seats."

Kevin Ryan, the serial entrepreneur who led DoubleClick from a twenty-person start-up to a global company with over fifteen hundred employees, calls this process addition by subtraction. He told me, "Part of building a great team is learning to recognize when individuals aren't working out and then letting them go." His advice: "Don't let a bad situation fester."

One reason I became obsessed with finding the right way to let the wrong people go is that for a long time I was not so good at finding the right people in the first place. To put it another way, I used to be bad at hiring, so I had to become good at firing. But while I agree with Jim Collins and Kevin Ryan in general—letting people go is necessary—my experience with entrepreneurs has led me to believe that there are better and worse ways of doing this.

First, working with founders in emerging markets, I learned that most people live and work in small worlds. Your employees are also your former classmates, your neighbors, the children of your mom's best friend, the kid who looked up to you down the block. You can't cruelly fire somebody and expect to do business, eat lunch, or go to the grocery store without incurring some bad karma.

Second, in the age of social networks, even an ex-employee is still a spokesperson for your brand. That person you just let go is posting about his or her experience on Facebook, broadcasting his or her views on Twitter, and leaving a digital trail of complaints that's forever available to the next recruit who types your company's name into Google. There are even sites, like Glassdoor.com, that serve as open bulletin boards for gossip about hours, working conditions, and who's got the worst boss. Forget the revolving door; these days the bigger threat to entrepreneurs are walls that talk. There are no secrets anymore.

All this has put more pressure on the art of letting people go. Nothing defines your culture more than how you treat people you no longer need or want around. The classic scene from the movies, one that's far too real for many people, involves employers cutting off their employees' e-mail, taking their keys, keeping their contact lists, and sending them on a perp walk with a lone cardboard box filled with droopy plants and water-stained photos of their kids. This kind of draconian action may be necessary in a few rare situations, say, at banks or security firms, where sabotage is an issue. Yet for nearly every entrepreneur I've ever met, this way of firing people is not only unnecessary but self-destructive.

There is a better way. You can move people out gracefully. Just because you make a swift decision to discharge people, that doesn't mean you have to rush their exits. You can allow them to use your office to find future work. You can offer to be a reference. You can let them notify others themselves. I'm not naive: It's still awkward and uncomfortable. I've practiced lots of termination speeches in the mirror. I've seen lots of tears. Anyone you force out is not going to leave singing your praises.

But if you handle yourself thoughtfully, people won't leave cursing you either. And in many cases, they'll thank you for the transition time. In today's hyperconnected world, that's vitally important. Our experience with entrepreneurs shows that when you're building a company, minimizing detractors may be even more critical than maximizing promoters.

This new way of letting people go is so crticial that even my daughters picked up on it. One day, when my girls were six, they were singing a silly song with some friends. The song was to the tune of "Happy Birthday."

> *My mommy hates work*
> *She fired a jerk*
> *She hired a monkey*
> *Who ate my homework*

At the end of the song, Tybee turned to her friend and said, "Well, actually, my mommy doesn't fire people. She just tells them they'll be happier elsewhere."

## — *IF YOU CAN'T BEAT 'EM, YOU KNOW, LIKE, JOIN 'EM #FOMO* —

One summer morning on the fifth floor of the iconic Puck Building in New York's SoHo district, a swarm of new employees from the fashionable eyewear brand Warby Parker gathered for their weekly company-wide meeting. "This is actually our biggest number of hires," said Neil Blumenthal, one of the founders. At thirty-three, he was probably the oldest person in the room. "Come on up," Blumenthal called to a recruit. "Give us your fun fact!"

Fun facts are a Warby Parker tradition and one of many ways the company has designed its workplace to fit the temperament of its youthful workforce. Younger employees are different. They don't like to wait; they don't like to pay dues; they don't like to do drudgery. And it's not enough to roll your eyes and insist they do it your way. Your way needs to adopt some of their ways, the most important of which is: Their work needs to matter—to them and to the world.

At Warby Parker, one way that message is conveyed is to make the workplace more collegial. One of the company's eight core values: "Inject fun and quirkiness in everything we do." Fun facts are an attempt to do that. While no one has topped an early hire's revelation that she once held Michael Jackson's infant son, Blanket, today's entries are eclectic and, more important, bonding. Kate, from product strategy, is a champion rodeo barrel racer. Natalie, from customer service, was a fan dancer for Beyoncé in the Super Bowl halftime show. Julie lost her sense of smell crowd surfing at sixteen.

Warby Parker sells cheap eyewear over the Internet and in a handful of retail stores. By the standards of contemporary business, its young employees should be undervalued. Instead, they are empowered, upbeat, and engaged. "I know that technically it's like a call-center job," said Mikayla Markrich. (Fun fact: She was a Segway tour guide in her native Hawaii.) "But it doesn't feel that way. You think of the call-center stereotype: The people are old; they're miserable; it's kind of a dead-end job. Here everyone is so young and so smart. And we aren't treated as though we're just the customer service representatives. We're viewed as part of the team."

What Blumenthal realized was that to succeed, he and his partners needed to give their young employees more than just safe jobs with good benefits; they needed to give them a feeling of belonging. Every new hire gets a gift certificate to a Thai restaurant (the cuisine of choice during the founding); a copy of Jack Kerouac's *The Dharma Bums* (Warby Parker is an amalgam of two Kerouac characters); and a free pair of glasses, whether they need them or not. Every week all employees tell their manager their happiness rating on a scale of zero to ten. Blumenthal surveyed employees asking why they were attracted to Warby Parker and why they stayed. "And to both of those questions, compensation was dead last," he said. "It was culture and opportunity to learn and have an impact."

Warby Parker's employees are mostly millennials, a term that describes anyone born between 1982 and 2000. They are the most intensely studied of contemporary workers in part because they're the fastest-growing group—millennials are now 36 percent of the American workforce and will reach 46 percent by 2020—but also because they're so baffling to older employees. Researchers have found that millennials display three fundamental qualities that distinguish them from others.

First, they came of age in an amped-up, always-on world, so they expect the same at work. They are consumed with speed; they want it yesterday. The good news is, they've never known nine to five, so they aren't bound by old-fashioned time clocks; they're much more willing to work at odd hours and to crash to get a job done.

Second, millennials care more about their personal brand than the company's. One lesson millennials definitely absorbed from their parents: They can achieve whatever they desire. If they can't find personal fulfillment at your company, they'll search for it elsewhere. In one study, millennials indicated they were deciding whether to stay or quit a new job within weeks. Boomers, by contrast, expect to spend up to four years in a job before moving on.

Because of this, younger workers want to believe they *matter*. A 2012 survey by Net Impact found that 72 percent of college students said that a job that allowed them to make an impact was very important to their happiness. Their parents may have been content with putting in long hours at a corporate office, then giving back at the PTA bake sale or the year-end charity drives. But millennials don't see the boundaries between their work and their service to society, and they don't want to work for anyone who does.

The FAA, the fifty-year-old Washington agency charged with overseeing aviation, learned this lesson reluctantly. For years the agency's recruiters used a pitch familiar to the federal government. As Ventris Gibson, the agency's head of HR, put it, "Our message has always been that you should come to work at the Federal Aviation Administration, become an air traffic controller or aviation safety inspector, and you will earn great benefits. To be honest, for my generation of Boomers, that message worked just fine."

But for new recruits the refrain fell flat. Younger workers were looking for meaning, not benefits, and they saw the agency as a stale bureaucracy. With a generation of veteran air traffic controllers reaching retirement age, the FAA faced a recruitment crisis. In 2008 the situation was so dire the agency resorted to hiring high school seniors to fill its ranks.

Then it dawned on Gibson and her team: The FAA wasn't a stodgy bureaucracy; it was the foundation of a functioning society. Nearly two million passengers a day board domestic flights in the United States. Aviation brings families together, expands individuals' horizons, and allows nearly every business in the country to thrive. The FAA is the backbone of the U.S. of A.

So Gibson introduced a new recruiting message. "Now we really hammer home the idea that if you come to work at the FAA, you can be part of changing the agency that will change aviation," she said. "We talk to millennials about how they can lead the aerospace industry and make their mark." The agency's Web site boasts, "Working at FAA offers a unique opportunity to experience a career where your impact not only reaches throughout the aviation industry but around the world as well." The new frame worked. "It used to take us a lot longer to recruit the best and the brightest," she said. "Now that we have changed our value proposition, they land on our doorstep."

Finally, millennials need to be connected with others at all times. Having grown up in homes where their families were teams, having gone to schools that had students work in teams, when they get to work they expect to be part of a team as well. Millennials aren't bothered by flow charts and chains of command. One department faced with a rapidly approaching deadline? They'll happily volunteer to help finish the job. They also want to feel as if they have a finger in every pot and a voice in every decision.

One way to handle this is transparency. At Warby Parker the entire team comes together on Wednesdays to hear updates from every department. At Endeavor, Fernando and I had to go a step further, adopting a technique we saw our entrepreneurs use: job rotation. Our employees were always antsy about what everyone else was doing, so we instituted a career path rotation. New hires start on our search and selection team; after twelve to eighteen months they move over to service our entrepreneurs; a year later they may move on to launch new countries or other departments. Thomson Reuters was having a hard time retaining recruits because the newbies wanted to understand the whole company and were unhappy about specializing. So now the recruits rotate through three positions for nine months each. Retention rates of associates at Thomson Reuters soared to 95 percent.

Another millennial device gaining popularity is the hackathon. Started in the software industry in the late 1990s, a hackathon (the word is a combination of "hack" and "marathon") is an around-the-clock, caffeine-fueled binge, usually lasting a day or two, in which workers come together in a mad dash to complete a project. Facebook was an early adopter, having hosted over thirty hackathons since 1996. The "like" button, chat, and video functions all grew out of hackathons. These events are the ultimate way to crowdsource a problem, a cross between *The Social Network* and *Animal House*.

Or at least they were. Nowadays they've gone mainstream and often involve a competition, with different teams vying for a prize.

- In 2013 British Airways assembled one hundred Silicon Valley luminaries (including the Endeavor entrepreneur Vinny Lingham) and tasked them with designing solutions to increase the number of women in STEM—science, technology, engineering, and math. The hack? They had to do it while thirty thousand feet in the air. The event took place aboard BA flight 9120 from San Francisco to London. After they landed, participants presented their ideas at an innovation summit.

- That same year a group of skunks inside Boston Children's Hospital approached MIT about collaborating on a hackathon to improve pediatric care. Over the course of a weekend doctors, nurses, clinicians, dieticians, engineers, and coders came together. Among the proposals that emerged: RightByte, a mobile platform that assembles recipes for families facing food allergies; eNgage, a dancing robot that reminds kids when to take their medicine; and the Comfy Ball, a "smart" ball children can squeeze to signal pain.

What's important about these hackathon occasions is that they break down traditional time sheets and appointment calendars. They create a spirit of teamwork and collective problem solving. They do things, in other words, on millennial time.

And millennial time and values are spreading beyond their own demographic. Take DreamWorks, where employees' average age is thirty-six. The studio releases only around three movies a year, and its stock fluctuates on box office performance, so the founders, Steven Spielberg, Jeffrey Katzenberg, and David Geffen, thought hard about how to cultivate workplace culture. The DreamWorks campus has the normal Southern California mix of breezy pathways, picnic tables, and Ping-Pong. Employees are grouped into two-pizza-size pods. The company runs classes on everything from yoga to improv.

But more important, DreamWorks has adapted its culture to meet the expectations of millennials, who constitute 20 percent of its workforce. The company avoids dividing employees into silos. Anyone is allowed to contribute to any creative endeavor. The company even trains every employee on how to deliver effective pitches to senior executives. That means the accountants can comment on plot twists in an animated movie, and assistants can recommend songs for the sound track of an Oscar contender. To prove the point, the company lists every employee in the credits of every film. These policies have helped DreamWorks maintain a loyal workforce, with a turnover rate under 5 percent. As the head of human resources explained, "Each employee is encouraged to be their own CEO."

And that's the point. Millennials are to other workers as entrepreneurs are to the rest of the economy: Their energy, zeal for disruption, and drive for collegial creativity are infecting everyone around them. These ideas may have begun in the hoodied crowd but they increasingly apply to everyone. You can't beat 'em, so you might as well, you know, like, join 'em.

#Withit.

## — PUT OUT YOUR FAMILY PHOTOS —

My final hard-earned truth about how to elevate your employees is equally simple in theory yet hard in practice: Tell them to get a life, or even better, get a life yourself and set a good example. And by life I mean a personal life that doesn't revolve around work.

About three years into Endeavor, after working around the clock for years, I went to visit our team in São Paulo, Brazil, where our managing director was even more driven as a leader than I was. She was running the most efficient office in our network. Her team was skilled; their productivity, off the charts. My first day hosted by Endeavor Brazil, I called everyone together to tell them how impressed I was. Afterward several team members pulled me aside. "We need to talk to you," they said. "Will you tell our boss to take a lunch break every once in a while? None of us ever leaves our desk. We're too afraid."

When I returned home to Endeavor's headquarters in New York, the first thing I did was book my first vacation in three years. I realized my team hadn't taken their vacations because they saw me working all the time and thought I expected the same of them. I noticed the difference immediately, with people returning from time off feeling refreshed and energized. I hadn't realized the signaling effect I had as a leader.

Today I make it known that I drop off my kids at school each morning and am home by dinnertime almost every night; if there's a ballet performance or a curriculum night, I will attend; I schedule regular family vacations. I may get up early; I may send e-mails before going to bed. But I prioritize work-life harmony. And my team can, too.

This lesson of setting boundaries is especially important in the always-on world of today. Americans receive an average of fourteen vacation days a year but take only ten, leaving nearly 600 million unclaimed vacation days a year. By contrast, the French get thirty days, they take all of them, and 90 percent still complain they feel "vacation deprived."

For the first time in my life I see evidence around me that Americans are growing more serious about stepping away. Zulily is an online deals site for parents and kids. Founded in 2009 by Darrell Cavens, a forty-year-old father of two, the site grew in its first five years to more than eight hundred employees. Cavens quickly learned that two things draw anxiety from team members: their paychecks and their chairs (specifically, where the chairs are located). "Don't screw up either," he said. But it took him longer to learn that a third thing was causing them anxiety, too: his around-the-clock schedule. Working on Saturdays? Check. Skipping vacations? Check. Sending e-mails in the middle of the night? Check. He did them all.

Until his wife made him stop. As he wrote in *Inc.* magazine, Cavens finally realized he was driving himself—and his team—into the ground. Now he leaves work early on Fridays and goes with his family to his wife's native Ireland every summer. "I've actually gotten better about not being attached to my phone over the weekend," he wrote. "That makes my wife happy, and it's been good for the team as well." Cavens continued: "Our chief merchant once admitted that getting emails I'd sent in the middle of the night or over the weekend gave her anxiety, because she felt pressure to respond." His effort to prioritize family time did not stand in the way of his company's growth. Zulily went public in 2013 at a market cap of $5 billion.

In recent years there's been a robust debate about the evolving relationship between work life and private life. By almost every measure, workers today value things that bring them joy and meaning. Foremost among these are friends and family. Younger workers especially may like to be "on" all the time, but they also like to turn off when they want. Two-thirds of millennials say they would like the ability to shift their work hours or occasionally work from home. And the clamor for flextime grows even louder as people grow older and have children. Among workers in the thirty-six to forty-two age range, 72 percent say that flexibility is key to their quality of life.

Going off the grid is the new status symbol.

That includes men. A 2013 study from BabyCenter, the leading parenting Web site, found that 79 percent of dads are involved in their children's bedtime routines, 61 percent put their families before work, and 75 percent make it home for dinner as often as they can. And these numbers are growing. The number of dads under thirty who say that being a father is important to them is twenty points higher than dads over forty.

While dads are coming out of the closet at work and declaring their love of family, women are too often still forced to conceal their interest in their families for fear of being passed over. In a study we did at Endeavor, the top three reasons women cited for leaving corporate jobs to start their own companies were: (1) need for more flexibility; (2) experiencing the glass ceiling; and (3) being unhappy with their work environments. One thing they especially disliked about their old workplaces: Their offices made working moms feel like second-class employees.

The two skunks at Clorox who combined their jobs into one, Suzanne Sengelmann and Mary Jo Cook, told me their company's willingness to offer flexible hours was a big reason they could attract top female candidates. "We discovered we had a competitive advantage by allowing women, particularly ones with children, to maintain a career while also spending more time with their children," Suzanne said.

This competitive advantage talk came as a surprise to me, given

Clorox's Bay Area location, which means that it competes head-on with the hottest Internet companies. But Suzanne explained, "Women were being recruited for dot-coms, which were seen as more creative, sexy, progressive, and entrepreneurial companies, but they insisted you work six days a week. We were able to maintain talent by focusing on quality of life."

In 2012 I gave a speech at a prestigious Wall Street firm. Before my talk, I was asked to lead a roundtable with thirty top female executives. These women expressed surprise when I told them that as an entrepreneur and CEO I fully integrated my family calendar and my work calendar, that my girls were regular fixtures around the Endeavor office, and that I often made references to Tybee and Eden in my speeches and annual letter to our network. This seemed completely alien to their experience on Wall Street. The most shocking thing several of these women told me: They didn't dare have photographs of their children in their offices for fear that it would make them seem less loyal to the firm.

Putting employees first means realizing employees are people first. That may be the most important point of all. At the end of the roundtable discussion, one of the women asked if I had any advice to pass on. "Yes," I said. "Put your family photos out!"

Until recently companies designed work environments to suit their needs and forced employees to adapt. These days, egged on in part by a new generation of employee-focused start-ups, companies are looking first at the needs of their workers and adapting their work environments to suit them. The smartest organizations are realizing that leadership is not the only key to a well-functioning enterprise. Something else is equally important.

It's employeeship. And it's time you got on board.

# CHAPTER 9

# *Go Big AND Go Home*

*Dear Eden and Tybee,*

As you know, I've spent a lot of time recently working on this book. I wrote it for anyone who dreams of trying something new. I wrote it for people who are joining companies, leaving companies, starting companies, or changing companies from within, and many who will never set foot in companies at all. I wrote it for anybody who wants to take risks but wants to do it without risking it all.

But deep down I was secretly writing it for you. I wanted you to know what I've been doing all these years and what I've learned along the way. I especially want to prepare you for the world you're about to enter. So as the writing draws to a close, I want to devote this final chapter to answering those questions directly.

First, a little background. As I sit down to write this letter in our Brooklyn home, you girls are downstairs, making rubber band bracelets. For the past few months you've been busy taking orders from friends, arranging your unsold wares on toilet paper tubes to make them look more presentable, and devising a discount pricing scheme: a dollar for one bracelet, 25 percent off for two. I suggested you raise your price, but you rebuffed the idea. "We want a lot of customers," Eden said. "People won't buy from us if we charge too much money."

At first, you called your enterprise KAO, for Kids Accessories Organization, but you decided you didn't want to suggest you weren't interested in profit, so you formed a company. You invited three friends and became BEETS Kids Crafts (BEETS being an acronym from the first initials of your names). You then developed a plan for a Web site and added a second product line, laminated bookmarks. You even asked for a Square Reader for your ninth birthday so you could accept credit cards! (I embraced your moxie, though when you tried to set up a table to hawk your merchandise in the playground nearby, I told you you couldn't do that without a permit.)

In short, you've become entrepreneurs.

Your timing couldn't be better. You are growing into a world that's quite different from the ones your grandparents and even your parents grew into. When your grandparents were your age, in Rhode Island, Maryland, and Georgia, they could expect to graduate from college and hold the same job for the next fifty years. Even when your dad and I were just starting out, people talked about following a career path, climbing the ladder, joining the rat race.

Today those paths are no longer straight; those ladders have tumbled; those rats are less willing to run someone else's race. As Tom Friedman said, "My generation had it easy. We got to 'find' a job. But, more than ever, our kids will have to 'invent' a job." Instead of following a course set by others, more and more people today have the opportunity to decide a course that they want to follow, then change it if that doesn't work, and pivot again if they choose. Rather than think of your life as following a single career track at all, you might be better off viewing your life as attempting to master a set of skills.

We don't yet have a good name for those skills. But we do know where they come from. They come from a group of outsiders who are committed to looking at the world a little differently and overturning traditional ways of doing things. They come from a collection of

"Davids," to use Malcolm Gladwell's term, who take on entrenched "Goliaths." They come from people who are not bound by convention, precedent, or habit but are committed to disruption, adaptability, and reinvention.

They come from entrepreneurs.

What I most want to tell you is that these skills will form the foundation of whatever path you choose to follow in your lives. It doesn't matter whether you start an enterprise, work for someone else, go into public service, or join a cause. (Or as is more likely, you mix and match among these.) As your mom I'll support you in whatever direction you choose (within limits, of course). What does matter is that you understand that accepting the world as it is will likely lead to a life that's, well, acceptable. If you want to have a more fulfilling life, you'll look at the world around you not as it is but as it can be. And then you'll take a step or two to turn that vision into a reality.

I have been helping dreamers do just that for most of my adult life, more than twenty years now. And I've picked up a few ideas for how to increase your odds for success. In the next few pages, I'd like to share with you what I believe are three key things you need to know to help your dreams come true. And because I'm your mom, I'm also going to remind you of what many entrepreneurs I know seem to forget: to find time to enjoy what you build with someone you love.

## *— GET GOING —*

A lot of people will tell you the first step to starting something new is to have an idea. I don't agree with that. To me the first step starts long before that. It's a commitment to looking at the world through rainbow-colored glasses. A rainbow, as you know, is a refraction of sunlight through rain. When the light comes from the sun it's white, but when it hits raindrops, it disperses into a spectrum. You long ago memorized the colors: red, orange, yellow, green, blue, indigo, violet—ROY G. BIV, an acronym, just like BEETS.

An entrepreneur is like a drop of rain to a beam of light: You take something that looks one way and transform it into something else entirely, something that makes the world around you more beautiful and everyone else say, "Wow!"

My favorite story lately is one you taught me. Sure enough, it involves rainbows.

By day Cheong Choon Ng crashed cars. A test engineer at Nissan, Ng spent hours hurling vehicles at hard surfaces: walls, concrete barriers, other vehicles. By night the Malaysian immigrant with a graduate degree in mechanical engineering tried to bond with his two adolescent daughters. He found it tough. One evening the girls were making bracelets out of small rubber bands. Ng thought he could use his design experience to impress his girls, but his fingers were too chubby. So he fetched a wooden board from the basement of their Detroit home, studded it with push-pins, and used a dental hook to crisscross the rubber bands. The result was a long, colorful braid, like a bike chain, only thinner and more flexible. To turn the chains into bracelets, he fashioned fasteners out of cut-up credit cards.

His daughters were suitably impressed, and soon the neighbors' daughters were as well. His girls urged him to sell the gadgets, but his wife said, "No way!" The couple had saved up $11,000 in an education fund for their daughters, and she wanted to preserve it. So he used his jerry-rigged contraption to weave his wife a ring (smooth!), and she relented. Ng spent $1,000 registering his invention, $5,000 having it manufactured in China, and $5,000 on colorful rubber bands. He called his creation the Rainbow Loom.

But as soon as the orders began arriving in the summer of 2011, the crash expert hit his own wall. The rubber bands came covered with a grimy dust, so Ng washed them, first in his bathtub, then in the washing machine. The hooks came in the wrong shape, so he spent hours fixing them with a hammer, one by one. There were good days and bad days, he told *Entrepreneur* magazine. "But most of the times, they were bad days." Soon those days got worse. Retailers had no interest in the odd-looking gizmos, and selling them online fizzled. Then he realized why: No one knew how to use the things. So Ng and his daughters posted a handful of explanatory videos on YouTube.

Finally a call came: The owner of a Learning Express franchise in Alpharetta, Georgia, wanted twenty-four looms. Two days later she called again and ordered forty-eight more. A week later she placed an order worth $10,000. Ng said, "My wife and I were looking at the computer where the orders came in. We were staring at it for three minutes." It was a year after he had made her the ring, and the couple had already earned back their daughters' college fund.

The Learning Express owner quickly spread the word to her 130 fellow franchisees. The crafts store Michaels caught wind of the trend. And in the summer of 2012 Rainbow Loom went viral at girls' overnight summer camps. As one retailer said, "The last time parents were this hot and heavy over a toy, it was Beanie Babies." Ng quit his job as a crash tester and went to work on Rainbow Loom full-time, as did his wife. Eventually they rented a seventy-five-hundred-square-foot warehouse. In 2013 the company sold 3.5 million units with a retail price of $16.99. You certainly did your share, girlies: You each have your own looms, and you've given and received more than a dozen more as gifts. As parents Dad and I like them because they're creative and social, and they keep you off electronic devices. Even better, the Ngs' entrepreneurial vision has inspired your own.

For his part, Ng said he was overwhelmed that Rainbow Loom had tapped into a generation. "I am still waking up every morning and asking myself and telling myself at the same time: 'Is this for real?'" His answer: "This is real. This is a dream come true."

Sometimes seeing things differently leads to starting a company, as Ng did. Sometimes it's taking anything that's been done the same way for a long time and upending it.

One of your favorite singers, Beyoncé, is a great example of how everyone, even those who are already on top, needs to take risk these days. Pop stars usually release albums with standard playbooks. They flood the radio with singles, pose for magazine covers, appear on TV chat shows, and partner with major retailers. This predictable buildup also comes with a downside: leaks, bootlegs, and digital piracy. Beyoncé did none of those obvious things (and faced none of those downsides). Instead, around midnight, ten days before Christmas, she simply wrote "Surprise!" to her more than eight million followers on Instagram, and her entire "visual album," containing fourteen songs and seventeen videos, appeared for sale on iTunes.

The stunt assured that the release was an event. The news generated 1.2 million tweets in twelve hours, helped by artists like Lady Gaga who were eager to further undermine traditional media. Katy Perry tweeted, "Don't talk to me today unless it's about @Beyoncé." Owning the album became a status symbol. One journalist wrote, "I like Beyoncé, but she's not my favorite artist. There's probably something else I could have done with the $15 I dropped on this. But because the availability of the album was a surprise, it became an impulse purchase." And the no publicity gambit assured that the publicity would follow. As one fan tweeted, "Beyoncé doesn't need publicity. Publicity needs Beyoncé."

The move wouldn't work for every artist, but that's not the point. The point is that by embracing measured risk, Beyoncé overturned the long, steady decline in record sales (hers included) and generated something rare—a pop culture moment. Her entrepreneurial creation was a new way of doing things. "I didn't want to release my music the way I've done it," she said. "I am bored with that."

And it succeeded, wildly. The album went to number one in ninety countries. It sold 80,000 units in its first three hours, enough to crash iTunes. It reached 430,000 copies on its first day, more than her first week's sales two years earlier. And it topped a million in its first week. One DJ said, "It's an instant classic, a game changer." He was right. Entrepreneurs don't reflect the world; they remake it in their image.

That's really the message I want to leave you with. The first step to acting like an entrepreneur is to look not at the writing on the wall but at the spaces between the writing. It's in the gap between what's being said (or done) and what's not being said (or done) that entrepreneurs thrive. Costica Bradatan, a philosopher and the author of *Dying for Ideas*, wrote that there is always a void left between what we are and what we can be. "Whatever human accomplishments there have been in history, they have been possible precisely because of this empty space," he said.

I wish for you girls the ability to see the gaps and the desire to fill the empty space.

But I also warn you: This will come with a backlash. Many will not understand. Some may even call you crazy. And you know what I say: If they *don't* call you crazy, you aren't thinking big enough.

If you don't want to hear this lesson from me, then hear it from Katrina Markoff. After graduating from Vanderbilt University with degrees in psychology and chemistry, Markoff traveled to Europe to pursue her love of food. She studied at Le Cordon Bleu and worked at the molecular gastronomy restaurant El Bulli under Ferran Adrià. He encouraged her to backpack around the world. Two things happened during Markoff's travels. First, she ate a beignet filled with frozen chocolate ganache. "That experience of eating this doughnut-crusty exterior and, when you bite down, this molten explosion of chocolate started piquing my curiosity about chocolate," she said. Second, she accumulated a suitcase full of exotic spices.

Back in the United States Markoff moved to Dallas and went to work for her uncle's mail-order catalog. He asked her to find an up-scale candy bar, and she quickly decided that there was little innovation going on in the world of chocolate. The global market was huge: $100 billion, with 20 percent of sales coming from the United States and most of those from women. (And if we're talking dark chocolate, count me among them!) But Markoff thought that "everything was just loaded with sugars and artificial flavorings and extracts and wax, and there was no story."

One evening she came home wearing a necklace from the Naga

tribe in India. "I was researching a little bit about the culture," she said. "Then for some reason I went into my kitchen and made a curry and coconut milk chocolate truffle and called it Naga. That's when it hit me that I could use chocolate as a way to tell stories about cultures, art, people, and the world."

That night Markoff ended up making twenty different flavor profiles, all based on her travels: saffron with white chocolate and sugar crystals to represent Gaudí's architectural masterwork in Barcelona; a Hungarian paprika and chocolate ginger. But she could find no one who shared her quirky taste. "Dallas in 1997 was still very much a BBQ town," she said, "and these people were like, 'I'm not trying that curry thing.'" Finally she found one woman who was willing to try her sushi special—chocolate with wasabi. "She took a bite and her face went from disgust and worry to awe and surprise to 'Oh my God, this is actually good.'"

That glint of encouragement was worth its weight in cacao. Markoff opened her first store in Chicago in 1998, and she now sells chocolates in two thousand outlets worldwide. Her annual revenues top $35 million. Besides her freshman class of curry, saffron, paprika, and wasabi, her high-end label Vosges Haut-Chocolat includes such mix-ins as olives, wattleseed, Himalayan sea salt, and bacon. She started a line called the Groove Collection influenced by African-American music and another inspired by *The Hunger Games*. She also developed a more mass-market all-American label called Wild Ophelia that sells four-dollar bars with classic American flavors like beef jerky, barbecue potato chips, and peanut butter and banana. It's now sold in Target and Walgreens.

To me, what Markoff represents is the fearlessness of the entrepreneur. About her offbeat flavor combinations and quest for good ingredients, she said, "Nothing is totally sacred to me. If I find a wattleseed supplier who has better wattleseed than Australia, I'll gladly go there. I'm constantly trying to innovate. I want to evolve. The recipe today will probably not be the same recipe ten years from now."

This bravado is especially important for women, Markoff said. "I think it's really important for women to have confidence in her individuality and not try to conform to being someone she thinks she needs to be." I would certainly love you girls to internalize that.

But mostly what I want you to learn is the courage to take your dream out of your head and put it to the test in the real world. Don't just think it; act on it. This notion may be best captured in a song we used to sing around the house. It comes from the ultimate candy bar story: *Willy Wonka and the Chocolate Factory*. And it's Willy Wonka's classic theme song, "Pure Imagination." "Come with me," he sings, into the land of pure imagination. There is no better life than the one you can conceive. "Want to change the world?" he asks. "There's nothing to it." Simply look around and imagine a better life.

As Willy Wonka says, "Anything you want to, do it."

## — GO BIG —

The second key skill you'll need to bring change to the world will really test your creativity, as well as your sanity, your patience, and your resolve. It has to do with how to take your dream and make it as real as possible. That may mean turning your accessories partnership into a worldwide craft-selling platform or starting an organic asparagus farm (if you ever eat asparagus) or rethinking the PTA or writing experimental music or inventing a cancer drug. It doesn't really matter what your dream is, "going big" means doing it to the utmost.

To do that, you need one thing: other dreamers to share your dream.

I've spent years helping risk takers think bigger, and from what I've seen, the biggest single mistake they make is not learning how to work effectively with others to refine their ideas, adapt them, pick them up after they fall to the ground, raise them to the sky so they can soar again, then let their success shine on everyone who's touched them.

Dreamers are good at motivating themselves. They're not always so good at motivating others. I know this because I had to learn it myself. And what I've come to believe is that in this era, when entrepreneurship is everywhere, a new type of leadership is emerging. When I started out, I had internalized an old-fashioned notion of what it meant to be in command: Leaders are strong, steady, domineering. Today that's changed. Instead of being invincible, leaders are open, at times even vulnerable. Instead of being rigid, leaders are nimble. Instead of bellowing from on high, leaders encourage creativity and influence to bubble up from below.

You've seen the fruits of this in your own lives. When you were born, you received a Radio Flyer wagon as a gift. On your first birthday, we put the wagon in the middle of the dining room table and filled it with flowers, diapers, pop-up books, and photos. Later you held the bar and pushed it around our house. You both loved that wagon, and it was incredibly durable, but the company that manufactured it nearly didn't endure. How it survived is a wonderful example of how to thrive in the age of reinvention: Make your dream a team effort.

Antonio Pasin was sixteen years old when he moved to the United States from Italy in 1914. The son of a cabinet-maker, Pasin started a similar business in Chicago, but the customers were more interested in the wooden wagon he built to carry his tools. They wanted wagons like it as toys for their children. So like any good entrepreneur, Pasin pivoted. The auto business was booming at the time, and he used some of the scrap metal that became plentiful to build a steel wagon. He called it Radio Flyer after two recent inventions, the radio and air travel. Helped by the 1933 Chicago World's Fair, Radio Flyers became a household staple. The business had sold nearly 100 million wagons by the time Pasin's grandson Robert took over in 1997.

The company was also at risk of going under at the time. Cheap plastic wagons were overtaking the market, replacing their steel ancestors. Radio Flyers had become as trendy as Saturday afternoon radio serials and Pan Am wings. Robert said, "We were a manufacturer, a steel stamper, and that's what we were good at. We weren't asking moms what they wanted in a new wagon."

This was Robert's leadership test: He could retool the company and survive or remain nostalgic and fade away. What he chose to do is instructive: First, he sat the entire team down and explained the situation. He let them know how serious things were but also provided reassurance, saying, "We're going to keep treating people here as well as we possibly can." Then everyone in the company joined in a year-long review. The process led to a decision to manufacture a plastic wagon and eventually to stop making the steel ones. Even more vital, it led to a rethinking of the company culture.

By the time I met Robert nearly a decade later, Radio Flyer was thriving. He was known as Chief Wagon Officer and had set up smile squads to organize team-building exercises like heritage days and company-wide volunteer efforts. Employees could nominate colleagues for Little Red Rule Awards for upholding the company motto, "Everytime we touch people's lives, they will feel great about Radio Flyer." Internal classes, called Wagon U, offered lessons on business. Robert himself taught one titled "Reinventing Radio Flyer Through Goof-ups, Growth, and Gratitude."

By reaching out to others instead of retreating, Robert remade the century-old company. Sales quintupled to $100 million, and Radio Flyer reached number thirteen on *Fortune*'s "Top 50 Best Small Places to Work." (He also started listening to moms. That wagon from your birthday party? Robert sent it to me and asked for feedback. I suggested a wagon that could hold more than one toddler, so you wouldn't have to take turns being pulled around. The next year he sent a Double the Love twins wagon.)

Radio Flyer's lesson about the need to actively engage employees and customers applies to all entrepreneurs, whether you're running a small company, redesigning a homeless shelter, or making letterpress invitations in your basement. It even applies when you're inside a big business. Some of the boldest entrepreneurial ideas these days come from within corporations. And to succeed, they, too, need buy-in from the group.

In 2009, three years before Taco Bell would celebrate its fiftieth anniversary, CEO Greg Creed was worried. "Our target audience is in their 20's," he told *Fast Company*. "Turning 50 makes us sound old, and I didn't want to sound old." He didn't want a celebration or a cake, he told his team. He wanted a new taco.

Tacos, with their bendable-breakable corn shells stuffed with ground beef, lettuce, tomato, and cheese, were simple but stale. Creed said, "If you look at all the buns the burger boys sell, and the bread at Subway, they are forever coming up with a new bread bun. The crunchy taco: It was yellow and made of corn. We sold a couple billion of them, but there was no innovation."

Creed's task was similar to Robert Pasin's: Reinvent something most people didn't think needed reinventing. And he took the same tack. He sat his team down and called for a group approach. Creed gave his team just under thirty-six months to reinvent the taco. The group began with an all-day brainstorming session at the company's headquarters in Irvine, California. Ideas included importing elements from burritos and nachos. But the wackiest idea was the one that broke through: Make a taco shell out of Doritos. The company's marketing director said, "It was like 'Holy crap!' Nobody had ever done this before: turning a Dorito into a taco shell."

But turning that idea into reality proved to be a nightmare. Problem number one: getting the flavoring onto the shell. The first thing the team members did was go to Home Depot and buy a paint spray gun, which they used to spray the orange dust onto the existing yellow taco. They quickly realized that wouldn't work because it would produce a nacho-cheese nuclear winter in the factory. The seasoning would have to be baked in. Problem number two: Doritos are made to be crunchy; taco shells are made to be malleable. Early prototypes were too fragile, too soggy, or too unevenly flavored. Problem number three: What did the public think? The first consumer taste test bombed. The team went back to work, then for the next round invited individual fans and bloggers, including an Arkansas man who had started an online campaign calling for Doritos tacos. This time the response was more encouraging. Finally, after forty recipes, the company rolled out a prototype. Customers went crazy. One Taco Bell addict drove nine hundred miles from New York to Toledo, Ohio, to taste it.

The company was eager to launch, except for problem number four: It had no formal contract with Doritos' parent, Frito-Lay. That would take months. So Creed invited the company's CEO to his office. The Taco Bell chief said, "We both realized that if we let the lawyers get involved, this thing would get slowed down and bogged down. So we did a handshake deal. Everyone was like, 'You can't launch without a contract.' And we were like, 'Just watch us.'"

Doritos Locos Tacos went on sale in early 2012. The company sold 100 million of them before the contract with Frito-Lay was signed. The product was so hot that Taco Bell had to hire fifteen thousand new employees to meet demand—two or three people per store. In year two the company introduced a second flavor, Cool Ranch. That year revenues from the Doritos line reached $1 billion, with more products on the way, including a burrito with Fritos in it. As Taco Bell showed, sometimes the key to going big is not thinking outside the box; it's getting more people inside the box and letting them think and solve problems together.

In school you girls learned about safety in numbers. When I asked what this meant to you, Tybee said, "When you have more people on your side—like a revolution or a new idea like BEETS Kids Crafts—you have better chances of winning." Well put.

Want to go big? Don't go it alone; go with others.

## — GO HOME —

And then the most important lesson of all: Go home. Make time for the ones you love.

The easiest thing to think about living like an entrepreneur is that these skills apply to only one part of your life: your job. That's a mistake. In the same way that entrepreneurs are redefining many of the traditional rules of the workplace, they're also helping to break down one of the most stubborn boundaries of all: the one between work and family. While it's popular to say you can have either a successful career or a meaningful personal life, I'd like to suggest you can aim for both.

I didn't always believe this; you girls taught me this lesson. Now it's one of the things I stress most to entrepreneurs. To make my point, I often use a twist on a familiar phrase.

In the early 1990s a small company in Southern California that specialized in motorcycle parts started making oversize exhaust pipes called Porkers Pipes. To capture their bravado, the package designer recommended the slogan "Go Big or Go Home." He later wrote, "Everyone from the company owner on down asked the same question, 'What does this mean?' My reply was, 'It doesn't mean anything.'" But the meaningless phrase entered California's hot rod culture and from there jumped to extreme sports. Soon it embodied the swagger of a new generation. (The designer, by the way, was like the woman who initially got only thirty-five dollars for designing the Nike swoosh. He received just fifty bucks for coining the catchphrase of a culture.)

For years I delivered this message to entrepreneurs and tried to follow it myself. Whatever happened, I pushed harder, faster, louder. "Go Big or Go Home!" I blared. I was like an X Games skateboarder, addicted to the thrill of the stunt. I occasionally retreated, like when Endeavor tried to expand to India and we encountered some resistance. I invoked Go Big or Go Home, and we pulled out. But in general, I knew one direction: higher.

Then I was on a business trip to Austin, Texas, and I called your dad. "I think I ate some spoiled guacamole," I said. "I threw up twice in the bathroom tonight." Well, it wasn't the guacamole. It was you! A few weeks later Dad and I went to see a doctor, and we learned we were having identical twins. We were overwhelmed, but we had little time to react. The next day I boarded a seventeen-hour flight to South Africa. Several months later my doctor put me on bed rest. "Tushie on the cushie," your dad cried out as I sat in our living room, two babies in my belly, two phones on my ear. I stayed that way until you arrived, at thirty-eight weeks and over six pounds each.

That's when I began to realize I would need a new slogan. I couldn't choose between my work or my family. But I couldn't give one up either. I would need to find a way to do both.

In *Built to Last*, Jim Collins and Jerry Porras say successful companies do not oppress themselves by what they call the Tyranny of the OR. Collins and Porras mention certain examples of such tyranny:

You can have change OR stability.
You can have low cost OR high quality.
You can invest for the future OR do well in the short-term.
You can create wealth for your shareholders OR do good for
    the world.

Instead, highly visionary companies liberate themselves with the "Genius of the AND," the ability to embrace two extremes at the same time. "Instead of choosing between A *OR* B," Collins and Porras argue, "they figure out a way to have both A *AND* B."

Entrepreneurs have the ability to do the same thing in their overall lives, I believe. It's one of the ways they can lead society at large. Instead of choosing career *OR* family, they can choose career *AND* family. Instead of aiming for work-life balance, they can strive for work-life integration.

Instead of choosing to Go Big *OR* Go Home, they can choose to Go Big *AND* Go Home.

Now, I'm not deluding myself. I know life is full of trade-offs. I know there are important work events I've skipped to be home helping you with your homework. I also know there have been times when I've wanted to make sure you were brushing your teeth and instead have glanced at my smartphone. (And you know it, too. One of your favorite ways to taunt me is to chant, "Mommy! Mommy! Mommy and her e-mails!") And I know I'm very lucky when I head off on a day-and-a-half trip to Dubai that your dad works from home.

I'm not perfect, but I do believe one of the benefits of being an entrepreneur is that it forces you to look at all aspects of your life as laboratories for reinvention. You keep trying. And if you make a mistake, you try even harder.

That's even more true today, when technology has opened up unimaginable new ways to time shift, delegate, share, and rejigger. I see more and more moms and dads scheduling early morning meetings or doing work late at night so they can be more present with their kids during the day. I see flextime, working from home, taking sabbaticals as ways for people to have fulfilling careers while spending more hours with their children. I see people giving up comfortable jobs in corporations to start risky ventures because they're no longer willing to work around the clock. I see the genius of the AND gaining favor all around.

Some people will tell you that you can't go big because you're women. I need you to know that they are wrong. Women have always been, and will always be, entrepreneurs. They're also daughters, sisters, wives, aunts, mothers, and grandmothers. Forget this notion that you have to "balance" these competing aspects. That term suggests some sort of fifty-fifty equilibrium, where you inevitably do each side poorly.

In the world of Go Big AND Go Home, you are called to manage both sides the best that you can.

Fortunately, there are role models. Tina Fey, the actress, comedian, writer, producer, and mom, wrote a book, *Bossypants*, mining the question of how working moms can survive in a male-dominated workplace. She fiercely defended the idea that women can go big. When she became an executive producer of *30 Rock*, she wrote, people asked her, "Is it hard for you, being the boss?" and "Is it uncomfortable for you to be the person in charge?" Fey added cheekily, "You know, in the same way they say, 'Gosh, Mr. Trump, is it awkward for you to be the boss of all these people?'" Her response: "I can't answer for Mr. Trump, but in my case it is not."

The secret to being a good boss, she continued, is hiring the best people and getting out of the way. "Contrary to what I believed as a little girl, being the boss almost never involves marching around, waving your arms, and chanting, 'I am the boss! I am the boss!'"

But what resonated most with me about what Fey shared is the extreme efforts she made to be successful at work AND at home. When her show first launched, she had doubts. "I now had an eight month old at home," she wrote, "and I wasn't sure that this new seventy-hour-a-week job was, as disgraced politicians say, 'in the best interest of my family at this current juncture at the present time.'" So she made adjustments. She had breakfast with her daughter, acted during the day, spent the evening with her daughter, then invited the writing team to her house until two in the morning, while her husband sat in the pantry writing the score for the show. And she would sometimes disappear into the kitchen and break down.

She wrote: "Of course I'm not supposed to admit that there is a triannual torrential sobbing in my office, because it's bad for the feminist cause. It makes it harder for women to be taken seriously in the workplace. It makes it harder for other working moms to justify their choice." But she also had friends who stayed home with their kids, and they also had triannual sobs. "So I think we should call it even." Fey's conclusion: She didn't want to give up her work; she didn't want to give up her family; she would have to find a way to have both AND.

These days more and more men are realizing that they, too, want to Go Big AND Go Home. The fashion designer Kenneth Cole is married to the filmmaker Maria Cuomo; they have three daughters. One day Cole was working in his home office when his youngest daughter, then eight, arrived home from school.

"What are you doing?" she asked.

"I'm working," he responded.

"Who gives you the work?"

"Well, I give it to myself because I have to get it done."

"Well, aren't you the boss?" she asked.

"Yes, that's why I give myself the work, and that's why I have to make sure it gets done."

His daughter strolled off, but the next day, at the exact same time, she walked into his office again. "What are you doing?" she asked. "Who gives you the work?" The two had the same conversation, then repeated it again two days later.

Not long after, Cole was telling the story to a friend. "She's a smart girl, but she just doesn't get it," he said.

His friend replied, "Or *you* don't. She spent a week trying to teach you a lesson, and clearly, you still haven't learned it."

When you're an entrepreneur, Cole concluded, it's especially important not to succumb to the temptation to work around the clock. "I've learned that I can't win 24 hours a day," he said. "I've learned that life is about finding a working compromise." Most of all, he learned not to subtly value his job over his family. And that's what I want you to remember.

Fortunately, you're the ones who taught it to me. One day, when you were five, I had just finished packing and was preparing to leave for a business trip. As the taxicab pulled up, Eden tugged at my leg and said, "Remember, you can be an entrepreneur for a short time, but you're a *mommy* forever."

I can't say it any better myself. Go big if you choose, girls. But don't forget to go home. (And come visit me and Dad every now and then.)

## — WHEN YOU WISH —

Nearly two decades ago I ventured out into the world to find dreamers who needed a little help making their dreams come true. Along the way I met a woman named Leila. She had been trained to sell hamburgers at a McDonald's in Brazil but wanted to help her neighbors in the slums of Rio, where she grew up, feel better about their hair.

The first time I met her, she was soft-spoken, timid, and intimidated by the world around her. She looked as if she might break. But with every barrier she crossed, every person she hired, and every milestone she achieved, she grew stronger. Today she runs an international company nearing $100 million in annual revenues, provides jobs for over twenty-three hundred people, and is a role model for entrepreneurs.

I saw Leila recently. She was beautiful, confident, and brimming with new ideas. She's already picked out the location for her first U.S. salon, in Harlem. And this time, when I looked at her, I thought of you, girlies. I thought of all the opportunities that people in your generation will have that so many generations, in so many places around the world, never had before.

If Leila can do it, you can, too.

Walt Disney, who had one of the greatest imaginations of the last century, used as his theme song, "When You Wish upon a Star." It captures the essence of being an entrepreneur, which is to be empowered by fantasy: to live within your own illusions, then strive to make them real. Anyone can see things others don't. The entrepreneur does that and so much more, making the ultimate leap from conjuring to creating to changing lives. And as Jiminy Cricket told Pinocchio, these days "it makes no difference who you are."

Take chances, girls. Take the journey with others. And don't forget to take time to enjoy what you create with those you love.

But mostly, believe that what you imagine can come true. Because it can.

But not if you don't try. So when you're ready, take the advice of Willy Wonka: Hold your breath. Make a wish. Count to three.

Jump.

I'll be cheering you on.

*Love,*

*Mommy*

# TEAM CRAZY

I want to begin by thanking the one thousand Endeavor entrepreneurs around the world. Your passion, enthusiasm, and doggedness inspire me every day. My goal has been to build a movement of, by, and for entrepreneurs—and you've done that. Special thanks to the many entrepreneurs (along with board members, mentors, and other supporters) who appear by name in this book, for sharing your stories, missteps, and triumphs.

Peter Kellner is a pioneer, partner, and friend, and his vision continues to shape Endeavor. Bill Drayton gave me the knowledge and push to start something on my own. George and Bicky Kellner never stopped believing. Stephan Schmidheiny, Peter Brooke, Bill Sahlman, Eduardo Elsztain, Beto Sicupira, and Jorge Paulo Lemann supported me before it was practical, or even rational. Jason Green and Gary Mueller were founding board members and steadfast guides. Kimberly Braswell was my ally and co-conspirator for many years.

I often speak of two eras at Endeavor: "Before Edgar" and "After Edgar." Since Edgar Bronfman, Jr., became our global board chair in 2004, I have been elevated by his mentorship, judgment, and camaraderie. A heartfelt hug to his incomparable wife, Clarissa.

I simply could not have built Endeavor—or written this book—without the breathtaking commitment from an extraordinary group of board members. You coached me, prodded me, schooled me, let me cry in front of you, gave tirelessly to our entrepreneurs, and took ownership of our idea. Beyond those already mentioned, thank you to Michael Ahearn, Matt Bannick, Nick Beim, Matt Brown, Wences Casares, Michael Cline, Paul Fribourg, Fadi Ghandour, Bill McGlashan, Arif Naqvi, Joanna Rees, Nicolás Szekasy, and Elliot Weissbluth. A hearty tribute to Reid Hoffman, who has steered me tirelessly through the publishing odyssey.

I am deeply grateful to Endeavor's partners: Bain, Barclays, Dell, EY, GE, SAP, Knight Foundation, World Economic Forum, Harvard Business School, and Stanford Graduate School of Business. A personal thank you to Pierre Omidyar and the incomparable Omidyar Network, and to the all-star team at ABRAAJ Capital. Without you, my dream would have stalled.

The heartbeat of Endeavor is the thousands of individuals in more than twenty countries who devote themselves to spreading the spirit of entrepreneurship. Led by an amazing squad of managing directors, these trailblazers serve on our boards, sit on our selection panels, spend countless hours mentoring entrepreneurs, and fervidly commit themselves to the idea that business can be a force for good. Though I am unable to thank you all by name, your passion infuses these pages.

I love coming to work every day and feeding off the enthusiasm of our 350 team members. They are smart, talented, opinionated, and exceptionally dedicated. They are led by a truly effortless commander, the incredible Fernando Fabre, who took the risk of moving his family from Mexico City to New York in 2011. (In February, no less!)

A number of those team members worked overtime as part of an Entrepreneurship Lab I set up at the outset of this book. Many thanks to Larry Brooks, Brian Chen, Joanna Harries, Julia Kaplan, Lucy Minott, Meghan Murphy, Beth Robertson, Todd Stone, and Tanvi Vattikuti. Teo Soares contributed to every chapter. Tyler Gwinn is my spirited and indefatigable chief of staff.

I am grateful for the inventive research of Endeavor Insight, led by Rhett Morris and Michael Goodwin. A robust thank you to our talented partners at Bain & Company, particularly Chris Bierly, Vikki Tam, Eric Almquist, Chris Zook, Paul Judge, Paul Markowitz, Ned Shell, and Lily West.

Others who helped bring this book to the world include Bianca Martinelli, Walt Mayo, Dustin Poh, Alphonse Tam, Allen Taylor, Daniela Terminel, and most especially David Wachtel.

David Black is an unwavering friend and an unrivaled agent. Every conversation with him packs the motivation of a great locker room pep talk. Thanks also to Sarah Smith and the gang at the David Black Literary Agency.

The moment I met Adrian Zackheim I knew my book had found its home. Adrian runs a creative and entrepreneurial (!) operation at Portfolio, and at every turn he lifted this project with his deep knowledge and incisive ideas. Maria Gagliano edited this book with precision and emotional intelligence. She pushed me to be more revealing, and I am so thankful that her voice helped shape my story. Will Weisser tenaciously and enthusiastically buttonholed everyone he could to enlist them in Team Crazy. Allison McClean became our spiritual leader, encouraging us all to be bolder. My gratitude also to Justin Hargett, Elizabeth Hazelton, and Rachel Moore.

Thank you to Goulston & Storrs, Royce Carlton, Tim Hawkins, Laura Norwalk, Chadwick Moore, and Natalia Sborovsky.

In addition to many listed above, I turned to a number of more experienced people to help me navigate the sometimes daunting process of getting this book onto the page. I am grateful for the fellowship and support of Bill Ackman, Marc Benioff, Tory Burch, Ben Casnocha, Joshua Cooper Ramo, Tom Friedman, Seth Godin, John Griffin, John Hamm, Mellody Hobson, Adi Ignatius, Van Jones, Jodi Kantor, Ron Lieber, Rob Reid, Sheryl Sandberg, Chris Schroeder, Dov Seidman,

Pattie Sellers, Dan Senor, and Whitney Tilson. Michael Dell has answered every call I've ever made, from helping our entrepreneurs to cheering me through bed rest. Ben Sherwood boosted this project for many years. Karen Kehela Sherwood lent her keen eye and big heart to sharpen these pages.

Countless times over the years, I've reached out to an unrivaled group of colleagues for advice. Thank you to Jennifer Aaker, Chris Anderson, Sunny Bates, Gina Bianchini, Matthew Bishop, Adriana Cisneros, Beth Comstock, Jonathan Cranin, Caterina Fake, Andy Freire, Wes Gardenswartz, Sal Giambanco, Deb Goldfarb, Taddy Hall, Matt Harris, Richard Hamermesh, Pamela Hartigan, Joi Ito, Dena Jones-Trujillo, David Kidder, Wendy Kopp, Cindi Leive, Simon Levene, Nancy Lublin, Sheila Marcelo, Jacqueline Novogratz, Paul Parker, Alan Patricof, Diego Piacentini, Maria Pinelli, Diana Powell, Gabby Rozman, Kevin Ryan, Garth Saloner, Lauren Schneider, Klaus Schwab, Susan Segal, Veronica Serra, Tina Seelig, Fred Sicre, and Tom Speechley.

I have friends from across my life who surround me with warmth, laughter, and love. Andrea Mail's cheerful phone calls brighten every week. I send hugs and appreciation to Nora Abousteit, Jeanne Ackman, Karen Ackman, Jenny Lyn Bader, Jonathan Baron, Piraye Beim, Karen Bloch, Carolina Brause, Campbell Brown, Marisa Brown, Belle Casares, June Cohen, David and Tracey Frankel, Melissa Glass, Mareva Grabowski, Amy Griffin, Paul Hilal, Dave Levin, Miriam Longchamp, Evie Lovett, Dani Lubetsky, Steven Mail, Rafael Mayer, the Mitchell family, Kyriakos Mitsotakis, Lia Oppenheimer, Florence Pan, Diego Panama, Rebecca Plofker, Marília Rocca, David Saltzman, Daniel Schwartz, Chip Seelig, Ken Shubin Stein, Jeff Shumlin, Devon Spurgeon, David Stemerman, Max Stier, Susan Tilson, Martin and Nina Varsavsky, Inci Yalman, Michelle Yee, and the late Joy Covey.

A shout-out to Team Brooklyn: Nuar Alsadir, Nils Anderson, Steve Bodow, Alison Carnduff, Nina Collins, Greg Dillon, Felicia Kang, David and Stacy Kramer, Liz Luckett, Andrew and Cindy

McLaughlin, Alex Posen, Katherine Profeta, JJ Ramberg, Samantha Skey, and Vince Tompkins.

Jane and Ed Feiler welcomed me as a daughter-in-law, infused me with a love for Savannah, and introduced me to the wonders of mystery weekends and Tybee Island summers. Andrew Feiler read this book in its earliest form, found every gap in logic, and loaned his extraordinary acumen to enhance the final version. Cari Feiler Bender has become a sister, and I'm so proud of her many contributions to Philadelphia. Rodd, Max, and Hallie Bender make slurp-offs and family plays more memorable and fun.

Debbie and Alan Rottenberg gave me the unconditional love that made my crazy dreaming possible. After that brief kitchen-table encounter, they actively supported my non-traditional path; and eventually, they even got what they craved: a son-in-law, grandchildren, and a (relatively) stable life for their eldest child! Rebecca Rottenberg Goldman shared this journey, and she has always been my closest confidante. Dan Rottenberg is the sage, poetic, and bighearted person every girl dreams of for a brother. My siblings-in-law (and love) Elissa Rottenberg and Mattis Goldman embody what it means to go big AND go home. Nate and Maya Rottenberg, and Judah and Isaac Goldman fill Cape House challenges and Eulinda's ice cream visits with joy.

My aunt Barbara passed away days before I finished this book. She would have enjoyed sharing news of her niece, *la chica loca*. Her spirit lives on.

In 2008, my husband, Bruce Feiler, received a life-changing call: "Your tumor is not consistent with a benign tumor." For the next eighteen months, Bruce underwent grueling, life-saving treatment, yet he still found a way to ensure that our girls knew his values and his voice. Then, once he was declared cancer-free, Bruce made another extraordinary decision: He resolved to help me find *my* voice. This dream was his before it became mine. I love you.

I wrote this book especially for my daughters, Eden and Tybee.

They stretch me, motivate me, test me, and fill me with pride on an hourly basis. They are remarkable young women, and I look forward to cheering on their crazy adventures for many decades to come. And, Girlies, I'll always remember what you taught me: I can be an entrepreneur for a short time, but I am a mommy forever.

# SOURCES

*C*razy Is a Compliment draws heavily on firsthand conversations, meals, interviews, and mentor sessions I've held with the nearly one thousand Endeavor entrepreneurs since 1997. I've also consulted the detailed records we have on our entrepreneurs, their histories, challenges, and changes of strategy. Before joining our network, entrepreneurs must go through a year-long search and selection process. Our local boards conduct in-depth interviews with them, and our global team writes detailed profiles. Next, candidates are invited to an international selection panel, where, over the course of three days, CEOs, investors, and top business thinkers grill them and debate whether to induct them into the Endeavor entrepreneur network. The records of these deliberations, many of which I moderated, have provided deep insight into the entrepreneurial process.

In addition, our research arm, Endeavor Insight, and our partners at Bain & Company have completed numerous surveys and follow-up interviews with our entrepreneurs. All these reports helped me tremendously, and the published studies are available at www.endeavor.org/blog/category/research.

For more insight into the Endeavor process, I encourage you to read the three cases at Harvard Business School that have tracked our history, growing pains, and impact (www.hbsp.harvard.edu/product/ cases). Stanford's Graduate School of Business has also studied our model; its case study can be found at gsbapps.stanford.edu/cases.

A number of the well-known entrepreneurs and business leaders who populate these pages are also members of the Endeavor network, have appeared at our events, and have provided personal guidance to me when I most needed it. They graciously shared their insights over countless conversations, telephone calls, and moments of desperation. An inadequate expression of appreciation appears in the acknowledgments section.

Finally, I have benefited tremendously from the flowering of writing about entrepreneurship in recent years and a wide body of secondary sources. To mine this literature, as well as the deep knowledge of the Endeavor network, when I first set out to write *Crazy Is a Compliment*, I assembled an entrepreneurship lab of Endeavor team members. Together, we spent more than a year scouring more than one hundred books, along with countless academic papers, research studies, and press accounts. What follows is a breakdown of the most helpful sources by chapter.

## — INTRODUCTION: WHY EVERYBODY NEEDS TO ACT LIKE AN ENTREPRENEUR —

Sam Walton's "Rules for Building a Business" are detailed in *Made in America* (1992), written with John Huey. The story of Earle Dickson and Band-Aids appears in Anthony Rubino, *Why Didn't I Think of That?* (2010). For the relationship between Steve Jobs and Bob Noyce, I consulted Walter Isaacson, *Steve Jobs* (2011) and Leslie Berlin's biography of Noyce, *The Man Behind the Microchip* (2005).

### Entrepreneurship Isn't Just for Entrepreneurs Anymore
Alexis Ohanian's quote "'I have a startup' is the new 'I'm in a band'" comes from an interview by Christine Lagorio-Chafkin in the October 2013 *Inc.*

*Gazelles.* The term "gazelle" first appeared in the chapter "Gazelle," written by David Birch and James Medoff, in Lewis C. Solmon and Alec R. Levenson, eds., *Labor Markets, Employment Policy, and Job Creation* (1994). For a more recent study, see the Zoltan Acs, William Parsons, and Spencer Tracy, "High-Impact Firms: Gazelles Revisited" (2008), available at http://archive.sba.gov/advo/research/rs328tot.pdf. The account of Michael Dell's return to his company is based on conversations I've had with Michael and Dell's chief marketing officer, Karen Quintos. For the topple rate of big firms, see Deloitte's 2013 Shift Index series, available online. For the average tenure of firms in the S&P 500, see the 2012 Innosight report "Creative Destruction Whips Through Corporate America."

*Skunks.* For the story of the Lockheed Corporation's Skunk Works, I consulted Ben Rich with Leo Janos, *Skunk Works* (1996). For more examples of skunks, see Scott D. Anthony, "The New Corporate Garage," *Harvard Business Review* (September 2012) and Paddy Miller and Thomas Wedell-Wedellsborg, "The Case for Stealth Innovation," *Harvard Business Review* (March 2013).

*Dolphins.* My conversations with Wendy Kopp began in 1989 and continue to this day. Wendy's 2012 commencement address at Dartmouth, available on YouTube, is a good source for the founding story of Teach For America. Bill Drayton was once my boss at Ashoka and remains a good friend. The quote I use in this chapter comes from an interview conducted by Gregory Lamb, *Christian Science Monitor* (May 16, 2011).

*Butterflies.* The latest statistics on firms with few or no paid employees are available online from the U.S. Census Bureau. The statistics on self-employed workers come from "The State of Independence in America," a September 2013 survey by MBO Partners. The 2020 number for independent contractors comes from research by the International Data Corporation, cited by Daniel Pink, *To Sell Is Human* (2013). The quote "I'm not a businessman; I'm a business, man" is a verse sung by Jay-Z in the Kanye West song "Diamonds from Sierra Leone."

For the number of species of butterflies, I consulted the *Encyclopedia Smithsonian*. The term "butterfly effect" comes from the talk "Predictability: Does the Flap of a Butterfly's Wings in Brazil Set off a Tornado in Texas?" by Edward Lorenz at the American Association for the Advancement of Science, Washington, D.C., December 29, 1972.

### The Secret Sauce of Entrepreneurship

In addition to the books mentioned in this section, I'd like to highlight three contemporary books about entrepreneurship that are already becoming classics: Eric Ries's *The Lean Startup* (2011), Chris Guillebeau, *The $100 Startup* (2012), and Reid Hoffman and Ben Casnocha, *The Start-Up of You* (2012). On the theme of what it means to be a woman in business, I also recommend Katherine Graham, *Personal History* (1998), Tina Fey, *Bossypants* (2013), and Sheryl Sandberg, *Lean In* (2013).

### You Don't Need a Hoodie to Be an Entrepreneur

In conceiving this book, I was also inspired by *Mastering the Art of French Cooking*, Julia Child, Simone Beck, and Louisette Bertholle.

## — CHAPTER 1: GETTING TO DAY ONE —

I've spent countless days in conversation with Wences Casares over the years, most delightedly at his legendary *asados*, where he kindly offers me a vegetarian option! Wences has also received abundant media attention over the years, and the quote I use in this chapter comes from Wences Casares, "Teach Your Children to Be Doers," *Wall Street Journal* (June 14, 2013). I also consulted Sara Lacy, *Brilliant, Crazy, Cocky* (2011).

Jeff Bezos's story, which appears in multiple places in the book, is based on a number of sources, including Brad Stone, *The Everything Store* (2013); Richard Brandt, *One Click* (2011); Alan Deutschman,

"Inside the Mind of Jeff Bezos," *Fast Company* (August 2004); and an interview by the Academy of Achievement of Washington, D.C. (May 4, 2001), available at www.achievement.org/autodoc/page/bez0int-1.

### The Distance Between Your Ears

For the story of Clorox Green Works, I conducted original interviews with Mary Jo Cook and Suzanne Sengelmann and consulted a number of secondary sources. Particularly valuable were Leonard Schlesinger, Charles Kiefer, and Paul Brown, "New Project? Don't Analyze—Act," *Harvard Business Review* (March 2012); Danna Greenberg, Kate McKone-Sweet, and H. James Wilson, *The New Entrepreneurial Leader* (2011); and Felicity Barringer, "Clorox Courts Sierra Club, and a Product Is Endorsed," *New York Times* (March 26, 2008).

Amr Shady's story comes largely from a panel we shared at the Milken Institute Global Conference in 2012.

### What I'm Supposed to Be

A word about the word "entrepreneurship": When I arrived in Latin America in the 1990s, there was no popular expression in Spanish or Portuguese for what in English (and French) was called an entrepreneur. Extensive interviews of hundreds of Endeavor entrepreneurs done by Bain and Endeavor's research arm confirmed that few who started before 1999 identified what they were doing as entrepreneurship or themselves as entrepreneurs. Part of Endeavor's mission was to expose and popularize this term.

In the early 2000s we received a call from the editor of the leading Portuguese-Brazilian dictionary saying that inspired by our work, he was adding the words *empreendedor* ("entrepreneur") and *empreendedorismo* ("entrepreneurship") into the lexicon. During this same period the Spanish terms *emprendedor* and *emprendedurismo* also gained currency, in part because of the media attention given to Endeavor entrepreneurs. (The Spanish word *emprendedor* had previously been used for explorers like Christopher Columbus, as several Mexican bloggers let it be known.)

### Fan the Foolish Fire

My chief sources for the Thomas Edison story were Ira Flatow, *They All Laughed* (1993), Ernest Freeberg, *The Age of Edison* (2013), Randall Stross, *The Wizard of Menlo Park* (2008), and Jill Jonnes, *Empires of Light* (2003). Here, as elsewhere, I also consulted Harold Evans's brilliant *They Made America*, coauthored with Gail Buckland and David Lefer. The quote predicting Edison's "ignominious failure" appeared in the *New York Herald* (April 27, 1879). The characterization of electric light as "death to the blonde" appears in *Gaillard's Medical Journal*, vol. 36 (1883).

Early opinions of Sam Walton's concept for Wal-Mart appear in Walton with Huey, *Made in America*. The Xbox story comes from Jeffrey O'Brien, "The Making of the Xbox," *Wired* (November 2001) and "The Xbox Story," Patrick Garrat, VG247.com (August 2011). The colleague who called Raymond Damadian's MRI project "harebrained" was Donald Hollis, a magnetic resonance expert at Johns Hopkins University Hospital. He is quoted in Evans, *They Made America*. The story of Jeffrey Braverman, of Nuts.com, comes from Ian Mount, "Forsaking Investment Banking to Turn Around a Family Business," *New York Times* (April 18, 2012).

I reencountered the quote by Niccolò Machiavelli in David Bornstein's bible for social entrepreneurs, *The Business of Changing the World*.

### Stop Planning, Start Doing

Endeavor has conducted substantial research on business plans. I also consulted Julian Lange et al., "Do Business Plans Make No Difference in the Real World?" delivered at the Babson College Entrepreneurship Research Conference (2005), which cites the *Inc.* 2002 survey. Intel's original business plan is available at www.businessinsider.com/intel-business-plan-from-1968-2012-12.

For the story of Pfizer's Jordan Cohen, I consulted Arianne Cohen, "Scuttling Scut Work," *Fast Company* (February 2008); Jena McGregor, "Outsourcing Tasks Instead of Jobs," *Bloomberg Businessweek* (March 2009); Ron Ahskenas, "How to Give Time Back to Your Team," HBR.org (July 2010); Paddy Miller and Thomas Wedell-Wedellsborg, "The Case for Stealth Innovation," *Harvard Business Review* (March 2013); and Jordan Cohen's own account of the story, www.managementexchange.com/story/getting-rid-busy-work-so-you-can-get-work.

Margaret Rudkin's story comes from Anthony Mayo and Nitin Nohria, *In Their Time* (2005). Lastly, I highly recommend Bill Sahlman's entertaining "How to Write a Great Business Plan," *Harvard Business Review* (July 1997).

## — CHAPTER 2: DERISKING RISK —

For Sara Blakely's story, I consulted two pieces by the *Forbes* staff writer Clare O'Connor: "Undercover Billionaire" (March 7, 2012) and "How Spanx Became a Billion-Dollar Business Without Advertising" (March 12, 2012). Also valuable were Stacy Perman, "How Failure Molded Spanx's Founder," *Bloomberg Businessweek* (November 21, 2007), Sara Blakely's appearance in *Inc.*'s Women's Summit in January 2012 (available in videos on the magazine's Web site), and Blakely's account of her story as told to *Inc.*'s Liz Welch (February 2014).

### Don't Bet the Farm
Ray Kroc's quote about risk taking has been widely documented, including Michael Masterson, *The Reluctant Entrepreneur* (2012).

Beyond Endeavor's own research on risk taking, I relied on insights from the 2013 Inc. 500 list (www.inc.com/magazine/201309/numbers-from-inc.500-companies-first-year.html0), as well as Eric Ries, *The Lean Startup* (2011) and Reid Hoffman and Ben Casnocha, *The Start-Up of You* (2012). The story of Nick Swinmurn, founder of

Zappos, comes from an interview given to the BBC (June 2010) and Dinah Eng, "Zappos' Silent Founder," *Fortune* (September 5, 2012).

The story of MTV Top Selection came from Paddy Miller and Thomas Wedell-Wedellsborg, "The Case for Stealth Innovation," *Harvard Business Review* (March 2013).

The primary source for CakeLove was Warren Brown's own telling of his story in the CakeLove Web site and through CakeLove's video podcasts. Other sources include Patrick Cliff, "Warren Brown, Cake Love and Love Café," *Inc.* (April 2005); Mike DeBonis, "The Butter Business Bureau," *Washington City Paper* (November 2005), and "From Lawyer to Baker," *Cubicle Nation* (2011).

### Friends Don't Let Friends Test-Drive Their Ideas

The story of Mel and Patricia Ziegler comes from their book *Wild Company* (2012) and Adam Wren, "How One Couple Turned $1,500 into a Billion-Dollar Global Brand," *Forbes* (June 24, 2013). The account of Maiden Preserves draws on Benjamin Wallace, "The Twee Party," *New York* (April 15, 2012). The study by researchers at Babson College and IPADE Business School is discussed in Vincent Onyemah, Martha Rivera Pesquera, and Abdul Ali, "What Entrepreneurs Get Wrong," *Harvard Business Review* (May 2013).

### Follow the Crowd

The story of Kickstarter is based on "In Conversation," with Perry Chen and Theaster Gates, *New York Times* (May 30, 2013); Om Malik, "Kickstarted," GigaOm.com (May 22, 2012); Max Chafkin, "True to Its Roots," *Fast Company* (April 2013); Rob Walker, "The Trivialities and Transcendence of Kickstarter," *New York Times* (August 5, 2011); Beth Teitell, "Kickstarter Boosts Funding and Angst," *Boston Globe* (April 9, 2013); and Chen's talks at TEDxTripoli and Do Lectures, on YouTube. The Anindya Ghose quote appears in Robert Strohmeyer, "The Crowdfunding Caveat," *PC World* (September 26, 2013).

For information on the Do Good Bus, I turned to StartSome

Good.com. For GE's partnership with Quirky, I spoke with GE's chief marketing officer, Beth Comstock, and consulted Joshua Brustein, "Why GE Sees Big Things in Quirky's Little Inventions," *Bloomberg Businessweek* (November 2013). Other discussions of crowdsourcing inside companies included Victor Luckerson, "This New Kind of Kickstarter Could Change Everything," *Time* (January 2014), "Crowdsourcing Happiness," www.cocacola.com, and Daniel Neville, "Crowdsourcing Beer—the Samuel Adams Crowd Craft Project," IdeaBounty.com.

### The Lost Art of Stalking
The material about Sam Walton's stalking the competition comes from Sam Walton with John Huey, *Made in America*. The advice about stalking competitors on LinkedIn comes from Meghan Casserly, "Stalking Competitors (and Nine More Things Entrepreneurs Screw Up on LinkedIn)," *Forbes* (January 22, 2013). The Post-it story draws on the book *3M, A Century of Innovation* (2002) and Nick Glass and Tim Hume, "The 'Hallelujah Moment' Behind the Invention of the Post-it Note," CNN.com (April 4, 2013).

Estée Lauder's story is told in her memoir, *Estée* (1985); Evans's *They Made America*; and Nancy Koehn, "Building a Powerful Prestige Brand," *HBS Working Knowledge* (October 30, 2000).

## – CHAPTER 3: CHAOS IS YOUR FRIEND –

For Walt Disney's story, my chief source was Neal Gabler, *Walt Disney* (2006). Also helpful were Timothy S. Susanin, *Walt Before Mickey* (2011) and Daniel Gross, *Forbes Greatest Business Stories of All Time* (1997).

### Champagne for Your Enemies
Cari Lightner's story is told on the MADD Web site. For Michael J. Fox, I consulted his two memoirs, *Lucky Man* (2011) and *Always Looking Up* (2011). Petra Nemcova's story was told most fully in Leslie Bennetts, "Petra's Story," *Vanity Fair* (May 2005).

The figures on Cairo traffic come from the documentary *Cairo Drive*. The CNN correspondent who tweeted was Ben Wedeman. In addition to Endeavor's own materials on Bey2ollak, I consulted Chris Schroeder's excellent *Startup Rising* (2013).

Marian Croak's story appears in Sarah Kessler, "The Surprising Link Between 'American Idol' and Text-to-Donate Fundraising," *Fast Company* (October 2013) and "Helping Disaster Victims with One Simple Text," an interview with Croak, TheDailyBeast.com (October 28, 2013).

For the Veuve Clicquot story, I consulted Tilar Mazzeo's wonderful biography *The Widow Clicquot* (2008). As background for how uncertainty and adversity promote entrepreneurship, I recommend Dan Senor and Saul Singer, *Startup Nation* (2009).

## Hug the Bear

The Warren Buffett quote about capitalizing on downturns appears in his op-ed "Buy American. I Am," *New York Times* (October 16, 2008). The Kauffman Foundation study is Dane Stangler, "The Economic Future Just Happened," (June 9, 2009). Their data on new-business formation come from the Kauffman Index of Entrepreneurial Activity, available at www.kauffman.org/what-we-do/research/kauffman -index-of-entrepreneurial-activity.

I have benefited tremendously from Jim Collins's books, *Built to Last* (1994), written with Jerry Porras; *Good to Great* (2001); and *Great by Choice* (2011), coauthored with Morten Hansen. His quotation in this chapter appears in Allan Cohen, "Forget the Recession. The Right Time to Start a Business Is Anytime You Have a Great Idea," CNN .com (February 4, 2002).

For background on the situation in Greece, I relied on the excellent report published by Endeavor Greece with Haris Makryniotis, *Entrepreneurship and Investment Opportunities in Greece Today* (October 2013). I also consulted Niki Kitsantonis, "With Start-ups, Greeks Make Recovery Their Own Business," *New York Times* (March 24, 2014).

The Johns Hopkins report is Lester Salamon, S. Wojciech Sokolowski, and Stephanie Geller, "Holding the Fort" (January 2012). Diana Aviv is the president and CEO of Independent Sector. Her quote comes from Catherine Rampell, "More College Graduates Take Public Service Jobs," *New York Times* (March 1, 2011). This article is also the source for statistics on AmeriCorps and Teach For America applications.

J. K. Rowling's story has been told by many outlets, but most revealingly by the writer herself in her 2008 commencement address at Harvard, available at HarvardMagazine.com. Other sources include Ian Parker, "Mugglemarch," *New Yorker* (October 1, 2012) and Rowling's own Web site, which includes several posts on the origins of the Harry Potter series.

### Admit You Screwed Up

L. L. Bean's story is told by Pat Taub, *100 People Who Changed 20th Century America*, ed. Mary Cross (2013); M. R. Montgomery, "The Marketing Magic of L. L. Bean," *Boston Globe Magazine* (December 27, 1981); and "Leon L. Bean," *Entrepreneur* (October 10, 2008).

The story of Bonobos's Cyber Monday crisis comes from: Andy Dunn, "Bonobos Founder," *Inc.* (June 28, 2012); Alystair Barr, "Bonobos Caught with Pants Down on Top Shopping Day," Reuters (December 21, 2011); and Jon Schlossberg's entry on Quora headlined "Why Did Bonobos Have Such an Epic Fail on Cyber Monday 2011?" (November 29, 2011). The adulating Facebook comment was posted on the company's profile page on November 30, 2011.

To tell the story of Reed Hastings and Netflix, I relied mostly on primary sources on the company's blog, including "Netflix Introduces New Plans and Announces Price Changes" (July 12, 2011), "An Explanation and Some Reflections" (September 18, 2011), "DVDs Will Be Staying at Netflix.com" (October 10, 2011). The quotes given to James Stewart appear in two *New York Times* columns: "In 2013: Rebounds, Traders and Rights" (December 27, 2013) and "Netflix Looks Back on Its Near-Death Spiral" (April 26, 2013).

I learned about the "apology watch" from Dov Seidman in early 2014. The effort was announced in two *New York Times* pieces on February 3, 2014: Andrew Ross Sorkin, "Too Many Sorry Excuses for Apology" and Dov Seidman, "Calling for an Apology Cease-Fire." I also consulted Dov Seidman, *How* (2007).

## Once upon a Time

Alfred Chandler's quote appears in John Seaman, Jr., and George David Smith, "Your Company's History as a Leadership Tool," *Harvard Business Review* (December 2012). For the story of Howard Schultz's return to Starbucks, I consulted Schultz, *Pour Your Heart Into It* (1997) and *Onward* (2011), as well as Adi Ignatius, "Howard Schultz on Starbucks' Turnaround," HBR.org (June 2010). Schultz's famous Valentine's Day memo is available through the *Wall Street Journal*: www.online.wsj.com/news/articles/SB117234084129218452. And I personally heard Adi Ignatius interview both Howard Schultz and Angela Ahrendts at the ninetieth anniversary celebration of the *Harvard Business Review* in November 2012.

Other sources for Angela Ahrendts's story include Ahrendts, "Burberry's CEO on Turning an Aging British Icon into a Global Luxury Brand," *Harvard Business Review* (January–February 2013); Rupert Neate, "How an American Woman Rescued Burberry, a Classic British Label," *Guardian* (June 15, 2013); Jeff Chu, "Can Apple's Angela Ahrendts Spark a Retail Revolution?" *Fast Company* (February 2014); and Jill Krasny, "Why Apple Poached Burberry's CEO," *Inc.* (October 16, 2013).

## Shift Happens

The study of businesses in emerging markets was conducted by Mauro Guillén and Esteban García-Canal and is discussed in "Execution as Strategy," *Harvard Business Review* (October 2012) and *The New Multinationals* (2011).

## — CHAPTER 4: YOUR ENTREPRENEUR PERSONALITY —

The material in this chapter is the result of a decade-long effort at Endeavor to define these profile types. I'm deeply indebted to our partners at Bain & Company, especially Chris Bierly, Vikki Tam, Eric Almquist, and Paul Markowitz, who have worked tirelessly over several years to test and refine our exclusive diagnostic process. While hundreds of Endeavor entrepreneurs have taken our self-assessment test to identify their types, the famous figures I use as examples throughout this chapter have not. Their types are based on my own evaluation of their careers and reputations.

For the story of the Myers-Briggs Type Indicator, I consulted Lillian Cunningham, "Does It Pay to Know Your Type?" *Washington Post* (December 14, 2012); the Web sites of the Myers & Briggs Foundation (www.myersbriggs.org) and CPP, the company that now administers the MBTI (www.cpp.com), as well as Mary McCaulley, "The Story of Isabel Briggs Myers," (July 1980) at www.capt.org/mbti-assessment/isabel-myers.htm. I also enjoyed Gary Chapman's bestseller *The Five Love Languages* (2008) and Anthony Tjan, *Hearts, Smarts, Guts and Luck* (2012).

### Diamonds

The story of Tesla Motors is adapted from Tad Friend, "Plugged In," *New Yorker* (August 2009) and Ashlee Vance, "Elon Musk, the 21st Century Industrialist," Businessweek.com (September 13, 2012). His feud with the *New York Times* was ignited by John Broder, "Stalled Out on Tesla's Electric Highway," (February 8, 2013). I also recommend Chris Anderson, "The shared genius of Elon Musk and Steve Jobs," *Fortune* (December 2013). The story of Jobs's reality distortion field is told by former Apple engineer Andy Hertzfeld at www.folklore.org/StoryView.py?story=Reality_Distortion_Field.txt. Jony Ive's quote appears in Isaacson's *Steve Jobs*.

**Stars**

The primary source for Wolfgang Puck's story was Emily Ross and Angus Holland, *100 Great Businesses and the Minds Behind Them* (2004). Other sources included Dinah Eng, "Wolfgang Puck's Dining Revolution," *Fortune* (November 20, 2013); Puck's story as told to Liz Welch, *Inc.* (October 2009); "Meet the Chef," *JustLuxe* (February 2012); and Randall Frost, "Wolfgang Puck: Recipe for Success," BrandChannel .com (February 3, 2003).

Lance Armstrong's story was widely covered in the media, and a number of sources are available. The drop in donations and the quote from Livestrong's external affairs officer come from Eriq Gardner, "Livestrong Struggles After Lance Armstrong's Fall," *Hollywood Reporter* (July 25, 2013).

**Transformers**

I consulted a number of sources for Herb Kelleher's story, notably, Kevin Freiberg and Jacquelyn Freiberg, *Nuts!* (1996). Others include Jennifer Reingold, "Southwest's Herb Kelleher," *Fortune* (January 14, 2013); Joe Brancatelli, "Southwest Airlines' Seven Secrets for Success," *Wired* (July 2008); "'Never Say Never' on Bag Fees," CNBC.com (January 24, 2013); and "Is Southwest Airlines Always the Least Expensive?" a study by Topaz International.

The story of Burt's Bees comes from Louise Story, "Can Burt's Bees Turn Clorox Green," *New York Times* (January 6, 2008); Jonathan Evans, "Burt of Burt's Bees Is Living in a Turkey Coop," *Esquire* (September 13, 2013); Roxanne Quimby with Susan Donovan, "How I Did It," *Inc.* (January 1, 2004); and a Brigham Young University case study, www.emp.byui.edu/nygrenm/B283/Roxanne%20Quimby%20Case .pdf. The Change.org petition decrying Clorox's takeover of Burt's Bees was created by Danise Lepard and is titled "Clorox, Make Burt's Bees Products Like They Were! Keep It HONEST!"

Ben & Jerry's admission that it is "beginning to look like the rest of corporate America" came in its 2004 "Social and Environmental As-

sessment," which is available at www.lickglobalwarming.org/company/
sear/2004/sea_2004.pdf.

## Rocketships

For a complete listing of Bezos sources, please see the works listed under
Chapter 1. The quote about Bill Gates comes from Evans, *They Made
America*. The Bill and Melinda Gates Foundation's annual reports and
grant-making policies are posted at www.gatesfoundation.org/How-We
-Work/General-Information/Our-Approach-to-Measurement-and
-Evaluation/Evaluation-Policy.

## – CHAPTER 5: THE WHITEBOARD –

The lessons in this chapter have been culled from years of selections
panels and services provided to entrepreneurs. In recent years studies
by Endeavor's research arm have found quantitative and qualitative
evidence to support many of the conclusions drawn here.

For Henry Ford's story, I consulted Douglas Brinkley, *Wheels for
the World* (2004); Michael Blowfield and Leo Johnson, *Turnaround
Challenge* (2013); Thomas P. Hughes, *American Genesis* (2004); and
Lindsay Brook, "Top 10 Ford Model T Tech Innovations that Matter
100 Years Later," *Popular Mechanics* (September 25, 2008).

## Close Doors

For the Liquid Paper story, I relied on Catherine Thimmesh, *Girls
Think of Everything* (2000) and Ross and Holland's *100 Great Businesses and the Minds Behind Them*. For more on Phil Knight and Nike,
see J. B. Strasser, *Swoosh* (1993); Chuck Salter, "Innovation: Phil
Knight's 'Not Exactly Textbook' Moves," *Fast Company* (July 18, 2007);
and Geraldine Willigan, "High-Performance Marketing: An Interview
with Nike's Phil Knight," *Harvard Business Review* (July 1992). His
quote about the swoosh design comes from Brian Clarke Howard, " 'I
Never Get Tired of Looking at It,' " *Daily Mail* (June 16, 2011).

### Fire Your Mother-in-law

In this section, I relied heavily on Endeavor's research, as well as statistics on family-owned businesses from the University of Vermont (www.uvm.edu/business/vfbi/?Page=facts.html) and the Family Firm Institute (available at www.ffi.org/?page=globaldatapoints).

Usher's interview with Oprah is available on YouTube. The chief source for Lucille Ball and Desi Arnaz is Thaddeus Wawro, *Radicals and Visionaries* (2000). In addition, I consulted Kathleen Brady, *Lucille* (2001); Karin Adir, *The Great Clowns of American Television* (2002), and Susan Schindehette, "The Real Story of Desi and Lucy," *People* (February 18, 1991).

### Minnovate

The term "minnovate" was coined by Dan Isenberg, and it appears in his book *Worthless, Impossible, and Stupid* (2013).

For more information on Gore, I suggest Lucien Rhodes, "The Unmanager," *Inc.* (August 1, 1982); Richard Daft, *Organization Theory and Design* (2007); Robert Safian, "Terri Kelly, the 'Un-CEO' of W. L. Gore, on How to Deal with Chaos," *Fast Company* (October 29, 2012); Alan Deutschman, "The Fabric of Creativity," *Fast Company* (December 2004); and "Gore: Success with Simplicity," *HR Insights* (July–August 2012). Gore's own Web site has a wonderful history of the company at www.gore.com/en_xx/aboutus/timeline/index.html.

Kleenex's story comes from Robert Spector and William Wicks, *Shared Values* (1997) and Burton Folsom, "From Kleenex to Zippers," *Freeman* (December 1, 2005).

For Barbie's story, I consulted Mary Cross, ed., *100 People Who Changed 20th-Century America* (2013) and M. G. Lord, *Forever Barbie* (2004).

### Drop the Pens

The California accelerator mentioned here is Blackbox. It issued two reports in 2011: Max Marmer, Bjoern Herrmann, Ertan Dogrultan, and Ron Berman, "Startup Genome Report" and "Startup Genome Report Extra on Premature Scaling." I also consulted Austin Carr, "Blackbox's Startup Genome Compass Uses Science to Crack the 'Innovation Code,'" *Fast Company* (August 29, 2011).

Sources for Jobs's story are Isaacson, *Steve Jobs* and Isaacson, "The Real Leadership Lessons of Steve Jobs," *Harvard Business Review* (April 2012). The Sony quote comes from Hiroko Tabuchi, "How the Tech Parade Passed Sony By," *New York Times* (April 14, 2012).

The LEGO story is told in Jay Greene, "How LEGO Revived Its Brand," *Bloomberg Businessweek* (July 23, 2010); Gregory Schmidt, "Lego Builds an Empire, Brick by Brick," *New York Times* (February 14, 2014); and Wharton School, "Innovation Almost Bankrupted LEGO," www.knowledge.wharton.upenn.edu.

### Dream Big but Execute Small

American Giant's story comes from Farhad Manjoo, "This Is the Greatest Hoodie Ever Made," Slate.com (December 4, 2012) and "The Only Problem with the Greatest Hoodie Ever Made," Slate.com (March 21, 2013); Kai Ryssdal, "Could Being Named the 'Best Ever' Be Bad?" NPR's *Marketplace* (March 26, 2013); and Kate Dailey, "American Giant," BBC.co.uk (March 10, 2013).

For the details on Blackbox's Startup Genome project see the sources mentioned under "Drop the Pens." The water buffalo quote by Mark Chang came from an interview in *Digital News Asia* in May 2013. Miguel Dávila's story is based on my interactions with him, as well as Isenberg, *Worthless, Impossible, and Stupid.*

### Eat the Elephant One Bite at a Time

For anyone interested in tales and tips about survival, I heartily recommend Ben Sherwood, *The Survivors Club* (2009).

## – CHAPTER 6: LEADERSHIP 3.0 –

### Agile

The history of agile comes from research conducted by my husband, Bruce Feiler, for *The Secrets of Happy Families* (2013), which has abundant examples of how we've used these techniques in our home, for better and worse. You can see Bruce's TED talk on these themes (with me in the audience) at www.ted.com/talks/bruce_feiler_agile_programming _for_your_family.html.

The story of Heier's potato-peeling washing machine comes from Navi Radjou, Jaideep Prabhu, and Simone Ahuja, *Jugaad Innovation* (2012). George Lois's insights on the power of small teams come from Justin Rocket Silverman, "Quit Your 'Group Grope' Now," *Fast Company* (August 12, 2013). For more on Bezos, see the works listed under Chapter 1. Bezos also shared his insights on agile leadership in a personal conversation with my husband in late 2013.

The 2013 survey on workers' fear of failure was conducted by the American Management Association, www.amanet.org/news/9206 .aspx.

I consulted a number sources for the WD-40 story, including Nicole Skibola, "Leadership Lessons from WD-40's CEO, Garry Ridge," *Forbes* (June 27, 2011); Ken and Scott Blanchard, "To Encourage Innovation, Eradicate Blame," *Fast Company* (August 20, 2012); and Helen Walters, "Three Innovation Lessons from WD-40," ThoughtYouShouldSeeThis .com (September 22, 2011).

Scott Cook discusses the birth of SnapTax in his talk "Leadership in the Agile Age," www.network.intuit.com/2011/04/20/leadership-in -the-agile-age. Also helpful was an April 2004 *Inc.* profile by Michael Hopkins on Scott Cook as part of the series "America's 25 Most Fascinating Entrepreneurs."

For Ratan Tata's prize for best failure, I relied on Rita McGrath, "Failure Is a Gold Mine for India's Tata," HBR.org blog (April 11, 2011).

## Accessible

The 2012 Dreamforce panel with Jeff Immelt and Colin Powell is available at blogs.salesforce.com/company/2012/09/gen-colin-powell-and-ges-jeff-immelt-talk-about-leadership-and-the-economy.html. The Weber Shandwick report on executive sociability is in "The Social CEO: Executives Tell All" (January 15, 2013).

For the story about Barack Obama, I consulted Bobbie Johnson, "Barack Obama to Use BlackBerry as President, According to Reports," *Guardian* (January 21, 2009); Joshua DuBois, "The Prayers Inside the President's BlackBerry," CNN.com (October 22, 2013); Michael Hastings, "How Obama Won the Internet," BuzzFeed.com (January 8, 2013); Laura June, "President Obama's Reddit AMA Reaches over 5 Million Pageviews," TheVerge.com (August 31, 2012); and Obama's AMA itself, available at www.reddit.com.

## Aware

The best resources on the power of powerless communication are Adam Grant, *Give and Take* (2013) and Susan Cain, *Quiet* (2012). I encountered the term "flawsome" at the 2012 Fortune Most Powerful Women conference, in a talk by Wendy Clark of Coca-Cola. Trend watching.com also has good material on the term at www.trendwatching.com/trends/flawsome/.

While the video that started the Domino's controversy has been taken down, the pizza relaunch Web site is still accessible at Pizza-Turnaround.com. The developments also received plenty of media coverage: Stephanie Clifford, "Video Prank at Domino's Taints Brand," *New York Times* (April 15, 2009); Bruce Watson, "Domino's Pizza Reborn?," DailyFinance.com (March 5, 2010); and Bruce Horovitz, "Domino's Pizza Delivers Change in Its Core Pizza Recipe," *USA Today* (December 16, 2009).

The Spoleto videos can be seen at www.youtube.com/watch?v=Un4r52t-cuk and www.youtube.com/watch?v=ebe-3s4TLfQ. My relationships with Danny Meyer and knowledge of his philosophy of hospitality began when my husband worked as a maitre d' in the Union Square Café. You can read Bruce's James Beard Award–winning article at www.gourmet.com/magazine/2000s/2002/10/therapistat thetable. The quotes in my book appear in Danny's bestselling book *Setting the Table* (2006).

### Authentic

Tony Dungy's moving personal story comes from his memoir, *Quiet Strength* (2008). Other accounts include Matthew Kaminski, "A Coach's Faith," *Wall Street Journal* (September 12, 2009); Pat Yasinskas, "A Dungy Story You May Not Have Heard," ESPN.com (January 12, 2009); and Gene Wojciechowski, "Dungy Delivers Profound Message in Son's Eulogy," ESPN.com (December 28, 2005).

Brené Brown, the author of *Daring Greatly* (2012), is today's leading voice on vulnerability. A report on her talk at *Inc.*'s 2013 Leadership Forum is available at www.inc.com/kimberly-weisul/leadership-why-the-best-leaders-are-vulnerable.html.

Finally, my husband has written widely, and beautifully, about how cancer affected him, me, and our entire family. I recommend his inspiring 2010 memoir, *The Council of Dads*, as well as " 'You Look Great' and Other Lies," *New York Times* (June 10, 2011) and "Cancer Survivors Celebrate Their Cancerversary," *New York Times* (December 6, 2013), which marks the moment he was declared cancer-free after five years.

## – CHAPTER 7: A CIRCLE OF MENTORS –

Mentorship is a crucial part of the Endeavor model, and we've spent years trying to make sure we do it as effectively as possible. Tom Friedman dubbed us "mentor capitalists" in a section on me and Endeavor in *The World Is Flat 2.0* (2006). I will always be grateful for his support.

The term "360° Mentoring" was the title of an article by Elizabeth Collins, in the March 2008 issue of *Management Update*, a newsletter from Harvard Business School Publishing. This article is also the source of the Kathy Kram quote about networked mentoring. I also consulted Kathy Kram's seminal *Mentoring at Work* (1985).

For Bill Campbell's story, I consulted Jennifer Reingold, "The Secret Coach," *Fortune* (July 21, 2008); a two-part article by Ozy.com's Carlos Watson titled "Guru of the Valley" (December 18 and 19, 2013); Miguel Helft, "Bill Campbell on Coaching RockMelt and Google vs. Apple" and "Coaching Silicon Valley," *New York Times* (November 8 and 15, 2010).

## Get Yourself a Simon Cowell

Nick Bilton's *Hatching Twitter* (2013) includes a gripping account of the early years of Twitter. The quotes on *American Idol* and *The Voice* come from Lara Martin, " 'X Factor' USA's Simon Cowell on Judges' Role," DigitalSpy.com (September 14, 2011); Cortney Wills, " 'X Factor' Finalists Alex & Sierra Notch iTunes No. 1, Show Sales Potential," *Hollywood Reporter* (December 12, 2013); and Carla Hay, "Christina Aguilera, Adam Levine Take Aim at Simon Cowell and 'The X Factor,' " Examiner.com (October 27, 2012).

## Cut the Cord

Beyond my many personal conversations with Ala' Alsallal of Jamalon, Fadi Ghandour, and Diego Piacentini of Amazon, I also relied on Christopher Schroeder's excellent telling of Ala's story in *Startup Rising*.

Gerry and Melissa Owen's story comes from Carol Shih, "Fourteen Eighteen Coffeehouse in Downtown Plano Has Already Become a Neighborhood Favorite," *D Magazine* (September 30, 2013); Peter Cohen, "3 Start-Up Tips from 'Yale's Professor of Coffee Shops," *Inc.* (September 17, 2013); Mark Oppenheimer "Taste-Testing a Second Career, with a Mentor," *New York Times* (September 15, 2013); and Duncan Goodall's profile on PivotPlanet.com, www.pivotplanet.com/advisors/486.

### Phone a Frenemy

The Kram and Isabella study mentioned in this section is titled "Mentoring Alternatives," *Academy of Management Journal* (March 1985). The British Telecom anecdote comes from Jeanne Meister and Karie Willyerd, "Mentoring Millennials," *Harvard Business Review* (May 2010). Larry Page's account of his last visit to Steve Jobs comes from Brad Stone, "Google's Page: Apple's Android Pique 'For Show,'" *Bloomberg Businessweek* (April 4, 2012). Walter Isaacson's account of the encounter comes from his biography of Jobs as well as his *Harvard Business Review* article "The Real Leadership Lessons of Steve Jobs."

### Not All Mentors Have Gray Hair

John Donahoe shared the story of his relationship with Brian Chesky to me over a dinner in 2012. He later recounted the tale at *Fortune*'s Brainstorm Conference in July 2013, www.tech.fortune.cnn.com/2013/07/23/brian-chesky-john-donahoe. I also drew from Mike Isaac, "eBay CEO John Donahoe on the Importance of Design," AllThingsD.com (July 29, 2013).

A good overview of this subject is Leslie Kwo, "Reverse Mentoring Cracks Workplace," *Wall Street Journal* (November 28, 2011). Chaudhuri and Ghosh's article on reverse mentoring is titled "Reverse Mentoring," *Human Resource Development Review*, vol. 11, no. 1 (February 2015). For the Mentor Up program at P&G, I consulted Tara Parker-Pope, "P&G Makes Pitch to Keep Women, and So Far the Strategy Is Working," *Toledo Blade* (September 10, 1998). In addition to Sheryl Sandberg, *Lean In* (2013) this new conception of career paths can be found in Patricia Sellers, "Power Point: Get Used to the Jungle Gym," *Fortune* (August 6, 2009).

## – CHAPTER 8: THE PURPOSE-DRIVEN WORKPLACE –

The story of Globant's headquarters comes from my many private conversations with two of the cofounders, Martin Migoya and

Guibert Englebienne. Also valuable were Ken Stier, "IT Outsourcer Globant Sells Innovation, Wows Google, LinkedIn," *Bloomberg Businessweek* (April 8, 2011) and a Harvard Business School case by Mukti Khaire, Gustavo Herrero, and Cintra Scott (2011).

## Psychic Equity

Beyond Endeavor's research on workplace culture, I relied on many sources. For those on W. L. Gore, please see the works listed under Chapter 5. I also have reviewed data available at the Gallup Web site; Rob Goffee and Gareth Jones, "Creating the Best Workplace on Earth," *Harvard Business Review* (May 2013), which cites the Hay Group data; and Shawn Achor, "Positive Intelligence," *Harvard Business Review* (January–February 2012).

For Dan Ariely's research, I consulted *Predictably Irrational* (2010), and Ariely's "What's the Value of a Big Bonus?" *New York Times* (November 19, 2008). Nancy Lublin discusses job titles in her book *Zilch* (2010). Also valuable were Ashley Ross, "Job Titles Retailored to Fit," *New York Times* (August 30, 2013); and ABC News, "Sugar High," *Nightline* (September 30, 2013).

Assorted strategies to foster psychic equity are discussed in Paul Kretkowski, "The 15 Percent Solution," *Wired* (January 23, 1998); Ryan Tate, "Google Couldn't Kill 20 Percent Time Even If It Wanted To," *Wired* (August 21, 2013), "Facebook's Wi-Fi Spreads in the Wild," *Wired* (June 18, 2013), and "LinkedIn Gone Wild: '20 Percent Time' to Tinker Spreads Beyond Google," *Wired* (June 12, 2012); Amanda Lewan, "Quicken Loans Innovates with a 'Small Business' Culture," Michipreneur.com (March 5, 2013); Jessica Lessin, "Apple Gives In to Employee Perks," *Wall Street Journal* (November 12, 2012); and Bo Burlingham, *Small Giants*, (2006), which profiles Jay Goltz.

Daniel Pink, *Drive* (2011) contains great insights on the science of motivation.

## Culture Club

Many of the strategies Jenn Lim discussed with our entrepreneurs also appear in Tony Hsieh, *Delivering Happiness* (2010). The story of Debbi Fields is told in Edward Horrell, *The Kindness Revolution* (2006) and Ross and Holland, *100 Great Businesses and the Minds Behind Them*. Jim Collins's *Good to Great* is a valuable resource for information on the value of assembling a strong team. I also recommend Reid Hoffman, Ben Casnocha, and Chris Yeh, "Tours of Duty," *Harvard Business Review* (June 2013), which contains interesting insights on hiring and firing in the entrepreneurial age.

Kevin Ryan has been a good friend for many years and shared insights on hiring and firing with me on multiple occasions. He expressed these eloquently in "Gilt Groupe's CEO on Building a Team of A Players," *Harvard Business Review* (January–February 2012).

## If You Can't Beat 'Em, You Know, Like, Join 'Em #FOMO

I have learned a tremendous amount about millennials from the many talented members of that generation who've worked at Endeavor and from the hundreds of young entrepreneurs we've supported around the world.

For much of the latest research, I am indebted to Lynne Lancaster and David Stillman, *The M-Factor* (2010), as well as Jeanne Meister, *The 2020 Workplace* (2010), both of which informed many of my ideas. *The M-Factor* is also the source for the stories about the FAA and Thomson Reuters. For the FAA, I also consulted Chuck Bennett, "FAA Kids Are in 'Control,'" *New York Post* (July 14, 2008).

The following sources provided information on Warby Parker's story: Jessica Pressler, "20/30 Vision," *New York* (August 11, 2013); Neil Blumenthal's interview for Adam Bryant, "Corner Office," *New York Times* (October 24, 2013); Neil Blumenthal, "Give Me More Millennials," *Inc.* (July 15, 2013); and Leigh Buchanan, "Warby Parker CEO," *Inc.* (June 2013).

For data on millennials in the workforce, I consulted the 2012

Jessica Brack report, "Maximizing Millennials in the Workplace," which is available at www.kenan-flagler.unc.edu, and a 2013 PricewaterhouseCoopers report, "PwC's NextGen," which is available at www.pwc.com. The Net Impact study is Cliff Zukin and Mark Szeltner, "Talent Report," available at https://netimpact.org/docs/publica tions-docs/talent-report-what-workers-want-in-2012-full-report. For data on Generation X, I consulted Marcie Pitt-Catsouphes, Christina Matz-Costa, and Elyssa Bensen, "Workplace Flexibility," a 2009 report by the Boston College Sloan Center on Aging and Work, which is found at www.bc.edu.

For information on hackathons, I consulted Drew Olanoff, "Facebook Shares the History of Its 'Hackathon,'" TheNextWeb.com (May 23, 2012); Alyson Krueger, "Hackathons Aren't Just for Hacking," Wired (June 6, 2012); and Pedram Keyani, "Stay Focused and Keep Hacking," Facebook.com/Engineering (May 23, 2012). For the British Airways hackathon, I consulted Zoe Fox, "The Hottest Spot for Hackathons? 30,000 Feet in the Air," Mashable.com (June 13, 2013). For information on the pediatrics hackathon hosted by the Boston Children's Hospital, I relied on the event's Web site, www.hackingpediatrics.com.

For DreamWorks's story, I turned to Jessica Grose, "The Animated Workplace," Fast Company (March 15, 2013); Joel Stein, "Millennials: The Me Me Me Generation," Time (May 20, 2013); Todd Henneman, "DreamWorks Animation Cultivates a Culture of Creativity," WorkForce.com (August 4, 2012); and Nancy Davis, "DreamWorks Fosters Creativity, Collaboration and Engagement," SHRM.org (July 5, 2012).

## Put Out Your Family Photos

I have known and admired Sheryl Sandberg for over twenty-five years. Her breakthrough book, Lean In (2013), ignited breakthrough conversations in my office and offices around the world. The Inc. magazine piece by Darrell Cavens of Zulily, "The Way I Work," appeared on April 30, 2013. The results of the BabyCenter.com study are available at www.babycenter.com/100_press-release-dad-survey_10383601.bc.

## – CHAPTER 9: GO BIG AND GO HOME –

The Tom Friedman quote appears in "Need a Job? Invent It," *New York Times* (March 30, 2013).

### Get Going

The Rainbow Loom story draws on a number of sources, including Catherine Clifford, "Inventor of the Wildly Popular 'Rainbow Loom' Weaves the American Dream with Rubber Bands in a Detroit Basement," *Entrepreneur* (August 26, 2013); Camille Sweeney and Josh Gosfield, "How a DIY Dad Took the Toy World by Storm with Rainbow Loom," *Fast Company* (August 21, 2013); Catherine Kavanaugh, "Rainbow Loom's Creator Weaves Success from Playtime Inspiration," *Crain's Detroit Business* (December 15, 2013); and Claire Martin, "Rainbow Loom's Success, from 2,000 Pounds of Rubber Bands," *New York Times* (August 31, 2013).

Beyoncé's stealth album release received considerable media attention, including Matthew Yglesias, "How Beyoncé Got Us to Pay for Music," Slate.com (December 13, 2013); Jon Pareles, "A December Surprise, Without Whispers (or Leaks)," *New York Times* (December 13, 2013); Ben Sisario, "Beyoncé Rejects Tradition for Social Media's Power," *New York Times* (December 15, 2013); and Matthew Perpetua, "Beyoncé Sold Nearly a Million Copies of Her New Album in Three Days," Buzzfeed.com (December 16, 2013).

Costica Bradatan's quote comes from his "In Praise of Failure," *New York Times* (December 15, 2013).

Katrina Markoff's story is informed by the following sources: David Burstein, "Vosges Unwraps Chocolate's Wild Side," *Fast Company* (February 9, 2012); Emily Bryson York, "Chicago Chocolate Artisan Known for Vosges Preps Wild Ophelia for Mass Market," *Chicago Tribune* (March 14, 2013); *Fortune*'s profile on Markoff in the 2011 edition of its "40 Under 40" series; and Becky Anderson, "Sweet Success," CNN.com (July 10, 2012).

## Go Big

I am grateful to Robert Pasin for sharing the Radio Flyer story with me and for sending us those wagons! I also consulted Reshma Memon Yaqub, "Backstory: Radio Flyer," *Inc.* (October 30, 2012); Kristin Samuelson, "Office Space: Robert Pasin, Radio Flyer," *Chicago Tribune* (July 23, 2012), "How Robert Pasin Dug Deep to Help Radio Flyer Evolve Its Brand and Its Products," *Smart Business* (January 2013), and "Radio Flyer Toys Bring Smiles, Create Memories," *Business Ledger* (June 10, 2010).

The story of the Doritos Locos Taco comes primarily from two articles in *Fast Company*: Austin Carr, "Deep Inside Taco Bell's Doritos Locos Tacos," (May 1, 2013) and Anya Kamenetz, "Taco Bell, the Late Todd Mills, and the Actual Invention of the Doritos Locos Taco," (December 5, 2013). Courtney Subramanian, "Taco Bell Sells $1B in Doritos Locos Tacos Because 'I Worked Late, I Deserve a Treat,'" *Time* (October 16, 2013) was also valuable.

## Go Home

The phrase "the genius of the AND" is discussed in detail in Collins and Porras, *Built to Last*. My thinking about the value of going home was shaped by Clay Christensen's beautiful and moving *How Will You Measure Your Life?* (2012).

The origin story of the phrase "go big or go home" is told anonymously by the packaging designer on the Web site Answers.com, available at www.wiki.answers.com/Q/Who_coined_the_phrase_'go_big _or_go_home'.

Tina Fey's story comes from the hilarious and thoughtful *Bossypants* (2013). Kenneth Cole shares the story of his incident with his daughter in Alison Beard, "Life's Work: Kenneth Cole," *Harvard Business Review* (December 2011).

## — JOIN #TEAMCRAZY —

Finally, if anything in this book has intrigued you about our work at Endeavor, I invite you to visit our Web site, www.endeavor.org. You can find abundant examples of our research, videos, ongoing studies of our impact, links to our country affiliates, and portraits of all the entrepreneurs we've worked with since 1997. For more information about me, this book, and my speaking schedule, as well as to contact me directly, please visit www.lindarottenberg.com or www.crazyisacompliment .com. You can also keep the conversation alive at www.facebook.com/ LindaRottenbergAuthor or www.twitter.com/lindarottenberg. I look forward to hearing about your crazy dream and how you managed to get going, go big, and go home.

# INDEX

# ERIC RIES

**THE LEAN STARTUP: How Constant Innovation Creates Radically Successful Businesses**

Most new businesses fail. But most of those failures are preventable.

*The Lean Startup* is a new approach to business that's being adopted around the world. It is changing the way companies are built and new products are launched.

*The Lean Startup* is about learning what your customers really want. It's about testing your vision continuously, adapting and adjusting before it's too late.

Now is the time to think Lean.

'Every so often a business book comes along that changes how we think about innovation and entrepreneurship. Eric Ries's *The Lean Startup* has the chops to join this exalted company.' Philip Delves Broughton, *Financial Times*

'Mandatory reading for entrepreneurs... loaded with fascinating stories and practical principles' Dan Heath, co-author of *Switch* and *Made to Stick*

'If you are an entrepreneur, read this book. If you are thinking about becoming an entrepreneur, read this book. If you are just curious about entrepreneurship, read this book.' Randy Komisar, Founding Director of TiVo

'*The Lean Startup* will change the way we think about entrepreneurship' Tom Eisenmann, Professor of Entrepreneurship, Harvard Business School

London, February
1988

# Reactions to the English Civil War 1642–1649

Each volume in the 'Problems in Focus' series is designed to make available to students important new work on key historical problems and periods that they encounter in their courses. Each volume is devoted to a central topic or theme, and the most important aspects of this are dealt with by specially commissioned studies from scholars in the relevant field. The editorial Introduction reviews the problem or period as a whole, and each chapter provides an assessment of the particular aspect, pointing out the areas of development and controversy, and indicating where conclusions can be drawn or where further work is necessary. An annotated bibliography serves as a guide to further reading.

# PROBLEMS IN FOCUS SERIES

FURTHER TITLES ARE IN PREPARATION

# Reactions to the English Civil War 1642–1649

EDITED BY
JOHN MORRILL

**M**
MACMILLAN

First published 1982
Reprinted 1986

Published by
MACMILLAN EDUCATION LTD
Houndmills, Basingstoke, Hampshire RG21 2XS
and London
Companies and representatives
throughout the world

Printed in Hong Kong

ISBN 0–333–27565–9 (hardcover)
ISBN 0–333–27566–7 (paperback)

# Contents

# Preface

I AM immensely grateful to all the contributors to this volume for their helpfulness, for their obedience over the length of their articles and over the time-limits set, and for answering queries so promptly and clearly. I was told that editing a collection of essays was one of the quickest ways to lose hair and friends: nothing could be further from the truth. I am particularly grateful to those contributors who made changes to their provisional titles and articles following changes in the initial 'team' and the need to accommodate two late changes of topic. My task has been made a simple one by the skill and understanding displayed by Sarah Mahaffy of the Macmillan Press. My wife agreed to our summer holiday in 1980 consisting of five weeks during which I spent the morning in record offices in some nice and some nasty county towns (the fruits of which are below) and the afternoons making amends to her and my children. For this, and much other forbearance in connection with the preparation of the book, she deserves my heartfelt thanks.

J.S.M.

# Introduction

## JOHN MORRILL

### I

IN his introduction to the companion volume to this collection of essays,[1] Conrad Russell laid down a challenge which has proved the most stimulating and widely discussed revision in early modern English history over the last twenty-five years. He distinguished between the two revolutions of mid-seventeenth-century England: the revolutions of 1641 and 1649. He committed himself and his team to explaining the first one only. His argument – admirably borne out by the essays in his volume – was that no one until the summer of 1641 expected, let alone wanted, a civil war to break out; and that those at Westminster whose actions in 1641–2 led to the creation of an organised Parliamentarian movement were essentially conservatives, reacting against the innovative administrative, fiscal, religious and cultural policies and actions of King Charles I. Much work in the past ten years has taken up Russell's thesis and the bulk of this new work has reinforced his conclusions and intuitions.[2]

Russell's book explicitly set out only to establish why civil war broke out in 1642. He did not attempt to explain the revolution of 1649.[3] Yet his book, so convincing in its revision of our views on the first crisis, made the second one even harder to understand. The question 'Why was Charles I executed?' has become easily the most difficult of the range of questions on Tudor and Stuart history with which those undergraduates I teach have to wrestle. If the Civil War came out of such a clear sky, if few wanted it and most of those who fought against the King did so for conservative reasons, why did things turn so *nasty*? Why was the King put on public trial and executed six-and-a-half years later? Why were monarchy, the House of Lords and the Church of England abolished?

The contributors to this volume were asked to bear these questions in mind and it is hoped that collectively they help to provide a context within which answers can be given. The purpose of this introduction is to introduce each of the articles and to offer a more general review of recent writings on the 1640s germane to our themes; it also seeks to review those aspects of the decade not comprehended by any of the essays. It is designed, in fact, to put a problem in focus.

II

We must begin by reflecting further on the ways recent work on the origins of the Civil War help to elucidate its nature.

The initial point is that few historians nowadays argue that the Civil War was long-planned or brought about wilfully and deliberately. This is as true of Marxist[4] as of 'revisionist' scholars. It is generally agreed that it came about because Charles I made a series of disastrous mistakes and miscalculations which drove into reluctant warmongering those who had continued until the last minute to hope for and to expect a peaceful resolution of their differences with him. There are, however, two broadly separate analyses of the reasons for Charles's blundering.

The first line of analysis denies that the King had any effective freedom of choice. His resources fell so hopelessly short of those needed for the tasks he was expected to perform that he was bound to fail. He could attempt to fulfil the expectations he had of himself and which his subjects had of him, but this would require him to arrogate to himself powers and resources which his subjects would not freely concede. Alternatively, he could live within his fiscal, legal and constitutional means, but would then be reviled for his failure to promote Reformation at home, the Protestant cause overseas, or even to protect his merchants from pirates.

The second line of argument grants Charles far greater freedom. Thus it can be shown that what caused civil wars in early modern Europe were disputes about titles or succession to the throne, foreign intrigues, underground churches, the centripetal tendencies for outlying provinces to pull away from the metropolitan base. Of all these dangers, none appeared to be a particular problem for England in the 1630s except, perhaps, for the last one. Certainly a comparison of the 1580s and the 1630s suggests greater potential for conflict in the former (with deep divisions over the succession, a predilection on the part of the Catholic powers to intervene in English affairs, a Puritan movement organising itself as a church-within-a-church and a Catholic minority confused in its political attitudes). By contrast, the 1630s saw Charles I with an unquestioned title to the throne, free from the meddling of foreign powers, facing a Puritanism no longer possessing an institutional coherence or clarity, and a tamed Catholicism. Furthermore, Charles's freedom of action can be seen as really quite considerable. The English administrative and legal system was the most unified in Europe, the social structure the most open and fluid in Europe. Even royal finances were really more healthy than they have often been portrayed as being. The Crown tripled its revenues between 1603 and 1639 (and doubled them even if inflation is taken into account); the budgets were balanced throughout the 1630s and Stuart indebtedness was less than that of any other Royal House in Europe (it is worth remembering too that royal bankruptcy abroad did not usually lead to civil war). Furthermore in the later 1630s Ship Money was the only source of revenue which was being even passively resisted, and that limited passive resistance did not prevent Ship Money from being an enormous fiscal success. In any case, Ship Money (paid not to the Exchequer but to the Treasurers of the Navy) was not an essential part of the budget and could have been abandoned at any point without sending the Crown into serious deficit. Of course, it is true that Charles I could not afford a militaristic foreign policy, but he did not have to have one. For the foreseeable future the Crown could pick and choose its quarrels with foreign rulers: no one was going to declare war on England. Most important of all, the long trend of rising prices and rising population was coming to an end (and not just in Britain). The English economy was moving into calmer waters.

All these factors would suggest that a civil war was unlikely in the conditions of the 1630s. Certainly the *potentiality* for breakdown, the extent of instability and political tensions, had been far greater in the early 1580s. Only Elizabeth's heartbeat kept England from civil war. But every political system has inherent weaknesses and there is always a *potentiality* for breakdown as well as a *potentiality* for evolutionary development. It is probably fair to say that no ruler since Henry V had so untroubled an inheritance as Charles I. The inherent strengths of his position were formidable and it took a remarkable inability to communicate and unerring bad judgement for Charles to find himself declaring war on his people in 1642. He was a necessary if not a sufficient cause of the war. The overwhelming majority of those contemporary observers who sought to explain the Great Rebellion saw no need to begin their search before 1625. Nor need we do so.

This does not mean, of course, that we need not study the long-term developments of the period 1540–1640: the major social, economic and institutional developments of that century determined the kind of civil war England had in the 1640s; they simply did not determine that England had to have a civil war. There were, of course, structural weaknesses in the Tudor and early Stuart state,[5] not least the dependence of the Crown on the voluntary support of the country gentry. Such men owed their offices to their birth, wealth and standing in their communities, not their standing in their local communities to their appointment as Crown officials. The demands made by the Crown increasingly appeared to such men as unreasonable. Charles's attempt to rule without Parliament was, indeed, as much symptom as cause of the collapse of the perceived identity of interest between Crown and political élites. The momentum of obedience which kept them serving the Crown in the 1630s could not disguise a growing anger and unease at the aspirations and aims of the Court. By 1640 it was overwhelmingly believed that Charles was an innovative and irresponsible monarch: that he tolerated the spread of Popery at Court and in government; that he sought to change the religion of Englishmen away from 'the pure religion of Queen Elizabeth and King James' by his support for Laudian clericalism; that his misuse of his prerogative powers constituted a threat to the security of mens' liberties and properties. Charles was a remote figure, unparalleled in his failure to communicate with his subjects. Civil war eventually broke out, however, only because all peaceful means of restoring a perceived identity of interest between King and political notions failed; the war was the final attempt to preserve the ancient constitution.

In 1640, there are a variety of possible ways the crisis could have been resolved. It seems likely however, that Charles's abject surrender of vital prerogatives and institutions in the first six months destroyed all hopes of a peaceful outcome. Although it was not until the autumn and winter of 1641–2 that anyone seriously contemplated the possibility (let alone the probability or desirability) of a civil war, the situation had already got out of hand. As late as May 1641, self-delusion was on every side: above all John Pym and his circle, having stripped the King of all contentious instruments of government, were still persuading themselves that the crisis would end once they took over as the King's chief advisers, committed to an expansionist policy on a shoestring budget. In fact, their prospects of harnessing backbench support for a programme which would endow the King with fresh fiscal resources and an effective administration were bleak. In any case, Charles's actions made it apparent that he would not stick by the concessions he had already made any longer than he had to. The only issue had already become what sort of anarchy England would dissolve into.

What do we need to conclude from the foregoing? In 1642 there were, in the Parliamentary leadership, no republicans, even covert ones (with the obvious exception of Henry Marten). Well over 90 per cent of all MPs who sided against the King were committed to a doctrine of mixed or limited monarchy (with sovereignty lying in King-in-Parliament: King, Lords and Commons); to a reconstituted national Church; and to the existing social and economic order. In 1642 the Parliamentarian leadership overwhelmingly saw itself as conservative, preserving the essentials of the constitution from Popery and arbitrary government.

Conservatives that they were, they had still to justify taking up arms against their anointed King. It is significant that it is only at the last moment, when events forced them to drastic actions, that theories of resistance were evolved.[6] It is, in fact, one of the strongest arguments which can be deployed against those who see the early Stuart period as one of an increasing radicalisation of the 'opposition' to the Crown, that there is so little evidence of anyone proclaiming a right of resistance to tyrants, let alone to James or Charles I. English Catholic apologists came largely to disown resistance theories and the only Protestant Englishman to argue a case sympathetic to active resistance *in extremis* was Ralph Brownrigg, subsequently a bishop and a Royalist.[7] Certainly generations of Puritans availed themselves of the rights of passive disobedience offered to them in the Anglican *Book of Homilies*;[8] whenever they were confronted by commands from civil or ecclesiastical authorities which were against their consciences, they passively neglected to obey and meekly took the consequences. For example, in the case of 'unconstitutional' taxation, they refused to pay, challenged the propriety of the writs in the courts, and finally submitted without violence to distraint of their goods or imprisonment of their bodies. Many men availed themselves of this doctrine to disrupt the attempts of Whitgift, Bancroft and Laud to achieve ecclesiastical uniformity, and of Salisbury, Buckingham and others to achieve fiscal conformity. It has never been demonstrated that there were more men engaged in acts of passive disobedience in the 1620s and 1630s than in the 1580s and 1590s (or for that matter than in the 1520s and 1530s); let alone that such obstruction was effective. There was no attempt, however, to justify physical, violent resistance to 'unlawful' acts by King or Church. It has been argued that when men lose their lives (or at least their ears) for less, one would not expect a full and frank exchange of views on the subject. Yet it is surely odd that in a land where Catholic recusants did die for saying such things, no Puritan can be found committing such a view to paper privately rather than publicly, even from the safety of exile.

Instead, it took the desperate atmosphere of 1642 for the more radical options to be considered, debated, embraced.[9] Only very reluctantly, in the wake of Parliament's claim to be solely responsible for the protection of the realm, was an ultimate right of self-defence articulated. In the course of 1642, three separate lines of argument were developed. The first was that the King was so affected by the venom poured into his ears by his wicked counsellors that he was no longer responsible for his actions. He had been, as it were, brainwashed, and had to be rescued and deprogrammed. This required others to rule in his name for a moderately long period – twenty years – by which time it could be safely assumed that he would be dead or recovered. This line of argument led John Pym seriously to investigate the precedents of the 1370s and 1450s, decades during which Edward III was senile and Henry VI mad.[10] The second justification derived from a radical reinterpretation of the doctrine of the King's two bodies. Charles Stuart the man was held to have betrayed the office which he held. Those who opposed Charles Stuart were opposing the body of the King but defending the office which he had betrayed. The purpose of the Civil War was to force the King to behave himself in accordance with the rights and duties of his office.

The final argument was that Charles had violated the original contract by which King and people were bound together. He had threatened, by his actions, the basic inalienable right of the people to security in their lives and goods, and the people could therefore withdraw their obedience until such time as the King undertook to act in ways consonant with their security.

It is worth stressing that although all these arguments were advanced in 1642 to justify limited resistance to the existing monarch, all of them could as easily be employed to advance far more radical remedies: deposition and/or regicide. There is not a shred of evidence that this was recognised at the time. Instead their use in 1642 confirms that the objective on all sides was to preserve the constitution and not to change it.

Both the Royalist and Parliamentarian parties were coalitions of conservatives and radicals, with the conservatives predominant at the outset. Studies of the Royalist party have for the past thirty years built on Brian Wormald's brilliant analysis of the movement of Edward Hyde (future earl of Clarendon) from oppositionist in the 1630s and in 1640–1 to constitutional Royalist in 1641–2.[11] The way in which the functional radicalism of Pym and his followers drove a great mass of moderate men back into the arms of the King and thus created the Royalist party is one of the best understood aspects of the period. There has also been agreement that the *mentality* and *instincts* of most Parliamentarians was to preserve the constitution. The aims of the majority were designed simply to ensure that fresh royal perfidy did not overturn the measures taken in 1640–1 to rebalance the constitution. Yet the intellectual justifications for that moderation remain obscure. We understand the constitutional Royalism of men like Hyde, Falkland and Colepepper. It is not so easy to find any defence of the Parliamentarian constitutionalism of those comparably great intellectuals and lawyers who opposed the King. The pursuit of moderate ends is seen as lacking a coherent legal and philosophical base; the Nineteen Propositions became an arid document, a hoarse war-cry, grounded in men's fears and ambitions and not in reason. If moderate Parliamentarians could give no credible intellectual account of their actions, could not defend their cause before an anxious and attentive nation, then their defeat in the later 1640s in the dialectic with the radicals (whose ideas, much studied, clearly did possess a cogency and internal logic) becomes less surprising.[12] But, in fact, there was a common-law case for the Militia Ordinance as well as one against it; the Royalists do not have all the best arguments. The importance of Richard Tuck's article in this volume is precisely that he shows how one influential figure – John Selden, most renowned of all living common lawyers – could take each new development in his stride, and how (in narrowly legal terms) the case for Parliament's actions was as rooted in the experience of the law as was the King's case, if not more so. It confirms that, in 1642, the objective on all sides was to preserve the constitution and not to change it. This could not be said of those who, in 1649, chopped off the King's head, abolished monarchy and House of Lords and set the seal on the abolition of the Church of England.

III

The realisation that the country was drifting into a civil war sank in gradually and reluctantly. The reaction of the majority was to keep the war at arm's length. Initially, most men assumed that it would be a short war: two armies would gather, they would march against one another and would fight a single great battle. The war would be over. They therefore based their behaviour on that assumption. They sought to neutralise their own area; or to secure it in the name of one side or the other, keeping the peace and awaiting the outcome elsewhere; or to barricade themselves into their homes and to defy all-comers; or to pay whatever either side demanded of them. Many enlisted on the assumption that it would be a short war, and that they would soon get back to their ordinary pursuits. All these groups assumed that when the armies of King and Parliament met, there would be an outright victor: most men had not considered the possibility of a draw, which is what the battle of Edgehill in southern Warwickshire on 23 October 1642 in fact was.

In the opening chapter of this book, Anthony Fletcher demonstrates how complex was the outbreak of hostilities in the various regions. The variety of responses, pressures, the very untidiness of the way that England went to war, has militated against all efforts to distinguish two coherent or distinctive parties.

There is little evidence that the English Civil War began as a social conflict.[13] The gentry were divided down the middle: attempts to distinguish the allegiance of greater and lesser gentry, rising and declining gentry, ancient and *arriviste* gentry, office-holding and 'mere' gentry have largely failed. This is partly because so many men followed the line of least resistance, simply obeyed orders, wanted to support both sides or neither, that the attempt to distinguish two clear parties is anyway an artificial one. If – as several historians have attempted to do – lists of Royalist and Parliamentarian gentry are drawn up from surviving lists of office-holders, of army officers, of those whose lands were confiscated by one side or the other for political obstructiveness, no identifiable difference (except one to which we shall return – religion) can be found between the two sides. All quantitative approaches have failed because they proceed to identify people on the basis of their activity rather than of their intention. If we were able to establish the names of those who believed either in the Royalist cause for its own sake or in the Parliamentarian cause for the sake of the achievement of a godly reformation in Church and State, then we might find clear distinctions. These listings could not be exhaustive. Such incompleteness is inevitable given that the sources are so often silent or misleading on questions of motivation. But they need not be exhaustive. A cross-section of each party is adequate. Family papers allow historians to identify the radical groups within Parliamentarian movements who were dedicated to victory and to a godly reformation. It would be possible to draw up lists of such men for many counties. Similar groups could be identified within the Royalist parties. The remaining members of both parties could then be examined independently and together and would quite probably look very much alike and would stand in clear contrast to both groups of militants. It is probable that in the north and west of England, the committed Royalists would appear as powerful groups of leading gentry, including dominant elements within the ruling élite, bound together by a fear of social revolution from below and the need to preserve hierarchy in Church and State, allied (with differing degrees of discomfort) to leading recusant families: and that the Parliamentarian radicals would be led by one or two leading gentry, but otherwise would be dominated by gentlemen of middling wealth, often from just outside the county office-holding circle, often of recent gentry origin with very strong commitment not simply to a reversal of Laudian innovation, but to the radical reform of the Elizabethan settlement and to the creation of a society influenced by godly Christian values and integrity. It must be stressed, however, that such an interpretation is likely to hold true only of the north and west.[14] In East Anglia, by contrast, control of the Parliamentarian movement remained in the hands of a moderate 'Puritan' establishment which looked initially for little social and economic reform, and for a limited reform of the Church.[15]

The 'honest radicals'[16] of the north and west (to take up David Underdown's terms for them) were drawn not only from amongst the gentry but also from amongst the yeomen and the rural and urban artisans – the 'middling sorts'. And they call into question the assumption that it is the gentry alone who determined the political alignment of a county in the Civil War. A good deal of recent work has shown a growing self-confidence and independence in the attitudes and behaviour of substantial yeoman-farmers, craftsmen and so on. The substitution of the parish for the manor as the principal unit of local government represents a transfer of effective authority from the generality of tenants and freeholders to an aristocracy of wealthy farmers and craftsmen, and it is clear that such men could and did wield considerable authority over the poor and rootless. Such men were often impatient at the failure of existing secular and ecclesiastical authorities to support their efforts to maintain order and discipline. Derek Hirst has stressed the growing political maturity and electoral volatility of freeholders and freemen (although it is clear that that volatility was only

effectual when the gentry allowed themselves to be divided).[17]
Interpretations of allegiance which rest content with analyses of
gentry activity are thus inadequate, and have been directly
attacked by Brian Manning and Joyce Malcolm.[18] Their work
makes it obvious that the 'middling sort' were capable of
independent action and that many did not wait upon the
gentry's decisions. Similarly, the idea that the labourers,
cottagers and others blindly followed their landlords' and
masters' lead needs important qualification. In my view,[19]
these recent works raise legitimate questions, but do not provide satisfying answers. Much more work needs to be done on
the question of non-gentry allegiance. Meanwhile, it would be
surprising if in fact the role of the 'middling sort' is decisive. For
it seems likely that the 'middling sort' were as divided as were
the gentry. The yeomanry, clothworkers and urban craftsmen
certainly included some very highly motivated and committed
radicals (particularly on religious questions), perhaps the most
highly motivated groups on either side. But equally there is
plenty of evidence that these very social groups displayed some
of the most committed neutral and anti-war sentiment. Not all
grand juries were packed, yet grand juries are frequently to be
found initiating neutralist petitions and leading neutralist
movements both in 1642 and 1645; the Clubmen risings of 1645,
whether they are treated as crypto-Royalist or neutralist,[20]
were the creation of the middling sort. Furthermore, there is no
evidence that minor officials (constables, churchwardens and
so on) obstructed Royalist more than they did Parliamentarian
administration, and in many counties assemblies of freeholders agreed to vote extensive contributions to the Royalist
cause. Nonetheless, while a majority of those below the gentry
probably accepted the leadership of the old élite, and while a
majority probably continued to look for the continuance of
known ways in Church and State, there is clearly more work to
be done on the extent and nature of popular movements before,
during and after the war.

The Civil War did not begin as a social struggle: it is not
much clearer how far it ended up as one. A large number of men
on both sides found the demands of war too disturbing, too
uncomfortable to their consciences, for them to continue to
serve. They retired from the fray. Equally, on both sides, there

was a recognition of the vitality and ruthlessness of a large number of men from minor gentry and non-gentry backgrounds and these men found themselves taking an increasingly prominent part in the fighting. There was also a great expansion in the number of administrative and executive posts available for such men. This is as true of the Royalist as of the Parliamentarian movements, as several recent studies have made clear.[21] Such a perspective will necessarily affect our judgement of the significance in the shift of the social basis of power in the 1640s. It is, furthermore, crucial to note that the change represents a shift of power *within* the gentry, not from the gentry: it is the middling squires, not the middling sorts, who governed England in the Interregnum.[22]

If the Civil War cannot plausibly be seen as a social struggle, neither can it be seen as a struggle between a 'progressive' south and east and a 'traditional' north and west. This view was plausible enough when it was believed that the early Stuart monarchy represented a feeble last stand of the old feudal–paternalistic order against progressive forces and incipient capitalistic virtues.[23] It becomes less plausible once that assumption is swept away. It is in fact not the case that the north and west were solidly Royalist and the south and east solidly Parliamentarian. As Anthony Fletcher shows below, the geographical pattern is highly complex and few areas were solidly behind one side or the other. Furthermore, it was the pre-emptive action of King or the Houses which quickly gave control to their supporters in some deeply divided counties. Kent and Somerset are two examples. In fact, the principal determinant of allegiance in 1642 is proximity to the King's person or to Westminster. Those counties within the immediate control of the Houses were quickly integrated into the war. It seems probable that in Kent, for example, a great majority of the county community – gentry and freeholders – were pro-Royalist. Certainly the petitions drawn up at quarter sessions and assizes in 1641–2 demonstrate a mounting anxiety over the drift of political events at Westminster and with religious iconoclasm locally and elsewhere. What proved decisive in cowing, if not converting, the majority was not popular radicalism (largely confined to the towns and inchoate). Rather it was the decisive action taken by a minority of gentry, organised and armed by the Houses, who seized the initiative. The repression which followed the legal petitioning of the winter and spring of 1641–2, involving astonishing abuses by Pym and his colleagues of legal forms and procedures, stunned the majority into an increasingly sullen acquiescence.[24] As Brigadier Peter Young said in a recent lecture, if London had been where Birmingham is, then Kent would have been Royalist.[25] Similarly, the King's strength in the north can be largely explained by his personal presence there and his peregrination of the north-midlands counties in August and September 1642. The West Country, Wales and the far north were not openly and solidly Royalist until some months later.

It does seem likely that work in progress on the 'ecology of allegiance' will lead to a far more subtle picture. Buchanan Sharp's study of grain and enclosure rioters in the west of England in the fifty years before the Civil War convincingly demonstrates that violent protests were generally led by rural artisans (artificers) particularly in the clothing trades, were located principally in the less closely structured and disciplined woodland and heathland areas, and were marked by very considerable hostility towards the gentry or at least towards particular gentlemen. His study of the renewed outbreak of enclosure rioting in 1641–2 and in the later 1640s has already been taken as support for the views of Christopher Hill and Brian Manning that the middling sort constituted the backbone of Parliamentarianism. It is an argument which Sharp specifically disowns: 'there is little solid evidence that the widespread outbreaks of popular disorder of 1641 and 1642 were in any real sense motivated by pro-parliamentarian political sympathies or viewed with anything but suspicion by prominent parliamentarians'; 'the second western rising demonstrates the indifference of many ordinary people in the west to the issues involved in the civil war.'[26] He further emphasises that what lay behind such disturbances was the weakening of traditional institutions of political and social control, together with the increased burdens war imposed. This conclusion is largely borne out by work in progress by David Underdown[27] which indicates that there was little to distinguish the popular support achieved by King and Parliament in rural areas of western England; but that popular support for the King was strong in

the market towns (including the decaying ones) while support
for Parliament was very marked in the clothing towns. It is too
early to comment on the significance of his findings, but once
again a connection with an ingrained radical religious tradition,
or else the connection between the clothing towns and a pattern
of recurrent economic crises exacerbated by clumsy and ineffec-
tual royal intervention, is suggested.

One must, however, be cautious about over-schematising the
reactions in towns, as in the countryside, particularly since so
little work has been undertaken on towns in comparison with
the burgeoning number of county studies. Roger Howell's
study below of urban responses is hesitant to reach firm conclusions and that is important and salutary. Too often it has
been asserted that towns were naturally more radical than the
county communities, that they witnessed earlier and more
violent struggles for control between ruling élites and groups of
less wealthy freemen. Howell shows that although there are
examples of towns where religious or economic radicals seized
power during the war, that is only one of several common
patterns. It is also possible that the threat which civil war posed
to the economic and trading interests of towns might lead to a
shelving of local disputes, a sinking of rivalries at least as long as
external threats jeopardised the common interest. My own
provisional researches also indicate that it just is not true that
most towns were Parliamentarian. If we take the Ship Money
assessments of the 1630s as a rough-and-ready guide to the
ranking of towns, we find that while Parliament gained control
of the great majority of ports, the King gained a majority of
inland towns assessed at over £100 in 1636.[28] It is at least
arguable that the Parliamentarian predominance amongst the
ports owed as much to the economic dependency of the outports
on London as it did to a greater measure of radicalism. To
declare against London was to threaten the local economy.
Since it is arguable that most large inland towns followed the
lead of their rural hinterland it can be hypothesised that the key
to much urban allegiance lies in their following the line of
immediate economic self-interest. David Underdown's work,
however, suggests that there are grounds for exempting the
small and middling clothing towns of the west country, Yorkshire and (less certainly) East Anglia from this pattern.

If there were profound differences between the two sides, they were over religion. In 1642–3 almost all those who can be found committed to (as against going along with) the King were either Catholic recusants or strong upholders of episcopacy. It may be that a majority of Catholics were non-participants,[29] but Catholics constituted a crucial element in the Royalist activists of the north of England and elsewhere; over one-third of the regimental officers in the six northern counties, for example.[30] Recent work also suggests the vital part petitioning in defence of episcopacy and the Prayer Book played in the formation of the Royalist parties throughout England.[31] On the Parliamentarian side can be found almost all those who campaigned against bishops and a great many who, while they were prepared to argue for a modified episcopacy, saw the structure of Church government as optional and negotiable.[32] More generally, there was an obsessive anti-Catholicism amongst most Parliamentarians, nurtured over decades in the struggle against Spain and the Jesuits, and now increasingly focused on the Court itself. The rhetoric of Pym and his fellow-leaders testifying to the Popish penetration to the very centre of power was not feigned: it was widely believed and not wholly foolish. The anti-Catholic riots throughout England were as much the product as the cause of the heightened perception that Charles had abdicated his responsibilities to guard his people from the Popish anti-Christ.[33]

The role of religion in creating and sustaining the Parliamentarian movement cannot be overestimated. Religious issues have too often been presented simplistically as a squabble over Church government. What advanced Protestants (Puritans if you like) at all levels of English society were concerned with in the 1640s was building a New Jerusalem, cleansing the political, legal, ecclesiastical and educational institutions of their corruptions and building a more godly society. This vision was held by those whom we would normally see as on the conservative wing of the movement (for example Simonds d'Ewes) as well as radicals. Most Puritans believed in the existing pattern of social and political institutions; they simply wished to make them work better and for this reason they demanded a better form of godly discipline: godly magistrates backing up the exhortations of godly preachers.[34] This is the mentality of those whom Brian Manning has dubbed the 'godly people' and David Underdown the 'honest radicals',[35] the gentry, yeomen, merchants and others – a cross-section of society – who were the Parliamentarian activists of the 1640s. They constituted the dynamic element which made the launching of the Parliamentarian war effort possible. Initially their programme of action was essentially concerned with the liberation of the preacher and the magistrate from anti-Christian constraints. But the war, by overthrowing so many certainties, so many intellectual and institutional walls, opened up unrecognised vistas.

Most dramatically, we can see this in the collapse of the Calvinist consensus: in 1641–2, few Protestant intellectuals would have dissented from the mainstream orthodoxy of the Reformation which laid stress on the total depravity of man, his intellectual and moral distance from God, and his inability to overcome his sinful nature in order to claim salvation, which was the free gift of God alone. In the course of the 1640s, men like John Lilburne and John Milton,[36] and many more, abandoned these views and came to see man as perfectible, rational, bathed in accessible grace and able to command it. The consequences for moral and pastoral theology, and for doctrines of Church government, were immense.

How did this liberation come about? In part it was clearly the consequence of the unprecedented freedom of expression and of the accessibility of heterodox opinions in hundreds of cheap pamphlets flooding the market. In part, it was also a consequence of the mental shock which the very fact of a civil war creates. When so many cosy certainties of life, when so many familiar institutions, cherished assumptions, unquestioned values, are overturned, everything that seemed established and ordered can become uncertain, unfixed. Charles Webster has demonstrated, for example, how the 1640s and 1650s produced an astonishing array of proposals for the fundamental overhaul of educational, medical and social institutions.[37] The connection between the dislocations accompanying a civil war and the collapse of an intellectual or theological consensus is suggested by the absence of any such theological disintegration in New England in the 1640s, free from the experience of civil war. The nature and extent of this collapse of Protestant unity powerfully reinforced the religious conservatism which is the subject of my own chapter below. But it also constituted one of the many ways in which the events of the decade created an entirely new intellectual climate and a fresh series of challenges in the late 1640s.

IV

From 1643 to 1646 England experienced full-scale civil war. Probably as many as one in ten of all adult males were in arms at any given moment during the summers of 1643, 1644, 1645 and perhaps one in four or one in five of all adult males bore arms at some point during the war.[38] The financial resources which were needed to pay, arm, feed and bury these men were beyond measure the greatest ever called forth from the English people. The administrative and legal tyranny which both sides licensed in order to liberate these resources also involved the violation of every clause of the Petition of Right and much that was held to be guaranteed by *Magna Carta*. The economy, particularly along the Severn and Thames valleys, was severely hampered. Although some regions saw far more of the fighting, far more quartering and plundering than others, no areas were immune from a military presence and a crushing fiscal and administrative yoke. Royalist areas may have seen more attempts to preserve traditional forms of local government, but they also experienced more serious collapses of military discipline. In this volume, Donald Pennington chronicles the greedy, peremptory demands of those fuelling the engines of war, and Robert Ashton discusses the way these demands were perceived and reacted against by most Englishmen.

By 1646 Parliament had gained a military victory over the King. Recent research has played down the purely military factors in that victory and has tended to stress logistic and administrative ones. Neither side developed new strategic or tactical methods; both sides had difficulty in maintaining their armies at full strength, although it is probable that the King had more difficulty in keeping a proper balance of infantry and cavalry;[39] both sides were desperately short of artillery and were constantly improvising supplies of small arms and ammunition (organ pipes had to be melted down to make bullets, bedcords stripped from mattresses in besieged towns to

provide match for the musketeers, while at the siege of
Gloucester, the King – desperately short of cannon – got Dr
Chillingworth to make a 'great store of engines after the manner
of the Roman *testudines*').[40] It is becoming plain that victory is
not to be ascribed to the discipline and godliness of the New
Model. Mark Kishlansky has shown that the creation of this
army in the winter of 1644–5 was more an administrative
reorganisation and rationalisation than it was a politico-
religious *coup*; that it was essentially a merger of three existing
armies with a regimental officer corps constructed on largely
non-political, non-religious lines and comprising a substantial
number of raw and reluctant recruits and ex-Royalist soldiers.
It was distinguished in 1645 not by its discipline, let alone its
godliness, but by its regular pay. The key is not radicalisation
but professionalisation[41] (a point of view reinforced by Ronald
Hutton in this volume when he demonstrates similar developments taking place in the Royalist armies). Not only was the
New Model a union of three existing armies: Royalist strategy
alone disrupted a plan to divide it into distinct campaigning units
in the summer of 1645. Other military factors are also of secondary importance. The contribution of the 20,000 Scots soldiers
who crossed into England in the winter of 1643–4 was disappointing, not least because they were constantly looking back
home, nervously watching the successful hit-and-run tactics of
Montrose and his Royalist Highlanders. The contribution of
the Navy, in supplying besieged Parliamentarian towns and
blockading Royalist ones, is also easy to overrate.[42]

More important to Parliament's victory is the contribution of
the capital. The support of London for the radicals in the two
Houses was, of course, essential to the achievement and con-
solidation of the constitutional revolution of 1640–2. This
support took the form not only of mass demonstrations and
picketing of the Houses at the time of crucial votes, but also the
vital takeover of city government itself by those sympathetic to
Pym and his aims. This was, however, only the beginning of
London's contribution to the Parliamentarian war effort. The
unemployed and the religiously committed (the proportions are
unknown) swelled the ranks of the earl of Essex's army (at least
6000 amongst the initial recruits). This manpower both
enabled Essex to be the first in the field and helped to maintain

numbers once the initial flow of volunteers elsewhere slowed
up. More important even than men was the money London
supplied. Seventy per cent of all customs duties were contributed by London; the assessments on London constituted
between a quarter and a third of all those received by the
treasurers during the war; the excise was settled in London and
hardly at all elsewhere. Crucially, the corporation and the great
livery companies continued to advance loans against future
revenues to keep the wheels of war turning. Almost three-
quarters of all revenues were anticipated in this way. By 1645 it
made all the difference to the financing of the two sides. If a
single cause of Parliament's victory had to be chosen, this would
be it.[43]

Most historians would also argue that Parliament generally
organised and deployed its resources more efficiently. Parliament evolved a committee-structure at county, regional and
national levels which was untidy, uneven but ultimately effective in releasing men, supplies and cash for the war. What made
the system work was less its intrinsic discipline and coherence
than its remarkable ruthlessness and arbitrariness. The King's
organisation was more bedevilled by overlapping jurisdictions
and conflicting responsibilities, but even more by its ultimate
lack of forcefulness. Ronald Hutton offers below an account of
the changing organisational structure which counteracts the
usual assertion that the Royalists became less and less efficient
as the war wore on. Hutton does not claim, however, that the
Royalists were as well organised as their enemies. They
improved, but continued to trail, in effectiveness.

An enormous amount could be learnt from a study that
looked at the 1640s from Charles's point of view, that set out not
to show why he failed, but what options were open to him at
particular junctures and how his positive acts required
responses from his enemies. All defeated chess-players have
made bad moves, but they have frequently enjoyed the initiative for long stretches of the game and their opponents have
sometimes had less play than they have had. This was arguably
the case, for example, in the nine months from the summer
1641: what if Charles had summoned Parliament to meet him at
York on his return from Scotland? What if he had refused to
leave London? It is one of the merits of Ronald Hutton's paper

that he demonstrates that the Royalist war effort had a coherence, a development, a logical progression of its own: it was not increasingly left behind by the growing sophistication of Parliament's armies and administration.

Hutton is concerned with the resilience of the Royalist war machinery; another chapter examines the resilience of the established religion to the Puritan challenge of the 1640s. Beneath the near-universal rejection of Archbishop Laud and his ecclesiastical aspirations, lay an enormous commitment to the hybrid religious forms and observances created in the mid-sixteenth century and now part of the daily and weekly experience of millions of Englishmen. My essay attempts to demonstrate that the godly reformation enacted in the 1640s was an abject failure. It was a failure, certainly, in part because of the growing disunity of the Puritans. But the hopes of the gentry-MPs for an orderly, seemly Protestant discipline were shattered just as much by an effective resistance from men at all levels of society, as by the impatience of the radicals. The Prayer Book and the celebration of Christmas and Easter proved as dear as the existence of the monarchy itself. The frustration and disillusion of MPs at the failure of their godly reformation was a powerful conditioning force in the crises of 1647–8.

v

Between the spring of 1646 and the summer of 1647 the Houses came to recognise that victory on the battlefield had solved none of the problems which brought about the war, but had created immense new problems.[44] They still had to treat with a king utterly insincere, utterly unchastened (except by the belief that his concessions of 1640–2 constituted a breach of his sacred trust and that the scourge of civil war was the consequence of his failures in those years) and deluded into imagining that he could divide and rule his enemies. In 1642, the problem had been difficult enough: how to obtain binding undertakings from so shifty a man that he would wield his personal authority responsibly. But the problem seemed manageable. Those who fought for Parliament seem honestly to have believed that if the King transferred certain powers to the keeping of the Houses he would be adequately restricted. The terms offered to the King in 1646–7 (and indeed 1648) were generically the same as those contained in the Nineteen Propositions.[45] Thus the precise extent of the powers to be transferred might change (from parliamentary vetting of royal nominees for office to parliamentary nomination and royal ratification); the period during which royal authority would be constrained might change; the nature of the reformed church might cease to be nebulous and negotiable and become a clear scheme worked out by an assembly of divines and amended by the Houses. But few new issues appeared in the terms, the most contentious being the fate of more than three thousand Royalist gentry and others who had had their estates confiscated. The basic premise remained the same: the way to restrain an arbitrary king was to expand the powers of a Parliament which was (in Henry Parker's phrase) 'the quintessence of the people', the guarantor of their liberties. In 1642 no one – not even Royalist apologists – queried that claim. After 1646 that assumption – still built into the Newcastle Propositions of 1646 and the Newport Propositions of 1648 – was widely questioned. The experience of war had taught men that Parliament was as capable of eroding liberties, of arbitrary actions, as the King had ever been. The violence and disruptions of war had already led to one backlash in the provinces: between February and November 1645, armed neutralist movements in twelve or more counties in southern and western England represented a determination to put an end to the administrative tyranny and material desolation occasioned by the war. Many of these Clubmen groups favoured one side rather than the other, but all were committed to an early peace, the removal of 'the insufferable, insolent, arbitrary power that hath bin used among us'. A preference for King or Parliament did not preclude a preference for peace above both.[46] Thus, increasingly throughout 1646–7, in petitions, especially those drawn up by grand juries (representing the general body of freeholders) at quarter sessions and assizes, the country clamoured for a restoration of normal government: the abolition of county committees and of new taxes, the restoration of jury trial and ancient local institutions, measures to restore regional economies. All these envisaged the restoration of the King to his proper powers and to his natural headship of his people. Nowhere was the feeling stronger than in the ring of counties around London, solidly Parliamentarian during the war, from which came petitions representing 'overwhelming demonstrations . . . of opposition to military government'.[47] To transfer power and authority from an arbitrary king to an arbitrary parliament in these circumstances was clearly a nonsense.

The pressures on Parliament were intensified by the deteriorating economic situation. Food prices in these years had reached a new high; plague and dearth stalked hand-in-hand; the dislocation of communications (probably a majority of the bridges on the king's highway had been destroyed or had collapsed) added to the problems of distribution so that trade was badly hit. All this affected the underemployed, particularly in the towns and most of all in London. The demobilisation of soldiers, many of them maimed by the war, would add to their number. Yet taxation was at a terrifying level. The assessment was intended to bring in each year a sum double the total income Charles I had inherited; to that was added excises on basic commodities (especially beer and salt) and attempts were being made to impose them effectively for the first time. In large areas in the Home Counties and East Anglia (but also throughout the north), the dispersed regiments and troops of the Army stood on free quarter (that is, taking board and lodging from the civilian population in return for paper promises of future payment). Yet the arrears of the Army were growing.

For a majority of Englishmen, then, the Civil War had solved nothing, and they yearned to wish it away, to get back to the old certainties and to hope for the best. Nothing demonstrates this better than the growing militancy of religious conservatives throughout England in the second half of 1647. There was a growing feeling that any terms from the King were better than none. But there was a radical alternative. If Parliament and King had both violated their trust, both must be called to account; if all existing institutions had proved arbitrary, then all must be swept away. The Levellers were amongst the first to claim that all existing contracts between government and governed were null and void, and that a fresh start had to be made. The starting-point for Leveller political thought was this: that there needed to be a new social contract, a new *Agreement of the People* (in a literal sense) by which all those who wished to enjoy political rights were to subscribe a new constitution which would guarantee fundamental rights. It would guarantee these rights by establishing a massive decentralisation and democratisation of power. All offices were to be held for short periods, all officers (judicial, administrative, military as well as law-making) were to be elected and all officers accountable directly to their electors at the end of their terms. Most functions of government were decentralised. The Leveller conception of democracy was emphatically not the modern one of legislative majoritarianism. Parliaments were to meet for short periods and their powers were to be attenuated by constitutional reservations which would bar them from discussing certain fundamentals (above all religious freedom). Just as the *Agreement* envisaged an individual subscription by all members of the community, so their model of democracy probably derived much more from their experience as members of gathered churches where all saints sought out a common agreement, or the primitive democracy of the manor, than it did from thoughts about expanding the franchise in parliamentary elections. True freedom would come more from free juries than from a free parliament. Such ideas are very clearly and expressly the outcome of experiences in the 1640s.[48] This programme – coupled with campaigns to protect the interests of independent small producers in town and countryside – understandably made little headway with MPs. It certainly made great, if temporary, progress in London, less progress in the provincial towns and little headway in the countryside. There has been much recent argument about the Levellers' penetration of the Army.[49] Most commentators now feel that – except briefly in the summer of 1647 – the Levellers never controlled more than a tiny minority of the soldiers, but the strength of the appeals from Leveller leaders to their comrades-in-arms certainly added further to the perplexity of MPs.

In the course of 1646–7, Parliament tried to meet the clamours of protest from across England: thousands of men in provincial armies were disbanded; the common-law courts were restored centrally and locally; a majority of the Royalists who had had their lands confiscated were allowed to negotiate the return of those lands in exchange for the payment of substantial fines and the swearing of oaths for their future good behaviour; the Scots were paid off and sent home (a necessary prelude to the attempt to disband the New Model); negotiations with the King were given a fresh urgency; agreement was finally reached on the new national Church to supplant the episcopal one and the first (unavailing) steps taken to make it a reality; finally the Houses set out to divide the New Model, with a plan to send 12,600 men to complete the settlement of the Irish problem and honourably to disband the rest. It was a coherent and sensible programme, backed by a great majority of MPs.[50] It seemed only a short distance from success when it foundered on the inability of the majority in the Commons to recognise the particular and proper anxieties of the soldiers of the New Model about the hazards of premature disbandment.[57] The soldiers were very conscious that their comrades in the provincial armies had been disbanded with vague promises of future payments of their arrears which had then been dishonoured. Their own arrears stood at over one million pounds. A precipitate disbandment would not safeguard this or other vital interests. For example, scores of soldiers were being vindictively sued or indicted in the courts for acts they carried out in time of war, and they looked to Parliament to protect them from such harassment; they wanted a clear commitment by Parliament that those who had served would not be recalled to arms; that widows and orphans were properly cared for; that disbanded soldiers be allowed to follow trades of their choice or be readmitted to tenancies over the wishes of hostile landlords. These were reasonable demands, but they required massive increases in taxation and extensions of the powers and responsibilities of county committees if they were to be implemented.

This was the unpalatable choice MPs had to make: to meet the legitimate demands of the Army at the expense of further alienating the provinces, or to meet the demands of the counties and to get rid of the Army for a pittance. In April and May 1647, the great majority opted for the latter, as the coping stone to a year of 'healing and settling' policies. But they handled the issue insensitively and unskilfully. The Army refused to be humiliated. After an exhausting few weeks of anxious self-examination, a majority of the soldiers and officers reached the conclusion that they had a right and duty to defend their own interests. They came to recognise in Parliament's actions an insupportable betrayal of trust. For a time, indeed, Leveller ideas gave the New Model a rationale of their mistreatment by, and a justification for defiance of, the Parliament. A large minority of officers who did not accept such arguments resigned or were cashiered, but the majority continued to act and speak for the rank and file. Mark Kishlansky's essay below examines the public declarations of the Army over the next eighteen months, and demonstrates how the Army came to rationalise and to justify its defiance of the Houses and its direct involvement in constitution-making.

The crucial decision was the one reached in late July/early August 1647: that the malignant spirits who had turned the Commons against its loyal Army should be expelled. For the first but not the only time, the Army marched on London, and plucked out the eleven leading 'incendiaries'. The great majority of MPs, who had previously backed the moderates, recognising now the brute facts of military power, swung round and voted the Army all the things it wanted. After heated exchanges in late October and early November within the Army, the vast majority endorsed the actions of the Grandees, and by the end of December a string of ordinances had set up committees with draconian powers to safeguard the pay, security and material interests of the soldiery and had shelved the problem of Ireland. The consequence of this new wave of taxes and arbitrary actions had the result that most MPs had always feared: a second Civil War which was far more than a desperate conjunction of the King with the Scots (who had convinced themselves that Parliament was reneging on its promise to bring in a strict church settlement consonant with theirs). This second Civil War was essentially a revolt of the provinces. It was not a series of insurrections by committed Royalists so much as a widespread revolt by all those who found Parliamentary tyranny insupportable. These included the whole county community of Kent, alienated Parliamentarian activists in East Anglia and South Wales, and a recrudescent Clubmen movement in the west.[52]

Yet when these uncoordinated risings were finally crushed or fizzled out in the autumn of 1648, the situation was exactly the same as it had been eighteen months earlier, except perhaps that the options were starker. At a practical level, only two

options were now viable: to give in to the King, to call him back
to head a government which would resolutely attempt to return
to the old certainties, to root itself in custom and precedent; or
to make a fresh start: to recognise that the Civil Wars had
revealed the failure of all existing institutions and had pointed
the way forward to entirely new possibilities. On the one side
stood all those who had fought to make the old order work and
who had now recognised that this would not be achieved by
force of arms. On that side too stood those who believed in
religious uniformity, in the necessary union of godly prince or
magistrate and godly minister. On that side stood all those who
had experienced war as proof of the old adage that resistance to
a tyrant brought on worse ills than did a meek submission to his
scourge.[53] On that side stood the great majority of all social
groups. On the other side stood that small minority who had
experienced the Civil War as a liberating experience, who
found that the collapse of the old order had freed them to plan
the building of a New Jerusalem – those who had experienced
the presence of God beside them on the battlefield, who had
experienced the freedom of worship and Christian witness
made possible by the religious anarchy of recent years. Such
men, who had prayed and deliberated in earnest about their
duty to bring about that which the Lord willed, included many
members of the Army. Mark Kishlansky's article shows how
that collective self-assurance came about. For them, and for
those beyond the Army (especially in the gathered churches)
who shared that vision, a surrender to the King was unthinkable, not only because it would constitute a betrayal of what the
providences of God foretold, but because they had come to
recognise, quite explicitly, that the guilt for all the sufferings
of England lay with the King and that peace and unity could
only be restored when expiation had been made. Before he
sentenced Charles I to death, John Bradshaw, President of the
High Court of Justice, reminded the King that 'I will presume
that you are so well read in Scripture as to know what God
himself hath said concerning the shedding of man's blood
(*Genesis 9 number 35*) will tell you what punishment is' – that
when a land is defiled with blood, it could only be cleansed by
the blood of the guilty.[54] When the majority in Parliament
moved to agree terms with the King no better than they could

have had at any time since 1642, it became imperative for those with the might to do so to strike him down. By December 1648 there were two choices only: capitulation to or decapitation of the anointed King.

# 1. The Coming of War

## ANTHONY FLETCHER

I

THE English Civil War broke out untidily and haphazardly. No-one had wanted it and the nation as a whole faced up to it slowly and reluctantly, seeking to preserve itself from the bloodshed, miseries and burdens that fighting was bound to bring. The initial military campaign between September and December 1642 cut a swathe of plunder across the midlands; it left some confusion and disorder in its wake yet it was a passing wind. This essay is concerned with provincial reactions to the war in the period between that campaign and the breakdown of the Treaty of Oxford negotiations in April 1643. It is focused on the local struggles that spluttered through the first autumn and winter of the war before becoming entrenched in the following summer, struggles that brought the war home to Englishmen living in every corner of the land.[1]

The catastrophic nature of the political crisis of 1642 became generally apparent when the King and Parliament spent the summer competing for control of the county militias and magazines. These militias were too makeshift and too locally orientated to form the basis of national armies, but both sides were convinced of the crucial propagandist benefits their allegiance could offer while field armies were being recruited. The story of the confrontation over the militias, which I have set out more fully elsewhere, can be briefly summarised.[2] The Militia Ordinance, Parliament's instrument for securing obedience, was enforced in fourteen counties between late May and mid-July 1642 and in a further nine between mid-August and late October. This enforcement involved the holding of musters, checking of arms and in many cases at least perfunctory training. The Royalist commissioners of array, though nowhere wholly unopposed, managed to hold musters in six counties during July and August. In twelve other counties Royalist gentry made unsuccessful attempts to execute their commissions: some commissioners, like the earl of Carlisle and Lord Lovelace, found themselves defeated by Parliament's superior intelligence and resources; others, like Lord Chandos and the earl of Bath, found themselves stoutly opposed by gentry and countrymen who were suspicious of the King's use of an unfamiliar constitutional device.

No coherent geographical pattern emerged from these musterings, though the strength of Royalist sentiment in the marches of Wales and of enthusiasm for Parliament in certain Home Counties, such as Buckinghamshire and Essex, was at once obvious. The allegiance of many counties was so fluid and uncertain in the summer of 1642 that categorical statements about commitment are hard to make. Early enforcement of the Militia Ordinance in Leicestershire and Warwickshire, for instance, did not secure either county for Parliament but was merely the beginning of a duel between the deputy lieutenants and the commissioners of array. In Cheshire and Lancashire both the deputies and the commissioners held musters; in Cumberland and Westmorland neither side held them. There is a striking impression of the vigour of a few men and the half-heartedness or even recalcitrance of many. Those who co-operated in organising the musters, as JPs, militia captains or high constables, mostly did so out of a sense of duty to their superiors rather than through any understanding that a declaration of allegiance was required. Among the mass of the gentry at this stage, perplexed and unprepared, allegiance could be shuffled off by obedience to the imperatives of local order and the customary processes of military preparedness.

II

In the six months following Edgehill the noise of war could no longer be ignored. It reached some families suddenly and ferociously with the arrival of plundering troops, others more surreptitiously with a knock on the door by a constable demanding money or supplies for the forces of one of the contestants. Garrisoning of towns and manor houses and mustering of volunteer companies, minor skirmishes and simmering factionalism were the characteristics of the local war in this period. But the predominant mood was localist: men were concerned above all for their lives, their property and the security of their immediate communities.

The King's heartland was Wales and its marches. Only Pembrokeshire, where the shire town held out against a siege led by the earl of Carberry in March 1643, escaped the Royalist hold.[3] By that time a string of garrisons at Shrewsbury, Bridgnorth, Bewdley, Worcester and Tewkesbury commanded the river Severn. In Herefordshire the gentry were decisively Royalist, with the exception of the redoubtable Lady Brilliana Harley, who awaited the threatened siege at Brampton Bryan. She was used by her social equals, she complained in one of a series of pathetic letters to her son, 'with all the malice that can be'[4] Shropshire was under the fierce rule of Sir Francis Ottley, governor of Shrewsbury: on 17 March he stepped up proceedings against forty-three gentry who had been 'backward or slack' in supporting the Royalist cause.[5] Worcestershire was administered equally vigorously by Sir William Russell, the governor of the county town. In March 1643 the Royalist commissioners of array there formalised their proceedings and met regularly, employing their own clerk, as a committee of safety.[6]

Ten counties were within the orbit of the King's headquarters at Oxford, in the sense that most of their territory lay within fifty miles of his capital. Parliament's forces wintered around Aylesbury, High Wycombe, Henley and Windsor. Thus three of these counties – Bedfordshire, Hertfordshire and Middlesex – received some effective protection from Prince Rupert's raiding parties. A resurgence of Royalism at St Albans in January 1643 was quickly crushed by Oliver Cromwell.[7] The other seven counties all felt the imprint of Cavalier plunder more or less harshly and continuously.[8] Northamptonshire and Warwickshire suffered least.[9] Oxfordshire and Berkshire, ringed with garrisons to secure the approach to the university city, were almost wholly at Charles's command.[10] Buckinghamshire north of the Chilterns seethed with soldiers of both sides.[11] Gloucester, carefully fortified by Parliament, was held throughout the winter by Edward Massey while a semicircle of towns and strongholds between it and Oxford – Tewkesbury, Sudeley, Cirencester and Berkeley – each in turn fell to the Royalists.[12] Prince Rupert's vicious sack of Marlborough in December was followed by further Royalist successes in March, when Devizes and Malmesbury were taken.[13]

During the first six months of the war Parliament had the upper hand in East Anglia, Somerset, the four south-eastern counties of Kent, Surrey, Sussex and Hampshire and parts of the midlands. Although the eastern counties were not politically homogeneous and some districts there showed hesitation and uncertainty, the fact remains that the region as a whole was the heartland of the Parliamentary cause.[14] The generous contributions forthcoming in rural Suffolk to the propositions for raising money and horse indicate the enthusiasm that activists could awake: the total of £995 raised in Waignford hundred in the north-east of the county included sums of over £100 from quite small villages like Mettingham and South Elmham All Saints and St Nicholas.[15] In Somerset at this stage the Parliamentarian caucus felt sufficiently confident to send forces under John Pyne and William Strode to assist the cause in Devon and Wiltshire.[16]

Once Sir William Waller had reduced the newly established Royalist strongholds at Winchester, Farnham and Chichester, the south-east was relatively quiet. New county bosses – Sir Thomas Jervoise in Hampshire, Herbert Morley in Sussex, Sir Richard Onslow in Surrey, Sir Anthony Weldon in Kent – were consolidating their rule by committee in preparation for the spring. The clash between Waller's army, marching into the west, and one of Prince Rupert's raiding parties at Alton in late February was in effect the beginning of the long 1643 campaign.[17]

In the midlands Parliamentarian control was surest in Northamptonshire and Warwickshire. A powerful garrison at Northampton kept the countryside in obedience and Royalist gentry fled to join the King at Oxford. Both the militia and volunteers were mustered and trained at Northampton, Kettering and Oundle in January 1643, a compelling gesture of solidarity.[18] The countrymen were ready to offer resistance to the plundering raids of the earl of Northampton and Prince Rupert, on one occasion acting to protect a large party of

carriers taking Cheshire cheese to London. The Northamptonshire committee co-operated with their Leicestershire ally Lord
Grey of Groby to root out pockets of Royalism on the borders of
the two counties and in Rutland.[19] Isolated Royalists who had
garrisoned their manor houses were seized: Henry Nevill at
Nevill Holt and Henry Noel at North Luffenham.[20] In Warwickshire Parliament's supremacy rested on the ideological
leadership of a radical peer, Lord Brooke, and his following
among the middling sort of people in the northern hundreds.[21]
The south, vulnerable to Northampton's garrison at Barnbury,
was at first less committed, but in February 1643 Brooke felt
sufficiently confident of support there to attempt the seizure of
Stratford-upon-Avon.[22] In early December 1642 the Parliamentary committee exercised unchallenged control of most of
Lincolnshire, but the establishment of the Royalist garrison at
Newark, just across the Nottinghamshire border, unnerved
their supporters and soon cast doubt on their hegemony. Gains-
borough fell to the Royalists in January, Grantham in March.
Newark was long to remain a thorn in Lincolnshire's side.[23]

A number of counties were bitterly and more or less continuously disputed during the period under discussion. The
pacification treaties that occurred or were discussed in them
testify to the ferocity of the local struggle rather than to perva-
sive neutralism. They were merely truces which gave both sides
a breathing space. Thus a protracted military conflict followed
Sir Ralph Hopton's march into the west in September 1642.
Having built himself a secure base in Cornwall, he spent
November and December trying to conquer Devon as well. But
Parliamentarian activists vigorously resisted him and the
negotiations for a cessation of hostilities which were opened
after his victory at Braddock Down in January indicated the
weariness of both sides. There was in fact another period of
skirmishing in south Devon before a firm truce for seven days
was agreed on 28 February. This led to a bolder and wider plan,
nothing less than the isolation of the whole of the four south-
western counties from the war, which was energetically
pursued by a few on each side during the next weeks. There was
insufficient trust for the scheme to succeed and the negotiations
only lasted into April because some were prepared to prolong
them as a way of playing for time.[24]

In three midland counties and two northern ones – Leicestershire, Nottinghamshire, Cheshire, Lancashire and Yorkshire – neither side achieved a lasting ascendancy during the winter of 1642–3. In each case, it is worth noting, actual fighting was preceded by a close-fought political campaign between two groups of gentry.[25] In Leicestershire the notorious feud between the Grey and Hastings families largely determined gentry allegiance. It also dictated the military balance of power: in the north Henry Hastings was in command – Royalist garrisons were established at Ashby-de-la-Zouche and Belvoir – while Leicester itself was held by Lord Grey for Parliament. The parties were nicely balanced, plunder was widespread, near-anarchy prevailed. On 14 January Hastings issued a declaration promising that he would do his utmost to prevent Royalist plunder of those who had obeyed the Militia Ordinance, if Grey acted likewise to protect the estates of those who had appeared for the King. Even this limited concession seems to have made no headway.[26]

The pattern within which the war would be fought in Nottinghamshire became apparent when the Royalist gentry began to fortify Newark and the Parliamentarians Nottingham. Desultory negotiations for a truce broke down after the Royalists failed to attend a meeting arranged for 24 December on neutral ground. It began to look as if Newark, reinforced by the earl of Newcastle from Yorkshire and ringed on the southeast by garrisoned manor houses at Thurgarton, Shelford and Wiverton, would quickly become impregnable. In late January, though, Newcastle was under such heavy pressure in the West Riding that he called his forces back there. The first unsuccessful attempt to storm Newark followed on 28 February.[27]

The two sides were also remarkably evenly balanced in Cheshire. Orlando Bridgeman held Chester for the King, with a considerable force at his command. The Royalists fortified at least a dozen manor houses late in 1642. But Parliament held most of the main market towns and had established garrisons of a kind at least at Knutsford, Nantwich, Northwich and Stockport. The demilitarisation treaty agreed at Bunbury on 23 December by two leading Royalists and two of the more moderate Parliamentarians testifies to the sense of stalemate in the county and the need felt by both sides for time to take stock.

But one of its fundamental weaknesses was that neither of the men whose ideological commitment went deepest, Sir Thomas Aston and Sir William Brereton, was involved. An awareness of the probable fragility of the treaty is evident in its terms: its subscribers would try to persuade Sir George Booth and all those active in either the militia or the array to support accommodation petitions to the King and Parliament and would attempt to ensure that 'all their friends, tenants and servants and all others in whom they have any interest' should obey the treaty's terms. It was in fact very shortlived.[28] Another abortive meeting of deputy lieutenants and commissioners planned to take place at Nantwich on 17 January merely opened the way to mutual recriminations. Yet the skirmishing of the next weeks showed that neither side had the military strength to dislodge the other.[29]

By the early autumn of 1642 the division of Lancashire on starkly religious lines had found a recognisable geographical expression. In the east, where many of the gentry were Catholic, the Royalists established garrisons at Eccleston, Ormskirk, Prescot, Warrington and Wigan. Parliamentarian strength was massed in the Puritan town of Manchester and its neighbourhood. Halfhearted negotiations for a truce in October came to nothing. From December to April there was almost incessant fighting, much of it brutal, as both sides sought to capture the middle ground of the shire from the Ribble southwards to the Mersey. In general the Royalists, deprived of many of their leading men who had joined the King's army, were being steadily forced back towards the coast.[30] Across the Pennines in Yorkshire the failure of the West Riding truce in September was followed by a running battle throughout the winter, which became focused on the control of the clothing towns such as Leeds, Bradford and Halifax. For a while the Parliamentarians not only had the upper hand there, but they were also sufficiently confident to extend their raids from their base at Hull across the Wolds into the North Riding. The intervention of the earl of Newcastle in December began to turn the scales. Yet he won no decisive victories in the first months of 1643.[31]

We are left with a few counties where determined efforts were made to keep the war at arm's length. The quietest county in the south was probably Dorset, where there seems to have been a fairly even division of opinion among the gentry and a distinct lack of ideological conflict. Men's general inclination, once the siege of the Royalist stronghold at Sherborne was over in September, seems to have been to sit tight on their estates. In early March Sir Thomas Trenchard and his brother-in-law John Browne discussed a neutralist agreement with the Royalist MPs Richard Rogers and Giles Strangeways. The intention was apparently to oppose any forces that might seek to enter the county. Trenchard and Browne were keen enough on the wider south-western pacification scheme mentioned above to travel to Exeter for a meeting appointed on 14 March of county representatives.[32]

Isolationism also had a particularly strong appeal in the far north, where their sheer remoteness tempted men to believe they might escape the national calamity. Not that the region was immune to the propaganda of both sides or lacked aware-ness of the issues at stake. In November 1642 some of the leading Parliamentarians in Durham complained in a petition to the House of Commons that because there was no 'visible authority that will grant commissions' in the county they feared that Papists and malignants from across the Pennines might any day 'break in upon them'. But there was a world of differ-ence between defensive worrying of this kind and the active participation in the war demanded by the earl of Newcastle, who spent the autumn raising a Royalist force in the north-east. The region as a whole reacted sullenly to his campaign: the earl of Northumberland's tenants in the border country ignored his warrants and some of them were even reported to have possessed themselves of Alnwick Castle in defiance of his inter-vention in their affairs.[33]

The leading gentry of Cumberland and Westmorland, while quarrelling among themselves, nevertheless managed to main-tain a neutralist stance under the cover of nominal Royalism from the start of the war until the intervention of the Scots in 1644. There was no garrison in either county during this time. In the summer of 1642 Newcastle appointed Sir Philip Musgrave, already colonel of a militia regiment, as commander-in-chief of the two counties. Against the advice of Sir John Lowther, another militia colonel who tried to dissuade him from any action at all, he did hold some perfunctory musters. The basic aims of these two men were probably similar. Neither was sufficiently energetic to raise volunteer forces and take them over the county borders. But issues of personal pride and jealousy led them into a long and vindictive feud that came to preoccupy gentry society. Both gained adherents among the leading families and the two counties became absorbed in a factional struggle that had little to do with the national contest going on elsewhere. Half a dozen or so activist Royalists meanwhile went south and fought for the King's cause.[34]

Finally two midland counties where neutralism was firmly rooted, which were only dragged unwillingly into the war early in 1643, deserve special notice. The Staffordshire gentry, led by Sir Richard Leveson, had pursued a cautiously neutralist policy throughout the summer and early autumn of 1642. The plan for raising a third force to defend the county against intruders, agreed upon by the JPs at a special sessions on 15 November, was the logical outcome of their endeavours. This was the most coherent expression any shire produced of the localist reaction to the war.[35] But Staffordshire had no coastline, mountain or fen to block the approach of outsiders: it lay open on all its borders. Thomas Crompton recognised the impracticality of the third-force scheme in a letter to Leveson on 28 November. The sheriff William Cumberford, he reported, had received a letter from the King ordering him to suppress all forces raised locally 'without our immediate warrant'.[36] In January Cumberford, acting in conjunction with the Yorkshire Royalist Sir Francis Wortley, garrisoned Stafford for Charles; other Royalist garrisons were soon established at Lichfield and Dudley. This divisive action provoked the moorlanders, Parliamentarian volunteers from the hill country towards Derbyshire, to besiege the county town. Outsiders like Sir William Brereton and Sir John Gell began to intervene. With the indecisive engagement on 19 March between the earl of Northampton's forces and Gell's at Hopton Heath, Staffordshire was finally embroiled in the war.[37]

The Derbyshire gentry were shocked, after managing to keep the peace among themselves by informal arrangements throughout the summer, by Sir John Gell's presumptuous expedition to borrow troops from Hull in October. Yet they still hoped, despite Gell's garrisoning of Derby on behalf of Parliament, that their local accommodation might be maintained. Tension grew in the last weeks of the year as the indiscipline of Gell's forces quickly became apparent. Sir John Coke, an active Parliamentarian at Westminster, tried to act as a mediator while he was at home visiting his father at Melbourne. But he merely earned the animosity of his colleagues on the county committee. 'He hath done us hurt in the cause but no good since he came down, neither can we conceive otherways of him but that his heart is against us and with those that oppose us', they wrote to Speaker Lenthall on 13 December. They were infuriated because Coke had only attended the committee once and on that occasion he had refused to sign a receipt for some money raised on the propositions. They alleged that this obstructionism, which had been well publicised, had led others to question their authority. [38] Meeting at Etwall in January, the gentry of the southern hundreds issued a final demand to Gell to dissolve his forces. It was his refusal to respond to this which meant that Derbyshire could escape the war no longer. During the next few weeks Gell's supremacy was challenged from two directions: from Leicestershire by Henry Hastings and from Nottinghamshire by the detachments that the earl of Newcastle had recently established at Welbeck.[39]

This then, insofar as something so constantly shifting can be captured in brief, is the outline within which the Civil War became established. The continual fluidity of the war needs to be stressed. Its ebb and flow never ceased in the months between Edgehill and the opening of the 1643 campaign and by the time the armies embarked on that campaign virtually every county was inextricably involved in the national struggle. It had proved impossible to achieve local pacifications that would endure for longer than a few days or weeks. Yet in a real sense the local war was and would remain a series of independent and often isolated contests, entered into by a minority of activists who imposed demands on their countrymen by cajolery, threats or force. The reaction of the localities to the outbreak of war has been described as 'confused, mercurial and at first sight incomprehensible'.[40] This account amply confirms that judgement.

III

Behind the complexity of the local story was the localism that governed men's approach to the war. This was manifested, in the first place, in the search for a settlement that would enable the gentry to restore rural and urban life to its normal pattern. Their personal correspondence shows that many of those most active in the war, let alone the doubters and waverers, longed for peace. Sir Marmaduke Langdale, for instance, writing to Sir William Savile on 9 November 1642, was disconsolate about the news he had heard that the Danes would invade to help the King when spring came, 'which is like to make this kingdom the seat of war for all the nations of Christendom'. Even after Edgehill, he could still dream of making an end of the troubles and distractions of Yorkshire by diverting the war elsewhere, 'that whatsoever foreign nations come they may be employed in the south, where the wellspring of our miseries began and where there is pillage enough to satisfy many armies'. The energetic MP for King's Lynn Thomas Toll ended a report to Lenthall on 19 December with his hearty prayers 'for peace and truth and a happy conclusion'. About the same time Edmund Walker, on the other side of the fence, wrote in similar terms from Oxford to the earl of Lindsey. The Royalist Edmund Verney's letters to his brother Sir Ralph are full of the sorrow that the war brought to divided families. He was 'tooth and nail' for the King's cause, but he was insistent that the conflict should not break the bond of love between them. He hoped for a quick peace 'that we may safely meet in person as well as affection'.[41]

Moderates on both sides expressed similar sentiments with even more force. Campaigning in the North Riding in January 1643, shortly before he changed sides, Sir Hugh Cholmley assured Lenthall of his fidelity and then added a desperate plea for accommodation: 'I profess it grieves my heart to see how these calamities increase and how I am forced to draw my sword not only against my countryman but many near friends and allies some of which I know both to be well affected in religion and lovers of their liberties.' 'If our religion be but firmly settled,' he asked, might it not be better 'to let go some things that in right belong to the subject' than for Parliament to prolong the war? Sir John Coke, a moderate Parliamentarian worried about his aged father's health, told him that he expected misery and confusion to befall the whole kingdom, 'if by God's mercy a settlement be not condescended upon very suddenly'.[42] If the war continued, Sir Richard Newport told his brother-in-law Sir Richard Leveson on 29 November 1642, there would be nothing but 'ruin and desolation'. 'God grant', he avowed, 'that that which is sour destroy not that which is sweet.' Rich and poor alike would suffer if peace were not made, the reluctant Cornish Royalist Sir William Courtenay asserted in a letter to his Parliamentarian friend Francis Buller in February 1643. The only way forward he could see was that God in his mercy might 'touch the hearts of some honest, wise and religious good men' so that a firm peace could be achieved. The localist element in his thinking comes out clearly in his conclusion that such a peace 'I know will advance the glory and true worship of God and the good of our nation and country in particular'.[43]

Lesser men, on the sidelines of the war, echoed all these views. 'I beseech God set an end to these miseries,' wrote his brother-in-law to Sir Simonds D'Ewes on 11 December. In an incoherent and anxious letter to his parents on 18 February a young Shropshire lad William Pritchard, who had gone to find work in London, reported the progress of the Treaty of Oxford negotiations. 'For my part,' he wrote, 'my daily prayers shall be to God that he may unite both the King and his parliament together and that there might not be one drop of blood spilt more in this civil war.' If the treaty failed, he knew that placed as he was at the centre of its operations he would have to fight for Parliament. He ended his letter with a request for his sister Anne to send him a pair of stockings 'for God knows whether I shall ever trouble you any more'.[44]

During the weeks following the King's advance to Turnham Green the municipality of London became divided between those who urged on Parliament more thorough prosecution of the war and those who urged it to seek peace. The petitions and counter-petitions of these groups were eagerly read in the nearby counties, some of which soon chimed in on the side of accommodation with petitions of their own. Those most earnest for peace in certain counties – Essex, Hertfordshire and Norfolk for example – addressed both the antagonists. Middlesex petitioned Parliament alone, Bedfordshire and Berkshire the King alone.[45] More belatedly distant counties like Herefordshire and Worcestershire added their voice. Cheshire, as we have seen, talked of doing so but the petitions seem never to have been formulated.[46] Some towns, like Bristol, Reading and Salisbury, mounted their own accommodation petitions.[47] There is nothing surprising in the breadth of this movement. Since 1640 petitioning had become a much favoured practice both in the towns and among the gentry leaders of the county communities.[48] Collection of large numbers of signatures was customary: in this case 6000 signed in Essex, 4000 in Hertfordshire, 3800 in Bedfordshire. But these totals should not be taken to indicate an authentic popular outcry. One Hertfordshire man who had put his hand to the county's petition readily confessed he 'never read it'. Many gave blind support. The whole business in Essex took a mere twelve days and the bulk of the hands came from parishes where the leading gentry who mobilised adherence had their estates.[49]

These accommodation petitions were based on a wide range of political viewpoints. The Essex one was the work of a group of moderate Royalists who up until this point had avoided provoking the Parliamentarian overlords of the shire into seizing or imprisoning them. The Herefordshire one, presented by the grand jury at the Epiphany quarter sessions, was quite openly Royalist. The county's bitter experience, it declared, was that, far from bringing peace and charity, rule by Parliament involved 'tyrannical oppressions'. The men at Westminster were requested to submit 'to such terms of accommodation as His Majesty will graciously yield unto'. The Bedfordshire petitions, by contrast, importuned the King to 'abandon all jealousies' and listen to Parliament's propositions; the Berkshire ones, taking the same line, hoped he would confide in Parliament's counsels, since they had no doubt that it would both 'settle a true and happy peace' and make the King's crown and dignity as famous as that of any of his predecessors. Hertfordshire, it seems uniquely in this series, managed to concoct a studiously neutral statement. The county earnestly desired that hostilities should cease and 'that some means of accommodation may be obtained' whereby both the King's honour and estate and the Parliament's just privileges might be preserved.

When it came to the arguments in favour of accommodation, though, all the petitions contained much the same message. All of them emphasised the harshness of the armies' demands and the insecurity that civil war brought to men's lives. 'No man enjoys his life, his wife, children, family or estate in safety this day,' declared the inhabitants of Bristol. Bedfordshire spoke of 'continual fears and perplexities'. The Thames valley, insisted Berkshire, had become 'the very theatre where all the tragedies which are derivative from the cruelty and barbarism of such a war as this must be acted'. In several cases the economic impact of the war was spelt out. Berkshire mentioned the collapse of the Reading grain market, Bedfordshire decay of trade and tillage, the people of Westminster their 'losses in their callings'.[50] Bristol described the interruption of foreign trade: 'our ships lie now rotting in the harbour . . . by reason of our home bred distractions . . . we being reputed abroad as men merely undone at home.'

Several of the petitions particularly urged the point that civil war was unnatural: 'those of the nearest relations', reflected Bedfordshire, 'are likely to imbue their hands in each other's blood and the whole kingdom (like a distracted man) lay violent hands upon itself'. Stress was put on the prospect of foreign states exploiting England's sudden vulnerability. Civil war, as a London petition put it, made way for 'a general confusion and invasion by a foreign nation while our treasure is exhausted, our trade lost and the kingdom dispeopled'. Pacific sentiment in East Anglia, it has been suggested, may also have been enhanced by fear of the social disorders that war was likely to bring to the region. The Stour valley riots in the summer had carried ominous overtones of class conflict. Those who wrote the Hertfordshire petitions certainly seem to have had this thought in mind: they predicted 'violence and rapine of unruly and dissolute multitudes which hope to raise themselves by the ruin of Your Majesty's good subjects'. The Norfolk petitioners warned MPs that the peril they ran was the 'miserable spectacle of a German devastation'.[51]

IV

During a period when it seemed to them that the Civil War lacked finality, many gentry who held office as JPs believed that their first duty was to do their utmost to maintain local order.

Yet the general sense of political crisis made some JPs reluctant to show their faces in public, so it was often difficult for the most energetic men to find a core of magistrates willing to act together. The usual administrative routine was becoming overlaid by political strife. Nevertheless the breakdown of the courts was only gradual. Although documentation is too patchy to allow firm conclusions, it seems that quarter sessions were held as usual in at least fourteen counties at Michaelmas in 1642 and that the Bench sat again in nine of these counties in January 1643.

In several counties these Michaelmas and Epiphany sessions can be seen as demonstrating the determination of JPs to put administration above politics. The Staffordshire sessions, as we would expect in view of the gentry's neutralist spirit, were a particularly impressive manifestation of solidarity in face of incipient disorder. Men who were soon to emerge as Royalist activists, like Sir Hervey Bagot, Sir Robert Wolseley and George Digby, sat together with Thomas Crompton who was at heart a convinced Parliamentarian. In October there was also the calming presence of Sir Richard Leveson; in January Lord Paget attended. The latter's interesting career in 1642 had included a phase as a positive lord lieutenant in Buckinghamshire and another as a recruiting agent for the King in Staffordshire. By the autumn Paget seems to have retired in disillusion from the military scene.[52] In Nottinghamshire few of those who occupied the Bench in the county town on 3 October, at Newark on the 5th and at Retford on the 7th, had yet shown their hand politically. The last entry in the quarter sessions files is dated 1 November. Thereafter the developing hostilities between the two parties based at Nottingham and Newark presumably brought parish business to a halt.[53] The Suffolk JPs were another group who conducted a valiant rearguard action against the chaos of civil war. Attendances at the autumn and winter sessions held in turn at Beccles, Woodbridge, Ipswich and Bury St Edmunds were lower than usual, but those present got through heavy agendas of settlement, apprenticeship and bastardy cases. Moderate Parliamentarians, like Sir Philip Parker and Sir Robert Crane, worked together with lesser men who had so far remained steadfastly neutral and with the latent Royalist Sir John Wentworth, who was shortly to be implicated in an abortive *coup* at Lowestoft.[54]

There were other counties where business was enacted as usual though the court was under the control of a solid group of magistrates committed to one side or the other. In Essex, Hampshire, Kent and Sussex Parliamentarian gentry were in charge; in Cheshire, Cornwall, Devon, Herefordshire, Wiltshire and Worcestershire Royalists held sway. Attendances in these counties varied widely. The Chelmsford sessions in January were quite exceptionally well attended with the earl of Carlisle, three baronets and twenty-one JPs in all present on the Bench. At Arundel, by contrast, the whole weight of business in the disrupted western rapes of Sussex was borne by two men.[55]

The creeping paralysis imposed by the war on the machinery of local government became striking between January and April 1643. The Essex sessions files contain a number of informations and examinations taken by JPs in their neighbourhoods in February and March 1643 and even some taken in the summer and autumn of that year. But there were no courts held between Epiphany 1643 and Easter 1644.[56] The interruption of proceedings in this strongly Parliamentarian county, which was relatively insulated from the fighting, has to be accounted for in terms of the general insecurity of the times and the heavy new responsibilities imposed on committed gentry and on parish officers by the Parliamentarian war effort. At Easter 1643 quarter sessions only survived in a few counties: in Kent and Worcestershire; at two of the Suffolk venues, Beccles and Woodbridge; in Devon, where the Bench concentrated on the appointment of constables, the foundation of parish order; at Lewes in Sussex where three justices worked their way through a normal agenda. It is probable that the court was also still meeting at Carlisle.[57]

There were a few attempts in this period to use the local courts for political ends. In Cornwall both sides bid for the support of the quarter sessions by bringing indictments against the other for disturbing the peace. But the grand jury was solidly Royalist and its foreman in his speech at Truro declared that 'it was a great favour and justice of His Majesty to send down aid to them who were already marked out to destruction'.[58] At both Chester and Hereford in January 1643 indictments were brought against certain Puritan ministers for their failure to read the Book of Common Prayer in their churches.[59]

At the Lent assizes at Shrewsbury in 1643 ten men, several of whom were substantial gentry, were charged with refusal to support the royal army or with uttering scandalous speeches against the King.[60] But such cases were exceptional. In general local government was kept going as long as possible not as a means of political advantage, but because gentry everywhere gave high priority in such desperate times to their traditional concern for good order in their neighbourhoods.

V

The essence of the localism that is so evident in the dealings of this period was county-mindedness. The most promising methods of raising forces were those most deeply embedded in the popular consciousness, which expressed the ancient imperative of defence of the shire. Thus John Grills was able to raise 3000 foot at short notice in the western hundreds of Cornwall in October 1642 by using his authority as sheriff to call out the *posse comitatus*. Sir Edward Ford seized Chichester in November and William Cumberford Stafford in January by the same method. Sussex gentry who had obeyed Ford's warrants, sent on pain of death, later argued persuasively that they had no choice in the matter. In Worcestershire Sir William Russell continued to use the device of the *posse comitatus* when he was well established as governor of the county town. His letter summoning it on 29 April 1643 used the pretext of the 'many unlawful and rebellious forces and riotous assemblies' in the county.[61]

Both sides of course sought to exploit the military might, such as it was, of the local militias in the areas that they controlled. The limitations of this policy soon became evident, since the war could not be fought within the self-contained administrative units of county government and there was a general sense that the militia's role was restricted to defence of the shire. In September 1642 the Cheshire trained bands refused to cross the Mersey and join in the earl of Derby's siege of Manchester. In October Sir Ralph Hopton was frustrated in his efforts to pursue the retreating Cornish Parliamentarians across the Tamar. Encouraged by Sir John Lowther's stance, the Westmorland freeholders also refused to serve outside the county.

The earl of Newcastle only obtained the co-operation of the Durham militia in his north-eastern strategy by promising them that they would not be asked to cross the boundaries of the Palatinate.[62] The plans laid by the Herefordshire Royalists to besiege Lady Harley at Brampton Bryan in February 1643 were balked by the refusal of the Radnorshire militia to go a few miles out of their own shire. Rowland Laugharne, desperate for forces with which to impose Parliamentarian control on South Wales in April, found that the Pembrokeshire militia was not prepared to do anything but defend its own territory.[63]

The letters, declarations and orders of the activists on both sides were full of the rhetoric and propaganda of localism. These men understood the grassroots of local opinion and sought to turn it to their own advantage. In a curt note to George Sitwell from his newly established garrison at Derby in November 1642, Sir John Gell asked what he was prepared to contribute 'towards your county's safety'. Gell explained that his commission from the earl of Essex permitted him to raise forces 'to be employed for the present securing the peace of this county'. Writing to John Smith on 9 December, the Gloucestershire Parliamentarian John Georges castigated the London administration for its 'cold and dilatory proceedings' and urged him to help redeem the failure of others by securing the shire, which now lay 'exposed to ruin and slavery'.[64] The carefully worded declaration issued by the earl of Cumberland and his Royalist supporters at York about this time indicates their sensitivity to the localist issue. They protested their affection for their 'native country' and their concern to pursue 'quiet and settlement'; they blamed the Hothams, the Fairfaxes and their associates for breaking the West Riding treaty and plunging the county further into bloodshed and misery.[65]

The same themes recurred in early 1643. The sheriff of Hertfordshire, Thomas Coningsby, tried to raise a Royalist force there in January by directing the lord lieutenant to use the militia to preserve the county from 'felonies and robberies' committed by Parliamentarian soldiers. The Westmorland militia colonel Sir Henry Fletcher explained to a colleague the same month that he looked for the assistance of gentlemen 'who have no desire but for the good and safety of their country'.[66] In a fascinating series of letters to the inhabitants of the Vale of the

Trent in March the activists, ensconced at Nottingham and Newark respectively, sought to woo those living in the disputed ground between the two garrisons with promises of effective protection. Both parties endlessly reiterated their zeal and concern for the good and the peace of Nottinghamshire.[67]

I have argued elsewhere that in the summer of 1642 localism was expressed in some counties through defensive arrangements which were accepted and welcomed by many of the gentry and were put into effect under nominal allegiance to one side or the other.[68] During the winter and spring the allegiance of ruling cliques who had engaged themselves in this way necessarily became more overt, even if their hold on their own community was still based on a declared policy of local autonomy and self-interest. Under the stress of the developing national conflict, neutralism on the part of leading families was less gracefully tolerated. Moreover the demands made on the counties by their masters greatly increased. Yet the basic principle of protection in return for at least minimal co-operation remained the same. This indeed was the principle on which the war in the localities was fought. When the central administrations and the local authorities were at odds it was often because defensive needs were believed to have been neglected. Thus the Suffolk deputy lieutenants decided in January 1643 that Captain Nelson, who had been sent by the earl of Essex to raise seventy cavalry for 'the service of the state', should remain in their company. His troop would be employed 'upon such service as we shall see needful for the peace of the county'.[69]

As the Royalists began to formalise their administration in the districts under their control the *quid pro quo* of resources in return for protection and a degree of county independence was sometimes spelt out. At Oxford on 21 December an elaborate set of arrangements was agreed by the grand jury of the county for billeting the royal forces through the winter. The King in return accepted that the countrymen should retain enough of their animals and stock to maintain their husbandry. He also promised not to impose on them any contributions for the garrisons in Berkshire. A few days earlier, the Royalist committee meeting at Preston in Lancashire had set out its programme for the 'safeguard and security' of the county: £8700 could be raised which would pay for a magazine and a force of

2000 foot and 400 horse to guard the inhabitants.[70] The Worcestershire grand jury agreed to a levy of £300 each month 'for the defence of the said county' at the Epiphany sessions. Although collection was proving slow and they were not satisfied that the 'outmost parts' of the shire were being adequately secured, they renewed the levy at the Easter sessions. The Staffordshire grand jury made a similar arrangement at their January sessions.[71] In February Prince Rupert imposed a monthly tax on Gloucestershire for the provision of the garrisons at Cirencester, Sudeley and Tewkesbury; in March the Cornish gentry and freeholders established a tax of £750 a week to sustain the Royalist cause beyond the Tamar.[72]

Parliament's committeemen, like their Royalist counterparts, hoped to cajole their countrymen by emphasising in their warrants that the new taxes necessitated by the war were 'for the defence of the county'.[73] Some continued to rely largely upon the unpaid local militiamen; others adopted their own expedients. In Hertfordshire, in November 1642, for example, the committee raised and taxed the county to support 200 dragoons 'to ride up and down for the safety of the county and give notice of any forces come in'.[74] During the autumn committeemen and deputy lieutenants were still basically dependent on the voluntary propositions of June 1642 for raising horse, money and plate. But between December and April a spate of ordinances put the Parliamentarian war effort on a proper footing. The two most important innovations were the weekly assessment and the sequestration of delinquents' estates. From the start a high proportion of the proceeds of the new taxes was diverted from the central treasuries by the exigencies of county defence.

VI

The period that has been discussed in this essay was a dark and uncertain one for all Englishmen who were in the least politically conscious. Perplexity and apprehension are the keynotes of personal correspondence. Many men began to wonder whether they had already committed or compromised themselves too far in a conflict which they believed could not be satisfactorily resolved by an outright victory for either side. Yet the reality of civil war was still too harsh for all to acknowledge. Our hindsight makes it hard for us to appreciate that it did not seem as obvious then as it does now that a war had actually begun. The appeal of localism was that it was everybody's common ground. Thus the temptation men felt to appeal for peace, to strive for the preservation of the normal routines of government and to emphasise the autonomy of their counties is entirely understandable.

# 2. The Royalist War Effort

## RONALD HUTTON

In previous years a certain anecdote has received frequent quotation in works upon the Civil War. It concerns a husband-man at Marston Moor, who was ploughing his fields when the rival armies drew up there to fight the biggest battle of the war. On hearing that the conflict was produced by a quarrel between King and Parliament he replied 'What, has they two fallen out again?' It is time that this engaging character vanished from the pages of history. Not merely does the incident not occur in any contemporary source, but it is inherently ridiculous. The land concerned lies a few miles from York, site of a Royalist garrison to which such a farmer would have been forced to contribute money for the previous two years. For the past three months it had been besieged by an army of nearly 30,000 men, some of whom would certainly have requisitioned supplies from the hero of the story. His ignorance is as incredible as the flippancy with which he is said to have greeted the news of the fratricidal conflict between the two traditional guardians of the Common Weal. In place of this happy portrait of rural insouciance, successive local studies are drawing a picture of the Civil War as a terrible and protracted conflict which imposed unprece-dented burdens upon the local community. Indeed, it is becoming obvious that there were two Civil Wars, the formal struggle between the rival partisans and the struggle between those partisans and the bulk of the population, whose support they attempted to enlist for their war effort. The purpose of this chapter is to examine the relationship between these different conflicts in the case of the Royalists. Did the King lose the war because he failed to mobilise the resources for it? If so, when, and why?

The area upon which the King based his war effort com-prised the six northern counties, almost the whole of Wales, and most of England west of, and including, Staffordshire, Worcestershire, Oxfordshire, Berkshire and Hampshire. In this huge region the Royalist war effort commenced in June 1642, when the King, based at York, began to issue Commissions of Array to each county, empowering certain gentry in that county to secure it in his interest. In the previous three months, with relations between King and Parliament deteriorating dramatically, people in this region had demonstrated considerable anxiety. Everywhere that a town corporation's records have survived, they show new attention being drawn to the fortifications. From most of the English counties petitions were sent to the King begging him to make peace with Parliament. In most counties family collections survive, and they show that the gentry possessed a genuine awareness of national events. However, except in Herefordshire, where clergy stirred up the population on the King's behalf,[1] there is little sign of commitment to the King's cause at this stage. A few gentry joined the King at York. The other future Royalists remained at home, expressing foreboding.

To these men the arrival of the Commissions of Array represented the moment of truth. In every county the Commission achieved its primary object, of persuading some gentry to declare for the King. They varied in status from great nobles to middle-rank gentry. Some, like the Herefordshire gentry or like Sir Thomas Aston in Cheshire,[2] seem to have been inspired by concern for the Established Church. Others, like Sir Thomas Salusbury in Denbighshire,[3] were concerned for the preservation of a strong monarchy. Most have left no record of their reasons for their espousal of the King's cause. In Herefordshire, with the aid of the clergy, and in most of Wales, for reasons that remain mysterious, these activists persuaded the bulk of the county community to co-operate with them. In Cumberland and Westmorland, most gentry likewise gave formal allegiance to the King, though they thereafter did virtually nothing to translate this into action.[4] In Northumberland and Durham the local leaders were generally equally inert, but the King was fortunate in possessing one active, powerful and popular local magnate, the earl of Newcastle, who took care to secure Newcastle for the royal cause.[5] In Lancashire also the greatest noble, the much-loved earl of Derby, succeeded in securing most of his county for Charles, though when he tried to remove the Manchester magazine the townspeople opposed him, and later formed a defensive alliance with the local Parliamentarians.[6]

Generally, however, the efforts of the King's adherents were a failure. In Staffordshire, Shropshire, Worcestershire and Cornwall the community as a whole remained aloof.[7] Likewise urban centres such as Chester, Worcester and Cirencester refused to admit Royalist troops.[8] Even in Yorkshire, where the Commissions of Array had been issued, some Royalist activists signed the local peace treaty with their opponents as soon as the King marched out of the county. In Cheshire, Somerset, Dorset and Devon several towns and many of the rural population forcibly opposed the Royalists when they began raising soldiers.[9] In the last three counties the insurgents co-operated with Parliamentarians to expel the Royalist troops, but having accomplished this task they displayed little enthusiasm for Parliament's cause.[10] Similarly, Gloucester was persuaded by its MPs to declare for Parliament, but when Parliamentarian troops arrived outside the city the inhabitants refused to admit them and the soldiers had to force an entry.[11] The only place in the future Royalist area which manifested aggressive and unequivocal support for Parliament was the small town of Birmingham, perhaps (as is often asserted but not demonstrated) because of its strong Puritan leanings. In general, the people of the future Royalist areas of England displayed no desire to involve themselves in the partisan conflict, and the clearest sentiment which they expressed was a distrust and a dislike of regular soldiers.

In this they were shrewd enough. The instrument which created the Royalist war effort was not the Commission of Array but the military commission issued by the King to one of his supporters to raise a regiment of regular soldiers for his service. Such men were assembled by private means, without reference to the views or interests of the community, which indeed they could, if numerous enough, coerce into co-operation. Each regiment began its existence as a form of joint-stock company, based upon the money, and sometimes the prestige, of its senior officers. Eleven regiments were commissioned by Charles in Wales and the Marches in the summer of 1642, and in

September he brought his existing troops into the area to be
united with them. Local partisans persuaded the corporation of
Shrewsbury to welcome him,[12] and the town became the base
for the gathering army. While it assembled, the King toured
north-east Wales and its March making tactful speeches to the
local people and sending soldiers to punish towns which had
forcibly resisted his adherents in the summer.[13] In this manner
the area was secured by the Royalists. Parallel developments
occurred in Cornwall, where a local peace treaty was broken by
the appearance of some Royalist horse under Sir Ralph
Hopton, which had been chased out of Dorset. Hopton
managed to avoid being expelled a second time by behaving
with scrupulous legality. He presented the Royalist case at the
Michaelmas sessions, standing trial himself as a disturber of the
peace, and, having secured his acquittal, indicted the local
Parliamentarians on the same charge. Nevertheless, regiments
of regular soldiers raised by Royalist gentry were required to
make the Royalist hold upon the county secure.[14]

Neither the Royalists nor Parliamentarians expected the war
to last more than a few weeks. Instead the fighting of the
autumn proved indecisive, and during the ensuing winter both
sides attempted to consolidate the territory they had secured.
For the King, now based at Oxford, this consisted of the four
northernmost counties, parts of Yorkshire and Lancashire, all
Wales and the Marches except Pembrokeshire, plus Worcestershire, Oxfordshire, Cornwall and parts of Gloucestershire and
Berkshire.[15] The most effective method of securing this area
was for Royalist gentry in counties upon its fringe to agree in the
name of their community to lay a rate upon its members to
support local garrisons. This was first achieved in Oxfordshire
in December, to pay the royal army now quartered there. Its
example was followed in Worcestershire, Gloucestershire and
all the Marcher counties by February.[16] In Cornwall, though a
formal rate was not imposed till April, villages were forced to
maintain troops nonetheless.[17] From the beginning this process
produced problems. In Worcestershire and Shropshire the rate
was soon in arrears, and in Cheshire its imposition produced an
armed rebellion, which culminated in the 'treaty' of Bunbury in
December 1642 by which the community agreed to withdraw
from participation in the national conflict. Likewise the winter

campaigns of the Cornish Royalists culminated in talks to unite all four western counties in an armed neutrality. Both these local attempts to contract out of the conflict were, along with the earlier Yorkshire pact, destroyed by Parliament, which saw them as a barrier to its prospects of invading Royalist territory and denounced them.[18] Put to the test, the gentry who favoured neutrality were not coherent and determined enough as a group to oppose forcibly both sets of partisans. It was one thing to withhold support from either of the two traditional branches of government when they attempted to attack each other. It was quite another to employ violence to resist the agents and commands of both, each claiming the sanction of law. The events of the winter of 1642–3 demonstrated both the strength of local sentiment for neutralism and the shallowness of its legal and ideological roots.

At the opening of the campaigning season of 1643 the King took further measures to ensure that his territory was well defended from attack and the communities within it en-couraged to support his adherents. Military administration in Oxfordshire and adjacent counties was co-ordinated by the royal Council of War, a mixed body of soldiers and civilians which dealt with problems arising from the imposition of martial rates and the quartering of troops. To provide similar control in the other Royalist areas Charles appointed, or recon-firmed the appointment of, six lieutenant-generals. Five were the greatest Royalist magnates of the areas committed to their care. Lord Herbert was given south-east Wales and its March, the earl of Carbery south-west Wales, the earl of Derby Lancashire, the earl of Newcastle the five other northern counties and the marquis of Hertford England west of and including Wiltshire and Hampshire. North and mid-Wales and their Marches, which possessed no obvious leader, were placed under a wealthy courtier, Lord Capel. All these men were inexperienced soldiers, chosen for their social status and local prestige, which would command inherent respect. Likewise local fortresses were placed in the hands of the local gentry, supplied by their fellows in their capacity as Commissioners of Array. In this fashion the King hoped to promote harmony within his local war machine, and between that machine and the local community.

In the fighting of 1643 and the following winter this hope proved illusory. The lieutenant-generals all raised local armies and persuaded the gentry in each county to agree upon local rates to support them. All but one then met with disaster. The exception was Newcastle, who did lead his army in conquering most of Yorkshire and Lincolnshire, though it was noted, then and later, that he heavily outnumbered his local opponents and may have deprived the King of total victory by the excessive caution of his movements. Even so, in comparison the record of his colleagues was miserable. Herbert's army was destroyed and his territory ravaged and demoralised. Capel lost most of Cheshire and north-east Wales and part of Shropshire, and so enraged the local populace that he dared not leave his base at Shrewsbury in case the citizens expelled the garrison in his absence.[19] Carbery lost the entire area committed to his care and Derby all but one garrison. At first sight Hertford seems to have fared better, for his army joined the Cornish forces and conquered Somerset and much of Devon and Wiltshire. These achievements, however, were really the work of his subordinates Hopton and Prince Maurice, while Hertford himself rapidly became unpopular with both his army and the local gentry.[20] Likewise serious quarrelling developed among the lesser Royalist leaders in Monmouthshire, Herefordshire, Worcestershire and Cornwall.[21]

Charles accordingly reversed his policy and placed his territory in the hands of men of proved military skill with no personal connection with the areas in their care, who could be expected to remain aloof from both local rivalries and local favouritisms. In July his nephew Prince Maurice replaced Hertford as lieutenant-general of the west. In December his brother Prince Rupert, reputedly the best Royalist general, replaced Capel, and in April 1644 Herbert's and Carbery's areas were added to Rupert's command, giving him control of all Wales and the Marches. Within this huge region he made a policy of ejecting the local gentry who had governed Royalist fortresses and replacing them with experienced officers loyal to himself. Maurice left undisturbed the local gentry whom Hertford had placed in charge of garrisons, but in appointing new military governors he followed the same policy as Rupert.[22] Between mid-1643 and mid-1644 the princes and their officers

did much to vindicate the new departure in military administration. Rupert and his junior generals restored Royalist
military supremacy in the Marches and south-west Wales.
Maurice reduced most of the remaining Parliamentarian
strongholds in Dorset and Devon while his field marshal,
Hopton, conquered all Wiltshire and much of Hampshire. Nor
was the princes' contribution to the local war effort limited to
military acumen. On entering into his command Rupert called
its communities to meetings to discuss problems in the administrative system with him.[23] These meetings produced considerable reforms. In Worcestershire the number of local
troops, prices of military supplies and days on which garrisons
were paid were all fixed.[24] In Shropshire and North Wales
Rupert permitted payment of the local rate in kind, and
standardised this rate at sixpence in the pound on all men's
estates.[25] The four western counties of Maurice's command,
Cornwall, Devon, Dorset and Somerset, were united in an
Association, with a Grand Committee of local gentry empowered to maintain general oversight of local administration
and settle disputes within it.[26] In this manner the princes hoped
not merely to place the local war effort in the hands of good
soldiers but to reduce the likelihood of tension between these
men and the local population. Both crowned their work of
reconstruction by raising large field armies for the campaigning
season of 1644.

This work was greatly assisted by a piece of good fortune, the
appearance of reinforcements of veteran soldiers. In September
1643 the King managed to arrange a truce with the Roman
Catholic rebels who had been in arms in Ireland for nearly two
years. This freed the army originally sent to fight these rebels to
return to England to assist the royal cause. The forces available
amounted to at most 6000 foot and 700 horse,[27] which was not
an overwhelming strength, and these were shipped over in
detachments to different theatres of war. Nevertheless they
were all experienced, disciplined and hardy soldiers, with good
officers, and gave considerable assistance to the Royalists
wherever they appeared. Some reconquered north-east Wales
and western Cheshire, and despite the loss of many men at the
battle of Nantwich, formed the nucleus of Rupert's new army in
the spring of 1644. Some garrisoned the coastal castles of North

Wales. Others made a blockade of Gloucester possible and formed the nucleus of Hopton's army in his winter campaign. Still more stormed and garrisoned Wareham to protect Royalist Dorset. Their appearance was particularly important in that it came at a time when all generals, of either party, were finding it increasingly difficult to attract new recruits to their colours.

Nevertheless, although the princes and their deputies could greatly improve the effectiveness of the war machine they could not solve its fundamental problems. These were of two kinds. First, as shown above, the population in general had never displayed enthusiasm for the war effort. Second, even had they shown this enthusiasm they would have found it difficult to co-operate cheerfully with the extraordinarily heavy demands made upon them. The strategic misfortune of the Royalists was that the early fighting had left them in command of a territory studded with Parliamentarian enclaves, so that continuous local fighting consumed much of the wealth of the region. Furthermore, the wealthiest counties were the most disturbed, whilst those which the Royalists held firmly, such as Cornwall and the Welsh shires, were also the poorest. Within Royalist territory every householder had to pay the rate to support local troops, itself considerably heavier than the heaviest taxation known before. In addition irregular levies, to pay for fortifications or convoys, were continuously imposed, and wherever field troops passed upon campaign, the area they traversed had to provide money, food, lodging and clothing for them. A crippling imposition of a different sort was the right of officers to conscript horses, carts and tools for military use, destroying the mechanisms which produced wealth at village level. Added to all these formal exactions the countryside had to endure the depredations of underpaid soldiers plundering for profit or survival, of Parliamentarians intent on destroying Royalist resources and of common brigands taking advantage of the breakdown of order to loot. To have co-operated loyally with all the demands of the Royalist war machine would have been suicidal.

That war machine, like its Parliamentarian counterpart, consisted formally of a series of civilian county committees staffed by local gentry.[28] The earliest, and most important, of these was the Commission of Array itself, which in the more strategically sited counties were granted more specific powers and duties in the course of 1643. Its duties were primarily financial, to supervise the collection and allocation of the local military rate. In July 1643 the King began to set up committees in each shire to exploit the property of local Parliamentarians to meet the expenses of the war. In practice they had been doing this since the previous war.[29] During the next year, the number of committees greatly increased. In November Charles began to empower local gentry to press men for service in the various Royalist armies, again formalising a practice commenced several months before.[30] In May 1644 he began to commission men in the wealthier, English, counties to collect the excise upon merchandise imposed by the Royalist Parliament at Oxford. The following month, acting upon a report requested to recommend ways to prevent waste and confusion in the financing of the war,[31] he began to set up new committees in each county to take accounts. Following, like the excise, a Parliamentarian precedent, they were intended to produce statements of all money received and spent in the royal service. With these committees the war machine was finally completed.

Despite several obvious similarities in structure and purpose, it differed in important respects from the Parliamentarian system. First, in concordance with the King's attempt to represent his cause as the more cautious and conservative, the formal construction of each part of the Royalist system was later than the equivalent stage of the Parliamentarian, and also more *ad hoc*. Whereas Parliament issued ordinances detailing the functions of the various bodies set up and listing the men who were to staff them, Charles gave new committees first to the counties immediately around Oxford and then to others over the following months in order of importance in the war effort. Second, whereas Parliament attempted to increase the efficiency of its committees by giving some, such as the committees for taking accounts, a different membership from others, the King staffed most with the same men. Usually, the committees for sequestration, impressment and taking accounts were headed by the same gentry, who were also among the most prominent members of the Commission of Array. By doing this the King may have intended to prevent bitter quarrelling between the various bodies, as certainly occurred in some

Parliamentarian counties, and the evidence of the local records suggests that he succeeded. The great weakness of the formal Royalist war machine was not that it was divided internally, but that it was often ineffective. Everywhere that the accounts and letters of Royalist military governors survive they reveal that the pay of their garrisons was in arrears from the day of their establishment, because the local rates were not fully paid. Even in sheltered counties at the opening of hostilities[32] the civilian commissioners had to call upon the troops to collect the rate by force. Just as the regular troops had made the provincial war effort possible, so they were needed to guarantee its continuation.

This situation considerably worsened during the campaigns of 1644. The Royalists were thrown onto the defensive everywhere. Their territory was the scene of continual fighting and manoeuvring. Newcastle's army was destroyed and with it all Royalist control over northern England; Reading, Abingdon, Weymouth, Taunton and Oswestry were lost. The King restored military supremacy in the west in September, but failed to retake the lost fortresses. Instead he placed his surviving strongholds in Wiltshire and Dorset under experienced officers from his army and left clear instructions for the organisation of local resources.[33] These measures, and the impact of his victory, prevented serious problems for the administration in the west during the following winter. In Wales and the Marches, however, the defeats continued, with the loss of Montgomery, Cardigan and Shrewsbury. The Royalist administration there became locked in a downward spiral. Local people, losing faith in the capacity of the King's supporters to win the war, began to reason that to lend them further support was only to prolong the war, and the suffering it produced, needlessly. Hence the letters of the defeated military governors of the area are filled in the autumn of 1644 with complaints of the now open hostility of the surrounding population, and its determination to deny them the resources to recover. By the early months of 1645 this discontent had been formally organised.

One of the forms taken derived, ironically, from an idea enacted by the King, calculated to utilise the growing desperation of the local populace with the war's burdens. In April 1644 some of the inhabitants of Hampshire petitioned Parliament to make peace with the King, threatening that henceforth they would rise en masse to oppose any disturbers of the peace.[34] This probably inspired the King to issue his proclamation to 'One and All' at the opening of an abortive march on London in October, calling on the populations of the counties on his route to rise and assist him in forcing Parliament to come to terms. The proclamation directly inspired some Somerset Royalist gentry to form the plan of joining the four western counties in a pledge to raise the population en masse to keep perfect local peace.[35] This scheme came to nothing, but it was copied with great enthusiasm by the Royalist gentry of the more disordered counties of Worcestershire, Herefordshire, Shropshire and Staffordshire, who united in a similar Association dedicated to raising a huge irregular army to impose order. In the prevailing situation in the Marches there was a considerable danger that this local force would provide the population with an ideal instrument for the ejection of the Royalist troops. Nevertheless the King approved the idea, perhaps because he believed that his adherents could control the Association, perhaps because he feared the consequences of refusal.[36]

Even while the gentry were preparing measures to impose order, certain groups of countrymen had begun spontaneously to enact them. There was nothing new about villagers resisting attempts by troops to enforce the levying of the local rates. They had been doing so in territory disputed and raided by both parties since early 1643.[37] What was different about the so-called Clubman risings in the Marches in early 1645 was their size and the degree of co-operation between settlements, and the fact that they took place deep within Royalist territory.[38] They were located in south-west Shropshire, west Worcestershire and north-east Herefordshire, hilly areas which had hitherto been insulated from the effects of the war, and appear to represent the reaction of backwoodsmen to attempts to integrate them completely into the war effort for the first time.[39] Elsewhere gentry represented the complaints of their neighbours to the Royalist leaders in the form of petitions.[40] The hillmen, lacking this channel of communication, had no other means of stating grievances than to enact the remedy. Even so, their risings differed in time and intent. The Shropshire Clubmen rose in December, demanding the evacuation of two local garrisons and the re-posting of a dissolute officer. Those of Worcestershire appeared in March and requested only the enforcement of existing disciplinary rules upon the regular troops. The Herefordshire rebels, also in March, were the most violent, besieging Hereford and demanding an exodus of all regular soldiers from the county. This dramatic development created great dismay among Royalist officers, and intensified the unrest in the local population all over the region.[41] It seemed as though the whole structure of Royalist administration in the area was about to collapse.

To avert this, the Royalists had to make some considerable attempt to restore and guarantee order and to prove the ultimate viability of their cause. This now occurred. In the winter the high command was reshuffled. Rupert was made general of the royal army, Maurice was given Rupert's command in Wales and the Marches and Hopton took over the west. Maurice reached Worcester in January, and spent three weeks codifying and rationalising all existing orders for the running of the local administration into a comprehensive set, stating exactly what soldiers and civilians had a right to expect in all matters. The war machine was remodelled to give a share of government to local gentry, and the projected Association was incorporated into it. These reforms were intended to remove many grounds for complaint.[42] In March Rupert joined Maurice with most of the royal army, and the princes restored military supremacy in the Marches in a rapid campaign. They then crushed the Herefordshire Clubmen and punished the county by quartering the army in it for the troops to refresh themselves at will. This object lesson was powerful. The other Clubmen movements and the Association submerged, and the local rate was probably more fully paid than at any time hitherto.[43] The royal army, swelled by new recruits, was able to take the offensive against Parliament as the campaigning season of 1645 opened. It reconquered northern Worcestershire, relieved Chester, received the surrender of Montgomery and stormed Leicester. A detachment sent into Wales retook Cardigan and took Haverfordwest.

Likewise the Royalists in the west made progress at this period. In March the prince of Wales was sent into the region with a panel of privy councillors to co-ordinate and accelerate administration, which they did with energy.[44] Hopton was replaced as military commander by an officer from the royal army, George Goring, who brought with him a section of that army. During the spring Goring used these troops to repel a Parliamentarian invasion of the west. The local Parliamentarian garrisons were then blocked up and Goring's army, existing local troops and new levies combined into a new western field force, with which Goring besieged Taunton.

This resurgence came to a violent end on 14 June, when the royal army committed suicide at Naseby. This dénouement was neither the obvious nor necessary course. When the Parliamentarian New Model Army approached, the King could easily have retired westward and either linked up with Goring's troops or those sent into Wales and rounded upon the New Model, or worn it out with manoeuvring. Instead, persuaded by his more reckless advisers, he ordered his army to charge uphill into a force nearly twice its numbers. Having destroyed the royal army, the New Model marched swiftly into the west and broke Goring's army at Langport on 10 July. On 1 August the Royalists of south-west Wales were defeated on Colby Moor.

Despite the unprecedented energy with which the Parliamentarians had followed up the victory at Naseby, the Royalists could still have recovered from their defeats. The King and his leading officers had survived the disaster to their army and fled to South Wales, where in the wealthiest and most sheltered remaining Royalist territory, they gave orders to the gentry to raise a completely new army. In doing so, they fell into the trap they had evaded in the spring. They were imposing heavier burdens than ever before upon a populace thoroughly weary of war, at a time when successive defeats again seemed to make any assistance to their cause futile. The crucial factor introduced by Naseby was that now they no longer possessed an army with which to enforce their will upon a recalcitrant local community. The Glamorganshire gentry vacillated through July and then raised an irregular army and coerced the King into removing his remaining regular soldiers from the county. The despairing monarch fled the region. A month later, when the New Model Army captured Bristol, the Glamorganshire gentry allied with Parliament and called in its troops. Their example was followed within two more months by the other gentry of South Wales, and of Monmouthshire and southern Worcestershire. The basis for a Royalist recovery in Wales and the Marches had been removed.

Events in the west followed a similar but slightly different course. During the early summer the continual fighting to which Wiltshire, Somerset and Dorset had become subject since the opening of Goring's campaigns resulted in the appearance of Clubman movements of villagers, intended to protect local property by force, of the sort which had appeared in the Marches. These seem to have followed the pattern of the Marcher risings in that they occurred in areas – the hills of the Wiltshire–Dorset border and the Somerset marshes – which contained few important gentry and many smallholders. In the former case the community had a tradition of communal action to resist innovation or attack which extended back to the anti-enclosure riots of 1629–31 and was to persist until the Captain Swing risings of 1830–2. The Wiltshire–Dorset Clubmen, who are by far the best-documented of all the Clubman groups, also represented the final stage of the integration of their community into the conflict. Their primary purpose was to prevent plunder by the recently established rival local garrisons by ensuring that the local rate was properly levied and delivered to the soldiers, a rational means of keeping them out of the countryside and a solution to the basic problem of military administration.[45] On the appearance of the New Model Army and its victory at Langport the mid-Somerset Clubmen, like the South Welsh gentry, declared for Parliament. The Wiltshire–Dorset Clubmen, by contrast, attacked the New Model for breaching local peace, and were crushed.[46] The simplest feasible explanation for this difference in behaviour is that it derived from a difference in experience. The troops with whom the Somerset Clubmen had consistently come into contact were the underpaid and unruly Royalists, to whom the uniquely well-paid and well-disciplined New Model would have presented a great contrast. The Dorset–Wiltshire borderlands, on the other hand, had been plundered not merely by Royalists but by the defeated and demoralised Parliamentarian invaders of the spring. Their people may thus have acquired a jaundiced view of all armies. In addition, the mid-Somerset Clubmen possessed a leader of unusual shrewdness and breadth of vision, Humphrey Willis.

By the end of 1645, the Royalist war effort was paralysed. The only sizeable body of field troops remaining to the King was the remnant of the western army, which the New Model was slowly pushing backwards through Devon and Cornwall. These troops were numerous enough to prevent an uprising of the sort that had removed the Royalist base in South Wales, and when rebellions did occur in Cornwall they were repressed. However, there was no real hope of rebuilding these defeated and unpaid soldiers into an army capable of taking the offensive, although the Royalist leaders worked desperately to this end. The New Model, with the resources of all south-east England to support it, had difficulty in maintaining its numbers and its pay was often in arrears. The western Royalists could not hope to oppose it with the resources of two war-torn and exhausted counties.[47] Two hopes remained to the King, that aid could be obtained by hiring mercenaries in Ireland or on the continent, or that the gentry who had defected in the summer might reverse their decision. The first proved completely vain, but the second came to pass in February 1646, when the gentry of Glamorganshire revolted against their newly acquired Parliamentarian allies. The latter, like the Royalists, had proved determined to keep regular soldiers in the county and to levy a heavy local rate to pay them. Unlike the Royalists, they had vested local power in a committee of minor gentry, thereby demonstrating their lack of trust in the established leaders, and outlawed the traditional ecclesiastical liturgy. The Royalists had threatened the peace and wealth of this community, Parliament seemed to menace its social and religious foundations as well. In rebelling, the gentry forgot that Parliament, unlike the King in the summer, still possessed troops to enforce its will. Three Parliamentarian forces converged on the shire and overwhelmed it.[48] A few weeks later the New Model Army finally overwhelmed the western forces and the last Royalist attempt to raise field troops from garrisons met with disaster. The King surrendered and his last fortresses were reduced. The formal war was over. The other struggle, between local populations and the military, remained. It was to be a prominent feature of English politics, affecting national and local events alike, until the regular soldiers finally vanished at the Restoration.

From this brief summary it may be seen how close, complex

and important the relationship between the two varieties of struggle was. In the last analysis it was the local community, not Parliament, which defeated Charles I, though from hatred of the war itself rather than of the Royalist cause. Yet the King's defeat in the field made this second defeat possible, and had he been victorious there the same process would have worked in his favour. Indeed, it did work in his favour only a few weeks before Naseby, and had done at other times during the war. The concept of a steady alienation of the local population from the Royalist cause is as misplaced as the concept of a basic hostility of that population to one or the other cause in particular. Nor can it be said that the Royalists failed to respond with energy or imagination to the problems of military administration, for their war machine too underwent no continuous process of decay and collapse. The history of the Great Rebellion is much more than a story of the actions of monarchs, ministers and MPs, but it is one in which, nevertheless, the decisions and personalities of individuals remain vital. This is as true at the local as at the national level.

# 3. Neutralism, Conservatism and Political Alignment in the English Revolution: The Case of the Towns, 1642–9

ROGER HOWELL

I

THAT towns were a significant element in the English Revolution goes without saying. It was not simply a matter of their parliamentary representation, much of it in the hands of the gentry and hence more a part of the history of the county community than a separate urban element in itself. Nor was it just the product of their strategic importance, though the numerous sieges of the war testify to the value contemporaries gave to that factor. Above all, it was the perception that the towns were intimately connected with the process of rebellion and sedition, the feeling that within the towns and especially within the middle mercantile strata of their population were to be found strong and active supporters of the Parliamentary cause. Thomas Hobbes suggested that merchants, looking at the examples of the United Provinces, had connected in their minds overthrow of the monarchy, the establishment of a republic, and the spread of commercial prosperity; Clarendon felt that the majority of the towns were naturally malignant and hence had been unusually receptive to Puritan infiltration and influence from the more radical sections of Parliament. In short, many people would have agreed with the comment that appeared in a news-sheet in 1643: 'most corporations, as we find by experience, are nurseries of faction and rebellion'.[1]

This contemporary view has been embodied in one way or another in much of the modern historical writing on the revolution.[2] There is, implicitly or explicitly, in many accounts of the war an assumption that the towns, or at least the progressive mercantile sections in them, were sympathetic to the Parliamentary cause, even if the governing oligarchies, for obvious reasons, tended to feel affinities with the Royalist position on which their monopolistic rights ultimately depended. From that assumption, which seems at least plausible given the rough geographical alignment of the two sides once fighting actually broke out, several further considerations can be derived. The alleged commitment of portions of the mercantile community to the Parliamentary cause suggests a relatively high level of interest in and information about the generalised grievances of the political nation as reflected in Parliament. Moreover, it suggests that within many towns one ought to find a conflict between the Parliamentary-inclined progressive elements and the ruling oligarchy whose overt sympathies should be Royalist. Given the victory of Parliament in the war, that same internal tension should be resolved in the late 1640s by some perceptible broadening of the oligarchical structure of the town corporations as the Parliamentary new men take over from the Royalist old men. Finally, this set of assumptions suggests that the relationship between the internal history of the towns and the events of the Revolution is explicable in terms of class; the solid middling elements emerge as the supporters of Parliament, while the social extremes opt for support of the King (although ultimately for rather different reasons).

There are, of course, exceptions to this simple model of the political behaviour of the English towns which even supporters of the model or some variant of it readily admit. But a more profound difficulty exists; the great diversity of towns in seventeenth-century England makes the construction of a single working model difficult, if not impossible.[3] Variations in size obviously affected the nature and sophistication of political life. Some 600 to 700 towns existed in England in the period, with more of a concentration in the lowland zone of the south and east than elsewhere. They ranged in size, complexity, and degree of specialisation from lesser market centres with a population numbered in the hundreds, through decaying boroughs with at best a localised influence to regional centres whose hinterland included a number of the lesser market centres, and a small group of large and rich towns whose status had become that of a regional capital. At the top of the urban hierarchy stood London, in size, complexity and importance a category all by itself and one that will not be considered in this essay. The structure of town government was a complex mosaic. At one extreme were small towns like Calne. There the chief executive power of the corporation was vested in the two guild stewards who served a one-year term; it was an office occupied by all the burgesses in turn, many serving several times during their lives. No evidence exists in the guild stewards' book to indicate that Calne was bedevilled by political rivalry or bothered by the intervention of the Crown to secure a corporation of a suitable political complexion. At the other extreme were towns like Newcastle-upon-Tyne, where there is abundant evidence for the existence of political rivalry and debate about the structure of town government from the 1590s; a complicated structure of government, involving a mayor, aldermen and court of common council had been established by successive charters, and an elaborate electoral system devised which virtually guaranteed the dominance of a select group of powerful mercers and coal-shippers. In the establishment of the tight oligarchy, the role of the Crown had been marked, and Newcastle provides a classic case in which Crown desires and the interests of the local inner ring went hand in hand, though even here, maintaining the fine line between royal support for the desires of the oligarchy and royal interference in the affairs of the borough had become a problem before the war. Norwich, on the other hand, presents quite a different picture. There, the government of the city had not been monopolised by a small and closed élite; on the contrary, a large and active citizenry had the constitutional right to participate in electoral politics and had periodically exercised that right in opposition to the magistracy before 1640.[4]

The case of Norwich suggests several other variables that make construction of a single model difficult. The presence of

the cathedral in Norwich added a complicating factor to the
working of local politics; conflict between the corporation,
which had close associations with nonconformity, and the
cathedral was predictable and gave a distinct, if hardly
unique, tone to the nature of local politics. In Worcester likewise the period before the Civil War had been marked by
conflict between the cathedral and the city authorities, with the
bishop supporting the city against the dean who had denied the
cathedral pulpit to the city preacher. Analogous conflicts in
attitude and jurisdiction between cathedral and civic authorities occurred in a number of other cathedral cities, such as
York, Salisbury, Chichester and Gloucester.[5] The case of
Norwich further suggests that the existence of extensive
commercial and personal ties with the metropolis was another
important variable in the political life of a provincial city or
town; in contrast to many provincial towns, Norwich showed a
pattern of concern for and response to national affairs, and it
would appear to be the case that a large and active Puritan
community sharing similar experience with that in London
provided the critical linkage. Yet relationship to London by
itself remains an insufficient explanatory tool for the behaviour
of a number of towns. Gloucester, Coventry and Birmingham,
for example, have also been seen as exceptions to the prevalent
localism noticed in so many towns; in their cases, the common
denominator would appear to be vigorous Puritan leadership
rather than relationship to London.[6]

Finally, the role of individuals in shaping the political
responses of towns should not be undervalued. Although the
evidence clearly suggests that in many towns significant
elements of the population sought to avoid commitments to
either side in the conflict, desired to follow the course of
neutrality as the safest stance, ultimately chose sides under
pressure and without deep conviction, and readily sought
accommodation with any regime that promised law, order, and
the preservation of local privileges, there were, of course, men of
principle and conviction whose intervention into the situation
had profound impact on the apparent loyalties of the town and
whose actions contributed to the important but not well understood process by which local grievances were merged with the
grievances of other communities, became generalised, and were

thus transformed into a growing interest in national affairs. The role of Edmund Prideaux in stopping the involvement of Exeter in the 1643 negotiations between the two armies in Devon and Cornwall for a cessation of hostilities provides a case in point, as do the roles of Sir John Marley in rallying Newcastle-upon-Tyne to the Royalist cause and George Peard in securing Barnstaple for Parliament.[7]

In short, the pattern in which the towns responded to the crisis was far from simple. If localism, neutralism and the preservation of established privilege were recurrent themes, they were modified by the intervention of other factors of various sorts, ranging from the degree of consensus within the community with respect to the appropriateness of historic forms of government to the degree of contact with the metropolis and to the strength of Puritanism within the corporation. If it is demonstrably simplistic to assume that the progressive elements in the town were active allies of Parliament and viewed the unfolding events in some sort of national perspective, it seems equally misleading to assume that they were therefore 'sub-political', that is that they reacted to exterior events virtually exclusively in terms of local perceptions. Between the poles of national perspective and sub-political behaviour, there was room for a wide variety of responses. The complex nature of the role of the towns between 1642 and 1649 can ultimately only be understood as a result of detailed, individual studies, of which there have been to date all too few. But some appreciation of what was happening can be gained from an examination of the responses of a sample of towns to the problems posed by the outbreak of hostilities, those posed by actual involvement in the conflict, and those raised during the vexed search for a new stability and order in the aftermath of the conflict.

II

The commonsensical observation of Thomas Povey in 1643 that 'no country, scarce any city or corporation is so unanimous, but they have division enough to undo themselves'[8] provides a useful starting point, especially if one considers that such division was not exclusively between those committed to one or the other side in the struggle but also involved those for whom non-alignment seemed the best course. Bristol provides a good illustration.[9] That the events in the country were leading to divisions within the population of Bristol is plainly evident; the wearing of colours or ribbons in hats to denote party allegiances is clear indication of that. On the other hand, it is important to note the majority response of the city authorities to such a development. Far from encouraging one party or the other, the mayor, aldermen, sheriffs and common council issued an order in November 1642 suppressing such behaviour in the hope that it would curb divisions into parties. Earlier in the year the common council had the intention of petitioning both King and Parliament, urging them to a mutual reconciliation of their differences. The project was not successful; the reality of political division was such that there were sufficient zealots on both sides to frustrate the project. But the response of the authorities to the decaying political situation was indicative, and both the motivation and the implications of that response became apparent in subsequent actions. It is clear from declarations made by the council in November that the division in the city was seen as a threat to the exercise of proper civic authority, while in December it was argued that the city should not be allowed to become a Parliamentary garrison, for this would invite retaliation on the part of the King. For many, the only sensible course was to attempt to stand aside and refuse to admit the forces of either side. When Bristol finally was garrisoned for Parliament in December, it was more a reflection of the fact that the city authorities no longer controlled the situation than a statement of loyalty to the Parliamentary cause. Even then, the Parliamentary forces under Colonel Essex were kept locked out for two days; the desire to remain uncommitted persisted until the very point of occupation.

This sort of response was hardly an isolated phenomenon. Both Parliamentarians and Royalists found Worcester initially unreceptive to their advances. A Parliamentary force was admitted there with obvious reluctance in 1642, but one soldier found his short-lived stay in the city so unwelcome that he felt compelled to compare Worcester to Sodom and Gomorrah.[10] On the other hand, the reception of the Royalists was no warmer; the city petitioned that no troops were to be billeted in the city and that no meetings of the King's commissioners were to be held there. In August 1642, when the King's commissioners were forced to accept this expulsion, there was little they could do but complain that 'the ill entertainment of the citizens of Worcester have so scattered our thoughts that they cannot be so suddenly recollected.'[11] The response of attempted neutrality appears to have been widespread in 1642 among the small Cornish boroughs, while Tewkesbury, despite the example of nearby Gloucester, seemed, as one disgruntled Parliamentarian remarked, to desire 'an everlasting neutrality'.[12]

Two observations need to be made about the attempt of many towns to remain unaligned. In the first place, neutrality was frequently misunderstood, both at the time and by later historians. As divisions grew in the country, it was unavoidable that neutralism came to be regarded as covert support for the other side from that against which it was exercised. Parliamentary supporters were quick to assert that neutrality was not an end in itself but rather a cloak for malignancy and a refuge for the cavalier. But as the Shrewsbury merchant Jonathan Langley discovered, it could cut the other way; his intention of not committing himself to either side was viewed in a Royalist stronghold as being covert support for Parliament, and he was forced to seek refuge elsewhere.[13] The assumption that neutrality was only a temporary stopping place on the route to open commitment (usually on the Royalist side) continues to appear in modern discussions of the period, but the widespread nature of the phenomenon would suggest that this reading of the situation is too simplistic. To be sure, the overwhelming majority of those who sought to follow the neutralist course eventually found themselves and their towns committed on one side or the other, and that points to the second observation that should be made; opting out was, in the long run, impossible for most. Yet the ultimate selection of a side should not be confused with an abstract desire to choose one, nor should political behaviour dictated by perceived necessity be confused with behaviour motivated by the holding of partisan principles. If nothing else, the continued resistance of towns to interference with the traditional way of doing things would indicate this; the preservation of local autonomy and the restoration of normal commercial conditions remained for the towns items of the highest priority, and the stress on them was, in many cases, nothing more than an expression of the same sentiments that had led to initial efforts to remain uninvolved.

Before turning to the behaviour of the towns after the fighting had enveloped them, two further points about the response to the outbreak of hostilities need to be considered: the actions taken by towns to commence fortifications and other sorts of defences and the nature of the emerging 'parties' in the towns as divisions did in fact occur. That most towns felt impelled to put themselves in a posture of defence as the situation decayed in 1642 in incontrovertible. The question is, however, what did such action mean? To assume that it was equivalent to a commitment either to the conflict in general or to one of the sides in it would be risky. Equally risky would be the assumption that all of the population perceived its importance and co-operated gladly in it. Given the prevalence of the idea that non-alignment would be the best course, it seems likely that for many towns the process of preparing defences was motivated primarily by a desire to put themselves in a position to maintain property and ultimately to protect themselves from both sides at a time when internal law and order were breaking down. Some towns appear to have been reluctant to face the fact that events had reached the point where such actions were necessary. Despite its obvious strategic significance, Newcastle-upon-Tyne displayed a seeming unwillingness to get down to the business of war-making, and when the earl of Newcastle arrived there, 'he neither found any military provision considerable for the undertaking of that work, nor generally any great encouragement from the people in those parts.'[14] The cases of Nottingham and Worcester are likewise suggestive. At the former, when the decision was taken to restrict the defensive work to the castle only, the townsmen protested openly and threatened to pull the castle down if they could not have 'their ordnance again upon their works'. Such actions could be easily misunderstood; to the Parliamentary commander it smacked of Royalist sympathy on the part of the townsmen, but a more detached judgement might suggest that it simply manifested the desire of the townsmen to have protection for their property.[15] This desire of a town corporation to keep control in some fashion of the town fortifications rather than leave such matters to a military garrison was openly stated at Worcester. The Royalist garrison was hardly settled in the city when the local authorities complained about being assessed for work on the fortifications and petitioned the military governor that 'he will be pleased . . . to have us to consider in what manner we may take course for the fortification of this city which we will presently endeavour to our powers'.[16]

Dorchester (Dorset) and Barnstaple provide further evidence of the varied reactions to the process of fortification. As early as January 1642 it was agreed in Dorchester that the townsmen should raise and continue a convenient number of soldiers for the defence of the town, but after only two weeks, many of the townsmen rated for the support of them refused to pay, some absolutely, others for more than one week. When more elaborate preparations were made later in the year with the clear intention of supporting the Parliamentary cause, the wealthiest inhabitants moved their goods out of town, apparently reasoning that defensive preparations were an incitement to attack and that the steps taken would prove insufficient to protect their property in such an event.[17] Barnstaple corporation decided on fortifying the town before a single Royalist soldier had entered Devon and before Parliament had committed itself to the war. But despite an order in January 1643 that those who refused to pay the necessary rates would be adjudged enemies of the town and proceeded against as malignants (an order in which the hand of the convinced Parliamentarian and MP for the borough George Peard is evident), the corporation encountered difficulty from owners and occupiers of land who resisted what they viewed as encroachments on private rights, and martial law had to be resorted to in order to forward the work of fortification. The earl of Stamford, commenting on the situation, touched on a significant element in the thinking of many townsmen when he remarked petulantly how they preferred 'their own private interest and commodity before the public and common good and safety'.[18]

If the towns had a tendency to put local interests first, and if such an attitude was more likely to be manifested in an attitude of non-alignment than it was in fervent enthusiasm for either side, it is nonetheless true that the towns did divide into parties, and it is important to consider what can be known about the nature of such parties. It is frequently argued that the divisions were reflective of class tensions and antagonisms. A considerable volume of contemporary comment would seem to lend strong support to the observation that the King's cause was favoured by the social extremes of the town, while Parliament and godly religion drew their support from the solid 'middling' sort. The divisions in towns as diverse as Bristol, Chichester, Bradford, Birmingham and Coventry have been explained in this fashion. But the situation is by no means so firmly established as its reiteration in the pamphlet literature of the time might seem to indicate. In Bristol, for example, those known to have been implicated in the Royalist plot of 1643 included a substantial number of people from precisely that middle rank which was supposed to be the core of the Parliamentary group.[19] There was, of course, a marked tendency for the grandest of the oligarchs, especially those with a hand in a monopoly like the Newcastle coal-trade, to identify with the Royalist side, but this should not be taken to indicate that those who opposed them were necessarily of a significantly different socio-economic level or that their opposition was the product of national issues. In a number of cases, the division into parties represents more a struggle of élites than it does a genuine class conflict. In Newcastle, for example, the division into Royalists and Parliamentarians was a new chapter in long-standing local battle over the control of the coal trade, but the new men who rode to power on the back of the Parliamentary victory were themselves already members for the most part of the wider commercial oligarchy of the town; they sought a modest extension of the monopoly privileges connected with the coal-trade, an extension that would include themselves, but they had no intention of abolishing the monopoly conditions nor even of opening them up more broadly to the middling orders. The split between Royalists and Parliamentarians in the nation provided the opportunity for pursuing an old battle under new banners, but it was not a battle that pitted the oligarchy against the middling orders.[20] The case of Chester was similar; there too the 1642 split into Parliamentarians and Royalists was 'the expression and outgrowth under national labels of the political struggle in which they had been engaged throughout the early seventeenth century'.[21] An exhaustive study of the opposed parties in Norwich has concluded that the leadership cannot be distinguished on the basis of social background, family connections, occupations or wealth. If Norwich differed from Newcastle and Chester in the fact that the divisions there were seemingly explicable in terms of ideological issues involving a national dimension instead of local issues dressed up in a new garb, it nonetheless bears a telling resemblance to the two northern cities in the absence of socio-economic issues as the root cause of the split.[22]

III

The opening phases of the war suggest, then, that the position of the towns was both different from and more complex than many contemporary observers allowed. It simply was not the case that the towns showed an overwhelming tendency to identify from the start with the Parliamentary cause; if anything, they showed a tendency towards neutrality. That tendency was, of course, the product of self-interest; for every merchant who thought as Hobbes speculated a merchant might think and conjured up an image of increased profit and trade deriving from a revolutionary change of government, there were obviously dozens who recognised that the breakdown of order would lead to destruction of property, interruption of trade, and interference with cherished privileges. The note was firmly struck by those townsmen of Hull who, in 1642, urged Sir John Hotham to surrender to the King because resistance would lead to the 'want of trade and victuals'.[23] The years of fighting meant for many the translation of such fears into realities. Under the conditions of warfare, the pressures for a policy of accommodation grew rather than diminished; if neutrality became in a practical sense impossible, the next best course was to seek a *modus vivendi* with the powers that be in the hope that such behaviour would produce the minimum degree of interference to the economic life of the town and to its traditional forms of government.

It is obvious that the conditions of civil war presented the towns with a host of challenges to 'business as usual'. Trade was interrupted. Tension between the traditional authorities of the town and other, imposed authorities, frequently of a military kind, was frequent. At times chaotic conditions, such as those attendant on a siege, produced a total breakdown in the normal governmental functioning of the towns. Property was destroyed, and the costs of war, in the form of extra taxation and supplies and loans extracted on a credit that was difficult to convert into hard cash, all plagued the inhabitants. The difficulty in enforcing such restrictive practices as the apprenticeship regulations or the prohibitions on trading by strangers not free of the corporation mounted. The readjustment of town corporations by the periodic purging of 'the other side' from the ranks of civil office holders not only threatened the continuity of municipal government, but raised that most unwelcome spectre of all, the intrusion of extramural authorities into the cherished independence of the towns.

That such pressures deeply affected the towns is everywhere apparent in the surviving records. While far more detailed research is necessary before a full economic balance sheet can be drawn up, the evidence of disruption to normal economic life meets one at every turn. In Newcastle,[24] for example, the prohibition of trade with London during the period the town was blockaded raised the prospect of economic ruin; fewer and fewer ships were able to clear the port, and this in turn adversely affected town income since the revenue from duties dropped severely. In April 1644 apparently only four ships cleared, and for half a month there were no receipts at all. When the Scots finally took the town later in the year, they were appalled by what they found; as one news-sheet reported,

> We had little news this day from the North, only that the letters from Newcastle speak that rich town, in which ten of the aldermen are knights, and as malignant as honourable, to be an object of pity, if malignants are to be pitied, there being in view nothing but many hundreds of almost naked people, wanting all things but misery.[25]

Of Leicester in June 1645 one observer commented, 'In the ruins of Leicester you may behold a large map of misery, the townsmen, from the richest to the poorest, being all of them despoiled of their goods.'[26] The damage was frequently indiscriminate. When Prince Rupert's troops looted Birmingham in 1643, considerable losses were suffered by Royalist towns-men because the troops were not careful to distinguish between foes and well-wishers.[27] There are, of course, exceptions to the picture of economic gloom; contracts for munitions were apparently of some importance to the economy of Birmingham while the war lasted, and some, like the West Riding chapman Thomas Priestley, who managed to make regular journeys to London throughout the war and brought home a clear profit on each trip, succeeded in making do even in the midst of the confusion.[28] But the general picture was clearly more grim. Nor were the conditions necessarily transient. The firing and des-truction of the mines around Newcastle and the sinking of ships in the river presented severe problems to the restoration of normal economic life long after the fighting was over, and if Birmingham had derived some war-related profits from muni-tions, there was a severe slump in local industry at the end of the war, to the extent the town could apply for relief at the quarter sessions in 1650 on the grounds of the 'deadness of trading'.[29]

The disruption to town government and the normal operat-ing of such regulations as those governing apprenticeship was equally marked. In Newcastle,[30] a steady drop in the enrolling of apprentices during the war years was paralleled by a marked drop in the same period in freeman admissions, and a similar situation was reflected in many other towns. Civic administra-tion frequently ground to a halt. In Newcastle, there were no recorded meetings of the common council between 20 October 1643 and 28 March 1645, although there may have been some informal meetings. The ecclesiastical administration of the town likewise suffered; the register of All Saints Church was broken off in 1643 and not resumed until January 1645 while the vestry book of Tynemouth church has no entries between Easter Monday 1642 and an unspecified date in 1645. In Worcester,[31] during the period in the autumn of 1642 when the town was occupied first by Parliament and then by the Royalists, no meetings of the corporation were recorded between 29 August and 7 October, though admittedly during the siege of the city (28 May to 23 July 1646) the level of council activity remained high, no fewer than twelve meetings being recorded. In Barnstaple, the sessions court records in 1642 end in the middle of an entry and the records for the next few years are either fragmentary or absent altogether, affording a strong suggestion that the regular government of the town was suddenly superseded by a military one.[32]

The presence of a military authority presented particular problems for the functioning of town government, and conflict between the two was frequent. The records of Nottingham suggest a steady pattern of conflict between the town and the governor.[33] There were similar tensions in Worcester.[34] In Hull,[35] the corporation complained to the Speaker of the House of Commons in 1643 about the 'tyrannical' government of Sir John Hotham, 'whose will was the rule of all his actions and by whose power all the liberties of this poor corporation were trampled underfoot'. Two years later the corporation, though declaring itself to be happy under the protection and government of Sir Thomas Fairfax, took strong exception to the proposal that Hull should be associated with the northern counties 'which they apprehend might prove very destructive and that thereby they should be brought into a dangerous and distracted condition by the various commands and other inconveniences that may happen'; through their recorder they pressed the argument that such an arrangement would destroy the liberties and freedoms of Hull, that the 'civil government will be trampled upon', and that Hull would be reduced to 'a parcel' of the East Riding. In the following year, the corporation was at pains to get a proviso inserted into the ordinance with respect to martial law that the provisions were not to extend to any civilian burgesses and that its exercise should not in any way prejudice the civil powers and government of the town.

If the conflict of authority was worrying even in the abstract its implications were most directly felt in the matters of taxation and the regulation of municipal office-holding. The problems of taxation require little elaboration. Both sides in the conflict pressed hard on the towns for necessary financial support, while the town's own expenses for fortifications and the repair of damages placed heavy strain both on municipal budgets and on individual burgesses. The nature of such special and unpredictable burdens can be illustrated by the case of Worcester.[36] Already subject to what appeared to be a sudden and drastic increase in taxation, Worcester faced in September 1643 a demand from the King for a loan of £4000, and while the corporation appointed assessors for each ward, they protested that it was impossible to raise such a large sum 'in respect of decay of trade of clothing, the weekly burdens and taxes laid on the inhabitants for making fortifications and scouring the ditches, etc.'. They undertook to raise if possible £2000, but the assessments amounted to only £1500, and at the end of the year they were petitioning for a further reduction or cancellation. In the following June the King demanded an additional £1000 as a grant, but at the end of the year both it and the £2000 from the year before were still in arrears. This was but one part of a larger picture, and even tiny boroughs of no strategic importance suffered the impact of similar extractions; Calne, for example, had to pay its share of the rates levied by both sides, and the constables' accounts of disbursements were swollen to a figure in the range of twenty times the normal amount during 1643–4 by such payments.[37]

That the war occasioned the purging of town corporations and interference with normal electoral procedures should occasion no surprise. In Newcastle,[38] Henry Warmouth, one of the most prominent Puritans of the borough, was removed from his aldermancy for neglect of duty in April 1643 and in September thirty-five freemen were disenfranchised for being incendiaries and treating with the Scots to invade. In Coventry,[39] the mayor was removed in 1645 for being disaffected to Parliament, and the governor of the town assumed the role of chief magistrate. At Nottingham,[40] an alderman and the town clerk were purged in August 1644, while in Worcester,[41] three aldermen were displaced during the brief Parliamentary control of the city, only to be promptly reinstated on orders from the King in March 1643 at the expense of those who had taken their places. Though there were numerous incidents of this kind, the significant feature is not their occurrence, but rather the reluctance with which the civil authorities co-operated with interference from outside. In Shrewsbury, for example, the King proscribed by name certain members of the corporation in October 1642. The town authorities agreed that the named aldermen and assistants should be sequestered from meetings until they cleared themselves, and, if they were not able to do so, new men should be elected in their place. A month later three of those named were removed on the grounds of non-residence, but no further action appears to have been taken against the remaining ten.[42] In Worcester, there was an evident reluctance to remove or to accept the resignation of anyone who remained resident in the city. The motivation for such reluctance was doubtless in part financial; it was essential to keep up the numbers of the common council in order to spread more evenly the heavy financial liabilities placed on it, but in major part the reluctance was clearly a reflection of a determination to maintain the chartered rights of the corporation against extramural interference.[43] Similar motives were probably behind the slowness of the removal of the town clerk in Nottingham; though loyal to the King's cause and indeed an active supporter of it, he was not voted unfit to hold his office until August 1644 and was not in fact physically removed from office until a year later.[44] For all the threat and reality of purging, the corporations on the whole displayed a distinct resistance to outside interference; to the Worcester authorities it seemed better that Parliamentary supporters should continue on the council of a Royalist-dominated city than that the corporation should allow its privileges to be interfered with, and few boroughs would have disagreed with the proposition.

Put together, the strains occasioned by the war could be severe for a town. In the face of them, ideological commitments often carried little sway and local self-interest looked far larger. It is striking how, in many towns, the mere prospect of a siege was sufficient to cause a considerable element of the population to urge an accommodation. The phenomenon was marked in Newcastle where some merchants were willing to make voyages to supply the Scots and carry coals to London as early as March 1644.[45] The same sort of thinking was reflected in Barnstaple during the period Parliament held the town in 1644; despite the allegedly strong Parliamentary feelings of the populace, no efforts were made to repair and strengthen the fortifications in this interval, and one can only conclude that the corporation had no inclination again to invite attack or a possible siege by displaying strong defences.[46] The hostile comments by the preacher Walter Powell about the behaviour of many towns described a style of action that might well have seemed to most of their inhabitants only common sense: 'Fear of plundering makes many stagger in respect of part-taking with either; if they reveal themselves, they are made a prey to the will of the adversaries; therefore, so they may sleep in a whole skin, they dread not the danger of a tattered conscience.'[47]

IV

The patterns of behaviour that appear to have characterised the towns during the actual fighting – reluctance to become involved, anxiety to seek an early accommodation in the hope of a return to more normal conditions, determination to preserve the town's liberty against outside authority – persisted into the period after the conclusion of hostilities. The assertion of parliamentary supremacy and the avowed intention to exclude delinquents from local office raised the last of these concerns in a particularly acute way. Two central questions need to be asked about this situation. First, did the years between the end of the first Civil War and the establishment of the Commonwealth see a major dislocation of urban government, with significant purging of the corporations taking place, either as the result of internal tensions or exterior pressures? Second, were the changes that did occur reflective of a national drift to the left in bringing men of a different socio-economic background and more radical political attitudes to positions of power in the towns?

Newcastle-upon-Tyne provides an example of the complexity involved in trying to answer such questions.[48] Certainly the reshaping of the corporation after the reduction of the town to Parliamentary control involved some violations of the chartered privileges of the corporation. The Royalist mayor Sir John Marley (whose own appointment by mandamus from the King in 1642 had already involved a charter violation) was removed from office by ordinance of Parliament, and Henry Warmouth, purged during the Royalist occupation, was substituted in his place without election. In March 1645, eight Royalists were ordered purged from the corporation by Parliament, though it was seven months before the official local enactment of their disfranchisement took place. How the corporation was actually reconstructed remains somewhat obscure. New appointees were named in a parliamentary Act, but at least two of them

were clearly acting in aldermanic office before the parliamentary ordinance named them, while one person named in that
document does not appear in the list of the corporation either at
this time or subsequently. One cannot avoid the impression
that the restructuring of the corporation was generated as much
from within Newcastle, where it represented the temporary
victory of the 'outs' in the long-standing battle for control of the
coal-shipping monopoly, as from without, in accordance with
national political loyalties. A further alderman, John Cosins,
was removed in 1647; he was a Presbyterian with close connections with the Scots, and hence it is tempting to see in his
removal a reflection of national political tensions. But close
examination of the town records suggests that the reasons for
his removal were connected with the local struggle between the
old inner-ring and the new men who had achieved power in the
wake of the Parliamentary victory; it is particularly telling that
it was more than three months after his expulsion when the
Newcastle authorities finally raised the 'national' issue that
Cosins intended to bring the Scots back into England embroil-
ing the nation once more in civil strife.

It is also important to note in the case of Newcastle a phenomenon that was widely reflected in other towns, namely the
survival through all the purges, both during the war and after,
of a core of town office-holders who adjusted skilfully to each
change of circumstance in turn. Such men formed what may be
termed a 'moderate–neutralist' bloc. They were frequently to
be found as the most vocal advocates of non-alignment at the
outbreak of hostilities and the chief spokesmen for accommodation under the pressures of war. Their loyalties were
doubtless baffling to their committed contemporaries, precisely
because they downplayed loyalty in respect to the divisive
national issues in favour of loyalty to and concern with the
specific local issues of the town. Nearly all towns experienced
some purging, though the slowness with which they responded
to exterior pressure suggests the importance of an essentially
local perspective. Weymouth and Melcombe Regis underwent
a major reshuffling in January 1649 when fifteen members of the
aldermen and common council resigned under pressure.[49]
What is most striking is not the size of the group forced out, but
the time it had taken to effect the change. They left office under

the terms of an ordinance of Parliament on 4 October 1647 banning from office all who had been in arms against Parliament or who had aided and abetted the Royalist cause. It was not until after the municipal elections in September 1648 that there was any local protest against their continuation in office; on that occasion only one who was objected against resigned, and even that resignation came more than a month later. In Worcester, the extent of the purging appears to have been modest and slow;[50] two of the leading Royalists, William Evetts and Sir Daniel Tyas, did not leave office until 1649, and though one prominent Royalist, Edward Solley, was removed from office in August 1646, both he and his colleague Sir Daniel Tyas continued throughout the Interregnum as trustees of the city lands.

The evidence for continuity in the towns, despite the existence of outside pressures, is strong. In Barnstaple, nearly 40 per cent of the known members of the common council of 1642 were still members of that body in 1650, and the first three mayors elected after the reduction of the town to Parliamentary control were all men who were active on the council before the outbreak of the war.[51] At Worcester,[52] the four mayors elected between 1646 and 1649 all had long service in the city government; all had been elected to the lower branch of town government, the Forty-Eight, by 1634 and two of them had become members of the Twenty-Four before the outbreak of the war. Although the established *cursus honorum* of town office-holding was occasionally disturbed in the years under consideration, more often than not familiar patterns were followed; when the House of Lords ordered in September 1647 that Edward Elvins, who had been mayor in the previous year, should continue in office until both Houses took further action, the directive was blithely ignored.

A prevalent conception about urban history in this period is that a distinctive drift to the left occurred, roughly coincident with the creation of the Commonwealth in 1649. The suggestion is that, in the process of purging, men came to the fore, not only in the central government but also in the local communities, who were far more radical in religion, politics and social attitudes than their predecessors had been.[53] It is admitted that such men were prepared to fight the traditional battles of their corporations, yet it is argued that there was a genuine radical-

ism in their careers, that they felt themselves in various significant ways free from the sorts of restraints which encumbered
those who had their roots in pre-war corporations. Despite the
existence of some well-known cases which seem to demonstrate
this pattern – the most frequently cited are Bedford, High
Wycombe and Wells[54] – the general phenomenon of the drift to
the left is far from established. In Newcastle,[55] the moderate
civic revolution in the wake of Parliamentary victory, a revolution which had no real social dimension, appears to have
quietened totally a sixty-year experience of conflict between the
upper and lower branches of town government and equally of
conflict between town government and the general body of
freemen. It can only be concluded that this reshuffling of élites
satisfied those in a position to make an articulate political
response and that a town corporation, not only protective of
inherited privilege but in most respects as closed and conservative as that which it replaced, was more than satisfactory to the
citizens. To label such a development a drift to the left is
seriously to confuse the issue. Nor does the experience of such
boroughs as Leicester and Exeter suggest a different picture. In
York and Barnstaple, the machinery of government continued
to function much as it had in the past; there is little, if any,
evidence of the alleged drift to the left.[56] Even Rye, which has
been described as a borough violently divided, turns out to be
something different; the essential division was between town
government and imposed authority, between the town officials
who sought to retain traditional forms and practices and the
military garrison. The causes of contention were disbanded
soldiers and strangers setting themselves up in various trades in
Rye, in violation of charter provisions; it was over this specific
issue that the mayor and jurats complained that the soldiers
were 'emboldened to despise and contemn all government and
ministers thereof'.[57] Even the situation in High Wycombe
should suggest caution about the alleged drift to the left.[58] The
conflict in the corporation was hardly a new one when it was
raised by a riot in September 1649. Nor was the outcome an
immediate triumph for the forces of a new radicalism; it was
only in 1650 that the Council of State intervened in the electoral
process and ordered the appointment of the mayor. Even that
order was resisted and, though the 'reform' mayor eventually

assumed his duty, his triumph formed no precedent since he was followed in office by a succession of supporters of the old order. When the popular movement finally made its impact on High Wycombe, it was not under the Commonwealth at all but at the height of the Protectorate. In Norwich, probably the most 'political' of the provincial centres, the drift to the left is not to be perceived. Although there was a considerable turnover in personnel in the late 1640s and 1650s, the type of person involved in city government remained extraordinarily consistent; those who came to civic power under the Commonwealth are basically indistinguishable on grounds of wealth, occupation or age both from those who preceded and from those who succeeded them. 'The new magistrates of the Interregnum were not men of politically obscure trades and they were not social upstarts. They had espoused no schemes for social and economic reform before 1649 and they introduced no radical programmes in these areas once they gained power.'[59]

The drift to the left remains an unproved phenomenon. Its absence in many boroughs underlines the general point being argued about the history of the towns in the period from 1642–9. They were not the natural spawning ground of the Parliamentary or popular cause. On the contrary, they were as divided and puzzled as was the nation at large when an unwanted and indeed dreaded conflict descended on them. There were zealots and committed men who spoke out and pushed them one way or the other, but their own overt commitment was more often the product of duress than of initial ideological enthusiasm. On balance, the older political structures of the towns showed a remarkable capacity to absorb the Revolution, and by the process of accommodation they managed to preserve against various forms of outside pressure a high degree of inherited privilege. In national terms the Revolution raised the question of broadening the base of political power; in the towns that initiative barely got off the ground in the vast majority of cases. The end result was that if the towns had any formative influence on the Revolution, it was not primarily of the progressive sort. With few exceptions, the urban response was conservative and defensive. And overwhelmingly, it was that stance that prevailed despite the outside pressures put upon it.

# 4. The Church in England, 1642–9

## JOHN MORRILL

### I

IN religion, as in politics, the Parliamentarians knew what they would not have, but not what they would have.[1] In 1640 there was a broad consensus that the Laudian experiment had to be halted and reversed, but no agreement whether to attempt to restore 'the pure religion of Elizabeth and James' or to make a fresh start. By 1642 most of those who joined the King were committed to the former, most of those who stayed at Westminster to the latter. From 1642–6 the House maintained an uneasy unity. The great majority were committed to the replacement of the Anglican[2] Church by a new form of national Church and were committed to the principle of uniformity within that new Church. There were few MPs willing to concede any toleration outside the new Church to the tiny minorities of separatists or sectaries. Their uneasy unity was shattered in the course of 1646–7 by the debates which settled the new national Church. While the great majority wanted a national Church, a considerable number disliked the one proposed by the Westminster Assembly and would have preferred a settlement which gave more autonomy at parish level, or more power to the laity. This minority had to decide whether to accept defeat and submit themselves to the Presbyterian scheme, or to demand a right to opt out. By taking the latter course this large minority made the cause of toleration far more general and powerful than it had been before it changed the course of English politics.[3]

These developments have been much studied, and they are very important. But there is another side to the ecclesiastical history of the 1640s – the commitment by the majority in Parliament to eradicate Anglican worship and observance. The will of Parliament was clear and unambiguous; but the programme was a miserable failure. Within the limited space available here, it is not possible to examine the complex problem of how far the aspirations of the Puritans in Parliament in the 1640s represented the articulation of a programme long cherished by Puritans among the gentry, urban oligarchs, the clergy. In order to impose limits to the discussion, the principal aim here will be to examine the effectiveness of a number of specific objectives laid down by ordinance between 1643 and 1649: the suppression of the Book of Common Prayer and its replacement by the Directory of Public Worship; the suppression of the old Christian festivals, particularly Christmas, Easter and Rogationtide; the substitution of one pattern of admission to holy communion by another; the removal or destruction of idolatrous and superstitious objects and images from the churches. It is the argument of the essay that all these ordinances were not only largely ignored but actively resisted; that despite the provision of penalties for non-observance, local committees and others charged with the enforcement found themselves unable or unwilling to carry out their duties. One is reminded of the inability of bishops, archdeacons and ecclesiastical courts in general to eradicate Puritanism in the half century before 1640. The tables were turned with a vengeance: Puritan non-conformity under Anglican harassment gave way to Anglican non-conformity under the Puritan yoke. The subject is an important one, yet historians have been so dazzled by the emergence of the radical sects (although it seems probable that at no point in the critical period 1643–54 did more than 5 per cent attend religious assemblies other than those associated with their parish churches)[4] that they have failed to recognise that the greatest challenge to the respectable Puritanism of the Parliamentarian majority came from the passive strength of Anglican survivalism. If the essay ignores the radicals, it is not because they are unimportant, but because the balance needs to be redressed.

This imbalance results from the nature of the evidence: the Anglicans did not publicise their defiance – there are no tracts drawing attention to their activities; those clergy who maintained the old services and practices did not keep diaries or write autobiographies; Puritan non-conformity before 1640 is recorded in the voluminous church court records while the comparable records of the 1640s, the county committee papers, do not survive. Conversely the basic sources upon which this paper is based have never been properly studied: church court records tell us about those who were disobedient, church-wardens' accounts tell us – very boringly in the main – about ordinary daily parish business and obedience. These accounts are scattered and it is only in recent years that they have been transferred in any number from vestry safes and cupboards to county record offices. Churchwardens' accounts have been used by historians of particular parishes, but not by historians of counties or dioceses, let alone historians of England. Study of them shows, however, that by 1640 most English parishes carried out the duties prescribed by law and by the Prayer Book conscientiously and often enthusiastically. The rhythms of the Anglican Year (itself deriving from more ancient custom), and the regular administration of the sacraments, were carefully observed, church ornaments and images cherished. These same accounts – even less used by historians of the 1640s and 1650s – will show the ineffectiveness of parliamentary decrees in very different regions.

Thus this essay rests upon the hypothesis that religious commitment is best observed in conditions of persecution. It is surely insufficient to portray the majority of Elizabethan and early Stuart Englishmen as wishy-washy, indolent, pale creatures besides the thrusting, vigorous Puritans and the dogged, ostracised Popish recusants. If three generations of Anglican practice meant anything to them, then the events of the 1640s would test their mettle. The essay also grew out of the puzzle that if Anglicanism collapsed so utterly in the 1640s and 1650s, how was it that it emerged so quickly, confidently and joyfully in most parishes in 1660–2? What becomes apparent to anyone who wades through surviving churchwardens' accounts all over the country for the Civil War and for the Restoration years was the spontaneity of the response in 1660 compared with the reluctant and partial acceptance of change in the 1640s. The strength of the Anglican reaction of 1660 lay not exclusively, or even principally, in the response of a gentry who craved the return of a hierarchical Church which would shore up a hierarchical government and society, but in the popularity of traditional religious forms at all levels of society.

What follows is a five-part discussion of religious policy for

and practice in the parishes in the 1640s. We will look first at
the way Parliament attempted to dismantle the old Church;
secondly, at the aborted Presbyterianism designed to take its
place; thirdly, at the failure of King and bishops to give a lead to
their flock; fourthly, at the background and experience of the
parish clergy; and finally at the evidence for Anglican revival
and resurgence in these unpromising conditions.

II

The old Church was dismantled piecemeal between 1641 and
1646. Laudian innovations in doctrine, government, discipline
and liturgy were overthrown, and ecclesiastical jurisdiction was
emasculated by the Acts abolishing the Court of High Commission and barring those in holy orders from holding secular
offices. Recent innovations in church furnishing (most notably
the railing of the altars in the east end) were ordered to be
reversed. The Houses assumed wide-ranging powers to sus-
pend ministers certified to them as scandalous in life or
doctrine, and they deliberated over several schemes for the
further reform of Church government and discipline.[5] Nothing
was actually done, however, expressly to challenge the basis of
the Elizabethan Acts of Supremacy and Uniformity.[6] The
attack on the defining characteristics of the old Church –
episcopacy, the church courts, the Prayer book, the Anglican
calendar – was undertaken step by step from 1643–6 in
collaboration with the Westminster Assembly (a body of 121
divines, 10 peers and 20 members of the Commons, to whom
Scots commissioners were soon added). This assembly was
asked to propose a settlement of the Church 'agreeable to God's
Holy Word' and to 'the Church in Scotland and other
Reformed churches abroad'.[7]

Despite the mass of anti-episcopalian propaganda and the
commitment of the assembly from the outset to alternative
forms of government, the office, title and authority of bishops
were not suspended or abolished until October 1646. In early
1643, the two Houses approved a *bill* abolishing the existing
frame (archbishops, bishops, deans, chapters and so on), and
this bill was sent to the King as part of Parliament's terms for a
settlement, but the bill was not converted into an ordinance. It

had no legal force. Fourteen of the twenty-six bishops had their temporal possessions sequestered by an ordinance of March 1643, but the remaining twelve were left free to enjoy their properties and powers; six of them were indeed invited (under their episcopal titles – for example, Dr Ralph Brownrigg, bishop of Exeter) to be members of Westminster Assembly; an ordinance for demolishing monuments of superstition in 1644 was to be superintended in the cathedrals by the deans. The most important effect of this failure to proceed to abolition was that the bishops retained sole right to ordain men to the ministry for most of the war, and those ordained up to October 1646 (in theory) and up to mid-1654 (in practice) were deemed qualified to hold a living in the national Church. Nonetheless, the situation was a confused one: ministers were deprived in Lincolnshire in 1644, for example, in part for upholding the office of bishops since it had been 'voted down by Parliament'.[8]

The abolition and replacement of the Prayer book (rather than its modification) seems only to have become certain after the alliance with the Scots. No formal ban on its use was attempted until January 1645 (although the two Houses ceased to use it in their own religious observances from early 1644). In January 1645 it was replaced by a new service book, the Directory of Public Worship, drawn up by the Westminster Assembly. This ordinance was almost wholly a dead letter, and probably less than 10 per cent of parishes had acquired the new book six months later. In August, Parliament publicly acknowledged this neglect in a further ordinance which required the knights and burgesses to send down to their county committees sufficient copies of the Directory to be distributed to each parish (who had to pay for them). County committees were in return to collect in and to destroy all copies of the Book of Common Prayer. Fines and imprisonment were prescribed for the continued use of the old book.[9] Despite the survival of relevant committee and quarter sessions papers (and the reiterated commands from Parliament) there is not a single known instance of these penalties being imposed and, as we shall see, little evidence that the Directory was distributed.[10]

The doctrinal formularies of the Church of England were abrogated in 1645. Unfortunately, although many parliamentary ordinances required proof of orthodoxy from those holding parish livings, no definition of orthodoxy was ever forthcoming. A Large Catechism (of 196 questions), a small one (of 107 questions) and a Confession of Faith were drawn up by the Westminster Assembly but were never approved by the Houses and thus never published by authority.[11] The Directory did not lay down any set forms, but offered a guide to the construction of do-it-yourself services. It did not even require the use of basic formularies like the Nicene or Apostles' creeds. The nearest thing to an agreed doctrinal statement approved during the whole period was the list of elementary truths, a knowledge of which was made a condition of admission to the Lord's Supper in October 1645.[12]

On 19 December 1644 the House of Commons realised that the next monthly Fast would fall on 25 December, Christmas Day. They rushed out an ordinance smugly entitled 'for better observance of the Monthly Fast, and most especially next Wednesday, commonly called the Feast of the Nativity of Christ' on which 'men took liberty to carnal and sensual delights, contrary to the life which Christ himself led on earth.'[13] The attack on the Anglican calendar was later extended by a comprehensive ordinance which banned the observance of Christmas, Easter, Whit, Holy Days and Saints Days; as also the Rogationtide perambulations of the bounds of the parish. Instead, the second Tuesday of every month was set aside as a day of Thanksgiving.[14] As we shall see, these decrees were widely disregarded.

Finally, Parliament set out to purify churches of Popish and superstitious objects and monuments. Parliamentary orders in 1641 had already ended Laudian experiments with east-end altars, and had ordered the removal of altar-rails and the levelling of chancels. Then in August 1643 they went much further, requiring the destruction of candles, tapers and basins from the communion tables, and all crucifixes, crosses, images, pictures and superstitious objects relating to the Virgin Mary, the persons of the Trinity and the saints (though not, curiously, representations of the devil or of Old Testament figures). In 1644 a further ordinance added vestments and other Popish relics such as fonts and organs. These new ordinances were directed against objects which had adorned the churches for centuries.[15]

It is instructive to compare the way the 1641 instructions were quickly and efficiently enforced by churchwardens and parish officers whereas the ordinances of 1643–4 were widely ignored until peripatetic commissioners came along. As we shall see, these commissioners often met active or passive obstruction from local congregations or parish officers.[16] The worst iconoclasm probably occurred in the cathedrals. At least fifteen of the twenty-six were seriously vandalised by detachments of the Army who went far beyond the instructions of Parliament. Some cathedrals were partly dismantled and their building materials used for other projects (for example, Lichfield, Hereford). The corporation of Yarmouth petitioned that Norwich cathedral be dismantled and the stone used to build a new workhouse and to strengthen the piers of Yarmouth harbour; at Gloucester a block and tackle were mounted on the tower as the first stage of a proposed demolition; the Rump three times debated the pulling down of them all. In the event, most were taken over as preaching centres (Exeter with a central dividing wall erected to keep apart rival Presbyterian and Independent congregations). Others were secularised: Lichfield, Durham and St Paul's were used as barracks or prisons (in St Paul's cavalry occupied the nave, but the cloisters were turned into a shopping precinct); while St Asaph was used as a wine shop and as a shippen for the local postmaster's oxen, and the font as a hog-trough (the bishop's palace at Exeter became a sugar bakery). All in all, the cathedrals suffered more than the parish churches, as we shall see.[17]

Let us conclude this section by pointing out what was not attacked: the parish system with its traditional officers (churchwardens, overseers, select and general vestries); lay impropriation (although Royalists who held rights to receive tithes and to present to livings had to surrender them, albeit in return for generous reductions in the size of their composition fines); the responsibility of all to pay tithes. This is another point to which we shall return.

III

In place of the Elizabethan Church, Parliament approved a new settlement which was intended to introduce a uniformity in government, discipline and worship binding on all.[18] What emerged was a four-tier structure. The ancient parishes were to remain as the basic unit, with the minister joined in the regulation of both worship and discipline by elders elected by all those parishioners who had taken the Covenant and who were not 'servants that had no families'. Parishes were to be grouped into 'classes' (roughly the size of the old wapentake or hundred and comprising between ten and twenty parishes), and the classes in turn were to be grouped into provinces, one for each county and one for the city of London. Each parish was to be represented in the classis by its minister or ministers and by one or two lay elders, and each classis was to send clerical and lay nominees to the provincial assemblies. Finally there was to be a national synod whose actions were subject to ratification by Parliament. This scheme was a heavily modified version of the proposals which came out of the Westminster Assembly. The Houses were determined to ensure that the laity were fully represented in every aspect of Church government and discipline, and they thus enhanced the power of lay elders at all levels. They also weakened the power of the classes and provinces and built up the autonomy of the parishes, in which the minister could be overborne by the elders, and strengthened the power of Parliament as the ultimate source of ecclesiastical legislation and jurisdiction. These changes led the Scots to dismiss it as a 'lame erastian presbytery'. Parliament required the use of the Directory in all churches, but never ratified the catechisms or Confession of Faith.[14]

The reorganisation never really got off the ground. Although it gained majority support in the Houses, there was no general support for it in the country. The problem was that the implementation of the scheme required the co-operation of local lay commissioners. The proposals allowed each county to decide for itself the most sensible way of grouping parishes into classes.[20] Groups of commissioners were expected to meet and to draw up proposals which were then vetted and approved by Parliament. It afforded massive opportunities for prevarication, for delay, and for producing unacceptable schemes. Furthermore, the will of Parliament to enforce the scheme disappeared in effect from the time of the Army's first occupation of London in August 1647. Without central backing, and with the achievement of *de facto* toleration from October 1647 and *de jure* toleration from 1650, the whole rationale failed.[21] Although the ordinances enjoining the Presbyterian order remained in force from 1645 to 1654,[22] they became increasingly inoperative after the winter of 1647–8. Eight of the forty English counties (plus London) produced Presbyterian schemes and made some effort to put them into operation (Cheshire, Essex, Lancashire, Middlesex, Shropshire, Somerset, Suffolk, Surrey) and two more (Derbyshire and – much later – Nottinghamshire) appear to have established a partially operative classical system without presenting it to Parliament for approval. Six other counties produced schemes which were never approved or implemented (Durham, Hampshire, Northumberland, Wiltshire, Westmorland, Yorkshire [West Riding]), but twenty-four counties made no formal response. Only in two areas (London and Lancashire) does the provincial machinery ever seem to have come into being, and it is probable that by the early 1650s only seven or eight of the seventy or so classes formally established in the years 1645–8 were still functioning.[23]

All was not total chaos, however. The civil power had established some supervision over aspects of parochial life pending the introduction of Presbyterianism, and much of this *ad-hoc* government persisted down to the introduction of the Cromwellian reforms in 1654. Existing rights of patronage to livings were protected except where the patron was the Crown, the bishops, the deans and chapters or sequestered Royalists. In those cases patronage was exercised by the committee of plundered ministers in London, either directly or through local county committees, or in response to advice from the parishes.[24] County committees – again supported by central bodies – had power to eject those whose religious practice, morals or political beliefs they found repugnant. The profits from dean to chapter and confiscated Royalist impropriations were made available within each county as a fund for augmenting the stipends of ministers in the poorer parishes, and tentative beginnings were made to the rationalisation of parish boundaries: large ones being broken up and small (mainly urban ones) amalgamated. Finally, much of the business of the old church courts was transferred to the JPs at quarter sessions. Much of this, however, was only formalised after 1649.[25]

This extension of lay control is one of the reasons why county committees were so reluctant to implement the parliamentary Presbyterianism. But there was another reason. The English Puritan gentry had probably always preferred a looser system of Church government giving effective autonomy for each parish in matters of worship and discipline (non-separating Congregationalism).[26] This is what the stalemate of 1648–54 achieved. It was then institutionalised by the Protectorate. But such a development contains a deep irony. If each parish was allowed to decide its own patterns of worship and observance, then those who wanted to maintain the old Prayer Book and the old rhythms of Anglicanism could easily get their own way. As we shall see, the county committees, after their initial enthusiasm for ejecting scandalous and insufficient men, were unable or unwilling to stamp out the old practices.[27]

IV

The cause of Anglicanism received surprisingly little help in the later 1640s from the King and the bishops. Although the King raised himself to claim a martyr's crown, he had done very little to guide those whose religious preferences were the same as those he professed. It is amazing – in view of the apparent earlier co-operation between them – how quickly Charles abandoned Laud. He left him to rot in the Tower and made no serious attempt to prevent his trial and execution (for example, by exchanging him for important Parliamentarian prisoners). By 1642, he had abandoned all the claims made for the Church by Laud and was openly identifying himself with an earlier tradition. He issued a proclamation (recording an oath he had taken immediately before receiving communion from Ussher, Archbishop of Armagh – most moderate of all the bishops, and allowed by Parliament to hold the office of chaplain to Lincoln's Inn throughout the 1640s), in which he pledged himself to maintain 'the established and true reformed protestant religion as it stood in its beauty in the happy days of Queen Elizabeth, without any connivance of popery'.[28] He nominated eleven new bishops between 1641 and 1643. Eight of them had been in trouble with Laud, and all of them were strict Calvinists in the mould of Grindal and Abbott. He also promoted several bishops, most notably Laud's arch-enemy on the Bench, Bishop Williams, who was transferred from Lincoln to York.[29] Apart from a flurry of proclamations in mid-1643, denouncing the Covenant and urging loyal subjects to withhold tithes from intruded ministers, he did very little to advise people how to respond to the changes imposed by ordinance.[30] His attachment to the old Church was not as inflexible as hagiography maintains. At various times between 1646 and 1649 he expressed a public readiness to contemplate an abandonment of the Act of Uniformity, to reduce the number of bishops to four, or to accept a Presbyterian system experimentally for three years. However temporary he privately resolved such concessions would be, they presented a poor impression to ordinary Anglicans as they struggled to find ways of being faithful to the Church. Most remarkable of all, Charles appears to have made little effort, during his captivity with the Scots and at Holdenby, to insist on the use of the Prayer Book. When his own chaplains forced themselves past his guards at Hatfield in the summer of 1647, it was the first time for over twelve months that he received the Anglican sacrament.[31]

The bishops gave little formal lead either. They spent much of 1641–2 striving to preserve their secular powers – their right to sit in the House of Lords and to hold office – and several of them spent long periods in prison (twelve were threatened with impeachment over the canons of 1640; another, overlapping, group of twelve were imprisoned for protesting that anything done by the Lords during their enforced absence – occasioned by the presence of an angry picket-line outside the House – was invalid; Laud was in the Tower from March 1641 until his death, Wren from 1641 to 1660). In every diocese (with the partial exception of Exeter) the diocesan machinery collapsed in the winter of 1642–3, although the routine business of nominating and collating to livings did continue. It is unlikely that more than two or three bishops remained in their cathedrals, even in Royalist areas. Several were at Oxford but they made no joint statements and offered no joint advice to those troubled by the Covenant or the ban on the Prayer Book or the sequestration of their minister and the intrusion of a parliamentary nominee. Three bishops spent the war years quietly in London, two were in arms, but most retired to country livings and kept their heads low. The 1640s and 1650s may have seen a great flowering of Anglican devotional literature and doctrinal works but the leading figures were not the bishops. Such works as the bishops themselves did write were personal utterances, not formal statements.[32] But the bishops made one crucial contribution: they continued to ordain.

## v

In the later 1640s, the people of England had been clearly instructed by the victors in the Civil War to abandon their old religious practices. The diocesan institutions which had upheld the old forms had crumbled and although no new ecclesiastical structure was operative in most areas, the civil power had assumed much of the old coercive power. They were given little help by the King or the bishops. Crucially, however, most of them still had their old clergy to lead them.

It has been reliably estimated that some 2780 clergy (including curates, lecturers and so on) were harassed by the authorities in the period 1641–60. But of these, 400 obtained new livings, 200 were pluralists allowed to keep one of their livings, 270 managed to stay on or were reintruded into their livings despite the orders of local or central committees, and 320 were only ejected after 1649. Thus, only 1600 were dispossessed in our period – less than one in five. If there was a normal death rate of ministers in the 1640s, then between three-fifths and two-thirds of all parishes had the same ministers in 1649 as they had had in 1642.[33]

Not all vacant livings could be filled in the 1640s. There were not enough men to fill them and (until the scheme for augmenting the stipends of poor livings was brought fully into operation in the 1650s) many livings were too poor to attract qualified preachers. From 1644 onwards, Parliament made provisional arrangements for ordination (by clerical commissioners in London and Lancashire), and from 1646 permanent arrangements (all classes were empowered to ordain those properly qualified and with a call from a parish). Men from more than half of the English counties were ordained by the 4th London classis in the years after 1646, for example. Nonetheless, the best estimate suggests that no more than 700 men had been ordained under the authorised arrangements before Cromwell introduced his Triers in 1654.[34] It is quite certain that the great majority of those who took up the ministry for the first time between 1644 and 1649 were episcopally ordained. The abolition of episcopacy did not slow down the flow of ordinands presenting themselves to the bishops in their rural retreats (at least ten bishops still held parish livings) and episcopal ordination – despite the disquiet expressed by the Lancashire province in 1649[35] – remained valid and sufficient in the eyes of authorities desperate to fill vacant livings. How utterly and ironically were the roles of Anglican and Puritan reversed! In Lincoln diocese alone, official listings at the Restoration show that ninety-two men who then held livings had been episcopally ordained since 1646; the records of London and Norwich dioceses provide comparable figures. Joseph Hall, bishop of Norwich, ordained over fifty men between 1646 and his death in 1654 who served in those two dioceses alone. Yet most of the ordinations were carried out by itinerant Irish and Scottish bishops. Among the English bishops, it is clear that it was the anti-Laudians who were most active, the only exception being Skinner of Oxford, probably the most energetic of all in his convenient nook close to the university city of Oxford. He is said to have ordained hundreds. Some of those ordained by the Presbyterians subsequently presented themselves for episcopal ordination. Surely the fact that – given a choice and given the legal and ecclesiastical complications – the great majority of the new clerics had sought out the bishop tells us something about the preferences of those who filled a majority of the vacant livings up and down the country.[36]

The pattern of persecution has recently been clearly established. What seems clear is that the distribution of ejections was determined less by the malignancy of the clergy than by the persecuting temper of local commissioners. Thus the highest percentage of expulsions were in solidly parliamentarian areas (London, Cambridgeshire, Suffolk and so on) and the lowest in solidly Royalist areas. Often the presence of an individual hardliner could lead to differential levels of sequestration within counties (as in Cheshire and Wiltshire). Secondly (as with iconoclasm), one needs to distinguish two phases of persecution. In the first two years of the Long Parliament, the initiative was often taken by outraged parishioners. Several hundred petitions were presented to Parliament in 1641 and 1642 and formed the basis of the first 200–300 ejections. From 1643 on, however, there was a different pattern. As Dr Green says: 'there are strong grounds for thinking that it was pressure from above rather than from below that triggered off most of the ejections.[37] Thus the instructions issued to the Lincolnshire commissioners admitted that 'it is found by sad experience that parishioners are not forward to complain of their ministers, although they be very scandalous.'[38] The stereotyping of the depositions against the clergy makes use of them difficult, but some points do emerge. Dr Green thinks that less than half of those sequestered were accused of Laudian practices or ceremonial innovation. He puts more stress on simple pastoral insufficiency and on political bias.[39] It may be, however, that he relies too heavily on an analysis of the earliest cases. A careful reading of the depositions from Suffolk, Lincolnshire, Essex and Wiltshire[40] suggests that the most important failings of those ejected after 1643 were insufficiency as preachers, Laudian practices and political unsoundness. Very few were ejected for upholding 'the true reformed protestant religion of Elizabeth and James' – for using the Prayer Book, for celebrating Christmas or Easter,[41] or for welcoming all their parishioners to the communion table – even after such actions were banned. In Dorset, for example, such ministers were remonstrated with, warned, but not suspended, and the same seems to have been true elsewhere.[42] Furthermore, although many were suspended for overt Royalism, many more were suspended for refusing to take sides: for reading Royalist and Parliamentarian declarations; for observing both Royalist and Parliamentarian fasts (and how far can one rely on depositions such as that against Mr Fisher that he read Royalist declarations 'audibly and distinctly', and Parliamentary ones 'with a low voice'?).[43] Isaac Allen of Prestwich, Lancashire, affords a good example. He was sequestered in November 1643 on nine counts, including failure to instruct his parish to support Parliament, answering a Royalist summons to a meeting in Manchester in June 1642, and hesitation before taking the Covenant. In each case this represents the attempts of a neutral to obey the law of the land as he understood it. His defence shows 'a man driven by force of circumstance out of the

attitude of neutrality he had endeavoured to adopt'. He subsequently regained his parish and remained there throughout
the Interregnum, stubbornly refusing to attend the vigorous
Manchester classis within which his parish lay, yet apparently
immune to its threats.[44]

Finally it should be stressed how frequently the attempt to
oust a minister led to resistance from parishioners. This sometimes took the mild form of a petition, but it could also take the
form of a tithe-strike against his successor, the physical protection of the parsonage against the attempts of a minister
intruded by the committee of plundered ministers to take up
residence, or even – after a period of disillusionment with a new
minister – the violent reintrusion of a sequestered minister,
usually with the Book of Common Prayer in hand. We shall
return to this subject at the end of the paper.

The great majority of the clergy, then, were men who had
served and conformed under Laud or who were episcopally
ordained in the 1640s when the decision to seek out a bishop
was a decision with very obvious political and ecclesiastical
connotations. How did these men respond to the challenges and
invitations laid down by Parliament?

VI

However much Parliamentarians differed over the religious
settlement they wanted, they were united in wanting to end the
Popish distractions in liturgy and observance that had marred
the old Church. They explicitly set out to break men's attachment to the Book of Common Prayer, to the Anglican calendar
and sacramental pattern. They created a number of offences
with civil penalties sharper than those held over Puritan nonconformists in the pre-war period. To find out how effectively
these prohibitions were enforced, I have examined the surviving records of county committees and quarter sessions, and also
150 surviving churchwardens' accounts for ten counties in
western and eastern England.[45] Churchwardens' accounts
record all the expenses incurred on such items as church fabric,
ornaments, vestments, service books, bread and wine for communions (and much else besides). They also frequently include
annual or irregular inventories of church goods. The survival of

such records for the mid-seventeenth century owes most to the vagaries of eighteenth- and nineteenth-century vicars and vestries in preserving their records. There is no reason to doubt that the 150 sets of accounts are a representative cross-section.

First of all, they help to demonstrate the continued use of the Prayer Book. Inventories record their survival in more than one-third of all parishes. This is an ambiguous finding. It could be that the Prayer Book was retained but not used; or that it was used in many more parishes but prudently not recorded with other parish effects. After all, possession of it was an offence, and an ordinance had required churchwardens to surrender all copies to county committees. It is perhaps striking that most inventories continue to record the preservation of Bishop Jewel's *Apology* and Erasmus's *Paraphrases* (which were not banned) but not the *Book of Homilies* (which was). It is perhaps also worth noting that in the period up to the Civil War four times as many churches possessed copies of Jewel's defence of the Elizabethan settlement as possessed Foxe's *Book of Martyrs*, with its puritanical expectation of a more perfect reformation. Certainly more churches possessed the Prayer Book than possessed the Directory: less than 25 per cent recorded purchasing the latter and less than 25 per cent of inventories record it. It seems to have widely been used only where either the classical system came into being, or where county committees made strenuous efforts to enforce the ordinance of August 1645 (as in Dorset and Gloucestershire where the travelling expenses of wardens summoned up to the committees to receive it are recorded as well as the eighteen pence or two shillings charged for copies: in contrast only one of twenty sets of accounts for Norfolk mention it).

More general evidence adds powerfully to the suggestion that the Prayer Book was widely used. John Evelyn had no difficulty in finding churches in London which used it throughout the 1640s and 1650s; Sir John Bramston wandered in off the street into a church in Milk Street and found the old liturgy in use. His father's carriage outside aroused interest, and soon the church was packed out. Churches in the very centre of towns continued quietly to use the Book, even in small boroughs like Abingdon, where a 'Puritan' corporation failed to prevent its use in one of the two churches. In both Oxford and Cambridge colleges the old service books were in frequent use down to the summer of 1647 if not later. Fragmentary evidence from many counties suggests that prudent observance was very common. Leading Anglican moderates like Robert Sanderson and Jeremy Taylor wrote out modified versions to evade the terms of the ordinances; others memorised the common elements in daily prayer and the communion service. Even where local authorities were informed of the continued use of the Prayer Book, they were too busy with other things, too desperate to fill pulpits, too pessimistic about the effectiveness of suspensions, to take effective action. The parallels with the impotence felt and ambivalent attitudes held by pre-war bishops to Puritan non-conformity are very obvious. To give an example: the Dorset committee were told in December 1647 about at least seven ministers who continued to use the banned liturgy. The seven were instructed to desist but no further action was taken against them, despite the specific penalties laid down in the 1645 ordinance. A petition of Presbyterian ministers in Essex in December 1647 spoke of the Prayer Book as being 'usually used' in the parish churches there, and a similar petition from Londoners was delivered to Parliament at the same time.[46]

Much more striking is the evidence of the continued observance of the established pattern of holy communion.[47] There are two aspects to this: the occasions on which communions are celebrated, and the rules governing admission to the sacrament.

Although customs varied from diocese to diocese, the general pattern before 1643 was for communion to be held on the three great feasts of Christmas, Easter and Whit (sometimes as part of a monthly celebration, more frequently as part of a basically quarterly pattern). The only parishes where communion was not celebrated at the great feasts before 1642 are those with incumbents known to have been Puritan nonconformists in other respects. The observance of these feasts was banned by ordinance in 1646 which reinforced the instructions of the Directory. The pattern of purchases of bread and wine suggest that in 1646 communions were still held on the major feasts in 85 per cent of all parishes; the proportion reached a nadir in 1650 when Easter communions are recorded in only 43 per cent of the accounts. From 1650 and particularly from 1657 the proportion of recorded Easter communions increases. In many places the old Feasts were very publicly celebrated: in godly Gloucester, one parish held special services with guest preachers every Easter Sunday while another rang its bells for the King's birthday every year down to 1648 and continued to deck out the church with rosemary, bay and holly to celebrate Christmas as late as 1650. The annual Rogationtide perambulations of parish boundaries were banned by ordinance in 1644 but persisted in over one-third of all parishes, including two in the city of Norwich.[48]

Parliamentary ordinances did not just ban holy communions on feast days; they attempted to restrict access to the communion table to those adequately prepared morally and spiritually.[49] Anglican practice had been to admit all those not openly scandalous, unrepentant and forewarned to stay away. Puritans denounced this as a 'promiscuous' practice and preferred a 'closed' or 'railed' communion. All those who wished to take communion had to present themselves for examination by the minister and elders on specific days immediately before the celebration. Formal docquets were given to those approved. In 1645 Parliament even drew up a list of doctrinal positions, knowledge of which had to be shown by those who came before the elders. Admission was thus by ticket only.

By 1650 the pattern of holy communions at Easter and (less frequently) at other major feasts was observed in 43 per cent of the parishes. In almost every case the amount recorded as spent on bread and wine was comparable with the sums spent before the Civil War. It seems as if the open-communion policy went along with the old pattern of celebration. Yet an alternative pattern of celebrations – at times other than the main feasts – is recorded in only 20 per cent of parishes. These celebrations were usually very infrequent – less than annually – and the Directory's recommendation of regular communions (by which was meant at least once per quarter) was extremely rare. In these 20 per cent of cases the amount spent on bread and wine was usually less than a third of the amount spent on the pre-war celebrations. This is evidence of 'closed' communions. Yet in 38 per cent of parishes, there is no record of any communions from 1646 (and often earlier) to 1650 (and often later). This could be because the change of open to closed communion resulted in a change of practice: it may be that the bread and wine were no longer paid for out of the rates but by the communicants at a special collection. There are occasional traces of this in the records. But there is more evidence that the silence of the records results from the suspension of the Lord's Supper. Many ministers felt unable to celebrate the sacrament (indeed disqualified from doing so) because they were unable to hold the necessary preparatory meetings until elders were chosen, which, as we have seen, they mostly never were. This could be a problem even where Presbyterian classes were established. But it could also stem from another consideration: the new system was all too likely to lead to divisions in the parish, with those refused admission witholding their tithes in protest. This is expressly the reason why Ralph Josselin held no communions from 1642 to 1650, when he finally held examinations and admitted thirty-four persons, less than one-tenth of those previously eligible. In 1646 he recorded that 'speaking concerning our intermission of the Lord's Supper I told them that perhaps some feared offending people in point of my maintenance they would deny me my stipend'.[50] Similar feelings appear to have underlain the tithe strikes in 1647 against many ministers intruded in previous years in East Anglia and elsewhere.[51]

Much of this stubborn liturgical conservatism may be simply a reaction against every manifestation of Parliamentarian interference in the localities. It does not necessarily indicate that long-established loyalties were being demonstrated. That it was in fact the latter could be demonstrated – if space permitted – from the evidence of the churchwardens' accounts of the period before 1640 and after 1660. Indeed, the increase in Easter communion as official pressure was relaxed in the 1650s is suggestive too. But the best evidence of a positive ingrained Anglicanism comes from the law courts. I have failed to find any prosecutions in the latter 1640s for use of the Book of Common Prayer: there are many indictments and presentments of ministers for *not* using it. In Norfolk at the midsummer quarter sessions of 1645, Peter Byng was presented by a grand jury for 'cutting and misusing the prayer book'.[52] There was a similar case in 1648, where the Elizabethan Act of Uniformity was invoked to enforce the use of the Prayer book.[53] In Cambridgeshire in 1648, six ministers were indicted for 'refusing to administer the sacrament but according to the Directory'. They were convicted and had to appeal to the parliamentary Committee of Indemnity.[54] At Beeston Regis in Norfolk, according to three eye-witnesses in 1648, William Feezer arrived at the church with a group of women and an ejected clergyman intending to baptise Feezer's child. The party was met by the vicar who asked why his offer to baptise the child had been ignored. Feezer asked whether the vicar would use the font, but was told that this was contrary to the Directory. Eventually the situation deteriorated into a scuffle.[55] The Directory barred any formal liturgy for the dead: kneeling by the grave, praying beside the corpse or the grave was banned, and 'meditations and conferences suitable to the occasion' were all that was allowed.[56] An alderman of Ripon who tried in 1648 to prevent the burial of a child by a vicar using the old burial service found himself indicted and convicted of assault and subsequently outlawed.[57] As late as 1658 Richard Cromwell was to issue a proclamation recounting the difficulties of godly ministers, some of whom were still being indicted in the courts for not using the old liturgy.[58] With the law – and the ingrained sensibilities of the Puritans – so widely flouted, it is clear that the yearning for a godly reformation was stillborn.

VII

It might be argued that most of the evidence for the survival of Anglican practice says more about the laziness of most parish clergy and a lack of zeal in most parliamentary agents. But there is a great deal of evidence of positive commitment to old values and practices.

Back in 1641–2, petitions in defence of the Established Church were circulated in over half the English counties (in addition to one from the six counties of North Wales). It is true that most of them were responses to anti-episcopalian petitions, but it is also true that many of the petitions were begun at, or approved by, meetings of the county community at quarter sessions or assizes. The initiative seems usually to have lain with the laity, usually with the greater gentry but sometimes with the minor gentry and freeholders who made up the grand juries. In that sense, the defence of the Church lay closer to the heart of the county communities than did the Puritan critiques. There is no more (though no less) evidence that the middling sorts swarmed to sign these petitions than to sign anti-episcopal ones. Most of these petitions contained not only reasoned (and often muted) defences of the office of bishop, but also defences of the Prayer Book, as yet under no parliamentary attack. The language used in the defence of the Prayer Book was usually warmer and more positive than that used in defence of episcopacy. It is clear that some Puritan petitions criticised the Prayer Book, but few or none had called for its abolition. It had been more violently attacked by itinerant preachers, or had fallen into disuse in particular parishes. Nonetheless, the threat was widely perceived and widely condemned. Finally, the petitions revealed, in Mr Fletcher's words 'that although they show no sympathy for Arminianism, they indicate that an alternative view of the church from the puritan one was held by substantial numbers of people'.[59]

By 1645, there was widespread revulsion against the war in a great swathe of counties across the south of England and along the Welsh Marches, as men banded together to halt the effects of war, to limit the demands made by the two sides or to neutralise their region. The appeals for a return to 'normality' in these areas were frequently led and articulated by yeoman-farmers, rural craftsmen, minor gentry. These Clubman risings coincided with Parliament's first efforts to suppress the Prayer Book. The demands of most Clubman groups include a defence of the old liturgy. In Wiltshire, for example, many clergy who had remained politically inactive up to that point, accepting orders from whoever controlled their area, joined the Clubmen emphasising the need to preserve the old ways in religion. Later in the year, many leaders of the 'Peaceable Army', an anti-war group in Glamorganshire who had banded together to drive out Royalists seeking to create yet another marching army after the débâcle at Naseby, and who had allied themselves to Pembroke-shire Parliamentarians to achieve that end, broke from their new friends in part because of attacks on the Prayer Book.[60]

Positive action was often more localised still. We have already noted that in 1641–2 there was a ready compliance by churchwardens and others in the dismantling of the Laudian innovations: churchwardens' accounts record the alacrity with which altar-rails were dismantled, chancels levelled and so on (though it should be stressed that in 80 per cent of parishes they had recently been erected with the same speed – many parishes purchasing cushions or carpets to enhance the appearance of the rails or for the ease of those who kneeled at the rails. It should also be noted that rails were built in 1641–2 in some churches – including some in unlikely places like Wroxeter, the Temple Church in the centre of Bristol, Sherborne[61]). The later enforced destruction of older ornaments and images was far less frequently implemented by the parishioners themselves: rather it had to await the arrival of special itinerant commissioners like William Dowsing.[62] Occasionally, as at All Hallows, Barking, the parish did act on its own. There, churchwarden Sherman was chided for allowing a statue of St Michael to remain. On consideration, he decided that 'it stood so many years and had done no miracle, therefore he conceived it was no saint,' a rather non-Puritan reason for iconoclasm. The leading authority on the subject, however, gives a series of examples of churchwardens obstructing commissioners or hiding idolatrous objects ahead of their visit.[63]

It has been said that the history of the English Revolution can be written around the history of tithes. There is truth in this. But – until the rise of the Quakers, if not later – the number of tithe-refusals based on Anglican scruples, that the minister was not discharging his proper duties or had an insufficient title, were more numerous than instances of refusals based on a radical critique of hireling priests. By the ordinances of November 1644 and August 1647, jurisdiction in tithe disputes was transferred to quarter sessions. It is clear that the second, and probably the first, was a specific response to a Royalist campaign to withhold tithes from intruded ministers. As early as May 1643, a royal proclamation had inhibited payment of tithes to anyone but the 'lawful incumbent', and this was much quoted in the summer of 1647. In Cheshire in September of that year the JPs, appraised that the inhabitants of Tattenhall had withheld tithes at the instigation of a group of Royalist clergy, recorded that they 'conceive the Ordinance for payment of tithes cannot be put into execution without bloodshed'. A dozen intruded clergymen in Dorset between 1646 and 1649 found themselves unable to collect tithes. In Cambridgeshire in mid-

1647 there were tithe strikes in favour of extruded ministers in at least four parishes. This was not just support for ejected ministers. It will be recalled that the main reason why Ralph Josselin did not celebrate the Lord's Supper in the 1640s was that he feared a tithe-strike by those excluded.[64]

But the best evidence of all of commitment to the old ways is that afforded by the reintrusion of ejected ministers in their parsonages and pulpits by their old parishioners. Many parishes lobbied so successfully that local committees dared not or chose not to enforce a planned ejection. Elsewhere men used force to keep out or to remove a nominee of the committee of plundered ministers. This could happen in the heart of London in 1647 and in Southwark in 1649.[65] As with tithe refusals, a high proportion of all reintrusions occurred in the months July to September 1647. What almost all the following have in common is that the ministers brought the Prayer Book back with them. Mobs of parishioners secured the return of ejected men in at least seven Essex parishes; at Soham in Cambridgeshire a major riot preceded the triumphant return of Richard Exeter to the pulpit from which he had been driven in 1644 for drunkenness, innovation and disaffection to Parliament. The neighbouring minister who assisted the operation kept his living up to and beyond the Restoration.[66] There were similar incidents elsewhere in Cambridgeshire. Sometimes those who assisted a minister to regain his living were amongst those who had helped to get him sequestered – as in the case of Meric Casaubon in Kent.[67] In Cheshire there were six reintrusions – the initiative coming from within the parishes, and sometimes from those involved in the earlier ejection. Let us conclude with two specific examples. At Aldenham in Hertfordshire, Joseph Soane was sequestered in 1643 and the living conferred by the committee of plundered ministers on John Gilpin. When the latter tried to hold a service on Whit Sunday 1643 (perhaps omitting the usual communion?) a multitude of parishioners drove him out and reinstalled Soane. Gilpin complained to the House of Lords who had Soane imprisoned, but he quickly submitted and was released. He thereupon reoccupied his glebe and parsonage. The county committee sought to arbitrate and finally persuaded both men to withdraw. The (Royalist) patron then presented a third man. So things rested until July 1647 when Soane reappeared and was reintruded by his parishioners, and despite attempts to oust him he stayed put until after the Restoration.[68]

At Bebington in Cheshire, Ralph Poole was ejected in 1646 for alehouse-haunting and preaching against Parliament, and the committee of plundered ministers nominated Josiah Clarke to take his place. In May 1647 a large number of men petitioned on behalf of Poole, and the committee suspended the payment of tithes until a decision was reached. In June, they decided in favour of Clarke. But in July, an aggressive picket-line kept the new vicar out and reinstated Poole. On 17 August the county committee admitted that they were powerless to act. The best the committee of plundered ministers could do was to refer the case to the arbitration of two MPs and the sheriff.[69] All this time, Poole had been receiving the tithes which were due.

What lay behind this surge of activity in the summer of 1647 were the rumours of an impending settlement between King and the Army that would lead to the revival of episcopacy and of the Prayer Book (albeit with a freedom for tender consciences outside the restored Church). Many of those involved in the reintrusions claimed to have seen a declaration from Sir Thomas Fairfax to that effect.[70]

That this militant resurgence of Anglicanism was widespread is further supported by the issuance of a new ordinance on 23 August 1647 which declared that

> whereas divers ministers in the several counties of the king-
> dom for notorious scandals and delinquency have been put
> out of their livings by authority of Parliament and godly,
> learned, and orthodox ministers placed in their rooms
> . . . the said scandalous and delinquent ministers by force or
> other ways have entered upon the churches and gained
> possession of the parsonages, tithes and profits.[71]

The Prayer-Book rebellion of 1647 was the prelude to the second Civil War. Several of the incidents which sparked off the provincial risings of 1648 were concerned with the suppression of Christmas or of the Prayer Book.[72]

VIII

There has been no space in the course of this essay to look at all the ecclesiastical developments of the 1640s. Instead I have concentrated on one neglected but major problem. A rounded account[73] would obviously attempt to show what happened in those parishes where the Presbyterian discipline was settled or where the old system collapsed but was *not* replaced by a Presbyterian discipline. It would have to look at the emergence and growth of the Baptist churches and of gathered congregations in towns and (to a lesser extent) the countryside; and at the peculiar religious situation in the New Model Army (which probably owed as much to the *lack* of chaplains as to the radicalism of its chaplains).[74] I have been rather vague about the social base of Anglican survivalism. It seems quite possible that this was not gentry-led but frequently owed its strength to the very middling sort who we are often told were the bedrock of Puritanism.[75] If this conclusion is borne out by the case studies on which I am now engaged,[76] it would confirm my belief that the middling sort were as deeply divided as were the gentry, though perhaps about different things.

Why does it matter that so many people *cared for* the Church of England; that after eighty years of maturation, a hybrid church, thoroughly if murkily reformed in its doctrines, un-reformed in its government, a mish-mash in its liturgy, had achieved not only an intellectual self-confidence but a rhythm of worship, piety, practice, that had earthed itself into the Englishman's consciousness and had sunk deep roots in popular culture? Attempts to destroy that tradition have been shown to have largely failed. One reason was that those charged to carry out the task had too much else to do. Another is that they had so little help from men and women who would voluntarily do no more than pluck off the cuttings recently grafted on to the healthy stem by Laud. Given this initial hostility to their aims, successive regimes lacked imagination. They reiterated all the 'thou shalt nots' without offering positive alternatives. In place of the old feasts, for example, they set aside the second Tuesday of every month as a day of Thanksgiving. The ordinance was almost wholly given over to proscribing forms of celebration.[77] No attempt was made to create a new public holiday to celebrate the Revolution. Throughout the 1640s and 1650s, the only event celebrated by the ringing of bells in almost all parishes was 5 November, the deliverance from Popery. No attempt was made to turn, say, 3 September (Cromwell's day of providences) into such a day. Successful religious revolutions adapt themselves to popular culture just as much as they change it. But the official reformation of the 1640s and 1650s was negative, sterile. As the 1650s wore on, an increasing number of parishes observed the old feasts and held open communion services. At Easter 1660, before Charles's return, there were celebrations of the sacrament in over half the parishes. During 1660 there was a spontaneity and responsiveness in the restoration of the old Church in most areas quite unlike the sloth (at best) in the previous period.

On Christmas Day 1656, John Lambert, speaking in Parliament, justified the Decimation Tax on the whole Royalist party by claiming that even as he spoke, the bulk of the Royalist party were in their homes, 'merry over their Christmas pies'.[78] For Lambert it was a symbol that they had not accepted the Revolution, had not turned away from old superstitions. He was right, but there was nothing he could do about it. On Christmas Day 1657, John Evelyn was at a communion service in central London when soldiers entered the chapel. They waited until the service was over, then arrested the leaders and took note of the rest. The leaders were questioned and then released.[79] It was an act of futile bullying. Further study may well show that the more the Puritans tried to abolish Christmas, the more certain their downfall became.

# 5. The War and the People

DONALD PENNINGTON

FOR most of the inhabitants of England and Wales the Civil Wars were an experience unlike anything they had known before. The Bishops' Wars had provided some alarming fore-tastes, not only in the parts of the north occupied by the Scots, but along the routes of the marching English soldiers and in the areas of intensive recruitment. Then, in 1642, life changed. The next four years brought to some places utter disaster; to others, perhaps not far away, little more than heavy taxation and alarming changes in the sources of authority and justice. Every-where the lord of the manor might be proclaimed a criminal to whom no rents must be paid, and the parson removed as idle, ill-affected, and 'scandalous'. Trade and industry became unsure; some men were persuaded, some were compelled, to serve in one force or another. Most of all there was fear – the new and inescapable fear that the soldiers would come. They could descend on a town, a village, or a house. They could stay for a day, or for weeks, or for years. They could take a few household possessions, or destroy the means of livelihood. Places from small country houses to large cities could become garrisons. In the end there were a few who fled from their homes, and a few who had on balance done well out of warfare. The majority accepted it as they or their predecessors had accepted fire, plague or dearth, and before very long had lived much as before. In many parts of Europe it would have seemed a short and muted specimen of a familiar calamity. In England it was unbelievable. We shall not be involved here in the great issues of social revolution or of land and capital that form the major historical problems of the Civil War. The effects of religious change have been investigated by Dr Morrill, and the practical and theoretical questions of legality by Professor Ashton.[1] There remains the more superficial topic of how this assortment of misery, fear and near normality was distributed and whether any objective assessments of it can be made. Even on this level it is only half a story: in many ways the worst misfortunes were those in the years between the first Civil War and the Restoration. By then the wars had become part of a greater event.

If the cries of distress could be taken literally, most of the country by 1646 seemed on the verge of a total collapse of its economy and government. 'Wasted, exhausted, and tired out . . .'; '. . . eaten up, undone, and destroyed . . .'; 'ready to give up the ghost . . .'; 'this wasted county . . .'; 'hardly anything left to cover their nakedness, or their children bread to eat . . . .'[2] The phrases may be no less heartfelt for being repetitive. Dr Morrill found evidence of 'systematic plundering' from thirty counties and petitions against the behaviour of the soldiers from twenty-two.[3] 'Plunder' was a word new to England, whose meaning depended on the circumstances. To the commander and administrator there was a firm distinction between the lawful gathering of necessities by his own side and the spoil and robbery mostly perpetrated by the other. It was less clear to the farmer, the tradesman and the householder. Soldiers demanding supplies did not readily explain whether they were buying them, for cash or promises, seizing them from their enemies, or indulging in sheer plunder for themselves. There was always some hope of redress: every civil and military authority faced the pleas and protests of citizens who had no clear idea of what legalities existed behind the plain fact that corn, fodder or household goods had been taken. It was not the most important question. The crucial difference, not apparent to the takers, was between the unhappy but tolerable removal of some of the year's crops or the household possessions and the disastrous losses that made it impossible or pointless to live as before. In theory all authorities tried to keep the economy functioning well, at least in their own territory. The instinct to preserve the land and the harvest was strong. Men notoriously deserted at harvest-time. In 1642 local forces could even be encouraged to leave the war to others and go home. But the habits of warfare assumed that a retreating army, unless it expected soon to be back, must make the countryside useless to the enemy. In 1645 the Committee of Both Kingdoms diverted both infantry and cavalry units to protect the growing crops.[4]

By then much of the economy depended on a few hundred inexperienced officials, the commissaries and commissary-generals who were supposed to keep the armies supplied with all the material resources they needed. Between them they had become the largest economic organisation in the country – perhaps the largest it had ever seen. Their work was regulated by a mass of orders, ranging from the great ordinances of Parliament and royal commands to the instructions of a captain. There were small men like the commissaries at Stafford for the magazine, for corn, for hay, for timber and for 'provisions'; and great men like Waller's commissary-general Nicholas Cowling whose stores in 1643–4 were collected from the inhabitants of eight counties.[5] Some of the confusions behind the system added to the uncertainties of civilians. It was never clear how far the soldier was expected to feed and clothe himself out of his pay, how far supplies were to be acquired for cash in the open market or how the promises of future payment were to be authenticated and redeemed. The notions of purchase, contributions – voluntary or not – and penalty for being in some sense on the other side were a chaotic addition to the all too simple process of a cartload of hay or a hundredweight of cheese being transferred from the producer to the soldiers.

The uncertainties were nowhere more evident than in the most widespread grievance of all – free quarter.[6] Here at least there was equality of a sort: castle and hovel were alike threatened with occupation by soldiers. Both sides claimed that billeting would be paid for, preferably on the spot. The householder faced with armed men demanding accommodation could only submit, and hope that he might be paid something. Hopton found that in Somerset there was no resistance to free quarter 'soberly taken'.[7] But this was in 1643, for an army on the move. The unluckily situated house that suffered continuous or successive occupation over five years or more could well be made uninhabitable. Detailed claims, perhaps supported by scruffy 'tickets', might – where Parliamentary soldiers were concerned – be set against arrears of tax. It was more unfortunate to have billeted Royalists, who in the end had no means of paying, or to be rated an 'enemy' to be punished rather than rewarded. The official view was reasonable enough. Commanders should realise that they could not extract more from a householder than he had: if it came in free quarter it would not come in taxes. In the end the debts could only be paid from money that had been collected somehow. It was not much comfort to Thomas Stocken and John Marshall of Wendover with their claims for more than thirty pounds each: 'three men and three horses for three nights, twenty foot-soldiers, one lieutenant . . .'. Moreover Major Fountain's troop had eaten up a meadow of mowing-grass worth £8.[8]

The wrecking of a house and the removal of food and drink could, if there was enough incentive, be repaired quickly. Most of the equipment for agriculture and minor industry did not take long to produce. But there were some commodities whose loss was an economic disaster. The greatest of them was the horse, a main weapon of war and an essential source of power for agriculture, and for the transport of goods and men. Even its manure was important. Commands, threats, money and prayer were powerless to reduce the time needed for a mare to produce and rear a foal. Troopers were expected to supply for themselves the animal and its apparatus, and were in theory responsible for replacing it if it was lost or unusable. In practice the army commissaries and commanders had to acquire most of the new horses needed. They were not likely to be the noble animals of equestrian portraits. Selective breeding of horses was only just beginning, and within limits they could be switched easily from one job to another. The army's rough classification as cavalry, dragoon or draught horses was not a rigid one: troopers could happily exchange their exhausted mounts for fresh ones from local farmers, on whatever terms they could impose. On paper there were detailed arrangements for horses to be valued and eventually paid for. A succession of ordinances and parliamentary instructions tried to regulate the levying of horses for general and local needs.[9] It was one of the first duties for which county committees were set up, in November 1642. An order for all stables in London to be searched was revoked after the two Houses admitted that there had been 'great abuses' in seizing horses on the pretence that they were for the army. In July 1643 the number to be raised in London and fifteen south-eastern counties for Manchester's army was fixed at 6500. The earl of Essex was authorised to raise 600 for the cavalry and 500 for artillery in the counties on his route to the west. For the New

Model Army Fairfax got wider powers to raise what horses he needed.[10] Protests continued. In May 1643 an ordinance again accepted that grievances were just. Some officers did not distinguish between supporters and enemies of Parliament; others allowed the horses seized to be sold, or took bribes to spare the best. The rules laid down were unconvincing: first find a horse, then find two deputy lieutenants with whose 'privity' it could be taken, then record in duplicate every detail of the animal and its capture. It must also be branded with the mark to be put on all the 'state's' horses.[11] No regulations helped much. The horse, obedient to every competent rider, was the easiest of possessions to steal. 'Protections' were readily granted and more readily ignored. There were endless pleas for redress – to commanders, committees, justices, even Parliament. Often the only answer that could be given was a warrant to find the missing animal and take it back. It was not likely to be identified too carefully.[12] The theft of horses was the largest category of offences for which, after the war, the Committee for Indemnity was called on to rescue soldiers from punishment by assizes and quarter sessions.[13]

Horses could still be bought: armies acquired a great many by purchase on the open market. The Eastern Association had its own agent for buying horses, who went round the towns of the whole area with ready money. London met the heavy demands imposed on it partly by buying from dealers who sold anything from ten to a hundred at a time. It did not, until 1645, lead to any drastic increase in price. A cavalry horse could sell for £10 or £12, a flea-bitten nag for under a pound. For bulk purchases £6 to £8 was acceptable. One complaint of army commanders was that the troopers sold their horses to civilians at 'under-rates', another that horse-stealers followed the camps and sold their booty back either to the soldiers or in the local market.[14] Many a horse must have led a harassed life of alternating military, agricultural and commercial duties; and somehow, in most places, the disruption of essential work was tolerated. 'They have no horses to plough and sow the land,' Samuel Luke wrote from Newport Pagnell in November 1644. In the same autumn Tavistock was said to be 'clean stripped of horses'. For the individual farmer it needed only one or two horse-collecting raids to upset the year's routine. If his plough-

team disappeared in the middle of a day's work he could spend
time and money trying to retrieve it and be left in the end with a
ruined harvest.[15] It was possible to plough with oxen, in areas
where food was available for them. Cattle were more troublesome to take away than horses, but the prospect of recovering
them was even worse. Owners were not always anxious to buy
more at the risk of losing them again. In Buckinghamshire some
of the Verney tenants refused to stock their land unless the
value of any cattle driven away was deducted from the rent.
Some of the 'beasts' driven into Oxford in 1644 were returned to
their owners because they could not be sold off at a fair price.[16]
Sheep were seized, sometimes in large flocks. (Lieutenant-
Colonel Michael Jones in 1645 reported that his soldiers had
returned with 6000 of them.) Like other livestock they could not
easily be hidden. Produce was most worth having if it could be
kept where strangers would not find it: some of the villages that
were thought by the armies to be totally without food proved
better supplied when they had gone.[17]

The survival or collapse of almost every economic activity
could depend on the behaviour at one moment of a small
number of soldiers; and nothing could be harder to predict. One
firm belief was that the Scots, and still more the small numbers
of Irish, were the worst cause of devastation. They were the
nearest equivalent England ever saw of the foreign mercenaries
common in European countries. Scottish armies appeared in
many parts of the north and midlands: Herefordshire in 1645
bore the brunt of Leven's unpaid army, for whom there was no
incentive to refrain from wrecking the countryside.[18] Differences between the behaviour of Royal and Parliamentary
armies are a more complex question. In 1642 both sides were
strongly aware of the need to keep as much goodwill as possible
and publicised their orders against taking supplies unneces-
sarily or without firm pledges of payment. Gradually the belief
grew that Royalist forces were more brutal than Parliamentarian. It was the view put forward by such Royalists as Sir John
Oglander and Henry Townshend, whose account of the war in
and around Worcester asserted that Royalist plundering went
unpunished while Parliamentarian soliders were better 'regulated'.[19] There were obvious reasons for such a difference to
arise. Royalist money and supplies had never been as well

organised as Parliamentarian, and the more their territory
shrank the greater the pressure on what remained. Defeated
forces were always less disciplined than victorious ones; unpaid
soldiers had to live on what they could take. As more 'delinquents' and their tenants came under Parliamentary control,
more resources could come from comparatively small numbers
of Papists and Royalist magnates.[20] By 1646 it was a costly
misfortune to have been associated with the losers: during the
fighting nothing mattered so much for the civilian as exactly
where he lived.

Some areas escaped the main armies almost completely. In
Kent, until 1647, local oppression and local conflict did not
amount to grievous disruption. The county committee got a
sharp reminder from the Committee of Both Kingdoms that
they had less to 'groan' about than other places nearer the
armies. Much of the southern half of Wales saw little of the
war. East Anglia contributed heavily in men and money, but
Royalist hopes of invading it never got far.[21] At the other
extreme it was soon realised that some districts were suffering
exceptional hardships. Northern Nottinghamshire, already a
partly uncultivated forest region, was devastated by successive
incursions of Royal, Parliamentary, and Scottish forces.
Lancashire in June 1644 was reported to have suffered more
than it could endure from Rupert's army.[22] Obviously places on
the regular routes of marching soldiers, or repeatedly changing
hands, were most at risk. But the unemployed army seeking
supplies and recruits and with time to spend on aimless
destruction could be at least as bad. There was some tendency
for the burden to be spread automatically as commanders
sought to quarter their troops and companies in districts not
already stripped of supplies. Waller and Haselrig in November
1644 thought north Somerset might still accommodate them
while the south and west of the county were in ruins. The King's
army set out on its disastrous eastward expedition in June 1645
partly because of the attractions of the hitherto unspoiled territory. By then feeding an army was a fearsome task. 'We are
called to march, march, march, that a plentiful country is still
before us,' Leven reported from Warwickshire to the Scottish
commissioners in London, 'but we find nothing by the way but
solitude.'[23]

Bad as it was to live in the zones crossed by field armies, the most inescapable and lasting misfortune for the civilian could be to find himself inside a garrison or in the area it dominated. Victory depended on control of territory. The outcome of the few decisive battles originated in the recruiting, supplying and movement of armies, and each of these was helped or hindered by the position and strength of garrisons. It did not mean that every garrison had a purpose clearly discernible to national or local powers, let alone to the population that maintained it. The smallest of them, the roughly fortified country houses defended by a few local soldiers, often originated in little more than an owner's zeal for preserving his property. Somewhere in his mind there may have lurked fantasies of the castles and retainers of his ancestors. 'Have store of bullet and powder, and get some body to lodge in the house that may defend it if need be,' Sir Edmund Verney ordered when he left to join the King; and he added a reminder to 'have a care of the harvest'.[24] There were many arguments about the value of the 'petty garrisons'. They were sometimes regarded as places where soldiers fortunate enough to be stationed there lived in comfort at the expense of the neighbouring villages. Certainly beds and bedding appear frequently in the lists of goods they seized. The Staffordshire county committee several times considered 'slighting' the petty garrisons but found their commanders reluctant to give them up. Clarendon was disgusted by the behaviour of some garrison forces on his own side: Campden House 'brought no other benefit to the public than enriching the licentious governor thereof' by his 'illimited tyranny' over the countryside. In Devon and Somerset infantry lived on the garrison stores and cavalry seized what they needed at random rather than organising a regular supply-system.[25] But small garrisons in general did make it easy to gather supplies even from a hostile countryside and sometimes to hold stocks for the armies. Winton Castle in Hampshire became a depot which in 1645 had '15000-weight' of cheese, '7000-weight' of biscuit, as well as beef, pork, salt and beer. Charles in March 1645 ordered Hopton to use the Royal garrisons in the west to get in and lay up corn. The foraging parties were to collect 'all that may be spared' – whatever that meant.[26] A county full of little garrisons had a steady but usually not intolerable drain on its resources.

In Shropshire thirty-four were counted in 1643. It was worse when a large house or castle became an outpost in enemy territory, held by several hundred horse and foot, besieged with varying severity, and eventually stormed. These were places like Lathom House, Lord Derby's home in west Lancashire, or Basing House on the main road from London to the south-west or Brampton Castle in Herefordshire, where the indefatigable Lady Brilliana Harley defied the besiegers until her death. The toughness of the defenders was not appreciated by the villages that were liable to be plundered both by the garrison and by the leaguer, or by two rival garrisons competing for territory. They could protest, but without much effort. When the inhabitants of Thoresby had their hay taken by soldiers from Stockton Castle their complaints went to the bishop of Durham, the committee at York, and the Committee of Both Kingdoms.[27]

Whatever the arguments about the military values of small rural garrisons, there was no doubt that to hold a town was often a major aim, and one for which the population inside the walls and in a wide area of country might have to pay heavily. Newark, defended by the Royalists in face of repeated Parliamentary attacks, was a main cause of the distress in its hinterland. The garrison, well supplied with cavalry, extended its raids into the territory of its rivals in Nottingham and set up out-garrisons of its own. 'The Newarkers' raided the countryside as far as Lincoln and Grantham, where the Parliamentary garrison alleged to exist purely for the 'annoyance of the king's good subjects' was destroyed. Newport Pagnell, originally fortified by the Royalists and captured by the earl of Essex, became for the Parliamentary strategists an essential defence of the routes northward and eastward, and for the population of eight counties an addition to the demands for men, money, and supplies. Its special ordinance in December 1643 led to a more widely spread system for maintaining its 1200 foot and 300 horses than ordinary garrison officers could ever hope for.[28] The few strategically important small towns like this were dominated by warfare while others of similar size and way of life could get away with interrupted trade, incessant levies of men, money and goods, and danger that came and went. For large towns and cities there was less chance of escape from major disruption. Any centre of commerce and industry was likely to

be worth holding. A town with ready-made fortifications –
especially, as at Warwick, a central castle – stocks of food and
materials, and a population that could be diverted into working
for the armies, could be defended against powerful attacks that
occupied large enemy forces. It meant absorbing new and
unrewarding economic activity, a population of soldiers and a
military government with ill-defined powers over the town
authorities. At any time there could be the danger of the
greatest horrors war could bring – blockade, assault, indiscriminate plunder, and conflagration. On the whole it was surprising how much of the normal city life was able to continue or
to recover quickly. Newcastle-upon-Tyne had almost every
source of misery. Professor Howell concludes that by 1645 its
economic life was 'severely shattered'; but he also shows how
complete disaster had been averted. Each of the occupying
powers saw the need to balance its demand for supplies against
the danger of alienating the population too much. A good deal
of trade went on with whoever had access to it – even the
Scots.[29] Gloucester after it was rescued from imminent Royalist
occupation in September 1643, remained under the threat of
blockade whenever forces were available. But life during most
of its siege was not unbearable. The stories of desultory artillery
fire that did little damage were no doubt good for the morale
of other siege victims; they contrast with the more common
journalistic exaggeration of sufferings. Fire-balls were said to
be extinguished with buckets of water, women and children to
work at the fortifications and tend the cattle in the 'little mead'
outside the walls with no great fear. The Londoners completed
their relieving mission in September 1643 by occupying
Tewkesbury 'till Gloucester had provided themselves of corn
and other provisions'. Thereafter Massey built up a system of
supporting garrisons able to control, or raid, enough of the
countryside to satisfy his needs. By 1645 he was able to report
garrisons at Stroud, Dymock, Strensham, Sudeley, Beverstone
and Slimbridge as well as 'five or six' in the Forest of Dean,
where they claimed to benefit the inhabitants by frustrating
the notorious plunderer Sir John Wintour, 'the plague of the
forest'.[30] Prince Maurice at Worcester was equally determined
to keep up a controlled and legitimate supply-system. Detailed
lists of requirements and strict orders against plundering were

supposed to define for the countrymen what exactions they must accept. But even a well-maintained garrison town was bound to show lasting effects of the war. Construction of fortifications involved demolishing houses, abandoning areas outside the walls to the enemy, and using up large amounts of material. York was largely saved from destruction by its surrender in July 1644; but streets in the suburbs were said to be burnt or 'broken down to the ground'.[31]

In terms of human suffering a prolonged blockade was probably the worst fate. In Carlisle, after six months of isolation, the stories that rats and dogs as well as horses were being eaten may conceivably be true. The Parliamentary committee found it, after its surrender to the Scots, 'the very model of misery and desolation, as sword, famine, and plague left it'. Large-scale destruction of inner cities came usually from an assault against determined resistance. Leicester, in May 1645, was captured by a Royal army that was then allowed to spend a day in unrestricted plunder. A house-to-house collection in London and twenty counties contributed to its relief. In the same month Taunton, after two long sieges, survived a Royalist attack. How much of it was destroyed in the fire that followed no-one recorded exactly: 'a third' according to Clarendon, 'a flourishing town almost ruined by fire' according to Sprigge.[32] Fire in streets of timber houses was a spectacle and a terror easy to describe with unqualified horror, and easy to ascribe to almost anyone. The destruction of half of Bridgewater was blamed by soldiers and inhabitants on each other. Lancaster was burnt too, apparently as deliberate destruction by the departing Royal army. Its inhabitants were promised £8000 out of the penalties imposed on Papists and delinquents said to have been present during the fire, as well as a public collection in London. Official recognition of need is as good evidence as any we can get of genuine destruction.[33]

It would be wrong to suggest that misery was the only effect of war on garrison-towns and their hinterland. The benefits of a sudden expansion of demand for goods and services were not confined to the few large-scale entrepreneurs. Money raised in the neighbourhood for the support of a garrison was largely spent there, and in one way or another was likely to be supplemented from national funds. If some of the soldiers' food and drink was taken as a forced contribution, a good deal was paid for at market prices. Garrison accounts usually show cash payments for bread, cheese, beer and most of the necessities available for immediate purchase. Individual soldiers were not only plunderers: they had often more money to spend than they were accustomed to earn as civilians. Officers, even when half their pay was 'respited on the public faith', were left with an impressive income. A large garrison was a major industry. To survive at all it had to make abundant use of local labour. Henry Townshend was grieved to find that at Worcester 'workmen, carpenters, and masons expect money now for their works – as if their lives and estates were not concerned if the city be taken by storm.'[34] Many of the materials needed for the fortifications were bought locally: spades, hammers, locks, brackets, nails, cords, thread and candles are a few of the regular items; raw materials include iron, lead, coal, charcoal and lime. The physician who supplied Colonel Massey with vomits, purges and cooling drinks for the sick soldiers in Gloucester may have appreciated the extra business as much as the masons, glaziers, blacksmiths and carpenters on almost every garrison's list of payments.[35] For the enterprising there were opportunities of steady profit. Carriers were always in demand: as long as they kept their carts and teams they were likely to make good in services to the army much of what they lost through the interruption of trade. Seizing of cattle by the soldiers was one side of the picture: the other was that Thomas Fisher of Warwick in six months sold to the garrison beasts worth £188 plus hides and tallow worth £143. Some of his fellow-citizens seem to have formed a syndicate: Thomas Little, Thomas Hunt, Francis Neale 'and their neighbours' regularly sold coals to the castle at 9d or 10d a hundredweight.[36] On a larger scale the war was a stimulus to all the trades involved in clothing. As the use of uniforms spread and the 'coat' with which recruits were traditionally provided proved insufficient for long service in the field, soldiers seem to have become much better dressed than most of them could have expected in civilian life. The three or four thousand coats, shirts and pairs of shoes that were in the Reading magazine in 1645 represented a demand that must have filtered down to numerous workers and tradesmen. When Richard Symonds arrived in Bewdley with the Royal army in

June 1644 he found that the only industry was the making of Monmouth caps, 'knitted by poor people for 2*d* a piece'. Henry Pomen, haberdasher, had contracted with Parliament for them in 1642 at 23*s* a dozen.[37] At Wells the mayor arranged for the corporation to contribute 500 pairs of shoes and stockings to the Royal army. The mayor, as it happened, was a shoemaker – but he appears to have fallen behind with the supply. Production of weapons and ammunition could be expanded much more easily than the supply of food. Charles's ambitions for the 'perfect militia' in the 1630s had already involved producing and storing arms in unprecedented quantities. Contracts that were made throughout the war with manufacturers and traders must have led to a good deal of new employment to set against the notorious 'decay of trade'. One city at least was temporarily transformed by the war. Oxford, apart from its role as the seat of Charles's Court and government, became the centre of his supply-system and armament manufactures. The iron-founders in Christ Church, the metal-smiths and gunsmiths in the Schools Tower, the swordmakers and the powdermakers drew materials from as large an area of the west as was accessible and sent out their products to the Royal forces with all the waggon-trains they could muster.[38] The large sums paid out to the contractors represented one of the many ways in which money was being circulated between the armies and every class of the community. Another was taxation.

This is not the place to describe the workings of the Royal and Parliamentary tax systems. For Parliament, Pym's creation of a money-raising machinery that made all the exactions of the 1630s look trivial by comparison was the greatest governmental achievement of the war. The King had at first greater access to gold and silver from other sources – contributions of plate, royal revenues, and some of the devices of the personal rule. His actual tax-gathering never seems to have been as successful as that of his enemies, and in the long run London was a better source of money and of financial organisation than anything under Royal control.[39] The wholly centralised collection of taxes envisaged in the parliamentary ordinances was intended to be equitable for the loyal subject and to extract as much as was practicable from the enemy. But in its original form it could never have worked. The picture of money being collected every week or fortnight from householders throughout the country, sent to London, and returned to the armies was not taken entirely seriously. The object was, or became, to maintain central supervision over an empirical and adaptable process. Perhaps the supervision went too far: the ponderous arrangements for taking accounts from every payer of money and every recipient or claimant used a lot of energy and created a mass of disputes and resentments. But it provides the historian with splendidly detailed glimpses of what was extracted from individuals and how it was spent.[40]

Taxation became an institutionalised version of the seizing of supplies by armies and garrisons from the countryside in their vicinity. Parishes, hundreds or towns were allotted, by central or county authorities, to units of the armies large or small. Collecting the money remained, legally, a civilian task. The county treasurer, the high collector and the parish constable were, under one title or another, familiar local figures. But a colonel or captain whose day-to-day solvency depended on the money from households in his area was usually very willing to help in making sure it was paid. The constable of Exall, in Warwickshire, described how he went on his rounds with Lieutenant Stephenson, Cornet Baldwin and William Morris to collect Captain Lovell's moneys. He told the three soldiers 'what was every man's due to pay', and they 'went away satisfied'. Only one of his taxpayers was ever in arrears, and that was a poor man who owed more than he was worth.[41] It was not always as easy as that. Complaints that the common people refused or evaded taxation were frequent from the beginning; 'covetous', Massey's chaplain at Gloucester, John Corbet, called them. In their reports to London, Parliamentary commanders were ready to accept that taxpayers might be simply unable to meet the official demands: Yorkshire in August 1644 was so 'miserably impoverished' that the latest levy of £20,000 a month was 'impossible to be paid'. (The only answer was that it had already been reduced from £30,000.) Fairfax was told by the Committee of Both Kingdoms that if he wanted Surrey inhabitants to pay their taxes he had better remove his troops from free quarter.[42] But the taxpayer was less aware of sympathy than of the increasingly unscrupulous threats and propaganda that were used to extract money.

Inhabitants could be assembled just to hear exhortations to pay. Atrocity stories were to be read in churches to encourage a liberal contribution. The individual who paid promptly could hope for protection, sometimes effective, against distraint or, most valuable of all, against free quarter. Inevitably as pressure and resistance grew persuasion and rewards turned into punishment and threats. The constable of Elmley Lovett received a demand for the parish's arrears in three days 'at your perils of pillaging and your houses fired and your persons imprisoned': he seems to have been left to guess whether his enemies or his superiors would behave in that way. The threat of allocating a house or a parish to the soldiers for free quarter was likely to prove as effective as any, especially when it was backed by the hint that the soldiers, for want of taxes, were unpaid and hungry. When Sir William Russell was ordered to send out his Royalist cavalry to collect money, the line between taxation and plunder had become very faint.[43]

The householder who meekly handed over the 'weekly pay' soon found that this was only the beginning of his financial burdens. Wherever he lived he was fairly sure to be faced with an unending succession of special levies for all kinds of purposes – some charitable and more or less voluntary, some imposed with the urgency that arose when there was desperate local necessity. Instructions for account-taking in the eastern counties eventually listed the levies and loans since 1641 under forty-seven headings. They included subscriptions for the British in Ireland, for maimed soldiers (the subject of many parliamentary orders), for providing red coats for soldiers, for carrying coals from Newcastle. Among specific military purposes were the fortifying of Cambridge, Wisbech and Ely, the maintenance of the Newport Pagnell garrison, the attack on the garrison of Crowland. They also included a total, which must have represented for individuals only the amount they paid directly, for the excise. The anger aroused by this novel form of taxation was notorious. In the excise commissioners and their agents there appeared for the first time civilian officials who were regarded collectively as vindictive and tyrannical. The popular impression of ruthless and prying collectors seizing the food and drink that the poor had struggled to produce at home made good propaganda, though the Royalists soon imitated the

tax they had denounced. Certainly the powers of the commissioners were alarming – to examine on oath anyone they chose,
to enter the cellars and storehouses of buyers as well as vendors,
to call in military assistance.[44] The amounts returned to the
treasurers were large enough to give some support to the complaints: £330,000 a year at the end of the war is one estimate.
But figures for all these taxes have to be treated with great
suspicion. Even the many totals that seem to show Parliament's
regular collections as highly efficient raises some doubts: the
pressure to produce a balanced account and the threat that the
collector or treasurer would be held personally responsible for
arrears made it more important to enter the required amount
wherever it could be found than to stick to the rules of assessment and separation of various funds. 'The gross sum is true,
though if you cast up the particulars . . . some of them differ a
little', the Herefordshire treasurer admitted. Totals were easily
confused by the practice of allocating and spending funds
locally. But the figures are consistent enough to give a relevant
impression. At the centre Sir Gilbert Gerard, treasurer-at-wars,
received between August 1642 and March 1644 £956,430 –
collected from the varying proportion of the country under
Parliamentary control. County treasurers, through whose
hands probably more of the total extracted passed, dealt with
such amounts as the £90,000 collected in Suffolk in 1644 for the
monthly assessment alone, or the £16,059 reckoned by the
Staffordshire treasurer from March 1643 to May 1645 ('if the
accounts be truly cast up, as I hope they be'). The inhabitants
of Sambourne in Warwickshire struggled to compile their payments between 1643 and April 1646: £15.12.0 from Hymphrey
Huggeford, gent., £12.0.4 from Walter Heynes, yeoman, £7.9.8
from Hugh Arrowsmith, husbandman. The total of £378 came
from about forty households; but it was made up of a great
variety of losses. 'We cannot rightly remember' was a fairly
common and honest answer to the enquiries.[45]

One provision of Parliament was, or should have been, of
crucial importance to the poorer taxpayer and to landlords. If a
rent was being paid to the full value of the holding, the whole of
the weekly pay and of some of the other taxes could be deducted
from it; if the rent was below the economic value the taxes could
be apportioned between landlord and tenant. The provision

was not widely advertised. Some efforts were made to protect tenants at the expense of their landlords. Thomas Smith of Fulford, who held his cottage 'upon a dear and hard rack', got an order from the Stafford committee for the landlord to abate the twopence per week assessed. But it was also important to compel tenants to pay the rent in order to deprive the recipients of an excuse for not paying his own taxes. To judge from the grumbles of landowners the war led many tenants to stop paying rent altogether. Henry Oxinden in 1644 wrote of 'most men being compelled to abate one part in three'. Lady Brilliana Harley's outrage at the refusal of the tenants to pay was a frequent theme of her correspondence.[46] Most rent problems were part of the larger question of the effects of sequestration. The theory of the parliamentary ordinance of March 1643 was clear enough. (There was nothing as comprehensive from the King). All property of active Royalists was to be taken over and used for the benefit of the Commonwealth. Tenants were to be 'saved harmless' from any penalties incurred through not paying rent to a delinquent landlord.[47] No-one at first seems to have thought how this would be administered. Some sequestration committees and their officials tried to manage estates themselves, and even to set an example of good husbandry. The profits could be allocated to an army commander in much the same way as taxes. The tenant could find one group of soldiers and their civilian allies demanding his rent and another his taxes while his landlord threatened him with eviction for non-payment. A military defeat might then bring the same demands from the other side. He could hardly be blamed for witholding as much as he could. It was easier for the authorities to let out an estate on a short lease – the procedure that led in 1645 to restoring Royalist land to its owners in return for a composition fine. The general cry then was that estates had been ruined – by neglect, by the depredations of soldiers or even of the 'poor'. Buildings, hedges and ditches had been wrecked, crops and herds neglected, trees cut down. Of all the sources of real wealth that were destroyed, trees were probably the hardest to replace. There were many efforts to prevent indiscriminate felling; but everything seemed to make timber the most tempting asset of the countryside to be removed. There was heavy demand, for the navy, for fortifications, and even for firewood. (London, when Newcastle coal was cut off, demanded unprecedented quantities of wood.) Forests as Crown property were open to confiscation. Temporary occupants of an estate could make quick profits from cutting down trees – and no-one could order them to be put back. If some landowners were appalled by the irresponsible destruction of trees that would take a generation and more to replace, some in urgent need of money resorted to ruthless felling for themselves.[48]

For many people and places the war destroyed normal life. But it is as easy for the historian as it was for contemporaries to overlook the limits to the general disruption. Perhaps the most important was that there was no prolonged breakdown in the legal system. Charles's proclamation in December 1642 adjourning the main central courts to Oxford conceded that there should also be some sessions at Westminster. Thereafter there were sporadic attempts by each side to thwart the major courts held by the other.[49] For the ordinary citizen, and the ordinary offender, the urgent questions were whether assizes and quarter sessions were held, whether justices of the peace, sheriffs, recorders and constables kept up their normal functions as well as the new ones that had been thrust on them, and what new authorities established themselves. Assizes and quarter sessions became irregular; but it was never assumed that they no longer mattered. Parliament suspended the assizes of 1643, but tried to hold some in other years. In Sussex there was plenty of business for the assizes held in 1644. Quarter sessions there continued throughout the war: the orders to maintain bastards, scour ditches, relieve the poor and close illicit alehouses give scarcely a hint that anything unusual was happening. Somerset too had assizes in 1644; but there it was under the King's commission and the county magnates temporarily given the status of judges enjoyed themselves by convicting their neighbours of treason. Experience of assizes becoming part of the conflict seems to have diminished their prestige, at least in the west; though the Cheshire committee in 1646 complained that 'we have not the benefit of Assizes as other adjacent counties have.' The scene at the Warwick quarter sessions of Michaelmas 1642 gave a fair indication of what justice in the areas of fighting was to become. Only two JPs turned up, and after an hour the noise of drums and trumpets so distracted the court that it adjourned to the Swan which was so full of soldiers that no business could be done. There were no more sessions until 1645.[50] It became a common complaint that there were 'no Justices of the Peace in this county', or that they, with other 'substantial inhabitants' had 'quite left the county'. The Staffordshire grand jury in 1645 asked that the commission of the peace should be directed to 'some gentlemen of quality' because no-one now had authority to swear new constables.[51] It was worse lower down the scale, where the holder of an office burdened with vast new responsibilities was often anxious to get rid of it. The strain on poor relief was enormous, and in areas where there were many new vagrants or disbanded and deserting soldiers the theoretical obligations ceased to make sense. But the assumption always was that the old institutions would return. The county committee, even though it seemed to the citizen an obnoxious new invention for organising taxation and many of the other oppressions, was in part at least a civilian body that could sometimes offer redress against the soldiers and act as a substitute for the JP in his various functions.[52] Essentially the institutions survived because the gentry survived. So, however justly they were denounced, did the lawyers. The communities, large and small, on which the old machinery of law and administration was based, were nowhere irreparably disrupted.

It is hard to guess, from the selective evidence, how serious a danger there may have been of lasting depopulation in the worst-affected places. Here and there local 'mortality crises' occurred in the war years, as they did at other times. Certainly the war increased the impact of disease. Plague was so common and so unpredictable in the period that it is hard to ascribe it directly to the war, even in a besieged city like Bristol from which it spread through much of the adjoining countryside. Disease in some towns must have been increased by the success of besiegers in cutting off the water-supply. The armies were a prolific base for infection of every kind: at Reading in 1643 both sides were said to have been immobilised by typhus. It all added to the misery, but without having demonstrably large effects on population.[53] The same is true of the food supply. For the poor and the 'middle sort' the loss of their stock of food was frightening. For the economy in general it had to be

remembered that food taken away was usually eaten by someone else, who would have eaten – perhaps less well – in any case.
Some was deliberately destroyed, some no doubt wasted by
bulk storage and transport; some – cheese especially – was
probably produced in greater quantities than ever before.
There is no decisive indication that wars were the main cause of
the dearth that threatened many areas in 1649 and 1650. Corn
prices then reached a peak after the trough of 1643 and 1644.
But the pattern in western Europe as a whole was much the
same.[54] It leads to the unhelpful conclusion that the war was
one of many factors in the cycle of abundance and scarcity.

'A kingdom . . . is not so easily ruinated,' John Greene wrote
in 1643.[55] But a town or village or household might be less
resilient. There was not much the victims of the war could do
about it. If life became insupportable they could go somewhere
else. Here and there reports came of what was thought to be a
large-scale exodus. How many people really fled across the
Pennines from west Yorkshire is impossible to say, nor how
soon if at all they returned. One account of Nottinghamshire in
1645 claimed that 'their cries are now of deserting their habita-
tions and seeking to live where charity will afford it.' From
burnt and pillaged cities many inhabitants took refuge in the
countryside. Again, it is easier to find descriptions of their
departure than any indication of what they did afterwards. To
those in authority much more important than movement of
people was the possibility of insurrection against the war and its
makers. We still need a comprehensive study of resistance in the
whole period. It would have to begin with the early neutrality
movements and the efforts to keep fighting out of a county and
local forces in. At that stage it was gentry initiative that
mattered. Alarm at the risk of popular revolt soon appeared,
especially in support of claims for help. 'The people stir with
fear,' Lenthall heard from Worcestershire in July 1643.[56] In
1645 the emergence of the Clubmen, with their varied aims and
actions, was closely linked with the distress caused by one side
or both.[57] It would be important too to sort out from the many
strands of the Leveller movement and radical Puritanism the
part played by specific war-time grievances. The whole topic
would have to extend into the second Civil War and the
Commonwealth. The great problem would still be to combine

the mass of local evidence into valid general conclusions. More perhaps than at any other time there is in so many aspects no history of England and not much of Yorkshire or Kent or the Cotswolds. There was John Robins of Tamworth who had his geese and poultry taken by the Scots, worked unpaid for the army for a fortnight, and lost twelve shillings by free quarter before his house was consumed by fire. There was Edward Watlin persuading Cromwell to sign a chit for the replacement of his lost horse; Ralph Josselin thanking the Lord that his child was safe while another was burnt to death; and Thomas Priestley carrying on his cloth trade between York and London without any harm 'all that dangerous time'.

# 6. 'The Ancient Law of Freedom': John Selden and the Civil War

## RICHARD TUCK

THERE were few people active in the political affairs of the 1640s whose intellectual activity both before and during that decade is so well documented that we can form a clear impression of their reaction to the Civil War. There were fewer still whose influence on their contemporaries was such that their own reactions can be taken to represent a not uncommon response. But there was one obvious and central figure of whom both these things are true, namely John Selden, the famous lawyer, political theorist and Parliamentary activist. An investigation of his behaviour at this time will clarify reactions to the Civil War in a way no other method of inquiry will allow.

In June 1642 he politely but firmly declined to accept an invitation from the marquis of Hertford to join the King at York, remarking that his going thither would constitute a 'disservice, by which name I call whatsoever will at this time (as this necessarily would) doubtless occasion some further differences 'twixt his majesty and that house of commons'.[1] It was a decision by which he was to abide for the rest of the war, but it was not a decision to adopt a neutral stance: between 1642 and Pride's Purge he was a continually active member of the House of Commons, serving on many important committees and associated frequently with men like St John, Pierrepoint, Glyn or Browne. It is even unclear that he was actually purged by Pride, though he did withdraw, and it was his name (along with St John's) that occurred to Oliver Cromwell in 1653 as the obvious author of a new constitution for England.[2] He died in 1654, at the age of seventy, but he had been intellectually and physically active until shortly before the end.

His behaviour in the 1640s prompts a number of questions. Here is the man upon whom Clarendon 'looked with so much affection and reverence, that he always thought himself best when he was with him', committing himself to a very different response to the crisis from his friend's; at a time when (we are told) there was little continuity with the issues of the 1620s, here is one of the few survivors of that generation of opposition leaders, still engaged in opposing royal policies; in a Parliament intent (we are also led to believe) on disregarding the legal order, and confronted by a King who appeared as the champion of the existing law, here is the greatest jurist of his age, 'the lawbook of the judges of England' as Jonson described him, throwing in his lot with illegality. If we can make sense of his conduct, then it is even possible that the politics of this complex decade may become generally easier to understand.[3]

Moreover Selden's influence was undeniably great. In his youth he had been a friend of Jonson, Cotton and Camden as well as a practising lawyer, and his acquaintanceship continued to include 'wits', both poets and historians, and professional lawyers. He was a friend of most of the group who gathered at Lord Falkland's house, Great Tew, during the 1630s, and who have come to be known as the 'Tew Circle'; like them, he enjoyed the friendship and patronage of Laud during the period when the Caroline government was making overtures to its former opponents, and it was to Laud that he owed his seat in the Long Parliament as member for Oxford University. In his profession, he was by 1640 a figure with immense influence over many younger lawyers: John Vaughan (thirty-seven in 1640), Matthew Hale (thirty-one) and Bulstrode Whitelocke (thirty-five) were figures particularly associated with him who were to achieve considerable eminence in the following decades. Other, rather more senior figures such as Henry Rolle and Edward Littleton (both fifty-one) were also close to him; they had worked together in the 1620s, when their ideas on the English constitution proved to be very similar, and Selden assisted Littleton in his antiquarian studies.

Although they all collaborated in working against the King in 1640–1, when the war came these friends were to move in different directions. Thus Falkland died for his King on the battlefield, while Rolle became the first Lord Chief Justice of the Commonwealth. But in the writings of many of them we can find distinct traces of the ideas of their friend, utilised to make different points but revealing the influence of his way of thinking about politics; and in the process revealing most strikingly that the ideologies of Royalist and Parliamentarian were often not as fundamentally opposed as might have been expected. After 1640, of course, Selden's ideas were in the public domain, and they were to be picked up by an equally wide range of writers from John Milton through Anthony Ascham to Jeremy Taylor – a reception which makes the same point.[4]

Any understanding of Selden's position in 1642 must begin from an account of the intellectual labours to which he devoted his life. As a young man he was one of a group of scholars who perceived the essentially discontinuous character of English history, and the absence of any 'ancient constitution', though his awareness of this fact was perhaps sharper than that of any of his contemporaries. He recognised that the present laws of England were clearly different even from those of the Normans, let alone of the Anglo-Saxons, and between 1607 and 1617 he wrote a series of books intended to explain the transition. Thus while many of his contemporaries believed that Henry I restored the laws of Edward the Confessor more or less intact, Selden believed that Henry 'restored and invented common liberties' – the creative side of medieval government was always obvious to him. Similarly, he was clear that *Magna Carta* had been won from John by force and represented a new settlement: he described it as an 'instrument of public liberties, through mediation of what is above all law, necessity'.[5] He appears to have seen the history of England as a series of conflicts between the various groups of English society, and in particular between the King and his nobles, alternating with settlements agreed to by the parties. These settlements constituted the law of each epoch. It followed that there were no immemorial or necessary rights either of King or of people: to determine what was legally valid one had to look at what was precisely and clearly laid down in current law, and not at some speculative history or the general principles of political science.

Moreover the common law was not in his eyes a different kind of thing from statute law. He spelt this out most clearly in 1617, in his famous *History of Tythes*: the 'common law of England' simply meant the laws which dealt 'with things and persons, as they have reference to a common, not sacred, use or society established in a commonwealth . . . in this sense the allowance of customs, and parliamentary statutes, as they ought, fall under the name of common law with us.'[6] Custom had to be allowed by the same authority that could make a new law; indeed, many apparently customary principles of the common law had, he believed, been established by legislative acts which had subsequently been lost.[7] Parliament was uncontentiously that authority in the seventeenth century, and Selden thought that in fact some kind of parliament-like assembly had usually been used in England since the Anglo-Saxon invasions for making law, though not before that time. Moreover its composition had frequently altered, being (for example) a purely feudal gathering under the Normans: even the source of legislation was in his eyes a matter of specific and historically variable agreements. Consequently he was quite unworried by parliamentary control over the common law; with his definition of the common law simply as the laws in force at any one time in England, it was obvious that Parliament could control it.[8]

It must be recognised that Selden's emphasis on the specific and historically determined character of the common law ran counter to one influential contemporary account of it. This was the view espoused *inter alia* by Coke, that the common law was the law of *reason* – that is to say, that its principles could be elucidated and (some people believed) extended in the light of general rational principles. The best example of this attitude is Sir John Dodderidge's text-book *The English Lawyer*, where he argued that the maxims of the common law were 'either conclusions of natural reason, or drawn and derived from the same'. It did not follow that anyone could be a lawyer; as Dodderidge said, in words close to the famous remark of Coke:

> the Law (as hath been before declared) is called reason; not that every man can comprehend the same; but it is an artificial reason; the reason of such, as by their wisdom, learning and long experience are skilful in the affairs of man, and know what is fit and convenient to be held and observed for the

appealing of controversies and debates among men, still having an eye and due regard of justice, and a consideration of the commonwealth wherein they live.[9]

Dodderidge pointed out that many of the law's maxims were in fact drawn from other 'rational' disciplines such as logic, natural and moral philosophy, and the civil and canon laws; Henry Finch, following him in this argument, added to the list theology, grammar and (most importantly from the point of view of what was to come) politics.[10] It is clear that given this view of the law, its great antiquity was unproblematical – for what could be older than human reason? – *and* it was capable of being expounded in terms of either the Commonwealth's present needs or the general principles of some political theory. Selden set himself firmly against both tendencies, but his older contemporaries such as Coke could not do so.

This became obvious during the parliamentary activity of the 1620s. Selden entered Parliament in 1623, and thereafter he assisted his aristocratic friends and patrons such as the earls of Pembroke and Arundel both in their extra-parliamentary legal affairs and in the opposition to Buckingham which they orchestrated within Parliament.[11] Selden's fiercest opposition was aroused by those arguments of his opponents which deduced the law of England from general theoretical principles, such as Sir Henry Marten's remarks on 19 April 1628 on the question of martial law. Marten said that 'Reason is the mother of the common law. Though I know not the law [he was of course a *civil* lawyer], yet no stranger to the mother, reason . . . . Martial law not lawful but when necessary; and when necessary, then lawful.' Selden replied to this, 'some speak of conveniency, some of necessity, and some of prevention. We are not now to consider what shall be, but to state the question as the law is.' Then, in a really remarkable anticipation of Leslie Stephen's famous observation that Parliament could legally order the execution of all blue-eyed babies, he argued that 'the same power that establishes the common law must establish martial law, and were it established here by act of parliament, it would be most lawful, for so it might be made death to rise before 9 a clock.'[12]

It is revealing that on 7 April, in the conference with the

Lords over the liberty of the subject which became so well known to contemporaries, Selden and Littleton were deputed to deal with statutes and precedents as the grounds for what the Commons claimed; Coke and Digges dealt with general reasons, Coke remarking: 'That these acts of parliament and these judicial precendents in affirmance thereof (recited by my colleagues), are but declarations of the fundamental laws of this kingdom, I shall prove by manifest and legal reasons which are the grounds and mothers of all laws.'[13] This and many similar remarks by Coke in 1628 display his unsurprising inability to disengage himself from his former way of talking about the law, and consequently his fundamental theoretical kinship with his political opponents. It was men like Selden and Littleton who made the ideological running in 1628, and in a sense Coke was captured by them.

When this period of his public life came to an end with the discontinuance of parliamentary activity, Selden proceeded to give his ideas on the law of England a foundation in terms of general political theory. This enterprise, of which the well-known *Mare Clausum* was one offshoot, culminated in the publication of *De Iure Naturali et Gentium juxta Disciplinam Ebraeorum* in 1640. In the eyes of its readers in the seventeenth and eighteenth centuries, both in Britain and on the continent, this was a major work of political theory to be compared even with Grotius' *De Iure Belli ac Pacis*, and they were not far wrong; there is little doubt, moreover, that the ideas put forward in it formed the background to Hobbes's political thought. Essentially, what Selden did was to show that there could be *no* general and universal rules governing a society, of the kind which his contemporaries had normally assumed. He did so by postulating a state of total natural freedom (a *hypothetical* state, as he emphasised), upon which laws of nature supervened; the laws were not innate, and had to be learned by man, so that the only condition which was truly natural to man was total freedom.

The laws were learned because (in Selden's eyes) no law could carry any obligation unless it motivated its subjects through fear of punishment – 'the idea of a law carrying obligation irrespective of any punishment annexed to the violation of it . . . is no more comprehensible to the human mind than the idea of a father without a child.'[14] But knowledge of punishments could not be innate, since it depended on the subject having a quite complex set of beliefs about beings or institutions with coercive power over him, beliefs which he had to acquire through instruction. In the case of the laws of nature, the source of punishment was God, and Selden's theory depended heavily on an account of God's dealings with mankind – an emphasis which might surprise some historians accustomed to thinking of him at the furthest possible remove from his Puritan contemporaries. The basic assumption which informs the whole work (and accounts for its idiosyncratic title) is that only once in history did God make plain to mankind what he would punish them for, namely after the Flood, when he issued the so-called *praecepta Noachidarum* to Noah's descendants. The Ten Commandments, which might have been seen as a rival promulgation, Selden dismissed as of purely Jewish interest – 'we read the commandments in the church-service, as we do David's psalms, not that all there concerns us, but a great deal of them does.'[15]

These *praecepta* were discussed most extensively in the Talmudic tradition, and Selden delved deep into post-Biblical Hebrew writings to elucidate them. The point of this was of course that if he could demonstrate the actual historical character of the *praecepta*, he would thereby demonstrate the content of the law of nature; pure, unaided reason could not be enough. His remarks on the subject during the 1640s were recorded later in *Table Talk*, and make the point neatly:

> When the school-men talk of *recta ratio* in morals, either they understand reason, as it is governed by a command from above; or else they say no more than a woman, when she says a thing is so, because it is so. The other reason has sense in it. As take a law of the land. I must not depopulate, my reason tells me so. Why? Because if I do, I incur the detriment.[16]

In practice, the essential command of God upon which Selden constructed his whole theory was the simple one *fides est servanda* (honour your contracts). Any contracts were possible, but once made they had to be kept; and the network of agreements, underpinned by this basic principle, which limited the absolute freedom of men in a state of nature, constituted the civil law of any state.

A number of significant propositions followed from this. First, it was not possible (Selden believed) to plead general considerations such as necessity against the settled provisions of a legal system. There was a long tradition in natural-law theory of endorsing such pleas of necessity as those of men who stole in order to avoid starvation: the settled rules of private property, it was held, did not apply in such circumstances. Selden was quite clear that they did, for one could not recede from an agreement when it turned out to be disadvantageous, 'If I sell my lands, and when I have done, one comes and tells me I have nothing else to keep me; I and my wife and children must starve, if I part with my land. Must I not therefore let them have my land that have bought it, and paid for it?'[17]

Second, it followed that *any* constitution was legitimate, even the most extensive absolutism, if it had been agreed on by the parties. There could be no general and residual right of resistance; all depended on the character of the legal system in which the subject found himself. As he said again at dinner:

> If our fathers had lost their liberty, why may not we labour to regain it? *Answer.* We must look to the contract; if that be rightly made, we must stand to it. If we once grant we may recede from contracts, upon any inconveniency that may afterwards happen, we shall have no bargains kept. If I sell you a horse, and you do not like my bargain, I will have my horse again.[18]

Selden thus lined up with Grotius as one of the most intellectually formidable defenders of at least the possibility of absolutism in the seventeenth century, though (also like Grotius) when it came to the constitution of his *own* country he was far from clear that it was absolutist in character.

Third, if the network of contracts failed, then war was the only alternative; and war could not be governed by rules of justice or fairness, since justice was a property of contractual arrangements. Thus he quoted with approval the Talmudic writers' views as follows:

> They believed that neither an injury, or some justification for vengeance, nor the need for self-defence necessarily had to

precede a war (as most Christian writers have thought). So in their opinion there was no race or land with whom there could be an unjust war, assuming that it was declared by the *Sanhedrin* (which they always took to be the relevant authority); nor were any grounds held to be necessary for the declaration of a war other than the extension of power.[19]

This would obviously be the case if the primary principle of the law of nature was the keeping of contracts, for in the absence of contracts men would be in the state of absolute natural freedom which he had postulated, and in which anything was legitimate. If nations were not bound by agreements of some kind, then they were clearly in that state, and the traditional idea of a just war disappeared from his theory just as it did from Hobbes's.

It is against this background of political theory that we must understand Selden's decision to adhere to Parliament in the 1640s. It is clear that his decision not to follow Hyde and Falkland into Charles's service (or to retreat into a form of neutrality) was made during the climactic months of March to August 1642, and that it was largely based on his understanding of the legal foundations for the military forces of the kingdom. Put briefly, Selden seems to have decided in 1642 that the King did not have law on his side, while the Parliament might; after 1642 he seems to have recognised that the constitution had broken down, but to have believed that its collapse left a Parliamentary victory as the best outcome.

It was as obvious to contemporaries as it has been to subsequent historians that the critical constitutional question over which the Civil War began was the question of the control of the militia. Parliament's decision on 5 March 1642 to pass an ordinance settling the militia in the hands of lieutenants nominated by the two Houses without the King's consent seemed to many to be the assertion of a new legislative power in the Houses alone. But it cannot be overstressed that it was not obvious that what the ordinance decreed was illegal, nor was it necessarily a claim to new legislative power: it was as compatible with the existing law, at least on one reading of it, as the previous arrangement of the militia under the King's lieutenants. The critical issue was not in fact the militia itself; it was the nature of the royal prerogative, an issue which many Parliamentarians (not unreasonably) believed to have been settled in the first year of the Long Parliament.

This was so because (as has recently come to be generally recognised) for at least three hundred years before the seventeenth century the right of the Crown to raise soldiers in circumstances other than the actual invasion of the country had rested on three possible bases.[20] One was feudal tenure, another was the normal process of contractual engagement (such as the hiring of professionals), and the third was a series of statutes which made explicit and precise the conditions under which the inhabitants of any county could be mustered: in particular, that they had to provide only a specified and limited set of arms and that troops could not be raised in one county to fight in another. The most significant of these statutes were passed in 1285 ('13.Edw. 1'), 1327 ('1.Edw. 3'), 1352 ('25.Edw. 3') and 1402 ('4.Hen. 4'), the last summarising and consolidating the others. The Marian government repealed all these statutes, but its statute of repeal was itself repealed in 1604, with the consequence that the former statutes came into force again. The statute of 13 Edw. 1 was repealed in 1624, but this apparently left the later statutes in force, though there could be (and was) argument about whether this was so. In the debates on the Petition of Right, it was generally recognised by the lawyers in the Commons opposed to the Crown that (as Coke put it on 12 May 1628), 'No act of parliament of force for the finding of arms. There is a negative law against it' (that is, against the methods followed by Charles and especially against the level of arms men were required to provide ).[21] The appeal in the Petition of Right against the illegal charges levied by lords lieutenant and commissioners of musters was after all based on the assumption that the levies were illegal precisely because there were explicit statutes against compulsory raising of troops except on a very limited and (by 1628) quite unworkable basis.

The response of the King's supporters in 1628 had been the same as that of some modern historians. The earl of Dorset put it best on 24 May: 'Yesterday, in the King's Bench a man was returned for refusing to contribute to the musters (upon a *Habeas Corpus*). Answered, because there is no law for it. So you see the King's prerogative is necessary.'[22] But to anyone who did not accept such a notion of the prerogative as the expression of the necessary and general powers possessed by any sovereign, Dorset's argument was wholly unconvincing: the arrangements for raising the militia under Charles I were straightforwardly illegal, though in the absence of any clear permissive legislation (which the Commons consistently failed to agree on) it might be prudent to wink at the illegality if the consequences were not particularly serious. But in 1641 the Long Parliament (with the King's assent) reaffirmed the state of the law when in the preamble to the Act for Raising Troops for the Defence of England and Ireland it declared that

> by the laws of this realm none of His Majesty's subjects ought to be impressed or compelled to go out of his county to serve as a soldier in the wars except in case of necessity, of the sudden coming-in of strange enemies into the kingdom, or except they be otherwise bound by the tenure of their lands or possessions.

As one would expect, Selden had been one of the keenest advocates of the line taken by the Commons in 1628. On 3 April he urged that only feudal tenures or contracts allowed the freedom of levy which Charles wanted,[23] and given his views on the nature of the common law it is obvious that he would find the idea that the King's prerogative had to fill the gap left by explicit law particularly unconvincing. In *Table Talk*, he referred to the king's prerogative, that is, the king's law.

> For example, if you ask whether a patron may present to a living after six months by law? I answer, no. If you ask whether the king may? I answer he may by his prerogative, that is, by the law that concerns him in that case.[24]

Prerogative was part of the law, and like the rest of it was (reasonably) clear and specific: it could not be stretched to cover new areas on the basis of general pleas such as necessity, without some explicit agreement to that effect in the legislative body. If the law left the military affairs of the country on an unsatisfactory footing, there was no remedy except a new law; bad bargains and agreements were struck every day, and necessity could not be pleaded to void them.

This legal background puts the ordinance of 5 March 1642 into a different light from that in which (for example) it was viewed by Clarendon.[25] It did not take away from the King powers that were clearly his, though it did seem to give Parliament powers that were not clearly theirs either. It avoided making a new *law* about the militia, but it also avoided a clear breach of an old law. The reasonable response to it was thus one of doubt rather than outright opposition – the response in fact of Bulstrode Whitelocke, who said in the debate on the ordinance that

By our law, as is declared by the statute of 1 Edw.3 [Whitelocke obviously took the repeal of 13Edw. 1 in 1624 to have left subsequent enactments in force] and by divers subsequent statutes, the King can compel no man to go out of his country, but upon the sudden coming of strange enemies into the realm . . . . Against insurrections at home, the sheriff of every county hath the power of the militia in him, and if he be negligent to suppress them with the *posse comitatus* he is finable for it.[26]

He concluded that the law left the matter of who controlled the militia in great obscurity, and that the wisest course of action was to attempt once again to negotiate an agreement with the King. In the event, when negotiation failed he voted for the measure, after hearing the 'solemn protestations of the most powerful and active members' that the purpose of the ordinances was purely defensive. In the aftermath of its passage he accepted a commission as a deputy under two Parliamentary lords lieutenant.[27] Edward Littleton, despite the fact that since 1641 he had been lord keeper, also voted for the measure, and moreover defended (plausibly, in fact) the legitimacy of proceedings by ordinance rather than Act.[28]

Selden himself does not seem to have spoken to the ordinance at this stage, and like Whitelocke he accepted a commission as a deputy lieutenant. On 14 March he was put on a Commons' committee to prepare a declaration in defence of the ordinance.[29] But also like Whitelocke he obviously had doubts, and they surfaced when the issue re-emerged during the negotiations over the Nineteen Propositions in June. One of the

Propositions was that the King should 'rest satisfied with the course that the Lords and Commons have appointed for ordering of the militia, until the same shall be further settled by a Bill'; on 2 July Selden made a major speech on this clause which is not at all well known but which makes his position clear.

> Mr Selden stood up and showed . . . that the King resting satisfied with the ordinance of the militia would not make it a law or add any further force to it, not though he should give his consent to it at York, but that which must make it a law must be [the] allowing of it in person or by authority of the Great Seal in the presence of the two Houses of Lords and Commons. That he conceived we ought no further to insist upon it, seeing the King had so solemnly expressed his dislike of it, and may justly so do in that we have desired in the said propostion that the ordinance of the militia may continue till a Bill be preparing, which may never be done for aught the King knows; and the people may justly dislike it for here is a power given by an ordinance to dispose of their goods and persons because they are to muster and train as often as they shall be required . . . . But whereas necessity is pretended to be a ground of this ordinance, that can be no true ground of it, for in that case where there is a true and an apparent necessity every man hath as great a liberty to provide for his own safety as the two Houses of Parliament; neither can any civil court pretend to do anything out of necessity which they cannot do by the ordinary rules of law and justice, so when such a real necessity comes there must be a stop of the courts of justice. And therefore he desired in conclusion that we would think of some way of accommodating all matters of difference with His Majesty . . . .[30]

It is apparent from this that Selden was most worried by the actual content of the ordinance, and would not have been happy about it even if the King had agreed to the Propositions. His unhappiness was obviously because it maintained the illegal militia system of the Caroline government, and was justified on the same grounds as its conduct had been, namely the bogus plea of necessity. It is striking that he avoided denouncing the measure as removing any right over the militia from the King; rather, he denounced it for depriving the *subject* of liberty, in words which were to be prophetic. But at least the measure was not (so to speak) any *more* illegal than the practice of the previous decades, and the enforcement of the ordinance at first respected the existing ban on leading troops from one county to another. The county association system was after all a reflection of Parliament's respect for this prohibition. The same could not be said about the attempts by the King at this time to raise his own army, and Selden threw himself with great energy and enthusiasm into the fight against them; it is obvious from both his writings and his actions in 1642 that he considered that the greatest threat to the legal order and the subject's liberties came not from Parliament, despite the Militia Ordinance, but from the King.

On 11 June Charles had issued Commissions of Array to leading Royalists in various counties, instructing them to raise troops and to conduct them 'as well to the coasts, as to other places, for the opposition and destruction of our enemies'.[31] His justification for using this method was purportedly the precedent of such commissions, with this wording, under the Lancastrian kings; he was probably advised to use it not by Hyde or Falkland, but by lawyers at York such as Robert Heath who had helped to organise the collection of Ship Money. On 18 June the Commons nominated a committee to draw up a declaration against the commissions, consisting of Selden, Glyn, Wilde, St John, Browne and D'Ewes (a smaller committee than had been usual for the drafting of declarations.) Selden and Glyn managed its affairs, and among Selden's papers are drafts for speeches and declarations against the commissions and an annotated copy of the King's reply to the parliamentary declaration. It is probable that the declaration as it was printed on 4 July and the answer to the royal reply, which Parliament arranged to be published in October but which appeared on 15 January 1643, was substantially Selden's own work.[32]

The Commons committee immediately perceived that the commissions, like all late-medieval military matters, had been governed by statute (in particular one of 1404, 5 Hen.4), and that the statutes prescribed the form they should take; and that the wording of the commissions seemed to assume that the troops were to be raised in accordance with the existing statutory provisions. Although the commissions of Henry IV's time allowed troops to be led out of their native counties, the committee argued that that was only to meet the specific threat of an actual invasion by the French or Scots. The crucial point upon which they insisted was that there was no evidence that the Lancastrian commissions were designed to overturn the existing basis of troop recruitment, and plenty of circumstantial evidence that they were not. Given this, it followed in their eyes that the statutory restrictions on recruitment were still in force, and that what the King was trying to do was clearly illegal; not only was he continuing the existing illegality of the militia system with regard to the level of arms which citizens had to find, he was also extending it in a crucial area by overriding the prohibitions on crossing county boundaries – a much more serious matter, given what we now know about local feeling.

On or about 20 July the King replied, and his answer was very revealing. First, it tried to argue that the statute of 5 Hen.4 had actually itself repealed all the previous medieval legislation; but then, recognising the implausible character of this argument, it attempted to show its faithfulness to them. But this was also an implausible line to take, and it is significant that its author had to turn to general arguments of political theory, just as his predecessors in the 1620s and 1630s had done.

> Since (as we hope none will deny) the kingdom must of necessity be ever in readiness (in time of danger at least) by power of arms to prevent or suppress rebellion at home and invasion from abroad; and to that end the subject must be armed and prepared beforehand, . . . and that this cannot be done without a command or government, we desire much to know in whom, out of Parliament, (for Parliaments are not always, nor can be called at all times, or meet on the sudden) this power can be, but in us as supreme governor; (as it is in all other states, be the persons of the governors one or more, according to the form of each state).[33]

The character of the government's views about the militia had seldom been made so clear.

The Commons committee leaped on this and similar passages. Selden's papers include a draft historical discussion of the problem of raising arms, arguing that even under the Anglo-Norman kings it was not uncontestably a royal power:

> every man knows out of the history of those times that there was great difference betwen the king and his subjects often touching their liberties, which were indeed never all settled at all till Magna Charta came to be settled. And it can scarce be doubted but that this very requisition of arms was one of the particulars so much complained of.[34]

The printed reply argues the same, and makes a remarkable deduction from it. The Anglo-Norman and Plantagenet kings had no straightforward legal powers to raise troops except by feudal tenures or contract – what else was the point of feudalism? So 'till 13.E1 there was no law to compel men otherwise to find arms, than as aforesaid [that is, by tenure or contract], and that law being now repealed as it was by the statute of 21. *Iacobi*, there is now neither common law nor statute law to compel any men to find arms, but those that are bound to do it by their tenures or contracts.' What about the existing practice? Commissions to muster troops

> have been often complained of, and never allowed in any judicial way, but have been upheld by power rather than law: for it had been easy to have tried the legality of them heretofore, upon defaults at musters, but the defaulters were ever presented to the Lords of the Council, and there punished . . . .[35]

So the committee had been led to say clearly for the first time that there was *no* legal basis for *any* militia, and to assert that the repeal of 13 Edw.1 meant a repeal of all subsequent enactments which confirmed it.

This was a wholly radical move, which also of course undermined the Militia Ordinance (no bad thing, no doubt, in Selden's eyes); but it was entirely in accordance with Selden's reading of the law of England. Indeed, it was based on a much more sophisticated sense of what feudalism was and the extent to which England remained legally a feudal country than his Royalist opponents were able to provide, and this point did not go unnoticed in the country at large. On 20 October 1642, before the Parliamentary reply was in print, an independent pamphlet *The Case of the Commission of Array Stated* appeared, stating clearly the feudal basis of the King's military power and arguing that anything beyond that must now be given solely by statute.

It is clear enough now why the greatest lawyer of his time chose to side with Parliament in 1642. Despite Clarendon's claims, made also and repeatedly in the contemporary pamphlet literature, that Charles now stood for the ancient constitution against innovation, this was far from being uncontestably the case. The Royal army, the crucial issue by 1643, was illegal, at least on Selden's account of what the law was. The Parliamentary army may also have been (though it should not be forgotten that he chose to serve as a deputy lieutenant), but in practice was more in line with a possible reading of the law. To support Parliament was to choose the lesser of the two legal evils. Selden was unhappy, of course, about supporting any army at all in 1642 – on 9 July he was a teller against the motion to raise 10,000 volunteers in London – and in this respect he again appears to have been like Whitelocke and his other friends in the House. But in 1643 he made a more definite commitment: on 6 June he took the Vow and Covenant to prosecute the war, on 18 July he was one of three members (the others being St John and Constantine) deputed to prepare an ordinance to implement the vote to raise 6500 horse, and on 19 July he was one of a committee of ten to consider a vindication of the Vow and Covenant.[36] From then until Pride's Purge he worked hard in the Commons, usually as one of the so-called Middle Group round St John, though with a consistent inclination to seek a negotiated settlement if one could be had without too much danger. He even took the Solemn League and Covenant.[37] In the crisis of July 1647, when the more radical members withdrew with the Speaker from the chamber under pressure from London Presbyterians, he seems to have played an eirenic role, staying in the chamber during the Speaker's absence but willing to work on the various committees set up in August after his return to sort out affairs.[38]

What led him to this commitment to war seems to have been his sense that while what the King was attempting was illegal, in the sense that it breached the legal rights of his subjects, Parliament's conduct was not illegal in the sense that it breached the *King's* rights. The agreement which constituted the laws of England had been broken by the King, and war was the only answer. A number of his remarks in *Table Talk* are suggestive.

> *Question*. Whether may subjects take up arms against their prince? *Answer*. Conceive it thus. Here lies a shilling betwixt you and me; ten pence of the shilling is yours, two pence is mine. By agreement, I am as much king of my two pence, as you of your ten pence. If you therefore go about to take away my two pence, I will defend it; for there you and I are equal, both princes. Or thus. Two supreme powers meet; one says to the other, give me your land; if you will not, I will take it from you. The other, because he thinks himself too weak to resist, tells him, of nine parts I will give you three, so I may quietly enjoy the rest, and I will become your tributary. Afterwards the prince comes to exact six parts, and leaves but three; the contract then is broken, and they are in parity again . . . .
> *Question*. What law is there to take up arms against the prince, in case he breaks his covenant? *Answer*. Though there be no written law for it, yet there is custom; which is the best law of the kingdom; for in England they have always done it . . . .[39]

These remarks are unequivocal: the King had attacked the rights of his subjects, and thereby destroyed the constitution. There was no question of his actions being warranted by the constitutional agreement, nor of the subjects encroaching on the prince's right.

There was of course a further element in the politics of the 1640s which must have obliged Selden to work with Parliament. Ever since the publication of his *History of Tythes*, he had been concerned with the threat to free inquiry and the secular way of life posed by an organised and powerful Church. The preface to the *History* contains an impassioned denunciation of the lazy and ignorant clergy who had persecuted Roger Bacon, Reuchlin, Budé and Erasmus,[40] and throughout his adult life Selden campaigned against ecclesiastical power. In February 1641 he

THE ANCIENT LAW OF FREEDOM'

at first opposed the abolition of episcopacy, but by the summer
he had swung round, perceiving the chance of a clearly state-
run Church under lay commissioners.[41] As he said,

> it does not follow we must have bishops still, because we have
> had them so long. They are equally mad who say that bishops
> are so *jure divino*, that they must be continued, and they who
> say, they are so antichristian, that they must be put away. All
> is as the state pleases.[42]

There was no doubt that if Charles won the old episcopal
regime would be reinstated, but the alternative was not so clear.
Like many of his contemporaries, Selden saw the threat of
ecclesiastical power as two-sided: one was a divine-right episcopacy, but the other was a Calvinist church government. After
the Westminster Assembly had been set up, Selden had to
devote a great deal of his time to ensuring that the Church
settlement eventually arrived at by a victorious Parliament
would not be Presbyterian. But he was obviously (and rightly)
confident that he and his supporters such as Whitelocke (again)
could bring this off, and that the ecclesiastical arrangements in
England would be far superior to the regime favoured by the
Royalists; such a prospect must have acted as a powerful motive
for remaining on the Parliamentary side.

    Indeed, there are signs of an increasing rather than a decreas-
ing radicalism on his part during the 1640s. The third part of his
*De Synedriis Veterum Ebraeorum*, which appeared posthumously
and was written after 1650, includes a remarkable discussion of
whether the kings of Israel could be tried by the *Sanhedrin* – and
not merely for crimes of which anyone could be guilty, such as
murder, but also for offences which only kings could commit.
He recognised that both Grotius and Salmasius had denied
this, but he quoted Maimonides and other Talmudists (with
some degree of approval) as maintaining that it was possible. At
the end, he refused to commit himself to the correctness of either
view: but this very judiciousness lent a weight to the anti-
monarchical position which it would not otherwise have enjoyed.[43] It was presumably this degree of sympathy with the
attitude of the new regime which led to Selden retaining the
favour of the Rumpers – in January 1651 it was reported that he

was among the absent members who were 'received in favour' and were not deprived of their seats. It was also presumably the knowledge of his position after 1649 that led Cromwell in 1653 to suggest (how seriously, we do not know) that Selden and St John should be approached to draw up a new constitution.[44] Many of Selden's friends, such as Rolle, Whitelocke and even Matthew Hale, were also reasonably happy to serve the new regime.[45]

It is also significant that Selden's ideas could at times be pressed into service by men with an extremely radical political commitment. The best example of this are Henry Ireton's arguments at Putney in 1647 against the Levellers. These arguments have often been misunderstood, and treated as merely a case of atavistic conservatism; but in fact they presuppose many of the points which Selden (and in 1647 more or less *only* Selden on the Parliamentary side) had made. Their central point was a denial of any natural right of property, or any other substantial, social right such as the right to participate in government. By nature, Ireton repeatedly insisted, men were *totally* free: a man 'hath the same right in any goods he sees – meat, drink, clothes – to take and use them for his sustenance. He hath a freedom in the land, the ground, to exercise, to till it; he hath the freedom to anything that anyone doth account himself to have any property in.'[46] All civil rights were the product of the civil constitution, the fundamental agreement men had entered into; if they were to be changed (and some *were* to be changed in the *Agreement* which had been accepted by Ireton and his opponents at Reading but which had now been reopened for discussion, much to Ireton's annoyance), then the grounds for such a change could not be any natural or 'birth' right but considerations of civil prudence and common interest. Those considerations, Ireton believed, precluded any substantial extension of the franchise; and it is a striking feature of the debates that the Levellers were consistently unhappy about operating on this kind of ground. They present in fact the spectacle of men familiar with a more traditional way of talking about the law of nature and its relationship to civil society, who had been caught out by Ireton's espousal of a new kind of theory.

It is hard not to believe that at least conversations with

lawyer friends such as Whitelocke (with whom Ireton was usually on good terms) lay behind his remarks at Putney; although his legal career is obscure, Ireton was seen as a member of 'the profession' by Whitelocke, and is likely through his membership of it to have come to a knowledge of Selden's ideas.[47] It should not be forgotten, moreover, that others of an unequivocally radical cast of mind could by 1647 approve of and use Selden's theories: in his *Doctrine and Discipline of Divorce* Milton spoke of

> that noble volume written by our learned Selden, *Of the law of nature & of nations*, a work more useful and more worthy to be perused, whosoever studies to be a great man in wisdom, equity, and justice, than all those decretals, and sumless sums, which the pontifical clerks have doted on,

while in *Areopagitica* he refers to the work's 'exquisite reasons and theorems almost mathematically demonstrative'.[48] A full awareness of the sympathy with which 'Puritans' like Milton could read Selden has often eluded historians such as A.S.P. Woodhouse, who have seen Selden as an obvious exception to the generally theological or religious character of seventeenth-century English thought.[49] But as we have seen, a belief about God plays a central role in Selden's political thought; he was sceptical about *churches*, it is true, but so were many Puritans, and his personal moral standards were freer than most Puritans (though by no means all) would approve of;[50] but his concern with God was real and important. The same is true of men like Whitelocke and Hale: after the Restoration, despite the social disadvantages attached to so doing, Whitelocke regularly preached at Dissenting meetings, and a volume of his sermons was published by William Penn in 1711. Hale (a close friend of Richard Baxter after 1660) also thought and wrote extensively on religious matters; he and his friends were pious laymen, with some unorthodox ideas but no hint of genuine scepticism.[51] Men like John Locke were their intellectual successors in this as in so many other respects.

We have seen that Selden's ideas could provide both himself and other people with reasons to support Parliament in the 1640s, and that doing so was (to them) a natural extension of

the kind of position they had taken up before the war in opposition to Charles's policies. What are we to make, then, of
Clarendon, whose firm belief it was that he himself had kept
faith with the principles of the constitutional opposition to
Charles while the other had betrayed them?[52] Selden's own
behaviour was obviously a difficulty for Clarendon; unwilling to
claim that it too was treachery, he had to emphasise Selden's
age and decrepitude as an explanation for it.[53] But we do need
to explain how Royalists too could utilise Selden's ideas and
believe that Selden must have been basically in sympathy with
their cause. I have demonstrated elsewhere the extent to which
they did so; the key figures here were the Tew habitués, who in a
series of pamphlets printed between 1642 and 1644 attacked
the Parliamentary case with arguments drawn from Selden's
general political theory.[54] They insisted that in a state of nature
men possess unlimited rights to all things, and that the state
was consequently one of war – as Henry Hammond put it, 'a
state of common hostility, . . . a wilderness of bears or tigers, not
a society of men'.[55] Upon this state supervened laws of nature,
decreed by God and acquiring their obligatory force from his
capacity to harm people; primary among them was the rule that
we must honour our contracts, and it was thus in our interests to
do so even if our own death resulted. As the young Dudley
Digges, the most impressive of these writers, said, 'if we submit
nature to religion, and be content to lose our lives for the
present, we shall receive them hereafter with great advantage.
So that charity to our neighbour, and love of our selves, do
sweetly kiss each other.'[56] Men in the state of nature perceived
that they needed a sovereign to bring the benefits of peace and
order, and that he could be created by a general commitment
not to resist his activities; the parties to this agreement were
then held to it even when the sovereign threatened them, by
virtue of the general requirement to honour their contracts.

But the Tew writers used this argument to deny the possibility of resistance to the King of England in 1642; and here
problems arose. It was the essence of Selden's argument that
the requirement of contractual obligation applied to kings as
much as to their subjects, and that the English king could be
guilty of breaking the agreement which constituted the government of England by acting against the common law. The Tew

writers had to show why contractual obligation did not apply to the King; they could not utilise the argument used by Hobbes later, in *De Vive* (1642) and *Leviathan* (1651), that the sovereign was not himself a party to the original contract and therefore cannot be bound by it, for in their eyes (as in Hobbes's in 1640, when he was closely associated with them) the crucial promise was a promise made *to* the sovereign not to resist him, on the understanding that he would act in some specified way towards his subjects – notably (but not necessarily exclusively) that he would protect them.[57] The sovereign was thus inevitably a party, and it was unclear what exempted him from the contract's obligations.

Digges confronted this issue in 1644 when he tried to answer the hypothetical objection that 'there is a mutual contract between king and subjects, and if he breaks the covenant, he forfeits the benefits of this agreement.' He could do so, however, only by asserting that the covenant between monarch and people was like that between husband and wife:

> as in marriage, so in monarchy there are two parties in the contract; though without a mutual agreement there could be no covenant, yet after it is once made the dissent of the inferior party, let it be not upon fancied, but real discontents, cannot dissolve the compact. Consent therefore joined man and wife, king and people, but divine ordinance continues this union; marriages and governments both are ratified in heaven.[58]

But of course, there was no reason to suppose that the contract between king and people was actually of this type; moreover Selden would have questioned whether marriage itself was.

What Digges's argument at this point reveals is that the Tew writers had to blend their 'Seldenian' ideas with something like traditional Royalism if they were to mount a successful defence of the King, and that the blending destroyed the distinctive characteristics of Selden's theory. I have given other examples of this process in my *Natural Rights Theories*, but it is worth drawing attention to the fact that Clarendon himself exhibited the same tendency, to an even more marked degree. In his *Transcendent and Multiplied Rebellion and Treason discovered by the Lawes of this Land*, which he published anonymously in November 1645, he asserted that the original of political authority

> is from God . . . and from none other, men or angels: for the creatures generally are under the commandments, *Thou shalt not kill*, *Thou shalt not steal*. And they cannot by any authority of their own, warrant any man to take away another's life without murder, nor his estate without theft. Only God, who . . . hath a natural dominion over all, can authorise in these cases: and he gives this authority to Kings and other supreme magistrates . . . .[59]

Elsewhere in the same work he argued about the English constitution that 'in some points of regality and sovereignty the King of England is already restrained and limited . . . but in all other things that are not expressly restrained by law, he is free and absolute, . . . as in providing for the present safety against sudden danger, and in levying of arms.'[60] Both these points are made explicitly by Digges and the other Tew writers; the former, about the need for God specifically to exempt magistrates from his general commandments, is a familiar argument of theirs and is entirely inconsistent with Selden's theory.[61] Clarendon's later pamphlets, such as his *Full Answer* to the Vote of No Addresses in 1648, and his critique of *Leviathan* published in 1676, make the same case for a traditional kind of divine-right theory far removed from anything Selden had countenanced.[62]

It seems in fact as if an undue concentration on Clarendon's *History* (from which, revealingly, its author omitted the projected Book dealing with general political theory[63]) has misled historians about the character of 'constitutional Royalism' and its links with the 'constitutional opposition' of 1640. There was a clear propaganda advantage in making the Royalism appear constitutional, and the direct successor of the opposition ideas of 1640; but as we have seen, in the eyes of at least one contemporary who ought to have known what he was doing, this was far from being a true description. In ideological as well as personal terms, Selden's career links the opposition of 1640, and even the opposition of 1624–8, firmly with an eirenic, Middle-Group Parliamentarianism and not with the Royalists. His intellectual legacy was of the same kind; it is no accident that it was John Vaughan, one of Selden's executors and in some ways his closest follower intellectually, who led the Commons' attack on Clarendon after the Restoration and who served as Chief Justice of Common Pleas under the Cabal.[64] Selden's ideas may not have won in 1649 or in 1660, but it is arguable that they did so in 1667 – and in some ways even in 1688.

# 7. Ideology and Politics in the Parliamentary Armies, 1645–9

## MARK KISHLANSKY

I

Much has been written in a general way about the ideology of the officers of the New Model Army. In historians' changing interpretations of the English Revolution the Army has always held a central place. Representation of its role and of its underlying motivations are as varied as those of the Revolution itself. The Army was composed of Saints in Arms whose aspirations were the culmination of the Puritan movement;[1] or of men from the forests and the fens who represented the hopes of the dispossessed in their struggle with the privileged few.[2] Service in the Army was a career open to the talents, accelerating the replacement of status by ability;[3] or it was the prototype for the armed citizenry, taking the first unsteady steps on the path towards participatory democracy.[4] In each explanation the New Model has been used as a symbol for a larger process of social change through which the meaning of the Revolution is revealed. It is many things to many men and this diversity mirrors the true heterogeneity of the Army's composition and conduct.

Much has been written about the ideology of the Army, but most of it has been misconceived. A principal reason for this has been that historians have assumed that the lowly social origins of many of the officers created a commitment to radical ideology This is false on both factual and logical grounds. There were men of low-birth among the New Model's officers, and much has been made of Pride the drayman and Hewson the cobbler.

More still might be made of obscure officers like Spooner and Creamer whose surnames suggest backgrounds in trades and service. The Army also contained a Cecil, a Sheffield, and three colonels who were knights. Yet careful study of the Army's social origins, which lends support to the view that they were more traditional in nature (of solid status in rural and urban structures) still does not meet the real objection to existing interpretations – the fallacy of social determinism. The man who seeks to level all property because he has none must always be balanced by the man who seeks to own more property because he started with none. Social outcasts and social climbers have the same origins. Similarly, is there a geographical component to anti-authoritarianism? Those who dwelt in forests and fens may be rugged individuals unused to the restraining presence of gentlemen and magistrates, but this will give us no general rule as to whether in the face of authority they will stand against it or in awe of it. The fact that the overwhelming majority of officers and soldiers whose geographical origins are known came from urban areas does not help to resolve the ecological fallacy. Nor, to compound confusion, is predictable behaviour – even when it can be established – the best guide to the actions of revolutionaries. To recast a fashionable parable: blind men have hold of an animal for which the sighted still have no name. In such circumstances it is best to be cautious.

So we must be with that more obvious component of ideology, ideas. Historians have worked assiduously to establish the radical quality of ideas available to the soldiers of Parliament's armies and, less successfully, to pinpoint those which indisputably made their way to the Army. It is less common, though far easier, to substantiate the stock of conventional ideas from which the soldiery were bombarded and to identify the more conservative preachers who sallied among them. It is widely accepted by intellectual historians that radical ideas may spread fastest not where they are given greater currency but where there is an audience preconditioned to accept them. Furthermore, it has been argued that radical ideology is more often the result of an extension of conventional ideas and of their implications than it is the introduction of novel ideas. The essentially conservative nature of much revolutionary ideology is thus frequently expressed in a phantasmagoric historicism like the Levellers' dreams of the halcyon days of Edward the Confessor. Thus conventional ideas newly perceived may be the ultimate source of radical ideology and the best preconditioning of radicals may be a tenacious hold on tradition.

Such paradoxes bring us no closer to the ideology of the New Model Army, but they have a salutary effect nonetheless. They serve to clear the ground of what we think we know and open wide vistas for us to gaze upon. Rebuilding will take time and will proceed slowly. The difficulty of answering the question makes it no less important. Perhaps the place to start to look for those ideas which motivated actions – our working definition of ideology – are the public manifestos in which the Army articulated to Parliament and the nation the reasons for its extraordinary actions.

II

The documents which the Army produced to define its goals and aspirations were all devised in an eighteen-month period beginning in June 1647. The first Civil War had ended a year before with the King's surrender of Oxford and was followed by nerve-racking political manoeuvring, first involving the King, his Scottish captors and Parliament, and later including the leaders of the government, of the City of London, radical London citizens and the Army. The fervent desires of the constituents of the Parliamentary cause for a settlement to recompose government were offset by fears of treachery in endless combinations, each at a different moment equally plausible. Thus Parliament and the Army feared that the King and the Scots would begin a new war; the Scots and important City leaders feared that the Army and Parliament would destroy the Presbyterian church establishment; Parliament and the City feared that the Army and the London radicals would overawe constituted authority; the Army feared that Parliament would ignore its material grievances and then that Parliament and the City would restore the King without a permanent settlement; the London radicals feared everybody and everything. The spring and summer of 1647 was a period of intense political turmoil, jangled and paranoid.

It was also a time of intense political examination, when the councils of the constituents of Parliament's cause plumbed the depths of their beliefs and desires. In the Army, this period witnessed the stirring of political consciousness among the soldiery and then the rapid development of a radicalised political body out of what had been a simple military organisation. The changes took place both in the modes of political expression and in the issues which the soldiers came to see as those central to their cause. At first the Army was organised into troops, regiments and brigades for efficient military action. From April 1645 to March 1647 there is almost no evidence of political activity within the New Model: for fifteen months the soldiers fought; for eight they waited. Indeed, the first stirrings within the Army, in March 1647, came when Parliament voted to begin a reorganisation of its forces which involved a large scale demobilisation. This led groups of soldiers, in scattered quarters, to initiate a petition, concerned with a number of material grievances, to be presented to their general, Sir Thomas Fairfax.[5] A similar petition had been presented to the earl of Essex when his Army was reorganised in 1644 and in March 1647 the only concerns of the soldiers, and the officers who subsequently came to be involved, were over issues like arrears of pay and judicial indemnity – essentially a pardon for civil offences committed under the necessities of war. When news of the soldiers' petition reached Parliament it was declared against as seditious and mutinous and ordered to be supressed ruthlessly.[6] This draconian response led to the development of new channels of organisation among the soldiery, first by the selection of regimental agents and then in a proposal to establish a general council of the Army.

More importantly, the material grievances which had first generated the desires for a petition to the Army leadership came to be generalised into demands for a vindication of the Army's honour. Not only should those who had ventured their lives and estates be given the back pay due them and assured freedom from harassment and imprisonment, but they should be honoured for their sacrifice rather than condemned for exercising their right, the right of all citizens, to petition – 'Our lives have not been dear unto us for the public good'. (*Declaration* of 2 August 1647.)[7] The elevation of specific material grievances into issues of honour and liberties was the first crucial step in the Army's radicalisation and it was taken confidently because the material grievances which gave it its strength were so incontrovertibly just. The next stride, though not as sturdy, was longer. If the Army's honour was to be upheld, and publicly proclaimed, in what did that honour consist? Certainly the victorious service in which the Army had engaged; surely the material deprivations which it had suffered; arguably the harsh treatment it had lately received at the hands of a group of parliamentarians; but in what did it consist fundamentally? Why had the Army engaged and suffered and been vilified? These were the questions which led, during a period of concentrated self-examination, to the statements of the Army's ideology – of the beliefs that had justified their action in taking up arms against the King and which now motivated them to seek a further transformation of English government. From disparate and inchoate ideas the Army formed its self-justification, and the process by which this happened, as do so many others of similar circumstance, remains mysterious.

We know little of the manner by which the Army's declarations and remonstrances were drafted and edited. Several of them were printed in Oxford with funds from the general's discretionary account and all were officially presented to Parliament.[8] But the methods of composition remain elusive. Thus in analysing these documents as statements of the Army's ideology, it is being assumed that the ideas being expressed in the documents were general to the Army rather than specific to the few who actually composed them. This is not to say that there was not disagreement and dispute over both principles and actions to follow on them. The records of these disputes, the Reading, Putney and Whitehall debates,[9] are well known and tell us much about the collective consciousness of the officers and soldiers as well as the issues upon which they contended. Yet each was followed by unified action or inaction upon which we can base our conclusion that there was an *Army* ideology.

Moreover, much circumstantial evidence lends credence to this assumption. In the first place, those who dissented from the generally expressed grievances of the Army had had an opportunity to withdraw in the weeks before the *Solemn Engagement* of 5 June,[10] which pledged the soldiers to stand united until their desires were secured, was taken. Several hundred chose this course. Secondly, much of the substance of the *Declaration* of 14 June,[11] the first statement of the Army's demands, was adumbrated in the many regimental petitions of mid-May when the soldiers of each regiment expressed their individual grievances and desires.[12] These documents are different in tone and content from later official representations, but not fundamentally in substance. Finally, no group of soldiers ever disavowed the Army's official declarations. The authors of the *Case of the Army Truly Stated*,[13] a radical pamphlet which precipitated the Putney debates over the first *Agreement of the People*,[14] accused the Army of falling off from its engagements. They did not claim that the Army's official proposals were not representative of the desires of the soldiery. It is not clear that the authors of the *Case of the Army* were mostly Army members, or that they commanded much of a following, but even at Putney, when the question of pre-engagements was bitterly disputed, there was never any suggestion that the Army's earlier commitments were unrepresentative of the views the officers and soldiers had held when they made them.

The accusations by London radicals that the senior officers, especially Cromwell and Ireton, had seized control of the deliberative mechanisms of the Army should not obscure the fact that the Army's August 1647 *Declaration*[15] as well as the *Heads of the Proposals*[16] were debated by large committees. The intimations that Henry Ireton had the chief hand in composing the *Heads of the Proposals*, suggested by Colonel Thomas Rainsborough at Putney, may well be the truth of the matter.[17] He was certainly a leading figure in the composition of the *Remonstrance* of November 1648,[18] the drafting of which had been assigned to a large and carefully constructed committee. Ireton's talents may have earned him a role of leadership, but the give and take within the committee on certain crucial issues is well documented. Perhaps the most important point to be stressed is that all of the Army's official representations, beginning in June 1647 and proceeding to the Army *Agreement of the People* in January 1649,[19] demonstrate a remarkable consistency of ideas and fundamental beliefs. As circumstances changed, particularly after the

second Civil War, the methods deemed necessary to secure the
safety of the nation's future changed as well. The Army's ideology was not static, especially as the implications of their ideas
and the necessity of events became clearer. Yet the principles
upon which they justified those demands – the trial of the King
being most notable – can be discerned in the *Declaration* of 14
June. If Ireton was the Army's ideologue he was also its
penman; he wrote to a long crescendo of voices in harmony with
each other. It is to the melody of the Army's ideology that we
must now turn.

### III

The Army's public manifestos were all self-consciously political. Each sought to justify impending actions or new sets of
proposals which the Army believed would secure a settlement
of the Civil Wars. Thus the documents have a reflective quality
as well as an assertive one, setting out the process of reasoning
or series of events which led to their articulation. The *Declaration*
of 14 June, the *Remonstrance* of 23 June, and the *Declaration* of 2
August 1647 all recount the history of the Army's sudden
intervention into the political process. The papers presented to
Parliament in June attempted to justify the Army's refusal to
disband, while the *Declaration* of 2 August was an explanation of
the march on London. The *Remonstrance* of November 1648, the
*Humble Proposals* of 6 December, and the Army *Agreement* of 15
January 1649 are set against the backdrop of the second Civil
War and Parliament's renewed negotiations with the King. *The
Remonstrance* was the fullest expression of the Army's final break
with the King; the *Humble Proposals* a justification of Pride's
Purge and the arrest or seclusion of half the members of the
Long Parliament, and the *Agreement* was the Army's draft con-
stitution. It was, in fact, a modified version of the *Heads of the
Proposals*, the first constitutional scheme devised by the Army,
and presented to the King at Windsor in July 1647. That the
Army felt the need to justify its actions rather than simply to
insist upon acceptance of them, gives all of these pronouncements a didactic purpose and elevates the ideology
expressed in them beyond mere rhetorical flourish. 'We doubt

not that the world shall see our actions answerable to our professions,' the soldiers declared in 2 August 1647 and the Army was frequently called to account, by both radicals and Royalists, when new professions appeared to contradict old ones. It was adherence to their beliefs which gave justice to their actions, and for this reason the officers and soldiers moved slowly and, at times, painfully with the leftward drift of events. As we shall see, it was the commitment to maintain the freedom and just rights of all Englishmen, including the King, which provided the greatest complication.

The Army's ideology had three elements: that all Englishmen had birthrights, freedoms and liberties inherent to them; that the authority of civil government resided in Parliament; and that the chief principle of social relations was the advancement of public good over private interest. Though distinguishable from each other, and at times given different emphases, these principles were interrelated and often inextricable. If the *Heads of the Proposals* of 1 August 1647 and the *Army Agreement* of 15 January 1649 emphasised parliamentary reform in precise and copious detail, it was because a purified representative would protect just rights and liberties and act to promote the public good. Similarly, the emphasis in the *Declaration* of 2 August 1647 and the *Remonstrance* of November 1648 upon freeing the nation from the corruption of private interest had as its intention the purgation – on the second occasion literally – of Parliament. Yet, as with all such basic principles, it would be a mistake to think that they were ideas clearly fixed and unchanging. Any man might know when he felt his just rights violated, but few could offer a compendium of what they were and the Army never did. Instead they enumerated examples of grievances which Parliament should resolve, the list that was appended to the *Heads of the Proposals*, for example. Though the Revolution itself turned on the interpretation of private interest, the concept contained more grey than black or white. Perhaps it is this ambiguous combination of beliefs shading into feelings that motivates men to leave off contemplation and take up action. Ideology is not only ideas.

By generalising its specific grievances into an ideology, the Army transformed its role in the political process. The petitions for redress of material complaints and even the insistence upon

the vindication of the Army's honour were at first circum-
scribed within its military experience. The gradual awareness
that settlement of these issues provided no guarantees for the
future changed both the purpose and emphasis of the Army's
concerns. As they were under order to disband – an order which
they fully intended to obey[20] – the soldiers began to think of
their condition when they returned to civilian life. Of course
their demand for judicial indemnity made this no great leap of
imagination; it was not as soldiers that they feared prosecution
in the localities for such actions as taking horses. Their refusal
to disband, therefore, was not justified by the failure of
Parliament to provide their back pay, but by their commitment
to enunciate their own desires for the establishment of a lasting
peace. These propositions, contained in the *Heads of the Proposals*,
were focused on issues of fundamental political importance,
institutional reforms and legal guarantees which thrust the
Army into negotiations between King and Parliament.

The identification of interest the Army found with the
citizens of the nation led to its belief that it was acting to secure
inherent rights and liberties:

> that we, and all the free-born people of this nation may sit
> down in quiet under our vines, under the glorious ad-
> ministration of justice and righteousness and in the full
> possession of those fundamental rights and liberties without
> which we can have little hopes (as to human considerations)
> to enjoy either any comforts of life, or so much as life itself.
> (*Declaration* of 14 June)

A part of these freedoms was directly related to the Army's own
grievances. The peremptory rejection of their March petition
made the soldiery sensitive to the difficulties experienced by
other petitioners in having their grievances aired. Throughout
the summer and autumn of 1647 groups of local citizens
brought their petitions directly to the Army in the hope that
Fairfax would act as a conduit between them and Parliament.
The right to petition was one liberty of Englishmen that the
Army declared for unequivocally: 'we desire that the right and
freedom of the people, to represent to the Parliament, by way of
humble petition their grievances . . . may be cleared and vindi-

cated' (*Declaration* of 14 June). Similarly, concerns about judicial indemnity led the soldiers to assert the fundamental liberty of Englishmen to be free from all arbitrary government, monarchical or parliamentary: 'the sum of the public interest of a nation in relation to common right and freedom, which has been the chief subject of our contest . . . [is] opposition to tyranny and injustice of Kings and others' (*Remonstrance* of November 1648).

The pledge to preserve the just rights and liberties of all Englishmen imparted a transcendent character to the Army's ideology and transformed a military body into a political force. It also propelled the Army into action. Initially, the defence of English liberties was made by standing up for its own rights and later by appealing to Parliament to ensure the rights of others. But by the end of the summer of 1647, the Army was able to make a more dramatic demonstration in defence of its countrymen's birthrights. At the end of July a mob of apprentices, former Parliamentary soldiers and others invaded the two Houses of Parliament and forced the members to pass a series of measures reversing earlier decisions.[21] While conservative MPs and their allies in the City briefly attempted to make political capital out of this reckless venture, other members, including the Speakers of both Houses, fled to Army headquarters demanding protection. This led to the Army's march on London in defence of the liberties of Parliament: 'it being our chief aim to settle peace with truth and righteousness throughout the Kingdom, that none may be oppressed in his just freedom and liberties, much less the Parliament itself' (*Declaration* of 2 August). The march on London provided the Army with an opportunity to demonstrate its commitment to parliamentary freedom, an occasion to prove that it was not a rag-tag assemblage of the unpaid and underfed – for its behaviour within the City was exemplary – and most importantly, a justification for its continued existence:

> the late example may evidence to all the world, who shall be masters of the Parliament's freedom and resolutions; and common reason will teach every man, who shall be masters of the birthrights of the whole kingdom when there shall be no Army on foot, when they have the confidence to dispute for

the mastery, notwithstanding such an army as this, to check and balance them in behalf of the kingdom and Parliament. (*Declaration* of 2 August)

The subtle change from advocate of the liberties of Englishmen to their defender led the Army to new efforts to articulate those rights which must be preserved in a lasting settlement of peace. After establishing its quarters on the south bank of the Thames, the Army publicly encouraged private citizens to meet with groups of officers and agitators for open discussions of these problems. The Army's own pronouncements of fundamental rights had been general ones: the right of petition; the benefit of the law; the taking off of arbitrary power; and the execution of public justice (*Declaration* of 14 June). Discussion between the various Army committees and civilians did not, with one significant exception, reveal essential disagreement over these issues, although a spirited debate took place at Putney on the details of parliamentary reform. The more important controversy, which was only briefly aired on the third day of the Putney debates, centred upon the future role of the King. On 14 June the Army had declared that

when his majesty in these things, and what else shall be proposed by the Parliament necessary for securing the rights and liberties of the people . . . shall have given his concurrence to put them past dispute, we shall then desire that the rights of his majesty and his posterity may be considered of, and settled in all things so far as may consist with the right and freedom of the subject.

On 2 August, less ambiguously, the Army pledged 'to assure unto the King his just rights and authority'. The consistency with which the Army had insisted upon the birthrights of Englishmen ensured its support for the birthrights of the King. 'We do not see how there can be any peace to this kingdom, firm or lasting without a due consideration of provision for the rights, quiet and immunity of his majesty, his royal family, and his partakers' (*Remonstrance* of 23 June). Where this same component of its ideology had propelled the Army into action in the spring and summer, it constrained them in the autumn.

Adherence to the just rights of the monarch posed one set of complications for the Army's political action, commitment to those of Parliament another. The Army's relationship with Parliament was tangled and complex. Parliament had called the Army into existence, had provided for its material wants, and had given it the justification for taking up arms against the King; from this point of view Parliament was the Army's master. Yet the Army had fought Parliament's wars – had literally saved the institution from oblivion and the members from traitors' deaths – had defended it against mob violence, and then from forcible dissolution; so from another point of view Parliament owed its existence to the Army. This mutual dependence might have been all to the good had not the confrontation in the summer of 1647 been between the Army and Members of Parliament whom the officers and soldiers believed had corrupted their public trust. This led to disobedience to parliamentary commands; to charges of impeachment against individual members; and to threats of force if particular pieces of legislation were not quickly adopted. Such acts were in direct violation of parliamentary authority and privilege, and these were but a pale shadow to Pride's Purge when a wholesale expulsion of MPs was necessary before a parliamentary majority could be secured to accept the demands contained in the *Remonstrance* of November 1648.

Amid such paradoxical and apparently contradictory actions, the Army remained unswervingly committed to Parliament and its authority. The belief that Parliament embodied the people's interest was a central component of the Army's ideology, a belief which intensified rather than weakened in the face of political crisis: 'we wish that the authority of this kingdom in Parliament (rightly constituted) that is freely, equally, and successively chosen, according to its original intention, may ever stand and have its course' (*Declaration* of 14 June). It was rooted in Parliament's own declarations which had provided justification for the first Civil War and which the Army frequently cited in defending many of its own proposals. It was rooted, perhaps more deeply, in the belief that Parliament was the respresentative of the people – 'this we speak of in relation to the House of Commons, as being entrusted in the peoples' behalf for their interest in that great and supreme power of the commonwealth, namely the legislative power, with the power of final judgment' (*Declaration* of 14 June). And it was manifested in the Army's actions; most directly in the fact that each of its public documents was presented to Parliament for its consideration, but also in its defence of parliamentary legitimacy against counterclaims that the power of the sword held equal sway. The *Declaration* of 14 June pledged the soldiery to defend the rights of Parliament – 'we shall hereby, for our part, freely and cheerfully commit our stock or share of interest in this Kingdom, into this common of Parliaments' – and each succeeding manifesto reiterated this vow.

From the Army's point of view, Parliament and its authority was tempest-tossed by a combination of elements. The most obvious of these was the King and his allies who endangered the very existence of the institution. Each of the Army's proposals for parliamentary reform contained a guarantee of successive Parliaments: 'that Parliaments may be biennially called and meet at a certain day' was the first heading of the *Heads of the Proposals* and the third clause of the Army *Agreement* of 15 January 1649. This proposal was similar in intent to the Triennial Act and ensured a continuity not only of sessions, but of legislative participation in government. Prior to the second Civil War, biennial Parliaments of between four and eight months' duration were designed to strike a proper balance between the King's governance with his chosen advisers and with those of the people. After the decision to incapacitate the monarch the balance was to be between the representative and a council of state which it would select and the duration of sessions was to be no longer than half a year (*Agreement* of January 1649). The specification of a set period for sittings spoke to the more potent danger the Army apprehended in adhering to parliamentary authority – corruption from within: 'we only offer . . . that from good wishes to the privileges of Parliament, to render them more lasting by being less innocent' (*Remonstrance* of 23 June). Free parliaments need protection not only from the actions of wilful kings but also from the frailties and presumptuousness of their own membership.

The Army's experience in 1647 had taught it to distinguish between Parliament as an institution and its members as individuals. This was not a semantic nicety behind which hid the realities of brute force. The strained relations between the Army and the men at Westminster might well have led to a *coup* and the establishment of a military regime had there not been a deeply held belief that the corruption of Parliament had been due to the overawing influence of individuals rather than the superfluity of the institution: 'through the powerful interest of the persons guilty . . . divers things lately done and passed from the Parliament against this Army . . . have brought insufferable dishonour upon the parliamentary authority and proceedings' (*Remonstrance* of 23 June). During different moments of crisis – July and October 1647, December 1648 – and against strong sentiments that the people's safety warranted a military take-over, the Army opted for action that adhered to their principle of parliamentary authority. Rather than dissolve the institution, the Army initiated selected excisions of members, first of Holles and his party followers in June 1647 and then Colonel Pride's more thorough purge in December 1648.

The Army's awareness that Parliament could be deflected from safeguarding the rights and liberties of the people informed the largest part of its proposals for parliamentary reform.

> That however unjust or corrupt the persons of Parliament men, in present or future may prove, or whatever ill they may do to particular parties (or to the whole in particular things) during their respective terms or periods, yet they shall not have the temptation or advantage of an unlimited power fixed in them . . . to the oppression and prejudice of the community and the enslaving of the Kingdom to all posterity; but that the people may have an equal hope or possibility, if they made an ill choice at one time, to mend it in another. (*Declaration* of 14 June)

Thus came the proposal for fixed sessions which could not be extended; the demand that Parliament set an early date for its own dissolution; and several proposals for the abolition of arbitrary courts and committees whose authority rested on that of Parliament. In the Army *Agreement* of 15 January 1649 Parliament was expressly forbidden to impress soldiers; exact retribution for acts committed during the war; cancel just public debts; arbitrarily intervene in the legal process; or 'level men's estates, destroy property, or make all things common'.

But the true protection against the corruption of Parliament by its members lay in the peoples' ability to choose fit and proper representatives who 'appear most righteous or most for the common good' (*Declaration* of 14 June) . . . 'men of courage, fearing God and hating covetousness' (*Agreement* of January 1649). Thus the Army held extensive discussions on the question of the proportions and qualities of the electors. It is often forgotten that the *Heads of the Proposals* of 1 August 1647 contained the provision 'that the election of the commons for succeeding Parliaments may be distributed . . . according to some rule of equality or proportion . . . to render the House of Commons as near may be, an equal representative of the whole.' The Army's suggestion then had been that such a proportion might be established on the basis of those who paid rates, but it was explicitly left to Parliament itself to establish the reapportionment and thus the principle on which it was to be based. The Leveller proposal that the franchise be 'more indifferently proportioned according to the number of inhabitants' (*First Agreement of the People*) revealed the ambiguity of the Army's suggestion and led to the historic discussions of the franchise at Putney. The result was that the Army *Agreement* of 15 January 1649 was more precise both in its geographical reallocation of seats and in specifying the qualifications which men would have in order to vote. Here the principle of male rate-payers was given pre-eminence in selecting a House of 400 members, 351 of whose seats the Army apportioned. By making free, successive Parliaments the centre of all their proposals for reform, the Army expressed its fundamental belief that Parliament would protect the rights and liberties of the citizenry and pursue the common good.

The advancement of the common good was the end of government and the underlying principle upon which the peoples' safety rested: *salus populi suprema lex*. This belief formed the third strand of the Army's ideology and knotted together its defence of just rights and liberties and its reforms of Parliament. Through two bloody wars the soldiers had sacrificed their personal interests – most literally in life and limb – to those of the nation at large, and from the beginning of their political

agitation they insisted that the same conviction guide the conduct of others: 'it cannot be imagined that so many of our
countrymen would have opposed us in this quarrel if they had
understood their own good' (*Agreement* of January 1649). From
its earliest declarations the Army repeatedly justified its own
actions in relation to the peoples' welfare, subsuming its particular grievances or comparing the loss of its rights to a threat
against those of the citizenry. One reason for disdaining private
negotiations with Parliament and for stating its beliefs and
desires so publicly was to demonstrate the Army's sincere
adherence to the advancement of the public interest. Thus the
officers and soldiers contrasted their motivations with those of
men of private interest, who worked individually through
corruption and covetousness or in combination through faction
and party. These the Army opposed consistently, leading to
confrontations with Parliament, the City government, and
ultimately the King.

Because the soldiers' politicisation began over issues specific
to their service in the war there was always the potential that
their agitation would result in a revolt for their backpay. This
was certainly a common misapprehension on the part of those
who came into opposition against them. In May and early June
1647 Parliament, dominated by Denzil Holles and his party,
voted numerous concessions to satisfy the soldiers' material
grievances; in the crisis at the end of July, City leaders offered
the Army security for all of its pay if it would not intervene after
the invasion of Parliament. Though more canny, the King also
attempted to persuade the Army to his ends by appealing to
their private interests, in his case to the desires of a segment of
officers and soldiers for a religious toleration. But the Army
expressly disavowed all such motivations and steadfastly
refused such deals. 'We appeal to all men,' they declared on 14
June,

> whether we seek anything of advantage to ourselves, or any
> particular party whatsoever, to the prejudice of the whole;
> and whether the things we wish and seek do not equally
> concern and conduce to the good of others in common with
> ourselves, according to the sincerity of our desires and in-
> tentions.

Against a chorus of accusations, after the impeachment of the
eleven members, that the Army was attempting to overawe
Parliament for its own ends this same sentiment was repeated in
the *Remonstrance* of 23 June: 'we never did nor do value or
regard our own injury or reparation . . . to the future security of
the common right and freedom of the nation.' Similarly, the
*Heads of the Proposals* and the Army *Agreement* of 15 January
were dominated by demands that would secure common rights
rather than particular ones. During the autumn of 1647 London
radicals even suggested that the Army's officers would sell out
the soldiers' material grievances for a compromise settlement of
the war.

As the Army stood ready to subsume its own interests to
those of the Commonwealth, it demanded that the other constituents of the Parliamentary cause do the same. The confrontation between Army and Parliament in the summer of
1647 had at its centre the issue of private interest. From the
rejection of the March Petition to the hasty order to disband the
New Model at the end of May, the soldiery developed the view
that Parliament had come to be dominated by a faction of
members who 'desire to advantage and set up themselves and
their party' (*Declaration* of 14 June). This led to the impeachment of the eleven members in hope that by eliminating
the leaders of faction the uncorrupted members would continue
to perform their public trust: 'that those worthies who have
formerly acted, and carried on things in Parliament for public
good, right and freedom, are now awed or overborn by a
prevailing party of men, of other private interests crept in'
(*Remonstrance* of 23 June). The *Declaration* of 6
December 1648, which justified Pride's Purge, began with a
statement of the same principle: 'having with others, for a long
while sadly beheld and tasted, in your proceedings, the
miserable fruits of councils divided and corrupted by faction
and personal interest, even to the neglecting, betraying and
casting away all public good'.

The fear of faction and party informed many of the specific
proposals the Army made to reconstitute Parliament. The
events of the summer of 1647 demonstrated not only the
potential for the corruption of Parliament's internal workings
by faction and party, but the ease with which outside interest

groups could influence parliamentary proceedings. The clash with the City which resulted in the Army's march on London in August came at the end of a long campaign of pressure by the City to gain control of appointments to its militia committee. While Parliament and the Army had nearly completed a set of proposals which it was hoped would end their own conflict and that with the King, the City, in pursuit of ends 'more suitable to the private bargains and undertakings of some men, than to the public welfare of the whole kingdom', made possible the invasion of the Houses (*Declaration* of 2 August). Thus when the Army created the Council of State to govern with the Representative, during its sessions and in the interim between them it expressly separated the functions of each: 'that to the end all officers of state may be certainly accountable, and no factions made to maintain corrupt interests, no member of a Council of State . . . shall, while such, be elected to be of a representative' (*Agreement* of 15 January). This, too, was the rationale behind fixing a limit to parliamentary sessions. Having observed the corruption of the Long Parliament, of men who had risked their lives and fortunes upon the same principles that the soldiers had risked theirs, the Army could no longer believe that good men would make good government:

> we cannot promise to ourselves, or the Kingdom, an assurance of justice, or other positive good from the hands of men, but those who for present appear most righteous, or most for the common good, having in them an unlimited power fixed in them, during life or pleasure in time may become corrupt or settle into parties or faction. (*Declaration* of June 14)

Finally, the Army's opposition to faction and private interests led to the conclusion, so long resisted, that the greatest faction in the kingdom, the overbearing private interest, was that of the enemy they had fought. After the first Civil War the Army did not extend its analysis of the corruption of party and faction beyond its controversies with its own allies. The just rights and liberties of Englishmen were obviously to be extended to the King's 'partakers' and the Army pledged to restore the King's own rights and liberties. Indeed, all of the Army's proposals for recomposition showed far greater leniency to the King's supporters than did those of Parliament. Parliamentary reform was the safest way to ensure that a proper balance was struck between the rights of the monarch and of his people; volatile issues such as control of the militia were moved into neutral ground.

But the experience of the second Civil War, especially the use of the Scottish troops, which the Army regarded as a foreign invasion, embittered the soldiery and led to a reassessment of their commitment to the rights and privileges of Charles I and his successors. Now the issue turned on interest and faction and in the *Remonstrance* of November 1648 the Army came to equate the motives of the King's acts with those they had opposed when they had appeared in Parliament and city: 'Against these matters of public interest, the King has all along his reign opposed and given himself up to uphold and advance the interest of his and his posterity's will and power.' In a public trial the King would have to demonstrate that 'what he has acted thereof has not been for the interest of his will and power, or not against the public interest of the people.' Once the Army came to extend the principles which justified their own actions to the evaluation of those of their enemies the King would have to be treated as ruthlessly as all of the others whom the Army had purged. 'What fruits can be hoped from such a reunion or renewed communion betwixt those contraries God had once so separated, viz. of principles of affections of liberty with principles of tyranny; principles of public interest with principles of prerogative and particular interest' (*Remonstrance* of November 1648).

IV

Many interesting and complex questions touching on the beliefs and actions of Parliament's Army remain to be explored than could have been treated in this brief essay. By grounding our analysis upon the Army's public manifestos and securing as beams those central doctrines which consistently inform the Army's actions, it is hoped that the remainder of the edifice can be more easily constructed. As yet we know little of the architects of this ideology and almost nothing of its numerous suppliers. The sources of the Army's ideas will be the most interesting for students of the history of ideas. What was the stock of theory from which the Army developed its beliefs? Did they antedate the Civil Wars or were they concurrent with them? Were they derived from Parliament's own justifications or those of London radicals? Were they traditional or innovative? Such puzzles remain to be pondered.

Nor will our structure be completed without regard to the other literature generated by the officers and soldiers: the records of their debates where some of the inchoate ideas we have isolated became formulated; the private papers of its leaders which, with the exception of Cromwell's, remain scattered and infrequently consulted; the masses of state documents that reveal the conditions which shaped the perceptions of the soldiers; the conflicting commentaries of observers, a kind of sandpaper often too coarse or too fine-grained to provide a proper finish. Disparate in nature, these sources will put rough edges on the surfaces which here appear smooth, and further honing of the points will be necessary. Both the tools and the materials of the historian are imperfect and it takes the hands of several craftsmen to fashion the work.

Finally a word must be said about religion, an element in the Army's ideology which has been passed over in silence. In the early months of the Army's agitation the officers and soldiers explicitly denied that they had any intention of overthrowing the Presbyterian establishment voted by Parliament. General statements about forbearance toward tender consciences appear in the *Heads of the Proposals* as the thirteenth point and toward the end of the Army *Agreement* in a number of clauses opposing persecution of Protestant Christians. It can be said equally that none of the Army's actions had a precise religious motivation and that all had a general one. Perhaps religion was one of the just rights and liberties that Englishmen held as fundamental; perhaps particular religious sects might be factious and self-interested. Parliament's rights to legislate religious matters was attenuated by the Army *Agreement*, but they were not abolished. Whatever its impact, religion does not appear to have held pride of place with the three fundamental components of the Army's beliefs so well summarised by the most famous passage in the Army's manifestos:

we were not a mere mercenary army hired to serve any arbitrary power of a state, but called forth and conjured by the several declarations of Parliament, to the defence of our own and the peoples' just rights and liberties. And so we took up arms in judgement and conscience to those ends, and have so continued them and are resolved according to your first just desires in your Declarations, and such principles as we have received from your frequent informations and our own common sense concerning those our fundamental rights and liberties, to assert and vindicate the just power and rights of the Kingdom in Parliament, for those common ends pre-mised against all arbitrary power, violence and oppression, and against all particular parties and interests whatsoever. (*Declaration of* 14 June)

# 8. From Cavalier to Roundhead Tyranny, 1642–9

## ROBERT ASHTON

### I

> . . . And assure yourselves, when Laws shall be altered by
> any other Authority than that by which they were made, your
> Foundations are destroyed. And though it seems at first but
> to take away my Power, it will quickly swallow all your
> Interest.[1]

THESE sentiments in an address by Charles I to the inhabitants
of Nottinghamshire at Newark in July 1642, on the eve of the
Civil War, were both to become a recurrent and increasingly
prominent feature of Royalist propaganda over the next few
years and to evoke an increasingly sympathetic response in the
minds of many of those who had sided with the Parliament
against the King in 1642. To his dying day Charles continued to
assert that his royal rights and the liberties of his subjects were
inextricably bound together. The Parliament which had withheld from him his property at Hull assuredly would not hesitate
to commit similar outrages on the property of his subjects. One
of Clarendon's most telling criticisms of the constitutional
usurpations of the King's opponents derived much of its force
from this frank admission of the ways in which the Crown itself
had gone too far during the eleven years of personal government
in the 1630s. What was now happening, he averred, was

> that the same principles . . . should be used to the wresting all
> sovereign power from the Crown, which the Crown had a

little before made use of for the extending its authority and power beyond its bounds, to the prejudice of the just rights of the subject. A supposed necessity was then thought ground enough to create a power, and a bare averment of that necessity to beget a practice, to impose what tax they thought convenient upon the subject by writs of ship-money never before known; and a supposed necessity now, and a bare averment of that necessity, is as confidently and more fatally concluded a good ground to exclude the Crown from the use of any power by an ordinance never before heard of; and the same maxim of *Salus populi suprema lex*, which had been used to the infringing the liberties of the one, made use of for the destroying the rights of the other . . . .[2]

During the controversy over the militia in the early part of 1642 the King, while admitting that he himself had been seriously at fault in attempting to justify his own arbitrary actions during the previous decade by reference to arguments from necessity, warned his opponents that they were in serious danger of 'falling into the same error upon the same suggestions'.[3] But as anyone who has lived through any war knows only too well, and as the parliamentary objections to the royal alterations to the articles for a cessation at the Treaty of Oxford emphasised on 27 March 1643, 'If the nature of War be duly considered, it must needs be acknowledged, That it is incompatible with the ordinary Rules of a peaceable Government.'[4] Thus to expect that men would be imprisoned only by due process was to expect too much, and, as one pamphleteer mockingly puts it, 'that Common Law, called *Salus populi* must be produced as a general warrant for all their undertakings; and that Statute Law . . . called *Lex necessitatis* must be made to justify all manner of severity and violence.'[5] He was not exaggerating. For instance, in his reply to the allegations of the imprisoned Royalist judge David Jenkins against revolutionary illegalities such as arbitrary taxes and imprisonment in 1647 the most distinguished of Parliamentarian political controversialists, Henry Parker, argued that 'tis not upon any particular law, but upon the general law of public safety that these warrants are grounded upon.'[6] Recourse to such arguments from necessity, protested a royal declaration of 8 December 1642, 'proves only

[that] they have undertaken somewhat they ought not to undertake, not that it is lawful for them to do any thing that is convenient for those ends'. The same declaration went on to hoist the Roundheads with one of their own petards by citing to good effect a passage from one of Pym's most celebrated speeches which pointed to the horrors which would follow from the disregarding of the law, as a result of which 'every man will become a Law unto himself. . . . Lust will become a Law, and Envy will become a Law, Covetousness and Ambition will become Laws, and what Dictates, what Decisions such Laws will produce may easily be discerned.'[7]

If the Parliamentarians required proof of this, they had only to look about them. One particularly flagrant example which Clarendon records of Roundhead disregard for the dignity and authority of the law was the celebrated case of Judge Thomas Malet. Malet, who was already in disfavour for encouraging a petition from the Kentish gentry in favour of the Prayer Book and for refusing to read the declaration in favour of the Parliament's Militia Ordinance and against the royal Commissions of Array at Maidstone assizes, was seized by a Parliamentary troop of horse on 4 August 1642, while he was actually presiding at the assizes at Kingston-on-Thames. He was consigned to the Tower, 'where he remained for the space of above two years, without ever being charged with any particular crime'.[8] There was abundant scope for the making of a great deal of Royalist political capital out of the contrast between this outrage and the King's refusal in the following February to comply with Parliament's request that 'in regard of the present distractions' – that is, of the war – 'the assizes and gaol-delivery might not be holden.' Parliament's suspension of the Lent assizes, disregarding the King's objection that this would involve denying justice to his subjects, is described by Clarendon as 'the first avowed . . . suspension of the public justice that happened.' Thereafter, he adds, admittedly with some exaggeration, 'the exercise of the law ceased throughout the kingdom, save only in some few counties, whither the King sent some judges of assize, and into others, his commissions of oyer and terminer.'[9]

Not only, it was complained, did the law sleep. What passed for legislation, in the form of parliamentary ordinances, not only had no constitutional validity, but sometimes added insult to unconstitutional injury by being retroactively applied. For instance, on 8 July 1645, the Committee of Both Kingdoms, sending instructions about the levying of 500 men to the county committee of Suffolk, also informed it that an ordinance had been passed for the execution of all deserters, and that it would be a useful deterrent to others if those deserters already in custody were punished accordingly.[10] Small wonder that one of the most significant requests of the Kentish petition of 11 May 1648, which marks the prelude to Kentish insurgency in the second Civil War, was 'That according to the Fundamental Constitution . . . we may . . . be governed . . . by the known and established Laws of the Kingdom and not otherwise.'[11] Such sentiments would have been echoed all over England in 1648, even if, unlike the Kentish men, not all of those who harboured them were prepared to push them to the point of renewing the war.[12]

II

By fully admitting the constitutional irregularities of royal government during the 1630s, Clarendon and others were both guarding themselves against Roundhead rejoinders about the throwing of stones by Cavaliers living in glass houses and helping to create the image of a reformed constitutional monarchy, of which the royal reply to Parliament's Nineteen Propositions in June 1642 is the most celebrated and impressive expression.[13] What might have been a Royalist weakness was turned by skilful propaganda into a source of Royalist strength via the insistence that it was now Parliament which was behaving arbitrarily, as the Crown had done in the 1630s. The Crown, by contrast, had now learnt its lesson and Charles had become a model constitutional monarch. It was not for nothing that Pym and his colleagues seized gleefully upon current royal actions which were inconsistent with this new moderate image, such as the appointment of the swashbuckling cavalier Lunsford as Lieutenant of the Tower in December 1641 and the attempted arrest of Kimbolton and the five members at the beginning of the following month. Such actions must have driven Hyde and Falkland close to despair, since they lent

themselves only too well to Pym's thesis of royal reversion to
type – to the extremism of the 1630s.

Embarrassing though such incidents might be to the King's
moderate advisers, they stuck to their guns, and the point made
so trenchantly by Clarendon in his *History* was reiterated over
and over again in Royalist tracts and official declarations.[14] Nor
was it confined to such sources. Beginning with the timid
legalistic complaints of Parliamentary peace-groupers such as
Sir Simonds D'Ewes against the attacks on the sanctity of
private property implicit in the Sequestration Ordinance and
against the excise, the weekly assessment and other taxes granted 'by a mere ordinance of both houses', as distinct from a
proper Act of Parliament which would, of course, have required
the royal assent,[15] the volume of complaints on the Parliamentarian side grew until it came, in the later 1640s, to
encompass a wide range of shades of political opinion from
conservative Presbyterians to radical Levellers. Thus the
Leveller John Lilburne in 1647 stressed a similar parallel
between the tyranny of Charles's Personal Government in the
1630s and that of the victorious Parliamentary regime in the
following decade to that voiced by the Royalist Judge Jenkins
and the conservative Parliamentarian Clement Walker, to cite
but three of many examples.[16] For instance, although the practice of prerogative courts such as Star Chamber and High
Commission of making suspects incriminate themselves by the
administration of interrogatories and the *ex officio* oath was
condemned in the Grand Remonstrance and in any number of
other parliamentary statements of the legal rights of the individual, their use was not abandoned by Parliament, quite apart
from its devising of new oaths such as the Negative Oath and
the Vow and Covenant. Complaints against such practices
came from a wide variety of sources. They are to be found, for
instance, in the Leveller remonstrance of many thousand citizens of July 1646 and petition of March 1647;[17] in the accusations both of the victims of the arbitrary actions of John Pyne
and the Somerset county committee[18] and of the House Committee of Examinations, chaired by the formidable radical and
later regicide Miles Corbet. Witness the incredulous outburst
on behalf of the Presbyterian MP, Sir John Maynard, who was
examined by the latter body in 1647.

Was it possible 5 years since . . . that the Parliament would have deviated so far from the rules of law and justice . . . as to examine any man upon interrogatories against himself in a criminal case? would any have believed . . . that this Parliament that hath deemed the Star-Chamber and the Council Tables names worthy to be a curse . . . because of their cruelty in censuring men for refusing to answer interrogatories, that this Parliament should urgently press Sir Jo. Maynard to answer interrogatories against himself . . .?[19]

Similarly, if Charles I had given room for serious doubts about the sincerity of his moderate constitutional intentions by having recourse to extremist action in the attempted arrest of the five members in January 1642, surely, as the royal declaration of 12 August pointed out, Pym and his party had little cause to complain of such breaches of privilege when they themselves made such frequent use of Pennington's and Venn's tumultuous assemblies 'to assault and terrify the Members of both Houses, whose faces or whose opinions they liked not'.[20] In recommending that Parliament should be adjourned to York, Oxford or some other place where its Members would be secure from such intimidation, Hyde was making a shrewd propaganda point.[21]

The summer of 1647 was to produce two further notable and flagrant examples of the violation of parliamentary privilege, the one revolutionary and the other counter-revolutionary. The former was the Army's forced exclusion of the eleven Presbyterian members which invited comparison with Charles I's action against the five members in January 1642;[22] the second was the counter-revolutionary tumults in London in late July which intimidated Parliament and drove away many Independent MPs as well as the Speakers of both Houses, an event which, counter-revolutionary though it was, recalled Pym's use of the London mob in 1641–2. It was in fact in the summer of 1647 that the phenomenon of the counter-revolutionary tumult, the precursor of the Church-and-King mob of the eighteenth century, made its first appearance on the historical scene, though on this occasion its triumph was cut short in a matter of days. But that very Army which put an end to it by occupying London in August had itself already been guilty of both unduly intimidating and flagrantly defying Parliament. In December of the following year it was to perform the ultimate act of violation of parliamentary privilege and freedom, beside which, as its victims, the secluded MPs, argued with force, the army plot of 1641, the attempts on the five members in 1642 and the eleven members in 1647, and the coercion of Parliament by disorderly bands of reformadoes and apprentices in July 1647, paled into insignificance.[23] Writing nearly twelve years after Pride's Purge, one of its more notable victims, William Prynne, puts it into true historical perspective as paving the way for the trial and execution of the King, the establishment of the republic, the dissolution of the resultant Rump by Cromwell in 1653 and again by Lambert in 1659. Here, he argued, was the ultimate violation of privilege, 'the very principal, essential, fundamental Privilege of Parliament', the right to vote according to conscience in the famous motion of 5 December that the King's answers to Parliament's propositions at Newport were fit grounds for prolonging negotiations.[24]

But if the view that the Army was the prime agency of the despotism of a minority of determined revolutionaries made sense in the context of 1649, even though it was a gross over-simplification of a very complex reality, things had looked rather different two years earlier. A pamphlet written in the spring of 1647, in answer to an Essex petition demanding the disbandment of the Army, vigorously repudiated the role of scapegoat for ruinously heavy taxation which a Presbyterian-dominated Parliament tried to fix on the Army. Far from being the root cause of fiscal oppression, it argued, the Army was the only safeguard against it. Not only were the oppressions of the Parliament far worse than anything perpetrated at any time by the King, but in addition it was asserted with some truth – given the Presbyterian plans to raise a counter-revolutionary force out of reformado and similar elements – that 'if this Army were now disbanded, the Parliament would still carry on the military charge, by raising them another in this Armies stead . . . So that the taking away this Army will not take away the military charge from you.'[25] Nor were such arguments confined to the New Model soldiers and their radical Independent allies in Parliament. The Royalist Judge Jenkins described the famous Cornet Joyce *coup* of 4 June 1647 as an honourable release of the

King from irksome Parliamentary captivity at Holdenby, con-
trasting the Army's willingness, with Parliament's refusal, to
allow the King the use of chaplains of his own choice and access
to all persons whom he desired to consult. Far from being the
cause of all the oppressions under which the nation groaned,
urged Jenkins, the Army was now the main ground which it had
for hope of the restoration of legality and constitutional rule.
This may seem an odd assertion in view of the ultimate outcome
of 1648–9, but it is not at all odd in the context of 1647 and the
determined attempts of Cromwell and the army grandees to
reach agreement with the King. Jenkins ended his *tour de force*
with an impassioned appeal to Fairfax to

> Remember what honour and glory the present age and all
> posterity will justly give to the restorer of the King to his
> Throne, of the laws to their strength, and of the afflicted
> people of this land to peace.[26]

How different history might have been if the role which was to
be played by Monck in 1660 had been taken by Fairfax in 1647!

### III

Fiscal oppression of one sort or another was one of the main
areas inviting comparison between the eleven years' tyranny
and the arbitrariness of Parliamentary government. Had the
King been at fault in the 1620s and 1630s in levying Tonnage
and Poundage not voted by Parliament? A royal declaration of
12 August 1642 was quick to point out that the Parliament was
at least equally at fault constitutionally in that its members
'presume to take Tonnage and Poundage by a pretended
Ordinance without Our consent, though they have so often
pressed it against us, that We took it without theirs . . .'.[27] Both
Professor Everitt and Dr Hassell Smith have drawn attention to
the role of the royal extra-parliamentary exactions of the 1630s,
and especially Ship Money, as providing a model for the modes
of rating later employed in the Parliamentarian weekly and
monthly assessments.[28] The arguments of Judge Jenkins, himself one of the foremost denouncers of Parliamentary fiscal
oppression – as of other forms of revolutionary illegality – in

1647–8, carried the more weight on account of the emphasis which he laid on his own earlier opposition to royal Ship Money and monopolies.[29] 'Did', argued what reads like a mock petition of April 1648 from the counties which had made up the Eastern Association, 'enforced Loan [sic], privy seals and monopolies grind the subject, and have not enforced assessments, and free-quarter grated them as small?'[30]

Of the exactions here listed, something has already been said about 'enforced assessments' and the Parliamentary debt to Ship Money and other royal extra-parliamentary levies of the 1630s. As to monopolies, these had, of course, been denounced by the Long Parliament in 1641 as one of the most characteristic evils of the days of royal misrule. But even the Long Parliament had made its exceptions, the most celebrated of which was those London soapboilers who were allowed to retain their exclusive economic privileges. However, it was to more exalted Round-head personalities that a royal declaration of 12 August 1642 drew attention as seekers after such concessions: to 'the connivance now given to Sir John Meldrum for his Lights, since his undertaking their service at Hull', and to the request of the earl of Warwick, who 'thinks fit to require the Letter-office to be confirmed to him for three lives, at the same time that 'tis complained of as a Monopoly'.[31] A complaint from the opposite end of the political spectrum in the later 1640s related to a quite different set of monopolies, the great chartered companies with area privileges in foreign trade, which had escaped from the successive anti-monopoly campaigns in the Parliaments of 1601, 1604, 1624 and 1641. But the rapport which was reached by these bodies with their former parliamentary critics during Charles's first three Parliaments and continued during the Long Parliament[32] did not save them from fierce attacks by the Levellers in the late 1640s. The Leveller petition of March 1647, for instance, was especially severe on the Merchant Adven-turers Company and the hardships wrought by its monopolistic practices on workers in the clothing industry.[33]

Like monopolies, forced loans did not entirely disappear from the scene with the advent of the Long Parliament. In its arrangements for advances totalling £200,000 to be made for the Scots army in 1644, Parliament leant over backwards to avoid the making of comparisons with the royal forced loans which had been condemned by the Petition of Right. Compulsion was to be used only if local authorities failed to raise the sums required of them on a voluntary basis.[34] Needless to say, compulsion proved to be necessary. Writing to the commissioners and committees of Norwich and Norfolk on 10 April 1644, John Ashe, on behalf of the central Committee for the Advance of Money at Haberdashers' Hall, chided them for their slowness in providing the £18,000 rated upon them towards the £200,000. Ashe stressed that

> it was hoped by the parliament that when the first ordinance passed for the free and voluntary loans that there would have been no need of the second to compel men to lend, and indeed in London we have made very little use of the second . . . [which] is only to compel the backward and ill affected, but if your county shall prove so far ill affected as that they must be wholly compelled, you may then expect speedily another ordinance to compel the payment of the residue . . . .

The Haberdashers' Hall committee was no doubt adding insult to injury in taking up the complaints of its clerk, whom it had sent down to Norfolk to expedite the business, that his expenses were not being adequately met locally. It was hoped that 'you will not suffer him to want that is Come so far to do you service'; a service which, since it involved the clear violation of the Petition of Right, the local authorities doubtless felt that they could well have done without.[35]

No less contrary to the Petition of Right was the practice of compulsorily billeting soldiers on householders. Quite early in the day, in his declaration of 12 August 1642, the King was quick to exploit Parliament's recourse to the same practice as had been condemned by its predecessor in 1628. The declaration gleefully recounted the disciplinary action taken by Parliament against the mayor and some of the aldermen of Hull who had cited the Petition of Right in support of their refusal to billet some of Hotham's Roundhead garrison.[36] There were, of course, complaints against both sides in this respect during the first Civil War, but, so far as Parliament was concerned, it was the continuance of the practice after the end of the war, first by the Scots,[37] and, after their departure in February 1647, by

English military establishments, which became a national grievance of first-rate importance. In particular, the free quarter exacted by soldiers who themselves, like the Scots before them, were owed heavy arrears of pay, accounted, more than any other factor, for the alarming growth of anti-army feeling, which the Presbyterian-dominated Parliament attempted to exploit so clumsily in its proposals for disbandment in 1647. It was also a prime cause of the growth of counter-revolutionary sentiments in the shires which was to culminate in the second Civil War in 1648. One complaint in January stated that the soldiers took in 'twice or thrice as much as their whole pay amounts unto, devouring like so many Locusts and Caterpillars, all our grass, hay, corn, bread, beer, fuel and provision of all sorts, without giving us one farthing recompense and leaving us ... to starve and famish ...'. Exactions were made for double and treble the number of troops actually involved, and free quarter taken 'for their wives, trolls, boys and those who were never listed'. As had been complained against the Scots before their departure, the ordinary countryman's fare was not good enough for these cormorants who 'will be contented with none but extraordinary diet, wine, strong beer, above their abilities with whom they quarter, thereby to extort money from them'. How dare the soldiers demand their arrears of pay, the complaint indignantly concludes, when they have already consumed these arrears in free quarter.[38] Another such declaration complains against the breaking into houses to get billets, since 'by the very statute and common law of the land, every man's house is and ought to be his castle.' In such circumstances the offenders were liable to capital punishment for breaking and entering, and the owners fully justified in defending their property by force of arms. The violation of these fundamental rights of Englishmen, it was claimed, 'renders our condition worse than any Turkey-Gally-Slave', a popular analogy, which, along with that of Egyptian bondslaves forced to make bricks without straw, was applied frequently to unfortunate citizens groaning under military tyranny.[39]

The Petition of Right had also condemned commissions for proceeding by martial law. The Civil War provides many examples of objections to the operation of martial law not

simply in the case of soldiers, but also of civilians. An example is
the objections of the corporation of Great Yarmouth to the
powers of proceeding by martial law against anyone refusing to
submit to the assessments raised by Colonel Francis Russell
whom the earl of Manchester had appointed as military governor of the town in December 1643.[40] One product of the rapidly
increasing political consciousness of the Army in 1647–8
was the soldiers' own objections to being subject to martial
law. The celebrated Leveller pamphlet, *England's Freedoms,
Soldiers' Rights*, denounces, *inter alia*, martial law as a means of
disciplining soldiers in peacetime, as contrary to both the Petition of Right and the principles of the Solemn Engagement of
the Army, as a result of which the Army was held together by
the 'mutual consent' of its members and not by the coercive
force of martial law.[41] It was stretching the Petition of Right
very far indeed to construe it as being applicable to such cases.
Much nearer to the original intentions of the petitioners of 1628
was a remonstrance against the quartering of soldiers, which
probably dates from 1648, and which complained that 'the
soldiers do pretend that they are exempt from the authority and
jurisdiction of any civil magistrates according to the course of
the Common Law . . . and are to be tried . . . according to
martial law as is used in armies in the time of war.'[42] Military
law is usually regarded as subjecting the military to additional
constraints and certainly not as exempting them from the
operation of common and statute law. Yet in 1647 as in the early
years of the reign, there was a well-founded fear that the military were becoming a law unto themselves and that the ordinary law of the land did not apply to them. As such the complaints against martial law are akin to those against the
ordinances which conferred indemnity upon soldiers for committing what in fact were civil offences which, as one such
ordinance of 7 June 1647 put it, 'the Exigency of the War hath
necessitated them unto,'[43] and which sometimes via the terms
of surrender granted by victorious Roundhead commanders
were also made to apply to offences committed by Royalist
soldiers against loyal Parliamentarians.[44] As a consequence of
the actions of the Indemnity Committee established in May
1647, Dr Morrill reminds us, 'the rights of both the government
and of the individual to seek redress for personal injuries or

criminal acts at common law were stayed. No King had ever claimed such wide powers to set aside the law.'[45] Nevertheless, as a radical petition to the House of Commons against the Treaty of Newport claimed in September 1648, many people were still in danger of prosecution for acts done in the war, 'the Law of the Land frequently taking Place and Precedency against and before your Authority . . . against which no Law ought to be pleaded'.[46]

Perhaps the most celebrated of all the provisions of the Petition of Right is that relating to arbitrary imprisonment, and Parliament's recourse to the practice which its predecessor had so roundly condemned in 1628 was naturally made much of in royal declarations and by Royalist pamphleteers.[47] But it was not simply from Royalist sources that complaints against arbitrary imprisonment by the Roundheads emanated. In 1647–8 the Presbyterian lawyer and MP, Sir John Maynard, was elo quent in his denunciation of the way in which he had been arbitrarily imprisoned,[48] as was his fellow Presbyterian, lawyer and MP, the indefatigible William Prynne, both in denouncing the arbitrary behaviour of John Pyne and the Somerset county committee, and in his attack on the imprisonment of himself and forty-three other MPs, following Pride's Purge. In a spirited letter of 3 January 1649 Prynne demanded to know of Lord General Fairfax whose prisoner he was that he might know against whom to take legal action for wrongful arrest.[49]

Among Sir John Maynard's fellow-prisoners in the Tower had been two persons whose political viewpoints were as far apart as could be, but who both had in common with Maynard a burning indignation about their arbitrary imprisonment by the Parliament. The first of these was the Royalist judge David Jenkins, who both protested at his imprisonment in defiance of *Magna Carta* and the Petition of Right and contested the authority of the court appointed to try him.[50] The second was nature's martyr, the Leveller John Lilburne, who was no less eloquent and a great deal more vociferous. Lilburne tells how on 1 February 1648 he contested

> For a legal warrant before I would go to Prison; but that mercenary Turkish Janissary Colonel Baxter laid violent hands upon me, telling me expressly he was not either to

reason or dispute the Houses' commands, but to obey them
. . . and in hauling of me away by force and violence he
stabbed *Magna Charta* and the Petition of Right etc. to the
very heart and soul.[51]

Needless to say, Lilburne was not the only Leveller to protest
against imprisonment; as witness Richard Overton's famous
appeal of July 1647[52] and the less well-known letter of protest
from Captain William Bray to Speaker Lenthall on 20 June
1649. Bray, who had been prominent in the Leveller agitation
in the Army in 1647–8, had been imprisoned in Windsor Castle
in March 1649 for an allegedly slanderous attack on Lord
General Fairfax. Significantly the texts which he cited in his
letter of protest were neither legal precedents nor constitutional doctrines, but Old Testament prophets and, above all,
that arbitrary, extra-legal process whereby 'the Lord Jesus, the
precious Son of the Most High and head of saints, was crucified,
butchered and massacred in the liberties, freedom and rights of
his humanity.'[53]

But in general it was the Petition of Right and *Magna Carta*
rather than the Old and New Testaments which made the
running in such arguments, with strong emphasis being laid on
the immemorial rights of Englishmen, confirmed over and over
again, most recently in the Petition of Right and most famously
in *Magna Carta*, but now violated by that very Parliament which
ought to have been their chief conservor. 'They have', urged a
Royalist pamphleteer in 1647, 'ravished *Magna Charta* which
they are sworn to maintain, taken away our birth-right, and
transgressed all the laws of heaven and earth.'[54] Nor were such
criticisms confined to Royalists. Sir John Maynard, as well as
claiming that his imprisonment was contrary to *Magna Carta*,
was also at pains to attack what he described as a widely held
view that 'the Parliament is above laws and statutes, yea *Magna
Charta* itself.' He emphasised that

> this great Charter hath a double consideration either as it is
> in part a Statute Law, and so it is subject to the pleasure of
> the Parliament, to be altered, repealed or confirmed, or as it is
> a Declaration of the Common Law, or common reason and
> equity and thus it is not prostrate at the feet of Parliament's
> will.[55]

IV

The arbitrary taxation and arbitrary imprisonment, against which the Great Charter and the Petition of Right were cited so often in vain, were among the principal complaints raised against the practices of county committees, which, according to one of their most eloquent Parliamentarian critics, 'trample Magna Charta under their feet'.[56] Thanks to the pioneering work of Professor Everitt and other county historians, it is now a commonplace that, among the most powerful of the factors which both contributed to the coming of the Civil War and made for the essentially conservative temper of many of those who sided with the Parliament, was reaction to what was regarded as Royalist centralising innovation. But the county gentlemen who had complained so bitterly about Solomon's whips were soon to be chastised with Rehoboam's scorpions. A great many of the bitterest complaints against the arbitrary practices of Roundhead government were, in fact, directed against its agencies in the localities: excise men, sequestration committees, and, above all, the county committees, or their equivalent lieutenancy commissions in the few counties such as Cheshire where no county committees *eo nomine* existed.[57] The instruments of royal centralisation of the 1620s and 1630s, the administrative patents, and the conciliar directives, the lieutenancy controls and pressures, were to be replaced by Roundhead centralising agencies which were no less contemptuous of the traditional local governors, the commissioners of the peace, than their early Stuart predecessors had been. The arguments of an apologist for innovations in parliamentary government, Edward Bowles, probably carried little conviction when he challenged, in a pamphlet published in 1646, the increasingly widespread view that Englishmen were

in a worse case in respect of Liberty than formerly, by paralleling Committees with the Star-Chamber, and Taxes with Ship-money .... For howsoever Committees may be guilty of partialities and miscarriages, yet their main intent is our preservation not our burthen as the other Courts were.[58]

To an increasing number of people such a distinction must have seemed forced, and there can be no doubt that the unpopularity of the county committees was a major factor in bringing about the localist counter-revolutionary disturbances of the so-called second Civil War in 1648. In June of the previous year the gentlemen of Glamorgan, engaged in one of a number of armed demonstrations which were ultimately to set South Wales on fire in 1648, affected to see the establishment of county committees as the origins of the troubles of which they complained, and urged that they might be 'permitted to re-possess and enjoy their Liberties and estates in such manner as was before the setting up of committees here.'[59] Making specific reference to their complaints as well as to Colonel Edward King's more publicised denunciation of the oppressions of the county committee of Lincolnshire, Clement Walker pointed out how the committee men engrossed the power of traditional local authorities ranging from sheriffs and JPs to churchwardens, and concluded

> If there be any intention to restore our Laws and Liberties and free us from arbitrary Government, it is fit that these Committees . . . be laid down . . . and that the old Form of Government by Sheriffs, Justices of the Peace etc. be re-established, and the Militia in each County settled, as before, in Lieutenants and deputy-Lieutenants or in Commission-ers.[60]

At the Michaelmas sessions in 1645 a Staffordshire grand jury had petitioned against the irregularities of the county com-mittee, and more especially the abuses incident upon a situa-tion in which 'almost all the Committees are Commanders and Captains,' which made them unresponsive to local people's complaints against their soldiers. The grand jury requested 'That the Commission of the peace may be directed to some gentlemen of quality in the County'; in other words, the putting into effect of a reform which Clement Walker was still demand-ing three years later; that local government should be the concern of those who by their birth and standing were the natural governors of the county community.[61]

Of course, the resuscitation and, in some cases, reintro-duction of the commission of the peace was not always attended by the results expected by moderates and conservatives, since, insofar as Royalists and neutralists were disqualified, there were far fewer local notabilities to choose from, and it was inevitable that men from below the level of the county gentry should get on to the commission, as they had on to the county committees. How could anything but arbitrary misrule be expected of such people, argued Clement Walker with his eye still mainly on the county committees, 'not having wit, manners, nor breeding enough, as being chosen for the greatest part, out of the basest of the people, for base ends, to satisfy men with an outside or Complement of justice'? If the complaint was formerly that 'our Princes are become thieves . . . now we must invert it and cry, that our thieves (mean and base people) are become Princes.'[62] Walker was, of course, by no means the first to stress the connection between revolutionary illegality and rule by low-born people. In September 1645 the Clubmen of Sussex had complained of

The insufferable, insolent, arbitrary power that hath been used amongst us, contrary to all our ancient known laws, or ordinances of Parliament . . . by imprisoning our persons, imposing of sums of money, light horses, and dragoons, and exacting of Loans by some particular persons stepped into authority who have delegated their power to men of sordid condition whose wills have been laws and Commands over our persons and estates by which they have overthrown all our English liberties and have endeavoured thereby to make us desperate.[63]

To conservatively minded Parliamentarians after the end of the first Civil War, the Army, deplored both as a status-elevator and – connected with this – a harbour for sectaries, – was yet another agency of social degeneration and revolutionary illegality in the provinces, not least via free quarter and the radical redistribution of wealth which was consequent upon the employment of the proceeds of the sale of Church and Royalist properties to meet alleged arrears of Army pay.[64] But it should not be imagined that the Army and the county committees were necessarily allied agencies in this process of social transformation. For at least as long as Fairfax and his senior commanders managed to retain a somewhat precarious control over the

Army, its declarations of policy were no less critical of the
arbitrary behaviour of county committees and other organs of
local government than they were of the Army's enemies in
Parliament such as Denzil Holles and his Presbyterian associates.[65]

Thus far the county committees have been considered as the
Roundhead equivalents of the royal centralising agencies which
had produced such strong opposition in the provinces to
Charles I's government in the 1620s and 1630s. However,
among the chief complaints against them was that they were
not so much the ruthless executors of the will of the central
government as the brazen defiers of parliamentary ordinances.
Now while it is undeniable that such defiance might betoken a
rugged localist independence of central dictation, this is by no
means incompatible with its being exercised in an arbitrary way
to the detriment of the rights and liberties of individuals.
Clement Walker charges the committees that they 'boldly and
avowedly . . . transgress all Orders and Ordinances of Parliament'.[66] In his justly celebrated charge to the Lincolnshire
grand jury at the Folkingham sessions on 5 October 1646,
Colonel King had been at pains to stress that it was he who was
the supporter of parliamentary authority against the unjust and
illegal proceedings of the county committee. It was, he argued,
unthinkable that Parliament 'should conspire to take away the
Law, by which they enjoy their estates, are protected from acts
of violence and power, and differenced from the meaner sort of
people'. Not so the county committee, plentifully peopled with
such lesser social breeds, whom he urged the grand jury to
present for their offences and their disregard of parliamentary
ordinances in oppressing the people.[67] Similarly, the Kentish
insurgents in the second Civil War in their declaration in May
1648 emphasised that their complaint was directed not against
the Parliament, but against the oppressions of the county committee, and not least its brutality towards those attempting to
draw Parliament's attention to their grievances by petition.[68]

v

But it was these same Kentish insurgents who finally took arms
against the Army of the Parliament with the cry of 'for God,

King Charles and Kent' on their lips. The absence of Parliament from this slogan is notable. Indeed it took an increasingly long stretch of the imagination to see the wartime and post-war Parliament as the same body as had been first called in 1640 and had promulgated the almost universally approved reforms of its first session of 1640–1. By contrast, as one Royalist pamphleteer put it in 1647, this makeshift assembly was 'no more Parliament than a pie-powder Court at Bartholomew Fair, there being all the essential parts of a true Parliament wanting in this, as fairness of elections, freedom of speech, fullness of Members, nor have they any head at all'.[69] By 1648 it was the King and not the Parliament who was becoming, for an increasing number of people, the guardian of English liberties as well as the symbol of the long-desired restoration of constitutional normality.

In his controversy with the Royalist judge David Jenkins in 1647, Henry Parker went to great pains to emphasise that the Parliament whose legality Jenkins was questioning because of both its incompleteness and its ceasing to render obedience to the King was the same body with precisely the same constitutional credentials as that called by Charles in 1640. On the point of its incompleteness, Parker claimed that the desertion of Royalist MPs from Westminster to the King at Oxford made for no more objections

> than might be made against the Husband, when the wife elopes and withdraws from his bed; shall that party which remains constant, and attends duly at the place assigned in the summons . . . suffer for that party's sake which proved inconstant, and neither observed the place nor business of the writ by which it was convened?[70]

The vividness of Parker's metaphor reflects his consciousness of how powerful a weapon the incompleteness of Parliament had been to Royalist controversialists since before the outbreak of the war. Indeed, spurred on by Edward Hyde, Charles I at the end of 1643 had attempted to make spectacular political capital out of this, when he summoned the so-called Oxford Parliament. The aim was not to create an alternative Parliament to that of Westminster, but to emphasise the patently incomplete

204 REACTIONS TO THE ENGLISH CIVIL WAR

and unrepresentative character of the latter by summoning all those who had been disabled from sitting at Westminster on account of their loyalty to the King, as well as any MPs still at Westminster who might change their minds and cross over. The latter objective was, it is true, singularly unsuccessful and, indeed, one of the objections of the MPs at Westminster to the Oxford assembly's appeal in April 1644 for conciliation via the medium of a 'free and full Convention of Parliament' was that by emphasising that such a full Parliament could come about only via an amalgamation of the two parliamentary assemblies, the appeal 'puts them at Oxford into an equal Condition with us'.[71] That indeed was the precise object of the operation, and while, from 1645 on, Parliamentarians might claim that Parliament's incompleteness had been remedied through the medium of recruiter elections, in so doing it laid itself open to the same retort as Jenkins made to Parker; that, insofar as the originally elected MPs were still alive, and the recruiters not elected to fill genuine vacancies but simply seats which had formerly been held by Royalist MPs, it was the latter and none else who were the rightful occupants.[72]

Of course, it was not simply in the enforced absence of many disabled MPs and peers that Parliament was incomplete, for it had no constitutional being at all without the King. But even if the King were restored the need for the royal assent to legislation might not amount to much; especially if, as Charles had complained in his answer to the Nineteen Propositions in 1642, he were to accede to the 'new Doctrine, that We are obliged to pass all Laws that shall be offered to Us by both Houses (howsoever Our own Judgement and Conscience shall be unsatisfied with them).[73] Henry Parker's defence of this doctrine of a toothless royal veto five years later is a characteristic piece of constitutional mysticism.

> The King has a power to assent and dissent: yet, without any impeachment of his liberty, he may, nay he must, assent to such Bills as are for the public good, and . . . dissent from such as are tending to the public detriment; the reason is, because the free choice of the King is to receive its determination from without from the matter of the Bills, not from within or from the propention of his own will: for the will

enjoys a more perfect liberty when it is attracted, and as it were necessitated by that object which is good, than when it is left to its own equilibrious motions, and so wavers indifferently betwixt good and evil . . . in the grand concernments of the Kingdom, wherein the King has not so great a share as the people has, tis more just that the reason of two Estates be satisfied than his . . . If there be any doubt in it, then the King ought not to oppose his single judgement, or rather opinion to the resolution of the Highest Court and Council of the Kingdom.[74]

There is not much scope for the independent exercise of the royal veto here. In his argument in favour of the retention of a similarly attenuated negative voice in the debate in the council of the Army at Putney on 1 November 1647 Henry Ireton was more brutally realistic, arguing not only that 'the King ought not to deny any [laws they offer to him]; it is his oath', but also that Parliament had 'gone thus much farther, that if he did not confirm them they were laws without him. Upon this there hath been a war made.'[75]

VI

'*Quaere*', urged Clement Walker, 'Whether our Laws, Liberties and Properties are not now as liable to an invasion from the Legislative power, as formerly from the Prerogative.' For now Parliament's 'little finger is heavier than the loins of the King'.[76] Committed in April 1647 to the Tower by the House of Commons to stand trial for treason for, as he put it, 'not acknowledging the power of the two Houses by adhering to the King in the War', Judge David Jenkins turned his accuser's arguments inside-out, arguing that if he submitted to examination by the House committee of that name, he would 'confess the supreme power to be in you; and so condemn myself for a Traitor'. But by the law of the land, which he had sworn to obey, Parliament had no power to examine him without royal writ, patent or commission.[77] In a constitutional world turned upside-down Charles had come to represent constitutional certainty, stability and normality. In arguing in 1648 that the restoration of the King to his traditional powers was the necessary condition of stability and that any other form of government was bound to lead to new tyranny Nathaniel Ward was echoing the views of many influential people up and down the land.[78] The view that the restoration of the rights of the individual was intimately bound up with the restoration of the King to his own rights was a central theme of any number of protests in the provinces in 1648: ranging from the January declaration of the inhabitants of Canterbury and the surrounding district against the high-handed action of that municipality in dealing with the demonstration in favour of the celebration of the previous Christmas;[79] through the petitions of Kent, Hampshire, Dorset and Sussex in the summer;[80] to the manifestos of the insurgents in the second Civil War in South Wales and northern England.[81] The King had become the prime symbol of constitutional propriety, of moderation, of a constitution in which the elements were judiciously and appropriately mixed. This idea, which had been so brilliantly exploited in the royal answer to the Nineteen Propositions in the summer of 1642, had never been popular with Royalist extremists. It had gone out of fashion at Royalist Oxford during the first Civil War[82] and probably found no favour with the Royalist extremists who did their best in 1648 to turn peaceful demonstrations such as the presentation of the Surrey petition to Parliament into acts of violence[83] and to ensure that protests against Roundhead illegality were, where possible, pushed to the point of armed insurrection. But, however successful they may have been in this aim, the restoration desired by most of the insurgents in the second Civil War was that of the reformed monarchy of 1641 not that of the personal rule of the 1630s.

At first it appeared as if the defeat of the insurgents might not be the death knell of such constitutional hopes, since, disregarding the protests of radical Independents and the Army, Parliament sought, via renewed negotiations with the King, to bring about that return to constitutional normality which all but Cavalier and radical extremists desired. It is not necessary to stress again that these moves were aborted by those supreme acts of revolutionary illegality beginning with Pride's Purge and ending with the illegal sentence of the illegal court which tried Charles I in defiance of the fundamental judicial axiom that the King can do no wrong.

The King cannot be tried by any superior jurisdiction on earth . . . The King denied the commons of England to be a court of judicature. He held the crown of England by descent for more than 1000 years. He was not accomptable to the people. They contrariwise insisted that he held it by election and had falsified his trust.[84]

While not denying the notion of a royal trust, Charles needless to say interpreted it differently. 'I have a trust committed to me by God, by old and lawful descent; I will not betray it to answer new unlawful authority.'[85]

This paper began with Charles in 1642 identifying his own with his subjects' interests over the Parliamentarian seizure of his magazine at Hull. Later in the same year, in his answer to the Nineteen Propositions, he followed up his statement that he did not wish the laws of England to be changed by the promise that 'We will be as careful of preserving the Laws in what is supposed to concern wholly Our Subjects, as in what most concerns Ourself.'[86] The most vivid and poignant expression of this connection between the legal rights of King and subjects was to come in his final outburst, when refused the right to speak after sentence had been passed upon him: 'I am not suffered for to speak: expect what justice other people will have.'[87]

# List of Abbreviations

| | |
|---|---|
| Add. MSS | Additional Manuscripts |
| BL | British Library |
| BL. E | British Library, Thomason Tracts |
| Bodl. Lib. | Bodleian Library, Oxford |
| BRO | Bristol Record Office |
| Clarendon, *History* | Edward Hyde, earl of Clarendon, *History of the Great Rebellion* (all references are to the edition of W. D. Macray; Oxford, 1888) |
| *CJ* | *Journal of the House of Commons* |
| CRO | Cheshire Record Office |
| *CSPD* | *Calendar of State Papers Domestic* |
| CUL | Cambridge University Library |
| *DNB* | *Dictionary of National Biography* |
| DRO | Dorset Record Office |
| *EcHR* | *Economic Historical Review* |
| *EHR* | *English Historical Review* |
| Gardiner, *History* | S. R. Gardiner, *History of the Great Civil War* (1893) 4 volumes |
| GRO | Gloucestershire Record Office |
| Harl. MSS | Harleian Manuscripts |
| HMC | Historical Manuscripts Commission Reports |
| *LJ* | *Journal of the House of Lords* |
| NRO | Norfolk and Norwich Record Office |
| PRO | Public Record Office |
| *TRHS* | *Transactions of the Royal Historical Society* |
| *VCH* | *Victoria County History* |

# Bibliography

The place of publication is London unless otherwise stated.

## INTRODUCTION

The best introductory surveys are B. Coward, *The Stuart Age* (1980), I. Roots, *The Great Rebellion* (1966) and R. Ashton, *The English Civil War, 1603–1649* (1978). The great classic narrative is S. R. Gardiner, *History of the Great Civil War, 1642–1649* 4 vols (1893), and the best modern narrative to integrate military and political history is C. V. Wedgwood, *The King's War, 1641–7* (1958). R. Ollard, *This War Without An Enemy* (1976), is the best short illustrated history. For developments within Parliament, particularly in the later 1640s (and the interaction of affairs in the provinces and at Westminster), see D. E. Underdown, *Pride's Purge* (Oxford, 1971), the best 'advanced' book on the subject. On religious developments, the standard guide is W. Haller, *Liberty and Reformation in the Puritan Revolution* (1938), but it is probably better to begin with the splendid introductions by D. M. Wolfe and R. Sirluck to volumes 1 and 2 of the Yale edition of the *Prose Works of John Milton* (1953, 1959), plus W. Lamont, *Godly Rule* (1969). Other key works are referred to in the notes to this essay or the bibliographies of other essays. For further reading, turn to *Bibliography of British History: Stuart Period*, ed. G. Davies and M. Keeler (1970), which lists some 8000 books and articles (published before 1962 for books, 1958 for articles); J. S. Morrill, *Critical Bibliographies in Modern History: Seventeenth Century Britain* (1980), which discusses 873 books published up to 1979 and lists 478 articles published since 1958; and G. E. Aylmer and J. S. Morrill, *The Civil Wars and Interregnum: Sources for Local Historians* (1979)

## I.  THE COMING OF WAR

The fullest narrative of this period of the war will be found in Gardiner, *History*. C. V. Wedgwood, *The King's War* (1958) provides a shorter account. Two recent studies which touch on various aspects of the theme of this essay are R. Ashton, *The English Civil War* (1978) and J. S. Morrill, *The Revolt of the Provinces* (1976).

For more detail it is necessary to turn to the numerous studies of the impact of the civil war on individual counties. The following stress the importance of localism: A. Everitt, *The Community of Kent and the Great Rebellion* (Leicester, 1966); A. J. Fletcher, *A County Community in Peace and War: Sussex, 1600–1660* (1975); C. Holmes, *The Eastern Association in the English Civil War* (Cambridge, 1974); C. Holmes, *Seventeenth-Century Lincolnshire* (Lincoln, 1980); R. W. Ketton-Cremer, *Norfolk in the Civil War: A Portrait of a Society in Conflict* (1969); J. S. Morrill, *Cheshire, 1630-1660* (Oxford, 1974).

There are three studies of western counties which provide reliable narratives: E. A. Andriette, *Devon and Exeter in the Civil War* (Newton Abbot, 1971); M. Coate, *Cornwall in the Great Civil War and Interregnum* (Oxford, 1933) and D. E. Underdown, *Somerset in the Civil War and Interregnum* (Newton Abbot, 1973). There are many older accounts of military events in the counties. Two have recently been reissued: E. Broxap, *The Great Civil War in Lancashire* (Manchester, 1973), and A. C. Wood, *Nottinghamshire in the Civil War* (East Ardsley, 1971).

## 2.   THE ROYALIST WAR EFFORT

By far the best existing general account of the machinery and problems of both Royalist and Parliamentarian war efforts is J. S. Morrill, *The Revolt of the Provinces* (1976). Dr Morrill's conclusions are, however, considerably sounder and better-documented for the Parliamentarians than for the Royalists, as his information upon the latter depends heavily upon the research of others, which he has had no opportunity to revise. Many of the recent local studies of the Great Rebellion contain information upon the Royalists, notably Roger Howell, *Newcastle-Upon-Tyne and the Puritan Revolution* (Oxford, 1967); E. A. Andriette, *Devon and Exeter in the Civil War* (Newton Abbott, 1971); D. E. Underdown, *Somerset in the Civil War and Interregnum* (Newton Abbott 1973); J. S. Morrill, *Cheshire, 1630–1660* (Oxford, 1974) and P. Styles, 'The Royalist Government of Worcestershire during the Civil War', *Transactions Of The Worcestershire Archaeological Society*, 3rd series, V (1976), 23–40. Of these, Dr Morrill's study is the most sophisticated. Professor Underdown's now seems the least satisfying, in that he attempts to fit his evidence, which otherwise accords with that of the other studies, into the old framework of the Civil War viewed as a class struggle. For a description of the evolution of the Royalist party as a whole, see Ronald Hutton, 'The Structure of the Royalist Party' forthcoming in the *Historical Journal*. Lastly, to gain a proper perspective upon the war efforts of both parties it is essential to read C. Holmes, *The Eastern Association in the English Civil War* (Cambridge 1974), for a reminder that activists faced considerable problems even in the best-protected and most loyal areas.

## 3.   NEUTRALISM, CONSERVATISM AND POLITICAL ALIGNMENT IN THE ENGLISH REVOLUTION: THE CASE OF THE TOWNS, 1642–9

In contrast to the large number of studies of recent vintage on the county community, writings on specifically urban politics in this period are disappointingly meagre. A useful introduction to the dimensions of the problem is to be found in Peter Clark and Paul Slack, *Crisis and Order in English Towns, 1500–1700* (1972), and Peter Clark and Paul Slack, *English Towns in Transition, 1500–1700* (Oxford, 1976). The first of these volumes contains (pp. 204–36) a suggestive essay on Chester by A. M. Johnson, 'Politics in Chester during the Civil Wars and the Interregnum, 1640–62'. The only two full-length studies are John T. Evans, *Seventeeth-Century Norwich* (Oxford, 1979), and Roger

Howell, *Newcastle-upon-Tyne and the Puritan Revolution* (Oxford, 1967). Some older accounts contain a good deal of relevant information though the sorts of questions asked of the material differ from current concerns. Useful in this regard are Richard W. Cotton, *Barnstaple and the Northern Parts of Devonshire during the Great Civil War, 1642–1646* (Chilworth, 1889), and John Latimer, *The Annals of Bristol in the Seventeenth Century* (Bath, 1970). General histories of towns frequently contain a chapter or two on the period but are often of limited value for the sort of detailed analysis required. J .W. F. Hill, *Tudor and Stuart Lincoln* (Cambridge, 1956) ch. 8, is an example, though Leonard J. Ashford, *The History of the Borough of High Wycombe* (1960) pp. 122–44, contains a useful account of the constitutional struggles there. Rather more useful studies have appeared in essay form: M. Coate, 'Exeter in the Civil War and Interregnum', *Devon and Cornwall Notes and Queries*, XVIII (1935) pt 8, 338–52; Roger Howell, 'The Structure of Urban Politics in the English Civil War', *Albion*, XI, 2 (Summer 1979) 111–127; C. G. Parsloe, 'The Corporation of Bedford, 1647–1664', *TRHS*, 4th ser., XXIX (1947) 151–65; Philip Styles, 'The City of Worcester during the Civil Wars, 1640–60', in his *Studies in Seventeenth-Century West Midlands History* (Kineton, 1978) pp. 213–57; John K. G. Taylor, 'The Civil Government of Gloucester, 1640–6', *Transactions of the Bristol and Gloucestershire Archaeological Society*, LXVII (1946–8) 59–118; and M. Todd, 'The Civic Government of Durham', *Durham University Journal*, XXVII (1930–2) 186–93, 276–80, 341–52, 431–41, and XXVIII (1932–4) 37–51. Many county studies contain useful material on the boroughs as well; in particular might be noted E. A. Andriette, *Devon and Exeter in the Civil War* (Newton Abbot, 1971); M. Coate, *Cornwall in the Great Civil War and Interregnum, 1642–1660* (Truro, reprint edn 1963); William J. Farrow, *The Great Civil War in Shropshire, 1642–49* (Shrewsbury, 1926); A. J. Fletcher, *A County Community in Peace and War: Sussex, 1600–1660* (1975); and J. S. Morrill, *Cheshire, 1630–1660* (Oxford, 1974). A number of general accounts likewise contain extensive material on the towns. Among these should be mentioned Robert Ashton, *The English Civil War, 1603–1649* (1978); Derek Hirst, *The Representative of the People?* (Cambridge, 1975); C. Holmes, *The Eastern Association in the English Civil War* (Cambridge, 1974); Brian Manning, *The English People and the English Revolution* (1976); J. S. Morrill, *The Revolt of the Provinces* (1976); and D. E. Underdown, *Pride's Purge* (Oxford, 1971). Fundamentally, the history of the towns must begin with the town records; a number have been printed and the most useful start into this sort of material is *The Chamber Order Book of Worcester, 1602–1650*, ed. Shelagh Bond (Worcester, 1974) which has a detailed introduction and a bibliographical listing of other such records in print at the time of publication.

## 4. THE CHURCH IN ENGLAND, 1642–9

For a balanced view of the ecclesiastical history of the period, this essay should be read alongside M. C. Cross, 'The Church in England, 1646–1660', in *The Interregnum*, ed. G. E. Aylmer (1975), a companion volume to this collection of essays. The best general introductions to the religious history of the period are

H. G. Alexander, *Religion in England, 1558–1662* (1968); M. C. Cross, *Church and People, 1450–1660* (1976); and F. M. G. Higham, *Catholic and Reformed* (1962). The third is the least well-known and easily the best, particularly on the Laudians and on religious thought generally. Two venerable works still provide the fullest descriptions of religious life in mid-seventeenth-century England and should be studied: J. Stoughton, *A History of Religion in England* (revised ed, 1882) vols I and II; and D. Neal, *History of the Puritans* (1822) vols III and IV. Both are condensed and improved in the admirable G. B. Tatham, *The Puritans in Power* (Cambridge, 1913). The fullest account of the institutional aspirations and reforms of the 1640s is in W. A. Shaw. *A History of English Church during the Civil War and under the Commonwealth* (1900). Volume I offers a cloudy narrative of the parliamentary debates on religion from 1640–3 and an admirable survey of all aspects of the work of the Westminster Assembly, 1643–7; volume II examines the implementation of the Presbyterian system and looks at changes in Church finance and patronage. There are a number of important appendices. The records of five classes survive and have been published (the London Provincial records survive unpublished). For the classes, see 'Register Book of the 4th classis in the province of London', ed. C. E. Surman (Harleian Society, LXXXII–LXXXIII, 1952–3); 'Manchester Classical Minutes', ed. W. A. Shaw (Chetham Society, XX, XXII, XXIV, 1888–91); 'Bury Classical Minutes', ed. W. A. Shaw (Chetham Society XXXVII, XLI, 1896, 1898), which also contains the records of the Nottingham Classis, 1656–60; 'Minutes of the Wirksworth Classis', ed. J. C. Cox, *Journal of the Derbyshire Archaeological Society*, II (1879).

The best introduction to the problem of the sequestered clergy is I. Green, 'The Persecution of "Scandalous" and "Malignant" clergy during the English Civil War', *EHR*, XCIV (1979), but the essential work is *Walker Revised*, ed. A. G. Matthews (Oxford, 1948). Walker was an early-eighteenth-century Tory cleric who gathered information from every parish about the nature and extent of clerical sufferings in the period 1642–60. Matthews expanded Walker's account from all the sources available to modern historians, and produced a *Who's Who* of the sufferers, arranged county by county. Anglican reactions to religious persecution are an important aspect of P. Hardacre, *The Royalists in the Puritan Revolution* (The Hague, 1955). Theological developments are well discussed in J. W. Packer, *The Transformation of Anglicanism* (1969), principally an intellectual biography of Henry Hammond. There are no biographies of leading Anglican clergy, but F. M. G. Higham, *John Evelyn* (1936), is a lovely work. Puritans have done better with several excellent and contrasted biographies of Richard Baxter leading the way (e.g. G. Nuttall, *Richard Baxter* [1966]; or W. Lamont, *Richard Baxter and the Millenium* [1979]).

Those who wish to round out their knowledge of the Puritan dimension of the Puritan revolution will have a vast literature to explore: the following are amongst the ones no-one can afford to miss: W. Lamont, *Godly Rule* (1969); G. Nuttall, *Visible Saints* (1957); C. Hill, *The World Turned Upside Down* (1972). Finally, those who want to encounter the period through accessible primary sources should start with *The Autobiography of Richard Baxter* (although all modern versions are seriously bowdlerised). The most accessible is in the Everyman edition (1975), edited by N. Keeble. *The Diary of Ralph Josselin*, ed.

A. Macfarlane (1976), is less easy to read but is engrossing. In the absence of any convenient matching Anglican clerical diary (the best – by Richard Drake of Radwinter, Essex – is in Latin and in manuscript in the Bodleian), the best introduction to Anglican sensibility is through any edition of *The Diary of John Evelyn* (less compulsive than Pepys but better reading than the memoirs of any modern Cabinet minister).

## 5. THE WAR AND THE PEOPLE

Two articles that cover similar ground to this, with many additional points and sources, are C. V. Wedgwood, *The Common Man in the Great Civil War* (Leicester, 1957), and Ian Roy 'The English Civil War and English Society', in *War and Society* ed. B. Bond and I. Roy (1977) vol. 1, pp. 24–43.

The most useful secondary work is to be found in county, town and parish histories. The *Victoria County Histories*, especially but not exclusively the more recent volumes, contain many fragments of information, though they still tend to treat the Civil War as a regrettable episode not deserving much space. Some of the old-style county histories have surprisingly detailed material on the war: George Lipscombe, *The History and Antiquities of the County of Buckingham* (1847) vol. 1, pp. 76–96, for instance, gives a fully documented account of the siege of Boarstall House. For many counties there is a study devoted to the war, or the war and the Interregnum. The older ones, such as J. Webb (ed. T. W. Webb) *Memorials of the Great Civil War as it affected Herefordshire and the adjoining Counties*, 2 vols (1879), are mainly concerned with the fighting, often with abundant references to the conduct and supply of the armies. The more modern approach still deals with gentry and government rather than the 'meaner sort'; but at its best relates the war to the whole community. A precursor was M. Coate, *Cornwall in the Great Civil War and Interregnum, 1642–1660* (Oxford, 1933). Outstanding recent examples are A. M. Everitt, *The Community of Kent and the Great Rebellion, 1640–1660* (Leicester, 1966), and J. S. Morrill *Cheshire, 1630–1660* (Oxford, 1974). D. E. Underdown, *Somerset in the Civil War and Interregnum* (Newton Abbot, 1973), describes the war with a constant awareness of its effects. C. Holmes, *The Eastern Association in the English Civil War* (Cambridge, 1974), includes a full account of taxation and supply. Histories of towns are still not as abundant as those of counties. Roger Howell, *Newcastle-upon-Tyne and the Puritan Revolution* (Oxford, 1967), and Philip Styles, 'The City of Worcester during the Civil Wars', in his *Studies in Seventeenth-Century West Midlands History* (Kineton, 1978) pp. 213–57, look at social as well as political questions.

Much of the work on the people has naturally been interested more in their active than in their passive roles. Brian Manning, *The English People and the English Revolution* (1976), is a persuasive demonstration of the influence of popular pressure. Two essays by J. S. Morrill, 'Mutiny and Discontent in English Provincial Armies', in *Past and Present*, no. 56 (1972) 48–74, and *The Revolt of the Provinces* (1976) ch. 3, show different aspects of the response to wartime deprivations. On the organisation of the armies and their supplies, C. H. Firth, *Cromwell's Army* (1902), remains a most valuable authority.

The amount of primary material available is immense, and a great deal is printed in one form or another. Letters and diaries of course come mainly from the propertied strata of civilian society and in the armies from officers. Examples of the various ways in which they have been published include F. P. and M. M. Verney, *Memoirs of the Verney Family during the Civil War*, 4 vols (1892–9), Eliot Warburton, *Memoirs of Prince Rupert and the Cavaliers*, 3 vols (1849), the letters of Lady Brilliana Harley in HMC, *Marquis of Bath MSS*, the *Diary of the Marches of the Royal Army . . . kept by Richard Symonds*, ed. C. E. Long (Camden Society, 1859), *The Letter Books 1644–45 of Sir Samuel Luke* (*HMC* JP4: 1963).

The vast number of pamphlets and propagandist newspapers raises the familiar difficulty of extracting reliable information from unreliable evidence. The lurid and entertaining stories from such publications as *Mercurius Aulicus* and *Mercurius Rusticus* have not been cited much here; but at the very least they are evidence for the kind of allegations that could plausibly be circulated. Much more revealing is the unprecedented quantity and range of the debris of government. Since the smallest as well as the greatest problems of the war could find their way to Parliament, the *Lords Journals* and the *Commons Journals* are important sources. The mass of business dealt with by the Council and later the Committee of Both Kingdoms is calendared abundantly in the *Calendars of State Papers Domestic*, 1641–43, 1644, 1644–5, and 1645–7. The legislative documents are collected in *Acts and Ordinances of the Interregnum* ed C. H. Firth and R. S. Rait, 3 vols (1911). But much of the best printed material is to be found in the publications of local record societies. In G. E. Aylmer and J. S. Morrill, *The Civil War and Interregnum: Sources for Local Historians* (1979), there are lists of assize, quarter sessions and other county records (in Appendix 3), city and borough records (in Appendix 4) and county and committee papers (in Appendix 5.) The Oxfordshire Record Society published *The Papers of Captain Henry Stevens, Waggon-Master-General to King Charles I*, ed. M. Toynbee (XLII, 1962) and the *Royalist Ordinance Papers 1642–1643*, ed. Ian Roy (XLIII, 1963–4); and the Worcestershire Historical Society *The Diary of Henry Townshend*, ed. J. W. Willis-Bund, 2 vols (1915–20.)

No-one has yet fully exploited the immense amount of manuscript material derived from the administrative activities of the armies and of local administrative institutions that were called on to provide money and supplies. One category alone, the Commonwealth Exchequer Papers in the Public Record Office (SP28) can provide details of the payments and losses of parishes and even of individual households as well as of money and goods received by troops, companies, garrisons and national treasuries. Royalist material is naturally less abundant and more scattered. Almost every local record office has its own sources, not always easily recognised, for so inexhaustible a topic.

## 6.   'THE ANCIENT LAW OF FREEDOM':
## JOHN SELDEN AND THE CIVIL WAR

There is very little modern work on Selden, largely no doubt because two-thirds of his writings were in Latin, and because in both his English and Latin works he used a notoriously difficult prose style. The basic edition is still that by the Whig clergyman David Wilkins (John Selden, *Opera Omnia*, 1726),

though there have been modern editions of his *Table Talk* (notably by Sir
Frederick Pollock for the Selden Society in 1927). The life by Sir Edward Fry
in the *DNB* is still the best account, though it has a number of relatively minor
inaccuracies. I have surveyed Selden's political thought in general and put it
into context in *Natural Rights Theories* (Cambridge, 1979).

On debates about the legality of Parliament's actions in the Civil War, the
best guide is Ernest Sirluck in his introduction to Milton's *Complete Prose Works*
(New Haven, 1959) vol II. There is also a cetain amount in W. M. Lamont,
*Marginal Prynne* (1963), in J.G.A. Pocock's famous *The Ancient Constitution and
the Feudal Law* (Cambridge, 1957), and in C. C. Weston and J. Greenberg,
*Subjects and Sovereigns* (Cambridge, 1981). Clarendonian 'constitutional
Royalism' is best depicted (but with an often misleading reliance on
Clarendon's own testimony) by B. H. G. Wormald in his *Clarendon* (2nd
edn, Chicago, 1976), but the ideas of what might be called 'constitutional
Parliamentarians' have not received the same sensitive treatment. Their
political activities on the other hand have been well covered: see J. H. Hexter,
*The Reign of King Pym* (Cambridge, Mass., 1941), D. E. Underdown, *Pride's
Purge* (Oxford, 1971), and V. Pearl, 'The "Royal Independents" in the
English Civil War', *TRHS*, 5th Ser., XVIII (1968) 69–96

## 7.   IDEOLOGY AND POLITICS IN THE PARLIAMENTARY
ARMIES, 1645–9

Standard accounts of the Civil War and of the Army's role in it include
Gardiner, *History*; C. H. Firth, *Oliver Cromwell and the Rule of the Puritans in
England* (1900), and *Cromwell's Army* (1902); R. Ashton, *The English Civil War,
1603–1649* (1978); J. S. Morrill, *The Revolt of the Provinces* (1976). For more
detailed aspects of events covered in this essay see D. E. Underdown, *Pride's
Purge* (Oxford, 1971); M. A. Kishlansky *The Rise of the New Model Army*
(Cambridge, 1979); and 'The Army and the Levellers: The Roads to Putney',
*Historical Journal*, XXII (1979); V. Pearl, 'London's Counter-Revolution', in *The
Interregnum*, ed. G. E. Aylmer (1972); J. S. Morrill, 'The Army Revolt of 1647',
in *Britain and the Netherlands*, ed. C. A. Tamse and A. C. Duke (1977); I.
Gentles, 'Arrears of Pay and Ideology in The Army Revolt of 1647', in *War and
Society* ed. B. Bond and I. Roy (1975) vol. I.

## 8.   FROM CAVALIER TO ROUNDHEAD TYRANNY

The most recent general history of the Civil War which touches on all the
problems raised here is R. Ashton, *The English Civil War, 1603–1649* (1978). So
does the best account of the politics of the 1640s, D. E. Underdown, *Pride's
Purge* (Oxford, 1971). On royal constitutionalism, see B. H. G. Wormald,
*Clarendon* (Cambridge, 1951); C. C. Weston, 'The Theory of Mixed
Monarchy under Charles I and After', *EHR* LXXV (1960) 426–43. On
Parliamentary conservatism, see especially J. G. A. Pocock, *The Ancient
Constitution and the Feudal Law* (Cambridge, 1957). For centralist pressures
before 1640, see L. Boynton, *The Elizabethan Militia, 1558–1638* (1967), and

'Billeting: the Example of the Isle of Wight', *EHR* LXXIV (1959) 23–40; S. J. Sears, 'Conscription and English Society in the 1620s', *Journal of British Studies*, XI (1972) 1–23; R. R. Reid, *The King's Council in the North* (1921); F. W. Brooks, *The Council of the North* (Historical Association pamphlet, 1953); P. Williams, 'The Attack on the Council in the Marches, 1603–1642', *Trans. Hon. Soc. Cymmrodorion* (1966) pp. 1–22; M. D. Gordon, 'The Collection of Ship Money in the Reign of Charles I', *TRHS* 3rd ser., IV (1910) 141–62. For centralising pressures and local communities before 1640, A. M. Everitt, *The Local Community and the Great Rebellion* (Historical Assocation pamphlet G70, 1969); W. B. Willcox, *Gloucestershire: a Study in Local Government, 1590–1640* (New Haven, 1940); T. G. Barnes, *Somerset, 1625–1640* (Oxford, 1961); A. J. Fletcher, *A County Community in Peace and War: Sussex 1600–1660* (1975). On Parliamentarian centralist exactions, see L. Glow, 'The Committee of Safety', *EHR*, LXXX (1965) 289–313; D. H. Pennington, 'The Cost of the English Civil War', *History Today* (Feb. 1978) 126–33, and 'The Accounts of the Kingdom, 1642–1649', in *Essays in the Social and Economic History of Tudor and Stuart England*, ed. F. J. Fisher (Cambridge, 1961) pp. 182–203. On the army and the militia after 1642, L. G. Schwoerer, '*No Standing Armies!' The Anti-army Ideology in Seventeenth Century England* (1974), and 'The Fittest Subject for a King's Quarrel', *Journal of British Studies*, XI (1971) 45–76; M. Kishlansky, *The Rise of the New Model Army* (Cambridge, 1979); J. S. Morrill, 'Mutiny and Discontent in English Provincial Armies, 1645–1647', *Past and Present*, no. 56 (1972) 49–74. On local communities and centralist pressures after 1642, A. M. Everitt, *The Community of Kent and the Great Rebellion* (Leicester, 1966), and *Suffolk and the Great Rebellion, 1640–1660* (Suffolk Record Society III, 1961); J. S. Morrill, *Cheshire, 1630–1660* (Oxford, 1974), and *The Revolt of the Provinces* (1976); A. C. Wood, *Nottinghamshire in the Civil War* (Oxford, 1937); M. Coate, *Cornwall in the Great Civil War and Interregnum* (Truro, 1963); D. E. Underdown, *Somerset in the Civil War and Interregnum* (Newton Abbot, 1973); G. C. F. Forster, 'County Government in Yorkshire during the Interregnum', *Northern History* XII (1976) 84–104; A. H. Dodd, *Studies in Stuart Wales* (Cardiff, 1971) pp. 110–76; *The County Committee at Stafford, 1643–1645*, ed. D. H. Pennington and I. Roots (Manchester, 1957); C. Holmes, *The Eastern Association in the English Civil War* (Cambridge, 1974) and 'Colonel King and Lincolnshire Politics', *HJ* XVI (1973) 451–84; R. Howell, *Newcastle-upon-Tyne and the Puritan Revolution* (Oxford, 1967). On political thought, J. W. Allen, *English Political Theory, 1603–1660*, vol. I: *1603–1644* (1938); M. A. Judson, 'Henry Parker and the Theory of Parliamentary Sovreignty', *Essays in History and Political Theory in Honour of Charles Howard McIlwain* (New York, 1967 edn).

# Notes and References

INTRODUCTION    *John Morrill*

1. *The Origins of the English Civil War*, ed. C. Russell (1973).
2. E.g. R. Ashton, *The English Civil War, 1603–1649* (1978); K. M. Sharpe, *Sir Robert Cotton, 1586–1631* (Oxford, 1979); *Faction and Parliament*, ed. K. M. Sharpe (Oxford, 1978); C. S. R. Russell, *Parliaments and English Politics, 1621–1629* (Oxford, 1979); J. S. Morrill, *The Revolt of the Provinces* (1976). For signs of a reaction against this so-called 'revisionist' approach, see D. Hirst, 'Unanimity in the Commons, Aristocratic Intrigue, and the Origins of the English Civil War', *Journal of Modern History*, L (1978); J. H. Hexter, 'Power Struggle, Parliament and Liberty in early Stuart England', *Journal of Modern History*, L (1978); C. Holmes, 'The County Community in Recent Stuart Historiography', *Journal of British Studies*, XX (1980).
3. But see another book in this series: *The Interregnum*, ed. G. E. Aylmer (1972). That volume contains two essays (by Valerie Pearl on London and the counter-revolution of 1647, and by Keith Thomas on the Levellers and the franchise) relevant to the themes of this volume. It is because of those articles that London and the Levellers get short measure here.
4. See, for example, the denial of the existence of any self-conscious revolutionaries in 1642 by C. Hill, 'A Bourgeois Revolution?' in *Three British Revolutions: 1641, 1688, 1776*, ed. J. G. A. Pocock (1980) pp. 110–11,134.
5. For a splendidly balanced review of the strengths and weaknesses, see P. Williams, *The Tudor Régime* (Oxford, 1979) esp. pp. 457–67.
6. See L. Schwoerer, 'The Fittest Subject for a King's Quarrel', *Journal of British Studies*, XI (1971).
7. I owe this point to Conrad Russell.
8. Most conveniently to be found in *The Tudor Constitution*, ed. G. R. Elton (Cambridge, 1960) pp. 15–16.
9. M. Judson, *The Crisis of the Constitution, 1603–1645* (New Brunswick, 1949); M. Mendle, 'Politics and Political Thought', in Russell, *Origins*, pp. 219–45; W. Lamont, *Richard Baxter and the Millenium* (1979) ch. 2. The greatest need is for a new and thorough study of the thought of Henry Parker: meanwhile see W. K. Jordan, *Men of Substance* (1942).
10. I owe this point to Conrad Russell.
11. B. H. G. Wormald, *Clarendon* (Cambridge, 1951).
12. For Pym, see J. H. Hexter, *The Reign of King Pym* (1941); for constitutional Royalism, see C. C. Weston, 'The Theory of Mixed Monarchy under Charles I and After', *EHR* LXXV (1960), and (with J. R. Greenberg) *Subjects and Sovereigns* (Cambridge, 1981).

13. What follows is drawn from two review articles: J. S. Morrill, 'Country Squires and Middling Sorts in the Great Rebellion', *HJ*, xx (1977) 229–36, and 'The Northern Gentry and the Great Rebellion', *Northern History*, xv (1979) 66–85. The first is principally concerned with B. S. Manning, *The English People and the English Revolution* (1976) and the second with B. G. Blackwood, *The Lancashire Gentry and the Great Rebellion* (Manchester, 1978).

14. See particularly D. Underdown, *Somerset in the Civil Wars and Interregnum* (Newton Abbot, 1972), and 'Community and Class: Theories of Local Politics in the English Revolution', in *After the Reformation*, ed. B. Malament (Manchester, 1980) pp. 147–66.

15. C. Holmes, *The Eastern Association in the English Civil War* (Cambridge, 1975).

16. D. Underdown, '"Honest" Radicals in the Counties', in *Puritans and Revolutionaries*, ed. D. H. Pennington and K. V. Thomas (1978) pp. 186–205.

17. K. Wrightson and D. Levine, *Poverty and Piety in An English Village: Terling, 1525–1700* (1979); K. Wrightson, 'Aspects of Social Differentiation in Rural England, c.1580–1660', *Journal of Peasant Studies*, v (1977); D. Hirst, *The Representative of the People?* (Cambridge, 1975).

18. Manning, *English People*; also 'The Godly People', in *Politics, Religion and the English Civil War*, ed. B. S. Manning (1973); J. Malcolm, 'A King in Search of Soldiers: Charles I in 1642', *HJ*, xxi (1978) – but see the reply by M. Wanklyn and P. Young in ibid., xxiv (1981); J. Malcolm, *Caesar's Due* (forthcoming).

19. Morrill, *HJ*, xx (1977).

20. Cf. Morrill, *Revolt*, ch. 3 , with D. Underdown, 'The Chalk and the Cheese: Contrasts Amongst the English Clubmen,' *Past and Present*, no. 85 (1979).

21. Blackwood, *Lancashire Gentry*, pp. 87–8, 165–6; P. R. Newman, 'Royalist Armies North of Trent' (unpublished D.Phil. thesis, York, 1978).

22. G. E. Aylmer, 'Crisis and Regrouping in the Political Elites: England from the 1630s to the 1660s', in Pocock, *Three Revolutions*, pp. 140–64.

23. E.g. C. Hill, *Century of Revolution* (1961; paperback edition, 1974) pp. 111–3.

24. A. M. Everitt, *The Community of Kent and the Great Rebellion* (Leicester, 1966), pp. 84–125; T. Woods, *Prelude to Civil War: Mr Justice Malet and the Kentish Petitions* (1980) *passim*.

25. At a day conference on the Civil War at the Tower of London in November 1979.

26. B. Sharp, *In Contempt of all Authority* (Berkeley, 1980) pp. 247, 264n.

27. D. Underdown, 'The Problem of Popular Allegiance in the English Civil War', *TRHS*, 5th series, vol. 31 (1981) pp. 69–94.

28. There were seventy such towns. For a full analysis, see J. S. Morrill, *England's Wars of Religion, 1637–1662* (provisional title; forthcoming).

29. K. J. Lindley, 'The Part Played by Catholics', in Manning, *Politics*, pp. 127–78.

30. P. R. Newman, 'Catholic Royalist Activists in the North, 1642–6', *Recusant History*, xiv (1977) 26–38, and 'Catholic Royalists in Northern England', *Northern History*, xv (1979) 86–92.

31. A. Fletcher, *The Outbreak of the English Civil War* (1981) ch. 9, and J. D. Maltby, in a Cambridge Ph.D. thesis nearing completion.

32. See below, p.89; also W. Abbott, 'The Issue of Episcopacy and the Long Parliament' (unpublished D.Phil. thesis, Oxford, 1981).

33. R. Clifton, 'Fear of Popery' in Russell, *Origins*, pp. 144–67; R. Clifton, 'The Fear of Catholicism during the English Civil War', *Past and Present*, no. 52 (1971); C. Z. Wiener, 'The Beleaguered Isle', *Past and Present*, no. 51 (1971); C. Hill, *Antichrist in the Seventeenth Century* (1971); and, most importantly, C. Hibbard, *Charles I and the Popish Plot* (forthcoming). Lamont, *Baxter*, ch. 2, is an important contribution to the anti-Catholic background to resistance theories in 1642.

34. W. Lamont, *Godly Rule* (1969) chs 4–6; Lamont, *Baxter*, ch. 3.

35. Manning, 'Godly People', in Manning, *Politics*; Underdown, '"Honest" Radicals', in Pennington and Thomas, *Puritans*.

36. M. Gibb, *John Lilburne the Leveller* (1946); J. Frank, *The Levellers* (1944); C. Hill, *Milton and the English Revolution* (1977) pt v.

37. C. Webster, *The Great Instauration* (1975).

38. These figures are based on a count of the numbers in the marching armies, Association armies and major garrisons set against figures for the number of males aged 16–60 provided by Roger Schofield of the Cambridge Group for the History of Population and Social Structure. A full justification will be given in Morrill, *England's Wars of Religion* (forthcoming).

39. Malcolm, *Caesar's Due* (forthcoming).

40. Morrill, *Revolt*, p. 87; information in lecture by Peter Young, above, note 25.

41. M. Kishlansky, *The Rise of the New Model Army* (Cambridge, 1979).

42. D. Stevenson, *Revolution and Counter-Revolution in Scotland, 1644–1651* (1977); J. R. Powell, *The Navy in the English Civil War* (1962).

43. V. Pearl, *London and the Outbreak of the Puritan Revolution* (Oxford, 1962); R. Ashton, *The City and the Court* (Cambridge, 1979); W. Harper, 'English Public Borrowing, 1640–1660' (unpublished M.Sc. thesis, London, 1929); D. H. Pennington, 'The Cost of the English Civil War', *History Today*, 18 (1958); Gardiner, *History, passim*.

44. The outstanding account and analysis of what follows is D. Underdown, *Pride's Purge* (1971).

45. For these separate sets of terms, see S. R. Gardiner, *Constitutional Documents of the Puritan Revolution* (3rd edn, Oxford, 1906) pp. 249–54, 290–305 (and cf. pp. 262–7, 275–86, 306–9, 311–16).

46. Morrill, *Revolt*, pp. 98–111.

47. Ibid., pp. 122–7; Underdown, *Pride's Purge*, pp. 79–83, 90–1.

48. The best introductions to Leveller thought are G. E. Aylmer, *The Levellers in the English Revolution* (1975); J. Frank, *The Levellers* (1944); Manning, *English People*, chs 9 and 10; C. Davis, 'The Levellers and Christianity', in Manning, *Politics*.

49. M. Kishlansky, 'The Road to Putney', *HJ*, XXII (1979); J. S. Morrill, 'The Army Revolt of 1647', in *Britain and the Netherlands*, ed. C. A. Tamse and A. Duke, vol. VII (1977); I. Gentles, 'Arrears of Pay and Ideology in the Army Revolt of 1647', in *War and Society*, ed. B. Bond and I. Roy, vol. I (1977); M.

Kishlansky, 'What Happened at Ware?' *HJ* (forthcoming).

50. It was originally planned that there would be a chapter in this volume on factionalism within the Houses in the later 1640s. Both this and a chapter on the second Civil War had to be substituted at a later stage. The groupings within Parliament have been subjected to innumerable different interpretations, mostly over-schematic. The safest method of proceeding is to rely on Underdown, *Pride's Purge* (with special attention to ch. 3), A. B. Worden, *The Rump Parliament* (Cambridge, 1974) pp. 1–19, and the articles of Valerie Pearl, notably 'Oliver St John and the "middle group" in the Long Parliament', *EHR*, LXXXI (1966), and ' "Royal Independents" and the English Civil War', *TRHS*, XVIII (1968). Ashton, *English Civil War*, chs 9 and 11, offers an excellent narrative. For points in this paragraph, see also P. Crawford, *Denzil Holles, 1598–1680* (1980) pp. 138–63.

51. For what follows, see the works cited above, notes 49 and 50. Also Pearl, 'London's Counter-Revolution', in Aylmer, *Interregnum*.

52. Morrill, *Revolt*, pp. 128–31; Ashton, *English Civil War*, pp. 318–31; Everitt, *Community of Kent*, pp. 231–70; A. Kingston, *East Anglia and the Civil War* (1910) pp. 252–71; R. Ketton-Cremer, *Norfolk in the Civil War* (1970) pp. 231–53; A. L. Leach, *The Civil War in Pembrokeshire and on its Borders* (1937).

53. Lamont, *Baxter*, pp. 100–3.

54. Crawford, ' "Charles Stuart, That Man of Blood" ', *Journal of British Studies*, XVI (1977) 58.

## I. THE COMING OF WAR    *Anthony Fletcher*

1. Gardiner, vol. I, pp. 23–88.

2. These two paragraphs are based on chapter 11 of A. Fletcher, *The Outbreak of the English Civil War* (1981).

3. HMC, *Portland MSS*, vol. I, 92–3, 96. R. Hutton, *The Royalist War Effort* (1981) pp. 33–40.

4. *The Herbert Correspondence*, ed. W. J. Smith (1963) p. 114; *Letters of Lady Brilliana Harley*, ed. T. T. Lewis (Camden Society, LVIII, 1853) p. 187.

5. *The Ottley Papers*, ed. W. Phillips (Shropshire Archaeological and Natural History Society, VII, 1895) p. 279.

6. *The Diary of Henry Townshend*, ed. J. W. Willis-Bund (Worcestershire Historical Society, 1915) vol. II, pp. 90–120; R. H. Silcock, 'County Government in Worcestershire, 1603–1660', unpublished Ph.D. thesis, London (1974) pp. 238–52.

7. C. Holmes, *The Eastern Association in the English Civil War* (Cambridge, 1974) pp. 53–4; H. G. Tibbutt, *Bedfordshire in the First Civil War* (Elstow Moot Hall leaflets, 3) pp. 4–5; HMC, *3rd Report*, p. 275.

8. 'The Journal of Prince Rupert's Marches', ed. C. H. Firth, *EHR*, XIII (1898) 731–2.

9. HMC, *Hastings MSS*, vol. II, p. 94; BL E85(9): *Special Passages*, 10–17 Jan. 1643; Clarendon, *History*, vol. II, pp. 472–3.

10. BL E84(29): *Kingdom's Weekly Intelligencer*, 3–10 Jan. 1643; A. Carter

and J. Stevenson, *The Oxfordshire Area in the Civil War* (BBC Radio Oxford, 1976); C. H. Firth, 'The Civil War in Oxfordshire, Buckinghamshire and Berkshire', *Proceedings of the Oxfordshire Architectural and Historical Society*, v (1980) 281–3.

11. HMC, *5th Report*, p. 68.

12. *Somers Tracts*, vol. v, pp. 305–11; R. E. Sherwood, *Civil Strife in the Midlands* (1974) pp. 46–7, 56; HMC, *Portland MSS*, vol. i, pp. 67, 71.

13. BL E83(11): *Truth in two letters*; E85(9): *Special Passages*, 10–17 Jan. 1643; E85 (37): *A letter from Sir Edward Baynton to the Earl of Pembroke*; G. A. Harrison, 'Royalist Organisation in Wiltshire, 1642–1646,' unpublished Ph.D. thesis, London (1963) pp. 104–72; J. S. Morrill, *The Revolt of the Provinces* (1976) pp. 61–2.

14. Holmes, *East Anglia*, pp. 33–68; R. W. Ketton-Cremer, *Norfolk in the Civil War* (1969) pp. 149–86.

15. East Suffolk RO, HD 224/1, fol. 8r.

16. D. E. Underdown, *Somerset in the Civil War and Interregnum* (Newton Abbot 1973) pp. 43–8, 121–6.

17. G. N. Godwin, *The Civil War in Hampshire* (1904) pp. 39–61; A. J. Fletcher, *A County Community in Peace and War* (1975) pp. 259–63, 325–39; A. Everitt, *The Community of Kent and the Great Rebellion* (Leicester, 1966) pp. 126–88; H. E. Malden, 'The Civil War in Surrey 1642', *Surrey Archaeological Collections*, XXII (1907) 105–14; D. and A. Hall, *Farnham and the Civil War* (Farnham Museum Society, 1973) pp. 7–15.

18. HMC, *Portland MSS*, vol. I, p. 89; A. Everitt, *The Local Community and the Great Rebellion* (Historical Association, general ser. 70, 1969) pp. 17–18.

19. BL E86(3): *Special Passages*, 17–24 Jan. 1643.

20. HMC, *Portland MSS*, vol. I, pp. 82, 94, 99; HMC, *5th Report*, pp. 76, 79.

21. A. Hughes, 'Politics, Society and Civil War in Warwickshire, 1620–1650', unpublished Ph.D. thesis, Liverpool (1980) pp. 250–62.

22. HMC, *Hastings MSS*, vol II, pp. 94–5.

23. HMC, *Portland MSS*, vol. I, pp. 80, 196; A. Garner, *Boston and the Great Civil War* (1972) pp. 1–7; C. Holmes, *Seventeenth-Century Lincolnshire* (1980) pp. 159–64.

24. M. Coate, *Cornwall in the Great Civil War* (Oxford, 1933) pp. 35–57; F. T. R. Edgar, *Sir Ralph Hopton* (1968) pp. 44–76; E. A. Andriette, *Devon and Exeter in the Civil War* (Newton Abbot, 1971) pp. 70–84.

25. Fletcher, *Outbreak*, pp. 302–410, *passim*.

26. Everitt, *Local Community*, pp. 11–17; HMC, *Hastings MSS*, vol. II, pp. 87–8.

27. Nottinghamshire RO, PR 5767: Thorpe constables accounts; A. C. Wood, *Nottinghamshire in the Civil War* (Oxford, 1937) pp. 29–42.

28. BL Harl. MSS 2135, fol. 96; E84(37): *The Unfaithfulness of the Cavaliers*; J. S. Morrill, *Cheshire, 1630–1660* (Oxford, 1974) pp. 65–9, 75.

29. BL E86(3): *Special Passages*, 17–24 Jan. 1643; HMC, *Portland MSS*, vol. I, pp. 95–6; *Civil War Tracts of Cheshire*, ed. J. A. Atkinson (Chetham Society, LXV, 1909) pp. 18–34; *Memorials of the Civil War in Cheshire*, ed. T. Malbon, (Lancashire and Cheshire Record Society, XIX, 1889) pp. 30–48; R. N. Dore, *The Civil Wars in Cheshire* (Chester, 1966) pp. 23–8.

30. E. Broxap, *The Great Civil War in Lancashire* (2nd edn, Manchester, 1973) pp. 53–85; A. J. Hawkes, 'Wigan's Part in the Civil War, 1639–51', *Transactions of the Lancashire and Cheshire Antiquarian Society*, XLVII (1932) 103–20.

31. HMC, *Portland MSS*, vol. I, pp. 63–4, 66–81, 84, 102; R. Bell, *Memorials of the Civil War* (1849) vol. I, pp. 21–40.

32. HMC, *Portland MSS*, vol. I, p. 103; A. R. Bayley, *The Civil War in Dorset* (1910) pp. 63–4.

33. HMC, *Portland MSS*, vol. I, pp. 69, 75–6; R. Howell, *Newcastle-upon-Tyne and the Puritan Revolution* (Oxford, 1967) pp. 144–8.

34. C. B. Phillips, 'The Royalist North: the Cumberland and Westmorland Gentry, 1642–1660', *Northern History*, XIV (1978) 170–3; C. B. Phillips, 'The Gentry in Cumberland and Westmorland, 1640–1665', unpublished Ph.D. thesis, Lancaster (1974) pp. 291–3.

35. Fletcher, *Outbreak*, pp. 384–6.

36. Staffordshire RO, D 593/8/8/1/7; William Salt Library, Stafford, Salt MSS 341/2.

37. *The Committee at Stafford*, ed. D. H. Pennington and I. A. Roots (1957) pp. lxi–lxii; Gardiner, vol. I, pp. 97, 106; D. H. Pennington, 'County and Country: Staffordshire in Civil War Politics, 1640–1644', *North Staffordshire Journal of Field Studies*, VI (1966) 16–18.

38. Bodl. Lib., Dep C MS 153, no. 111.

39. BL E85(45): *Certain Informations*, 16–23 Jan. 1643; E89(4): *Certain Informations*, 6–13 Feb. 1643; E90(28): *Certain Informations*, 20–7 Feb. 1643; A. J. Fletcher, 'Petitioning and the Outbreak of the Civil War in Derbyshire', *Derbyshire Archaeological Journal*, XCIII (1973) 39–41.

40. A. Everitt, *Change in the Provinces* (1969) p. 8.

41. HMC, *Portland MSS*, vol. I, p. 70; Bodl. Lib., Dep C MS 153, no. 115; HMC, *Ancaster MSS*, p. 411; Gardiner, vol. I, p. 79n.

42. HMC, *Portland MSS*, vol. I, p. 90; HMC, *Coke MSS*, vol. II, p. 329.

43. Staffordshire RO D 868/3/13a; *The Buller Papers*, ed. R. N. Worth (1895) p. 91.

44. BL Harl. MSS 382, fol. 206r; 383, fol. 207r; Phillips, *Ottley Papers*, pp. 261–2.

45. BL E84(39): *Petitions of Bedfordshire and Hertfordshire to the King*; E85(6): *Petition of Berkshire to the King; LJ*, V, 545; HMC, *Coke MSS*, vol. II, p. 328; Holmes, *East Anglia*, pp. 42, 53–4, 61; Gardiner, vol. I, pp. 74–5, 78, 81–2; V. Pearl, *London and the Outbreak of the Puritan Revolution* (Oxford, 1961) pp. 250–75.

46. J. Webb, *The Civil War in Herefordshire* (1879) pp. 354–5; Willis-Bund, *Diary of Henry Townshend*, vol. II, pp. 94–5; Morrill, *Revolt*, p. 161.

47. BL E84(31): *Petition of Bristol to the King; Reading Records*, ed. J. M. Guilding (1896) vol. IV, p. 70; Salisbury District Council Muniment Room, Ledger book D, fo. 10r.

48. Fletcher, *Outbreak*, chs. 3, 6, 8, 9 and *passim*.

49. Bodl. Lib., Dep C MS 165, no. 119; Holmes, *East Anglia*, pp. 42, 248–9.

50. BL 669 f 6(96): *Petitiion of Westminster to the Commons*.

51. Holmes, *East Anglia*, pp. 43–5, 61.

52. Staffodshire RO, Quarter Sessions Order Book, pp. 142, 151;

Pennington and Roots, *Committee at Stafford*, pp. xviii, xx, xxii, xxviii, 7, 297; Fletcher, *Outbreak*, pp. 362–3, 384–6.

53. Nottinghamshire RO, QSM 12, pp. 152, 160.

54. East Suffolk RO, B 105/2/1, fos 50r–57r; Holmes, *East Anglia*, pp. 49–52; Ketton-Cremer, *Norfolk*, pp. 182–4.

55. CRO, Quarter Sessions Order Book, fos 81r, 85r; Kent Archives Office, Q/SO WI; Morrill, *Cheshire*, p. 60; East Devon RO, Quarter Sessions Order Book, 1640–51; HMC, *Portland MSS*, vol. III, p. 106; HMC, *Various MSS*, vol. I, p. 109; Essex RO, Q/SR 318–9; B. C. Redwood, *Quarter Sessions Order Book, 1642–1649*, Sussex Record Society, LIV (1954) pp. 18–30; J. S. Furley, *Quarter Sessions Government in Hampshire* (1937) p. 81.

56. Essex RO, Q/SBa 2/49; Holmes, *East Anglia*, pp. 69–88.

57. HMC, *12th Report*, appendix, pt. VII (Le Fleming MSS) p. 19.

58. *Bellum Civile: Sir Ralph Hopton's Campaign in the West*, ed. C. E. H. Chadwyck-Healey (Somerset Record Society, XVIII, 1902) pp. 20–1.

59. BL E86(3): *Special Passages*, 17–24 Jan. 1643; HMC, *Portland MSS*, vol. III, p. 106.

60. Phillips, *Ottley Papers*, pp. 269–73.

61. Chadwyck-Healey, *Bellum Civile*, pp. 21–2; Fletcher, *County Community*, pp. 260–1; William Salt Library, Stafford, Salt MSS 341/2; Pennington, 'County and Country', 16–17; Birmingham Reference Library, Hanley Court MSS, Box 5, no. 398325.

62. C. V. Wedgwood, *The King's War* (1958) p. 125; Phillips, 'Royalist North', XIV (1978) 172; HMC, *5th Report*, p. 69.

63. HMC, *Portland MSS*, vol. III, p. 104; Hutton, 'Royalist War Effort', p. 74.

64. Sir G. Sitwell, *Letters of the Sitwells and Sacheverells* (1900) vol. I, pp. 19–20; GRO, D 2510/11.

65. BL E244 (18): *The Declaration of the Earl of Cumberland*.

66. *CJ*, vol. II, p. 1004; Holmes, *East Anglia*, p. 54; HMC, *12th Report*, appendix, pt. VII, p. 19.

67. Nottinghamshire RO, DD 294/1 (photocopies of documents owned by Mr R. I. Duncan).

68. Fletcher, *Outbreak*, pp. 369–406.

69. A. Everitt, *Suffolk and the Great Rebellion 1640–1660* (Suffolk Records Society, II, 1960) 38–9; Holmes, *East Anglia*, p. 52.

70. *Lancashire Civil War Tracts*, ed. G. Omerod (Chetham Society, II, 1844) 66–7; BL E83(32): *The Requests of the Grand Jury of Oxfordshire*.

71. BL 669 fo. 5(132): *The Agreement of the Grand Jury of Worcestershire*; HMC, *Various Manuscripts*, vol. I, p. 321; Hutton, 'Royalist War Effort', pp. 86–8; Pennington and Roots, *Committee at Stafford*, p. 341.

72. G. A. Harrison, 'Royalist Organisation in Gloucestershire and Bristol', unpublished M.A. thesis, Manchester (1961) pp. 64–73; Chadwyck-Healey, *Bellum Civile*, p. 36.

73. E.g. Northamptonshire RO, Isham MSS 246: Committee at Northampton to colonels and captains, 2 May 1643.

74. HMC, *7th Report*, p. 442.

75. *Acts and Ordinances of the Interregnum*, ed. C. H. Firth and R. S. Rait vol. I, pp. 46–137.

## 2. THE ROYALIST WAR EFFORT *Ronald Hutton*

1. *Letters of Lady Brilliana Harley*, ed. T. T. Lewis (Camden Society, 1853) nos 143–58; HMC, *14th Report*, appendix 11, pp. 86–92.
2. J. S. Morrill, *Cheshire, 1630–1660* (Oxford, 1974) pp. 49–51.
3. National Library of Wales, MS 5390D.
4. C. B. Phillips, 'The Royalist North: The Cumberland and Westmorland Gentry, 1642–1660', *Northern History*, XIV (1978) 170–4.
5. *The Life of William Cavendish, Duke of Newcastle* ed. Sir Charles Firth (1886) pp. 10–11; Roger Howell, *Newcastle-upon-Tyne and The Puritan Revolution* (Oxford, 1967) pp. 144–6.
6. For details of this process, see my paper 'The Failure of the Lancashire Cavaliers', *Transactions of the Lancashire and Cheshire Historical Society* CXXIX (1980) pp. 47–62.
7. Shropshire Archaeological and Natural History Society Transactions, VI (1894) pp. 34–7; HMC, *5th Report*, appendix, p. 141; *The Diary of Henry Townshend*, ed. J. W. Willis-Bund (Worcestershire Historical Society, 1915–20) vol. I, p. 75; *LJ*, vol. V, pp. 314–15.
8. BL 669 fo.6(55); BL E113(6); Willis-Bund, *Diary of Henry Townshend*, vol. I, pp. 84–9.
9. BL Harl. MS 2135 fo. 65: *Declaration of Cheshire Neutrality Movement*, 30 June 1642; *Bellum Civile: Sir Ralph Hopton's Campaign in the West*, ed. E. H. Chadwyck-Healey (Somerset Record Society, XVIII 1902) pp. 1–18.
10. *CSPD*, 1641–3, p. 361; *CJ*, vol. II, pp. 783, 864.
11. *Somers Tracts*, vol. V, p. 306.
12. Shropshire Archaeological and Natural History Society Transactions, VI (1894) pp. 41–3; XII (1900) pp. 4–5.
13. J. Rushworth, *Historical Collections* (1659–1701) pt. III, vol. II, pp. 5–11, 20–1, 23; BL E119(3).
14. Chadwyck-Healey, *Bellum Civile*, pp. 19–23; *The Buller Papers*, ed. R. N. Worth (1895) pp. 60–84.
15. For a different emphasis, see chapter 1, pp. 29–38.
16. F. Madan, *Oxford Books* (1912) vol. II, nos 1134, 1187; Bodl. Lib., Tanner MS 303, fos 113–15: Fitzwilliam Coningsby's Defence; *CSPD*, 1641–3, pp. 442–3; Willis-Bund, *Diary of Henry Townshend*, vol. I, pp. 96–7; BL Add. MS 36913, fos 122–3: Protest of Cheshire Gentry; HMC, *10th Report*, appendix 11, pp. 403–4.
17. Chadwyck-Healey, *Bellum Civile*, p. 35; R. Granville, *A History of the Granville Family* (1895) pp. 248.
18. *CJ*, vol. II, pp. 916–17, 987, 998–1000.
19. Bodl. Lib., Carte MS 7, fo. 424: Archbishop Williams to marquis of Ormonde, 12 Nov. 1643.
20. Edward Hyde, earl of Clarendon, *The Life of Edward, Earl of Clarendon* (1827) vol. I, p. 195n.
21. Bodl. Lib., Clarendon MS 21, fo. 202: Thomas Hughes to Edward Hyde, 17 Mar. 1643; MS 26, fo. 163: Joseph Jane's Relation; Willis-Bund, *Diary of Henry Townshend*, vol. I, pp. 131–57; Bodl. Lib., Tanner MS 303, fos 114–15: Fitzwilliam Coningsby's Defence.

22. E.g. for Weymouth, W. D. Christie, *A Life of Anthony Ashley Cooper* (1871) vol. I, pp. 45–6.

23. William Salt Library, Stafford, Salt MS 551: Letter of Prince Rupert to all local officers, undated.

24. Worcestershire RO, 705/24/876: 'Prince Rupert's Orders'.

25. HMC, *6th Report*, appendix, p. 472.

26. Bodl. Lib., Wood 376 (55): HMC, *Somerset MSS*, pp. 73–4.

27. *Somers Tracts*, vol. v, p. 333; Chadwyck-Healey, *Bellum Civile*, p. 62; BL E44(6); Bodl. Lib., Firth MS C6, fo. 11: Col. Broughton to Col. Lloyd, 22 Feb. 1644; Bodl. Lib., Carte MS 7, fo. 533: Col. Erneley to (marquis of) Ormonde, 19 Nov. 1643; Bodl. Lib., Carte MS 11, fo. 16: Ormonde to Archbishop Williams, 27 May 1644.

28. Details of which are in Bodl. Lib., Dugdale MS 19.

29. E.g. *LJ*, vol. v, p. 669; Cornwall RO, Basset MS 2: Commissioners of Array to Francis Bassett, 1 Dec. 1642.

30. E.g. Shropshire Archaeological and Natural History Society Transactions, VII (1895) pp. 324–5; M. Coate, *Cornwall In The Great Civil War and Interregnum* (Oxford, 1933) pp. 65–6.

31. Bodl. Lib., Clarendon MS 23, fo. 8: 'Propositions . . . For Revenues'.

32. Bodl. Lib., Rawlinson MS D924, fos 150–2: Minutes of Meetings of Commission of Array, 28–30 Mar. 1643.

33. Sir E. Walker, *Historical Discourses* (1705) pp. 43–106.

34. BL E45(10).

35. Walker, *Historical Discourses*, pp. 96–104.

36. Willis-Bund, *Diary of Henry Townshend*, vol. I, pp. 182–205.

37. E.g. in Buckinghamshire, BL Add. MS 18980, fos 66, 68: Lord Wentworth to Prince Rupert, 15 and 16 May 1643.

38. BL E258(6), E274(2), (24); BL Add. MS 11043, fos 19–20: Proclamation of governor of Hereford, 19 Mar. 1645; BL Egerton MS 787, fo. 93: Demands of Herefordshire Clubmen, 19 Mar. 1645.

39. R. Hutton, 'The Worcestershire Clubmen in the English Civil War', *Midland History* 5 (1980) 39–49, develops this argument.

40. E.g. *Harleian Miscellany*, vol. VII, p. 557; National Library of Wales, Wynn MS 1744; Clwyd Valley Petition, 12 Dec. 1644.

41. E. Warburton, *Memoirs of Prince Rupert and the Cavaliers* (1849) vol. II, pp. 385–7; BL Sloane MS 1519, fos 76–7: Lord Byron to Prince Rupert, 3 Apr. 1645.

42. Willis-Bund, *Diary of Henry Townshend*, vol. I, pp. 206–15.

43. Hereford RL 3668, fos 561–73; Warrants of Col. Devilliers, 9 Nov. 1644 to 23 May 1645; Webb MS 1, fos 129–91: Accounts of Walter Powell, 11 Dec. 1644 to 19 Apr. 1645.

44. William Salt Library, Stafford, Salt MS 45: Minute-Book of Prince of Wales' Council; Coate, *Cornwall*, pp. 181–4.

45. Bodl. Lib., Tanner MS 60, fos 163–4; Resolutions of Clubmen, 28 May and 24 June 1645.

46. J. Sprigge, *Anglia Rediviva* (1854) pp. 61–90; Bodl. Lib., Wood 378 (8), (11).

47. Sprigge, *Anglia*, pp. 145–63; Bodl. Lib., Clarendon MS 25, fos 19–234,

*passim*: thirty-seven letters to or from Lord Goring, Sir Richard Grenville and the Prince of Wales' councillors, July–Oct. 1645.

48. HMC, *Portland MSS*, vol. I, pp. 348–52.

3.  NEUTRALISM, CONSERVATISM AND POLITICAL
    ALIGNMENT IN THE ENGLISH REVOLUTION
    *Roger Howell*

1. Clarendon, *History*, vol. II, p. 226; Thomas Hobbes, *Behemoth*, in *The English Works of Thomas Hobbes*, ed. Sir W. Molesworth, 11 vols (1839–45) vol. VI, p. 128.

2. This is shown particularly in the well-known text by C. Hill, *The Century of Revolution, 1603–1714* (Edinburgh, 1961) esp. pp. 121–5, and by B. S. Manning. *The English People and the English Revolution* (1976). A healthy corrective to the view is provided by A. M. Everitt, 'The County Community' in *The English Revolution, 1600–1660*, ed. E. W. Ives (1968) pp. 48–63; R. Ashton, *The English Civil War, 1603–1649* (1978) chs. 3 and 10; and J. S. Morrill, *The Revolt of the Provinces* (1976). By 1640 there was a growing interest, especially in the larger towns, in national affairs even though many issues of primary importance remained local rather than national. D. Hirst, *The Representative of the People?* (Cambridge, 1975) pp. 45, 54–9, 110, 136, 145–53, 182–3.

3. The following material is drawn from *Crisis and Order in English Towns, 1500–1700*, ed. P. Clark and P. Slack (1972) pp. 1–56, and P. Clark and P. Slack, *English Towns in Transition, 1500–1700* (Oxford, 1976) pp. 1–16.

4. On Calne, see *Guild Stewards' Book of the Borough of Calne 1561–1688*, ed. A. W. Mabbs (Wiltshire Archaeological and Natural History Society Records Branch, 1953) pp. xiii–xiv; on Newcastle see Roger Howell, *Newcastle-upon-Tyne and the Puritan Revolution* (Oxford, 1967) ch. 2; on Norwich see J. T. Evans, *Seventeenth-Century Norwich* (Oxford, 1979) chs 1–3.

5. Evans, *Seventeenth-Century Norwich*, esp. pp. 84–104; *The Chamber Order Book of Worcester, 1602–50*, ed. Shelagh Bond (Worcestershire Historical Society, 1974) pp. 45–6, 324; Clark and Slack, *English Towns in Transition*, p. 136.

6. Clark and Slack, *Crisis and Order*, p. 25.

7. E. A. Andriette, *Devon and Exeter in the Civil War* (Newton Abbot, 1971) pp. 82–4 and n. 102, pp. 102–3; Howell, *Newcastle*, ch. 4; R.W. Cotton, *Barnstaple and the Northern Part of Devonshire during the Great Civil War* (1889) pp. 211–16.

8. Thomas Povey, *The Moderator* (1643) p. 11.

9. The following is drawn from John Latimer, *The Annals of Bristol in the Seventeenth Century* (Bath, 1970) pp. 154–65, and from the Bristol Common Council Books, 1627–42, fos 119v and 122; 1642–9, pp. 5, 6, 13, 21 (BRO).

10. P. Styles, *Studies in Seventeenth-Century West Midlands History* (Kineton, 1978) p. 216.

11. *The Diary of Henry Townshend*, ed. J. W. Willis-Bund (Worcestershire Historical Society, 1915–20) vol. II, p. 84.

12. J. Corbet, *An Historical Relation of the Military Government of Gloucester* [1645] in *Bibliotheca Gloucestrensis* (Gloucester, 1825) p. 24.

13. *Neutrality is Malignancy* (1648) p. 8; W. J. Farrow, *The Great Civil War in Shropshire, 1642–49* (Shrewsbury, 1926) pp. 28–9.

14. Margaret, Duchess of Newcastle, *The Life of William Cavendish, Duke of Newcastle*, ed. C. H. Firth (1886) p. 19.

15. Lucy Hutchinson, *Memoirs of the Life of Colonel Hutchinson* (1848) p. 157.

16. Bond, *Worcester Chamber Order Book*, pp. 363–4.

17. Arthur R. Bayley, *The Great Civil War in Dorset, 1642–1660* (Taunton, 1910) pp. 95–103. That the wealthiest moved their goods out of town is indicated in Bodl. Lib., Tanner MSS 62, fos 218ff.

18. Cotton, *Barnstaple*, pp. 49, 110, 162; Bodl. Lib., Tanner MSS 62, fo. 48.

19. R. Howell, 'The Structure of Urban Politics in the English Civil War', *Albion*, xi (1979) 115.

20. Howell, *Newcastle*, chs 4–5.

21. A. M. Johnson, 'Politics in Chester during the Civil Wars and Interregnum, 1640–1662', in Clark and Slack, *Crisis and Order*, p. 204.

22. Evans, *Seventeenth-Century Norwich*, pp. 138–43.

23. BL 669 fo. 6 (52): *Truths from York, Hull and Other Places* (1642).

24. The following on Newcastle is drawn from Howell, *Newcastle*, pp. 154–7.

25. *Parliament Scout*, no. 72, 31 Oct. – 7 Nov. 1644, p. 565. The figure of ten knighted aldermen is an exaggeration.

26. Nehemiah Wallington, *Historical Notices of Events Occurring Chiefly in the Reign of Charles I*, ed. Rosamund A. Webb (1869) vol. ii, p. 263.

27. Conrad Gill, *History of Birmingham: Manor and Borough to 1865* (1952) p. 53.

28. Ibid., p. 54; Herbert Heaton, *The Yorkshire Woolen and Worsted Industries* (Oxford, 1965) pp. 211–12.

29. Gill, *Birmingham*, p. 54.

30. The following on Newcastle is drawn from Howell, *Newcastle*, pp. 155, 160.

31. Styles, *Studies in West Midlands History*, p. 222; Bond, *Worcester Chamber Order Book*, p. 17.

32. *Reprint of the Barnstaple Records*, ed. John Roberts Chanter and Thomas Wainwright (Barnstaple 1900) vol. i, p. 20.

33. *Records of the Borough of Nottingham*, ed. W. H. Stevenson *et al.* (1882) vol. v, pp. 221–2, 228–32.

34. Styles, *Studies in West Midlands History*, pp. 238ff.

35. The following is drawn from *The Hull Letters*, ed. T. Tindall Wildridge (Hull, 1888) pp. 37–8, 70, 74, 140–1.

36. The following material on Worcester is drawn from Styles, *Studies in West Midlands History*, pp. 227–8; Bond, *Worcester Chamber Order Book*, pp. 370–1, 375, 381.

37. Mabbs, *Calne Guild Stewards' Book*, p. 61. Cf. pp. 65, 66–7, 68, 70, for more normal levels of expenditure.

38. Howell, *Newcastle*, p. 148.

39. Frederick Bliss Burbridge, *Old Coventy* (Birmingham, 1952) p. 247.

40. Stevenson *et al.*, *Records of the Borough of Nottingham*, vol. v, pp. 223–4.

41. Bond, *Worcester Chamber Order Book*, pp. 358, 364–5.

42. Hugh Owen and John B. Blakeway, *A History of Shrewsbury* (1825) vol. I, p. 431.

43. Styles, *Studies in West Midlands History*, p. 231.

44. Stevenson *et al.*, *Records of the Borough of Nottingham*, vol. v, pp. xv, 223–4, 237.

45. Howell, *Newcastle*, pp. 157–8.

46. Cotton, *Barnstaple*, p. 303.

47. Walter Powell, *Newes for Newters* (1648) p. 22.

48. Howell, *Newcastle*, ch. 5; R. Howell, 'Newcastle and the Nation: The Seventeenth Century Experience', *Archaeologia Aeliana*, 5th ser., VII (1980) 22–4.

49. *Weymouth and Melcombe Regis Minute Book 1625 to 1660*, ed. Maureen Weinstock (Dorset Record Society, 1964) pp. 73, 74, 76.

50. Bond, *Worcester Chamber Order Book*, pp. 416, 447, 448; Styles, *Studies in West Midland History*, p. 241.

51. Joseph B. Gribble, *Memorials of Barnstaple* (Barnstaple, 1830) pp. 202–3, 444, 463.

52. Bond, *Worcester Chamber Order Book*, p. 60.

53. D. E. Underdown, *Pride's Purge* (Oxford, 1971) ch. 10.

54. *The Minute Book of Bedford Corporation, 1647–1664*, ed. C. G. Parsloe (Bedfordshire Historical Society, 1949); C. G. Parsloe, 'The Corporation of Bedford, 1647–1664', *TRHS*, 4th ser., XXIX (1947) 151–65; Leonard J. Ashford, *The History of the Borough of High Wycombe* (1960) pp. 122–4; *The First Ledger Book of High Wycombe*, ed. R. W. Greaves (Buckinghamshire Record Society, 1956) pp. 132–58; D. E. Underdown, 'A Case Concerning Bishops' Lands: Cornelius Burges and the Corporation of Wells', *EHR*, LXXVII (1963) 18–48.

55. Howell, *Newcastle*, pp. 214–15.

56. *Records of the Borough of Leicester, 1603–1688*, ed. H. Stocks and W. H. Stevenson (Cambridge, 1923); HMC, *Records of the City of Exeter; VCH Yorkshire, City of York*, p. 183; Cotton, *Barnstaple*, p. 542.

57. F. A. Inderwick, 'Rye under the Commonwealth', *Sussex Archaeological Collections*, XXXIX (1894) 1–15; A. Fletcher, *A County Community in Peace and War: Sussex, 1600–1660* (1975); HMC, *Corporation of Rye*, esp. pp. 216–37. Cf. Underdown, *Pride's Purge*, p. 321.

58. Ashford, *History of High Wycombe*, pp. 126–42.

59. Evans, *Seventeenth-Century Norwich*, p. 191.

## 4. THE CHURCH IN ENGLAND, 1642–9 *John Morrill*

1. Much of the expense incurred in researching this paper was met by a generous grant from the Archbishop Cranmer Fund of the University of Cambridge, which I gratefully acknowledge. Earlier versions of the essay were read at seminars in Cambridge (at Peterhouse History Society and at Professor Christopher Brooke's ecclesiastical history seminar), in Oxford (at

the Stubbs Society), and in Bristol (at the Acton Society). I am grateful to the contributors to the discussion on all those occasions for their helpful comments. The final draft was read by Anthony Fletcher, Chris Haigh, Patrick Higgins and Blair Worden and gained enormously in content and presentation thereby. Several members of my own graduate seminar have generously provided me with references: Patrick Higgins, Judith Maltby, John Twigg, Tim Wales and especially Paul Gladwish.

2. The word 'Anglican' is used throughout to mean conformity to the canons and constitutions of the Church of England as they had developed since 1559. It was used in this sense by contemporaries – for example, Charles I, in a proclamation of 14 May 1644, undertook to defend 'this most holy religion of the Anglican Church'. See D. Neal. *History of the Puritans* (1822) vol. III, p. 77.

3. For this paragraph, see all the general works given in the bibliographical essay, above all W. A. Shaw, *The History of the English Church during the Civil War and under the Commonwealth* (1900) vol. I, pp. 1–384; see also, A. Fletcher, *The Outbreak of the English Civil War* (1981), *passim*, and W. Abbot, 'The Issue of Episcopacy and the Long Parliament', unpublished D.Phil. thesis, Oxford (1981).

4. This is a complex and controversial point which I intend to argue elsewhere. The figure may well be too low once the Quakers emerged in the mid-1650s.

5. Shaw, *English Church*, vol. I, pp. 1–144; vol. II, pp. 295–300; J. Stoughton, *A History of Religion in England* (revised ed., 1881) vol. I, chs 1–4; F. M. G. Higham, *Catholic and Reformed* (1962) pp. 181–210.

6. These Acts were not repealed until 1650 – C. H. Firth and R. S. Rait, *Acts and Ordinances of the Interregnum* (1911) vol. II, p. 423.

7. Ibid., vol. I, p. 180. For its deliberations, see Shaw, *English Church*, vol. I, pp. 145–384.

8. Firth and Rait, *Acts*, vol. I, pp. 106, 176, 180, 425, 879; Shaw, *English Church*, vol. I, p. 138; J. W. F. Hill, 'The Royalist Clergy of Lincolnshire', *Lincolnshire Architectural and Archaeological Society, Reports and Papers*, no. 2, pt I (1938) 59. See also below, pp. 101–3.

9. Firth and Rait, *Acts*, vol. I, pp. 582–607, 755. The best brief account of the Directory is in Higham, *Catholic and Reformed*, pp. 217–20.

10. See below, pp. 104–5.

11. All three, together with other papers from the assembly, were published in a collective volume entitled *The Confession of Faith* (Edinburgh, 1885).

12. Firth and Rait, *Acts*, vol. I, p. 789.

13. Ibid., vol. I, p. 580.

14. Ibid., vol. I, pp. 420–2, 607, 954.

15. Ibid., vol. I, 265, 425; Shaw, *English Church*, vol. I, pp. 103–10.

16. For the journal of the leading iconoclast, see *The Journal of William Dowsing*, ed. E. H. Evelyn-White (Ipswich, 1885), for his tour of Suffolk, and J. G. Cheshire, 'William Dowsing's Destructions', *Cambridgeshire and Huntingdonshire Archaeological Society Transactions*, III (1914), for Cambridgeshire. There is a good summary in A. Kingston, *East Anglia in the Great Civil War* (1897) pp. 329–32. My impressions are formed from an

232    REACTIONS TO THE ENGLISH CIVIL WAR

analysis of 150 sets of churchwardens' accounts in western and eastern England (see below p. 233, note 45).

17. J. R. Phillips, *The Reformation of the Images* (Berkeley, 1973) pp. 192–200; V. Staley, *Hierurgia Anglicana* (revised edn, 1902–4) vol. i, pp. 92–101, 185–6; vol. ii, pp. 256–70; Stoughton, *History of Religion*, vol. i, pp. 313–6; M. E. C. Walcott, *Traditions and Customs of Cathedrals* (1872) pp. 29–42; G. B. Tatham, *The Puritans in Power* (Cambridge, 1913) pp. 256–63; *A History of York Minster*, ed. G. Aylmer and R. Cant (York, 1977) pp. 211–5, 439–40, 503; J. F. Chanter, *The Bishop's Palace, Exeter* (Exeter, 1932) p. 93; R. W. Ketton-Cremer, *Norfolk in the Great Civil War* (1969) pp. 224–38.

18. Firth and Rait, *Acts*, vol. i, pp. 749, 833, 1062.

19. Shaw, *English Church*, vol. i, pp. 145–384. The best brief account is in Higham, *Catholic and Reformed*, pp. 213–23.

20. Shaw, *English Church*, vol. ii, pp. 1–33, 365–400. For important modifications, see G. Yule, *The Puritans in Power* (forthcoming) appendix ii, and C. E. Surman, 'Classical Presbyterianism in England, 1643–1660', unpublished M.A. thesis, Manchester (1949) pp. 35–59.

21. Yule, *Puritans*, conclusion.

22. For the Cromwellian reform, see C. Cross, 'The Church in England, 1646–1660', in *The Interregnum*, ed. G. E. Aylmer (1975) pp. 104–5;

23. For surviving records, see bibliographical essay.

24. W. A. Shaw. *The Financial Administration of the Revenues of the Disendowed Church* (Manchester, 1893); also his *English Church*, vol. ii, pp. 175–286.

25. See e.g. A Fletcher, *A County Community at Peace and War: Sussex, 1600–1660* (1975) pp. 113–7.

26. See the suggestive remarks of P. Collinson, 'The Godly', paper to *Past and Present* conference on Popular Religion (1966) p. 22 (cited in Fletcher, *Sussex*, p. 117).

27. See below, pp. 103–12.

28. R. R. Steele, *Bibliotheca Lindesiana: A Bibliography of Royal Proclamations of Tudor and Stuart Sovereigns* (Oxford, 1910) vol. i, p. 295.

29. P. King. 'The Episcopate during the Civil War, 1642–1649', *EHR*, LXXXIII (1968) 526–48; J. H. Overton, *The Church in England* (1897) vol. ii, pp. 95–7; *DNB*.

30. Steele, *Proclamations*, vol. i, 292–303.

31. King, 'Episcopate', 54–7; Abbot, 'Issue of Episcopacy', ch. 6; A. Kingston, *The Civil War in Hertfordshire* (1894) p. 72.

32. King, 'Episcopate', 528–33; see also the chapters on ecclesiastical history in many *Victoria County History* volumes, as *Cheshire* iii and *Cumberland* ii; *DNB;* R. Bosher, *The Making of the Restoration Settlement* (1951) chs 1–2; J. Packer, *The Transformation of Anglicanism* (1969) *passim*.

33. I. Green, 'The Persecution of "Scandalous" and "Malignant" Parish Clergy during the English Civil War', *EHR*, XCIV (1979) 525.

34. Firth and Rait, *Acts*, vol. i, pp. 521, 865; Surman, 'Classical Presbyterianism' chs 2 and 3; H. Smith, *The Ecclesiastical History of Essex under the Long Parliament and Commonwealth* (Colchester, 1932) pp. 121–6; 'Register Book of the Fourth Classis of the Province of London', ed. C. E. Surman (Harleian Society, LXXXII–LXXXIII, 1952–3) p. xiii.

35. Ibid., p. 15.

36. Smith, *Essex*, pp. 326–30, 410; K. Major, 'Lincoln Diocesan Records', *TRHS*, 4th ser., XXII (1940) 56; King, 'Episcopate', 531–2; *DNB*; *Autobiography of Simon Patrick* (1839) p. 38.

37. Green, 'Persecution', 509–13, 518.

38. BL Add.MSS 5829 fos 6–8.

39. Green, 'Persecution', 511–2.

40. C. Holmes. 'The Suffolk Committee of Scandalous Ministers, 1644–1646' Suffolk Records Society, XIII (1970) 19–24 and *passim*; Hill, 'Royalist Clergy', *passim*; Smith, *Essex, passim*; BL Add.MSS 5829; Add.MSS 22084; Tatham, *Puritans in Power*, pp. 65–92; A. Tindal-Hart, *The Country Clergy, 1558–1660* (1958) pp. 120–5.

41. But cf. A. M. Everitt, *The Community of Kent and the Great Rebellion* (Leicester, 1966) pp. 231–2, 243.

42. *The Standing Committee of the County of Dorset, 1646–1650*, ed. C. H. Mayo (Dorchester, 1900) *passim*.

43. BL Add.MSS 5829, fos 36–7.

44. Tatham, *Puritans in Power*, pp. 264–7; 'Manchester Classical Minutes', ed. W. A. Shaw (Chetham Society, XX, XXII, XXIV, 1888–91) pp. 26, 32, 109, 111, 116, 208, 251–3, 284, 289, 293, 296–302.

45. I have examined all extant accounts in the following county record offices: Cheshire, Worcestershire, Herefordshire, Gloucestershire, Wiltshire, Dorset, Cambridgeshire, Norfolk and Suffolk. I have seen some Cheshire and Norfolk accounts still held by the parishes themselves. In addition, Paul Gladwish generously made available his notes and transcripts of the accounts of Shropshire and Bristol.

46. *Diary of John Evelyn*, ed. E. S. de Beer (Oxford, 1955) vols. I and II, *passim*; Higham, *Catholic and Reformed*, pp. 257–8, 264–72, Overton, *Church*, vol. II, pp. 119–21; 'Autobiography of Sir John Bramston' (Camden Society, XXXII, 1845) pp. 91–7; Ketton-Cremer, *Norfolk*, pp. 332–8; A. E. Preston, *The Church and Parish of St Nicholas, Abingdon* (1929) p. 97; Tatham, *Puritans in Power*, chs 4 and 5; Neal, *History of the Puritans*, vol. III, pp. 365–9; CUL Baker MSS 25/167; Stoughton, *History of Religion*, vol. II, pp. 83, 103–4, 280–92, 322–4; Fletcher, *Sussex*, p. 111; Mayo, *Standing Committee*, pp. 318–9, 376; Smith, *Essex*, p. 84.

47. Based on sources in note 45.

48. NNRO PD 58/38 (St Lawrence); NNRO PD 59/54 (St Gregory). GRO P 154/14 CW 2/1 (St Michael); CRO P154/11 CW 2/1 (St Mary). For earlier complaints, see Staley, *Hierurgia Anglicana*, vol. I, p. 257.

49. Firth and Rait, *Acts*, vol. I, pp. 789, 833, 852; and Neal, *History of the Puritans*, vol. III, pp. 245–7.

50. *The Diary of Ralph Josselin, 1616–1683*, ed. A. Macfarlane (1976) pp. 77, 96, 234–6.

51. See below, pp. 101–2.

52. NNRO C/53/box 37, bundle 1, unfol.

53. PRO SP 24/1, fo. 187.

54. PRO SP 24/3, fos 118, 152; SP 24/4, fos 68, 77; SP 24/78, unfol.: petition of Wm Stephenson *et al*.

55. NNRO C/83/40: depositions of W. Greene, P. Rickman, A. Nicholls.

56. Firth and Rait, *Acts*, vol. i, 604.

57. PRO SP 24/2, fos 98, 171; SP 24/3, fo. 42.

58. Steele, *Proclamations*, vol. i, p. 374.

59. This paragraph is based on Fletcher, *Outbreak*, ch. 9, supplemented by a reading of Sir Thomas Aston, *A Collection of Sundry Petitions* (1641) (in BL E E.201 [26]); J. S. Morrill, *The Revolt of the Provinces* (1976) p. 151; J. S. Morrill, *Cheshire 1630–1660* (Oxford, 1974) pp. 35–7; BL Add.MSS 36913 fos 136–41; CRO QSF 1642 no. 4 fos 23–4.

60. Morrill, *Revolt*, pp. 92–9, 201.

61. Shropshire RO 2656/18(Wroxeter); BRO 0065(22) Ca15(1) (the Temple Church, Bristol); DRO P 155 CW 113 (Sherborne).

62. See above, pp. 94–5.

63. Smith, *Essex*, pp. 174–193, 408; Phillips, *Reformation*, pp. 184–9.

64. Firth and Rait, *Acts*, vol. i, pp. 567, 996; Steele, *Proclamations*, vol. i, p. 292; 'Plundered Ministers Accounts', ed. W. A. Shaw (Lancashire and Cheshire Records Society, XXVIII, 1894) pp. 185–7; Mayo, *Standing Committee*, pp. 108, 120, 353, 384, 419, 430, 438, 442, 448, 452, 453, 475, 500; *Walker Revised*, ed. A. G. Matthews (Oxford, 1948) pp. 79–84; Kingston, *East Anglia*, pp. 393–5.

65. M. Coate, *Cornwall in the Great Civil War and Interregnum* (Oxford, 1940) pp. 333–4; Tindal-Hart, *Country Clergy*, pp. 128–9; PRO SP24/77 unfol.: petition of D. Souton; BL Add.MSS 15671, fo. 240.

66. Smith, *Essex*, pp. 157–61; Kingston, *East Anglia*, pp. 326–8; Matthews, *Walker Revised*, p. 81.

67. Tatham, *Puritans in Power*, pp. 58–9, 69; Tindal-Hart, *Country Clergy*, p. 120.

68. Kingston, *Hertfordshire*, pp. 164–7.

69. Shaw, 'Plundered Ministers Accounts', pp. 175–182, 189.

70. E.g. ibid., pp. 183–9; Smith, *Essex*, pp. 162–3.

71. Firth and Rait, *Acts*, vol. i, p. 999.

72. Everitt, *Kent*, pp. 231–240; Ketton-Cremer, *Norfolk*, pp. 337–40; Morrill, *Revolt*, pp. 125–30, 207.

73. See, e.g., Cross, 'Church in England', in Aylmer, *Interregnum*, pp. 99–120.

74. I owe this point to discussions with Dr Anne Laurence and to the paper she delivered to my graduate seminar in Cambridge in November 1980.

75. Cf. B. S. Manning, 'The Godly People', in the book he edited, *Politics, Religion and the English Civil War* (Manchester, 1973).

76. To be reported in *England's Wars of Religion* (forthcoming).

77. Firth and Rait, *Acts*, vol. i, p. 905.

78. *Parliamentary Diary of Thomas Burton*, ed. J. T. Rutt (1822) vol. i, p. 240.

79. Higham, *Catholic and Reformed*, p. 270.

## 5. THE WAR AND THE PEOPLE    *Donald Pennington*

I am grateful to Dr R. E. Hutton for permission to make use of his thesis on the *Royalist War Effort* (soon to appear as a book), to Dr J. S. Morrill for advice far more valuable than his editorial duties required, and to Mrs Marjorie Pennington for indispensable help in reading sources and typing chaotic drafts.

1. See pp. 89–114 above; pp. 184–208 below.

2. HMC, *Portland MSS*, vol. I, p. 718 (Yorkshire); *The Diary of Henry Townshend*, ed. J. W. Willis-Bund (Worcestershire Historical Society, 1915–20) vol. I, p. 239 (Worcestershire); Bodl. Lib., Tanner MSS 60, fo. 75 (Gloucestershire); Bodl. Lib., Tanner MSS 60, fo. 220 (Cheshire); *CJ*, vol. III, p. 625 (Lancashire).

3. J. S. Morrill, 'Mutiny and Discontent in English Provincial Armies, 1645–1647', *Past and Present*, no. 56 (1972) 53, 63.

4. *CSPD*. 1645–7, pp. 4, 5, 8; *Sir Francis Ottley's Papers*, ed. W. Phillips (Shropshire Archaeological and Natural History Society, 2nd ser., VI, 1894) p. 43.

5. C. H. Firth, *Cromwell's Army* (1902) ch. 9; *The Royalist Ordnance Papers, 1642–1643*, ed. I. Roy (Oxfordshire Record Society, new ser., XLIII, 1963–4); *Acts and Ordinances of the Interregnum*, ed. C. H. Firth and R. S. Rait (1911) vol. I, pp. 41–2, 247, 655; *The Committee at Stafford*, ed. D. H. Pennington and I. A. Roots (Manchester, 1957) pp. xliv, 340; PRO SP28/126/3: Accounts of commissioners for victuals in Windsor Castle; PRO SP28/135: Accounts of Nicholas Cowling; *The Papers of Captain Henry Stevens, Waggon-Master General to King Charles I*, ed. M. Toynbee (Oxfordshire Record Society, XLII, 1962) pp. 17–18 and *passim*.

6. See R. Ashton, pp. 192–5 below.

7. D. E. Underdown, *Somerset in the Civil War and Interregnum* (Newton Abbot, 1973) p. 51.

8. Firth and Rait, *Acts*, vol. I, pp. 938, 945, 1048–9; Firth, *Cromwell's Army*, pp. 217–8; PRO SP28/129: Allowances to towns for quartering soldiers of the earl of Manchester; PRO E315/481: Losses of inhabitants of Wendover; SP28/126: Allowances for quartering; *LJ*, vol. VIII, p. 265; R. E. Hutton, 'The Royalist War Effort in the West Midlands and Wales, 1642–1646', unpublished D.Phil. thesis, Oxford (1980) p. 135. HMC, *Portland MSS*, vol. I, pp. 283–5; *CJ*, vol. III, p. 583.

9. Firth and Rait, *Acts*, vol. I, pp. 41–2, 155–6, 163, 650; Bodl. Lib., Rawlinson MSS, D 918; *The Agrarian History of England and Wales*, ed. J. Thirsk (Cambridge, 1967) vol. IV, p. 604; Claud Cockburn, 'The Origins of British Bloodstock', *History Today*, II (1952), 761–9.

10. *LJ*, vol. V, pp. 46, 526, 568, 570–1; *LJ*, vol. VI, p. 88; *CSPD*, 1644, p. 1; PRO SP28/130: two books of horses listed in the London area; SP28/131: commissaries' book of horses.

11. Firth and Rait, *Acts*, vol. I, pp. 155–6; *LJ*, vol. V, pp. 661–2.

12. *CJ*, vol. III, pp. 40, 49, 58; *CSPD*, 1644, p. 184; Bodl. Lib., Tanner MSS 60 fo. 80; Bodl. Lib., MS. Eng. Hist. 53 fo. 162; Pennington and Roots, *Committee at Stafford*, pp. xliii–xliv, 254.

13. The figures were calculated by Dr Morrill from PRO SP24/1–3.

14. C. Holmes, *The Eastern Association in the English Civil War* (Cambridge, 1974) pp. 149–50; PRO SP28/129, pt 10; Firth, *Cromwell's Army*, pp. 241–5; Pennington and Roots, *Committee at Stafford*, pp. 144, 246, 253.

15. HMC, *Letter Books of Sir Samuel Luke*, p. 354; HMC, *4th Report*, p. 308; *LJ*, vol. VIII, p. 265; *CSPD*, 1641–3, p. 481.

16. Thirsk, *Agrarian History* vol. IV, pp. 164–5; F. P. Verney, *Memoirs of the Verney Family during the Civil War* (1892) vol. II, p. 156; Toynbee, *Stevens Papers*, pp. 30, 31.

17. *Biblotheca Gloucestrensis*, ed. J. Washbourne (Gloucester, 1825) pp. 184, 261; J. and T. W. Webb, *Memorials of the Civil War . . . as it affected Herefordshire and adjacent counties* (1829) vol. II, p. 175; Clarendon, *History*, vol. III, p. 171; Ian Roy, 'The English Civil War and English Society', in *War and Society* ed. B. Bond and I. Roy (1977) vol. I, p. 41.

18. Bodl. Lib., Tanner MSS 59, pt I, fos 113, 152, 145; 60 fo. 556. Webb, *Herefordshire*, vol. II, pp. 221, 378, 397; Gardiner, *History*, vol. II, p. 309.

19. *A Royalist's Notebook*, ed. F. Bamford (1936) pp. 117–9; Willis-Bund, *Diary of Henry Townshend*, vol. I, p. 139; J. Rushworth, *Historical Collections* (1691) pt III, vol. II, p. 670; J. Engberg, 'Royalist Finances during the English Civil War', *Scandinavian Economic History Review*, II (1966) 93.

20. Hutton, 'Royalist War Effort', pp. 109–10.

21. A. M. Everitt, *The Community of Kent and the Great Rebellion, 1640–1660* (Leicester, 1966) p. 219; *CSPD*, 1644, pp. 222, 283. Hutton, 'Royalist War Effort', pp. 110–40; Holmes, *Eastern Association*, ch. 3.

22. Bodl. Lib., Tanner MSS 60, fos 518, 520; *CSPD*, 1644, pp. 230, 231, 237; 1644–5, pp. 83, 191; *LJ*, vol. VIII, p. 97; A. C. Wood, *Nottinghamshire in the Civil War* (Oxford, 1937) p. 112; *Tracts relating to . . . Lancashire during the Civil War* (Chetham Society, II, 1844) pp. 196–182.

23. Underdown, *Somerset*, p. 81; Bodl. Lib., Tanner MSS 60, fo. 206.

24. *Verney Memoirs*, vol. I, p. 94.

25. Pennington and Roots, *Committee at Stafford*, pp. liv, 68; Clarendon, *History*, vol. IV, pp. 37-8; D. G. Hey, *An English Rural Community: Myddle under the Tudors and Stuarts* (Leicester 1974) p. 198.

26. PRO SP28/129, pt 10; Bodl. Lib., Rawlinson MSS C125, fo. 10.

27. Webb, *Herefordshire*, vol. II, p. 131; Bodl. Lib., Tanner MSS 60, fos 17, 52; *CSPD*, 1641–3, p. 470; *Lancashire Civl War Tracts*, p. 211; P. Young and W. Emberton, *Sieges of the Civil War* (1978) pp. 59–66, 89–100; HMC, *Bath MSS*, vol. I, pp. 1–40; HMC, *Portland MSS*, vol. III.

28. Wood, *Nottinghamshire*, pp. 32–3, 44, 136–7; *Mercurius Aulicus*, 27 Mar. 1643; Firth and Rait, *Acts*, vol. I, pp. 353–4; PRO SP28/153: levies for Newport Pagnell.

29. R. Howell, *Newcastle-upon-Tyne and the Puritan Revolution* (Oxford, 1967) pp. 164, 165, 168.

30. Washbourne, *Bibliotheca Gloucestrensis*, pp. 172, 211, 217, 222, 261, 263; Roy, 'Civil War and Society', in Bond and Roy, *War and Society*, vol. I, pp. 36–7; *CSPD*, 1644–5, p. 269; Brian Manning, 'The Peasantry and the English Revolution', *Journal of Peasant Studies*, II (1975) 141; Gardiner, *History*, vol. I, pp. 198, 206.

31. Willis-Bund, *Diary of Henry Townshend*, vol. II, p. 206; Simeon Ash, quoted in P. Wenham, *The Great and Close Siege of York* (Kineton, 1970) p. 98.

32. I. Tullie, *A Narrative of the Siege of Carlisle* (1840); Firth and Rait, *Acts*, vol. I, p. 799; Underdown, *Somerset*, pp. 93–5; J. Sprigge, *Anglia Rediviva* (1647)

p. 19; Clarendon, *History*, vol. III, p. 49.

33. Underdown, *Somerset*, pp. 108–10; Sprigge, *Anglia Rediviva*, p. 74; *Lancashire Civil War Tracts*, pp. 84–9, *CJ*, vol. III, p. 623; vol. IV, p. 168.

34. PRO SP28/127: accounts of work at North Crawley; SP28/128: goods delivered at Lyme Regis; Willis-Bund, *Diary of Henry Townshend*, vol. I, pp. 130, 174.

35. PRO SP28/228, pt 4, fo. 674.

36. PRO SP28/183: (coals etc. carried to Warwick Castle).

37. PRO SP28/126, pt 1; *Diary of . . . Richard Symonds*, ed. C. E. Long (Camden Society, 1859) p. 14; Firth, *Cromwell's Army*, pp. 235–6; *LJ*, vol. v, p. 599.

38. L. Boynton, *The Elizabethan Militia, 1558–1638* (1971 edn) pp. 257–62; Underdown, *Somerset*, p. 81; Firth and Rait, *Acts*, vol. I, p. 272; Roy, *Royalist Ordnance Papers*, vol. I, pp. 25–9 and *passim*.

39. J. S. Morrill, *The Revolt of the Provinces* (1976) pp. 80–4; Engberg, 'Royalist Finances', 79.

40. Everitt, *Kent*, pp. 157–8; A. Fletcher, *A County Community in Peace and War: Sussex, 1600–1660* (1975) pp. 336–9; J. S. Morrill, *Cheshire, 1630–1600* (Oxford, 1974) pp. 94–138; D. H. Pennington, 'The Accounts of the Kingdom, 1642–1649', in *Essays in the Economic and Social History of Tudor and Stuart England*, ed. F. J. Fisher (Cambridge, 1961) pp. 182–220.

41. PRO SP28/236/32, fo. 2.

42. Washbourne, *Bibliotheca Gloucestrensis*, p. 17; Bodl. Lib., Tanner MSS 61, fos 57, 74; *CSPD*, 1644, p. 428; *CSPD*, 1645–7, p. 8.

43. *CSPD*, 1641–3, pp. 417, 442; *The Royalist Government of Worcestershire during the Civil War*, ed. P. Styles (Worcestershire Archaeological Society, 3rd ser., v, 1976) pp. 27, 34; Willis-Bund, *Diary of Henry Townshend*, vol. II, pp. 238–9; Bodl. Lib., Rawlinson MSS D 924, fo. 152.

44. PRO SP 28/152: Answers of Thetford, Chatteris and Ely St Mary's to the 47 Articles; Firth and Rait, *Acts*, vol. I, pp. 292–314, 274–83; E. Hughes, *Studies in Administration and Finance* (Manchester, 1934) pp. 116–36.

45. Gardiner, *History*, vol. III, p. 194; PRO E101/676/52; Holmes, *Eastern Association*, pp. 136–7; Pennington and Roots, *Committee at Stafford*, p. 325; PRO SP28/129: accounts of Thomas Blaney, fo. 85; PRO SP28/182: contributions of the inhabitants of Samborne.

46. Firth and Rait, *Acts*, vol. I, pp. 96, 120, 153, 237, 617; T. S. Willan, 'The Parliamentary Surveys for the North Riding of Yorkshire', *Yorkshire Archaeological Society Journal*, XXXI (1933) 231–3; Pennington and Roots, *Committee at Stafford*, pp. 51, 155, 170, 191; *The Oxinden Letters*, ed. Dorothy Gardiner (1937) pp. 9–10, 14–15, 22–3, 68; HMC, *Portland MSS*, III, 103–4.

47. Firth and Rait, *Acts*, vol. I, pp. 106–17, 254–60; P. H. Hardacre, *The Royalists during the Puritan Revolution* (The Hague, 1956) pp. 17–38; H. J. Habakkuk, 'Landowners and the Civil War', *EcHR*, 2nd ser., XVIII (1965) 130–51.

48. Firth and Rait, *Acts*, vol. I, 303–5, 422–3; *CSPD*, 1641–3, pp. 421–2; *CSPD*, 1644, p. 321; *CSPD*, 1644–5, p. 289; R. G. Albion, *Forests and Sea Power: the Timber Problem of the Royal Navy, 1652–1862* (Cambridge, Mass., 1926) pp. 127–8; Pennington and Roots, *Committee at Stafford*, pp. xliv–xlv, 28–9, 113,

181 and passim; F. W. Jessup, *Sir Roger Twysden* (1965) p. 71.

49. Rushworth, *Historical Collections*, pt III, vol. II, pp. 98–100; Firth and Rait, *Acts*, vol. I, pp. 66, 191, 372–3.

50. J. S. Cockburn, *A History of English Assizes, 1558–1714* (Cambridge, 1972) p. 241; Firth and Rait, *Acts*, vol. I, p. 191; Fletcher, *Sussex*, p. 340; Underdown, *Somerset*, pp. 67–71; Bodl. Lib., Tanner MSS 59, pt 2, fo. 426; E. A. Andriette, *Devon and Exeter in the Civil War* (Newton Abbot, 1971) pp. 102–3; *Warwick Quarter Sessions Order Book*, ed. S. C. Ratcliff and H. C. Johnson (Warwick County Records, 1936) vol. II, pp. 125–6; *Sussex Quarter Sessions Order Book*, ed. A. C. Redwood (Sussex County Records, vol. III, 1954) p. 38.

51. Wenham, *The Great and Close Siege of York*, p. 196; Pennington and Roots, *Committee at Stafford*, p. 343; Bodl. Lib., Tanner MSS 59, pt 2, fo. 426.

52. Morrill, *Cheshire*, pp. 92–3, 228–9; Bodl. Lib., Tanner MSS 59, pt 1, fo. 52; Everitt, *Kent*, pp. 126–42; Fletcher, *Sussex*, pp. 325–8; J. H. Hexter, *The Reign of King Pym* (Cambridge, Mass., 1941) pp. 13–30.

53. A. Everitt, 'The Local Community and the Civil War' (Historical Association pamphlet G70, 1969) p. 26; Morrill, *Revolt*, pp. 37–8; A. E. Wrigley and R. S. Schofield, *The Population History of England, 1500–1850* (1981) pp. 680–1.

54. Roy, 'Civil War and Society', in Bond and Roy, *War and Society*, vol. I, p. 31; J. Walter and K. Wrightson, 'Dearth and the Social Order', *Past and Present*, no. 71 (1976) 29–42; Thirsk, *Agrarian History*, vol. IV (statistical appendices) pp. 814–65.

55. E. H. Symonds, 'The Diary of John Greene', *EHR*, XLIII (1928) 391.

56. Jonathan Priestley, 'Some Memoirs Concerning the Family of the Priestleys' (Surtees Society, LXXVII, 1886) pp. 9, 18; *The Autobiography of Joseph Lister*, ed. T. Wright (1842) pp. 23–8, 39; 'Three Civil War Notes', ed. T. W. Hanson, in *Papers, Reports, etc. read before the Halifax Antiquarian Society, 1916*, 253–5; Bodl. Lib., Tanner MSS 60, fo. 518.

57. D. E. Underdown, 'Clubmen in the Civil War', *Past and Present*, no. 85 (1979) 25–48.

## 6.    'THE ANCIENT LAW OF FREEDOM':
### JOHN SELDEN AND THE CIVIL WAR    *Richard Tuck*

1. Bodl. Lib., MS Selden supra 123 fo. 159. The quotation in the title to this essay comes from ibid., fo. 70b.

2. David Underdown in his *Pride's Purge* (Oxford, 1971) p. 385, has Selden as secluded; but his name appears only on the list of 26 Dec. 1648 and not in Prynne's *Vindication* (see ibid., p. 212). As Underdown says, the list of 26 Dec. includes members who were abstaining as well as those who had been secluded by Pride. For Cromwell's thoughts about Selden and St John, see Blair Worden, *The Rump Parliament* (Cambridge, 1974) p. 339.

3. Clarendon's remark is in his *Life* (*The History of the Rebellion . . . Also his Life* [Oxford, 1843] p. 925); Jonson's in his conversations with Drummond of

Hawthornden (*Ben Jonson*, ed. C. H. Herford and P. Simpson [Oxford, 1925] vol. I, p. 149).

4. For information on Selden's friendships and influence, see R. Tuck, *Natural Rights Theories* (Cambridge, 1979).

5. The main works are *Analecton Anglo-Britannicon* (written 1607, published 1615), *Jani Anglorum Facies Altera* (published 1610), *Englands Epinomis* (written c.1610, published 1683), *Titles of Honour* (published 1614), notes on Fortescue's *De Laudibus Legum Angliae* (published 1616) and *History of Tythes* (published 1617). His remarks on Henry I and John are both from *Englands Epinomis*, in his *Opera*, ed. D. Wilkins (1726) – henceforth 'Wilkins' – vol. III, cols 20 and 41.

6. Wilkins, vol. III, cols 1329–30.

7. He gives as an example in *Titles of Honour* the ordinary's (i.e. the appropriate ecclesiastical court officer's) power of granting administration of intestates' goods (Wilkins, vol. III, col. 742). It is worth noting that this view of the common law became standard in the eighteenth century, largely through its expression in the works of Matthew Hale – see his *History of the Common Law of England*, ed. C. M. Gray (Chicago, 1971) p. 4.

8. On the history of Parliament, see *Jani Anglorum Facies Altera*, Wilkins, vol. II, cols 1026–7, and *Titles of Honour, ibid.*, cols 729ff.

9. J. Dodderidge, *The English Lawyer* (1631) sig. Iiiv. It is clear from internal evidence that this part of the work was written before Coke's *Reports* began to be published.

10. H. Finch, *A Description of the Common Laws of England* (1759) p. 52. This is the first translation of his *Nomotechnia*, published in Law French in 1613.

11. Selden probably owed his Parliamentary seats in Wiltshire to Pembroke; he was legal adviser to the earl of Kent, brother-in-law to Arundel, from (probably) 1619 – see Bodl. Lib., MS Selden supra 113.

12. *Commons Debates, 1628*, ed. R. C. Johnson *et al.* (New Haven, 1977) vol. II, pp. 572, 574, 576.

13. *Ibid.*, p. 356.

14. Wilkins, vol. I, col. 106 (my translation).

15. Ibid., vol. III, col. 2069.

16. Ibid., col. 2065.

17. Ibid., col. 2041.

18. Ibid., col. 2024.

19. Ibid., vol. I, col. 660 (my translation).

20. The medieval situation is discussed in M. R. Powicke, *Military Obligation in Medieval England* (Oxford, 1962); the sixteenth-century position by L. O. J. Boynton, *The Elizabethan Militia* (1967). See also the sensible remarks by Conrad Russell, *Parliaments and English Politics, 1621–1629* (Oxford, 1979) pp. 76–8.

21. Johnson, *Commons Debates, 1628*, vol. III, p. 375.

22. *Debates in the House of Lords, 1621–8*, ed. F. H. Relf (Camden Society, 3rd ser., XLII, 1929) p. 203.

23. Johnson, *Commons Debates, 1628*, vol. II, pp. 279–80.

24. Wilkins, vol. III, col. 2063.

25. See Clarendon, *History*, vol. I, p. 570.

26. B. Whitelocke, *Memorials of the English Affairs* (Oxford, 1853) vol. I, pp. 160–1.

27. Ibid., p. 171. On Whitelocke, see Ruth Spalding, *The Improbable Puritan* (1975), though the extent to which Whitelocke rewrote his own past still needs to be determined.

28. Whitelocke, *Memorials*, vol. I, pp. 171–2.

29. For his commission, see ibid., p. 172, and Anthony Wood's life of Selden in *Athenae Oxonienses*, ed. P. Bliss (1817) vol. III, col. 368. His membership of the Commons committee is recorded in the *CJ*, vol. II, p. 478.

30. D'Ewes's diary, BL Harl, MSS 163, fo. 254v.

31. J. Rushworth, *Historical Collections* (1721) vol. IV, p. 658.

32. See *CJ* vol. II, p. 632, for the committee to draw up the reply. The answer to the royal reply was ordered to be printed on 25 Oct. (*LJ*, vol. V, p. 423). For the date of the royal reply, see F. Madan, *Oxford Books* (Oxford, 1912) vol. II, p. 163. The most accessible texts of the declarations are in *An Exact Collection of all Remonstrances . . . beginning . . . in December 1641, and continued untill March the 21, 1643* (1643) sig. Ccc4v–Eee2 for the first parliamentary declaration, sig. Eee2v–Kkk4 for the royal reply and sig. Qqqqq4–Xxxxx4 for the second parliamentary declaration. That the parliamentary declaration was Selden's work was known to contemporaries: see Wood, in Bliss, *Athenae Oxonienses*, vol. III, col. 371. The Bodl. Lib. MSS are Selden supra 123 and 124, with the annotated copy of the King's reply being fos 120ff. of Selden supra 124. The Clark Library of the University of California, Los Angeles, possesses another manuscript which seems to belong to this enterprise.

33. *An Exact Collection*, sig, Eee4v.

34. Bodl. Lib., MS Selden supra 124, fo. 43v.

35. *An Exact Collection*, sig. Ttttt1v, Xxxxx3v.

36. See *CJ*, vol. II, p. 663; vol. III, pp. 118, 172 and 173.

37. Rushworth, *Historical Collections*, vol. V, p. 481. (This fact has been ignored by every biographer of Selden.)

38. On this crisis, and the Middle Group generally, see of course Underdown, *Pride's Purge*, together with Valerie Pearl, 'The "Royal Independents" in the English Civil War', *TRHS*, 5th ser., XVIII (1968) 69–96.

39. Wilkins, vol. III, col. 2076.

40. Ibid., p. 1073.

41. See W. A. Shaw, *A History of the English Church during the Civil Wars and under the Commonwealth, 1640–1660* (1900) vol. I, pp. 43 and 95.

42. Wilkins, vol. III, col. 2015.

43. Ibid., vol. I, cols 1676–9.

44. Underdown, *Pride's Purge*, p. 289; Worden, *Rump Parliament*, p. 339.

45. Rolle of course became Lord Chief Justice of the Commonwealth; Whitelocke served on its Council of State. Hale, despite having been counsel for many Royalists (and also, it should be said, for the Eleven Members), took the Engagement and chaired the famous 'Hale Committee' on law reform under the Rump. Under the Protectorate Whitelocke and Hale were obviously entirely at home (Rolle died in 1656). See the *DNB* for their lives, and Worden, *Rump Parliament*, pp. 107ff. for the Hale Committee.

46. *Puritanism and Liberty*, ed. A. S. P. Woodhouse (1951) p. 58.

47. Ireton does not seem to have practised at the Bar – see *DNB*. Whitelocke defended the memory of Ireton as one of 'the profession' in 1660 – see Spalding, *Improbable Puritan*, p. 219 – and was his friend in 1649 (ibid., p. 116).

48. *The Complete Prose Works of John Milton*, ed. E. Sirluck (New Haven, 1959) vol. II, 350, 513.

49. Woodhouse, *Puritanism*, p. (38). See also W. M. Lamont, *Godly Rule* (1969) p. 176.

50. He lived with the countess of Kent until her death in 1651, and various scurrilous stories were told about his sex life: see J. Aubrey, *Brief Lives*, ed. O. Lawson Dick (Harmondsworth, 1962) p. 331.

51. For Whitelocke, see Spalding, *Improbable Puritan*, p. 248; for Hale, the *DNB*.

52. See his *Life*, p. 924, for his remarks about e.g. Thomas May.

53. Ibid., p. 923.

54. See Tuck, *Natural Rights Theories*, pp. 101–18.

55. *Works of Henry Hammond*, ed. W. Fulman (1684) vol. I, p. 311.

56. Dudley Digges, *The Unlawfulnesse of Subjects, Taking up Arms against their Soveraign*, (n.p., 1644) sig. Q2.

57. For Hobbes, see Tuck, *Natural Rights Theories*, pp. 119–32.

58. Digges, *Unlawfulnesse of Subjects*, sig. P1.

59. [E. Hyde], *Transcendent and Multiplied Rebellion and Treason discovered by the Lawes of this Land* [Oxford] (1645) sig. A2. The identification of this anonymous work as Hyde's was made by Macray in his edition of Clarendon's *History*, vol. II, p. 292.

60. Ibid., sig. C1.

61. See Tuck, *Natural Rights Theories*, pp. 107–8.

62. Ibid., p. 109.

64. Clarendon, *History*, vol. II, p. 292.

64. For Vaughan, see J. Gwyn Williams, 'Sir John Vaughan of Trawscoed, 1603–1674', *National Library of Wales Journal*, VIII (1953–4) pp. 33–48, 121–46, 225–43.

7. IDEOLOGY AND POLITICS IN THE PARLIAMENTARY ARMIES, 1645–9 *Mark Kishlansky*

1. Leo Solt, *Saints in Arms* (Stanford, 1959); William Haller, *Liberty and Reformation in the Puritan Revolution* (New York, 1955).

2. Christopher Hill, *The World Turned Upside Down* (1972).

3. C. H. Firth, *Cromwell's Army* (1902); Hill, *The World Turned Upside Down*.

4. Michael Walzer, *The Revolution of the Saints* (New York, 1968).

5. M. A. Kishlansky, *The Rise of the New Model Army* (Cambridge, 1979) ch. 7.

6. *CJ*, vol. V, p. 129.

7. J. Rushworth, *Historical Collections*, 8 vols (1721) vol. VII, pp. 744–9.

8. William Clarke's Accounts, Chequers MSS 782.

9. For the records of these debates see *The Clarke Papers*, ed. C. H. Firth, 4 vols (1891–1901); A. S. P. Woodhouse, *Puritanism and Liberty* (1938).

10. Rushworth, *Historical Collections*, vol. VI, pp. 510–12; A. L. Morton, *Freedom in Arms* (1975) pp. 101–10.

11. Rushworth, *Historical Collections*, vol. VI, pp. 564–70; William Haller and Godfrey Davies, *The Leveller Tracts* (New York, 1944) pp. 52–63. The additions to this tract (bracketed on pp. 60–1) should not be considered authentic.

12. Worcester College, Oxford, Clarke MSS, vol. XLI, fos 105–27.

13. Reprinted in Haller and Davies, *Leveller Tracts*, pp. 65–87.

14. S. R. Gardiner, *Constitutional Documents of the Puritan Revolution* (Oxford, 1906) pp. 333–5; Woodhouse, *Puritanism and Liberty*, pp. 443–5.

15. Rushworth, *Historical Collections*, vol. VII, pp. 744–9.

16. Gardiner, *Constitutional Documents*, pp. 316–25; Rushworth, *Historical Collections*, vol. VII, pp. 731–6.

17. Firth, *Clarke Papers*, vol. I, p. 349.

18. *The Parliamentary or Constitutional History of England*, 24 vols (1751–62) vol. XVIII, pp. 161–238.

19. Ibid., pp. 519–36.

20. The Army very nearly did disband twice during this period: at the end of July and in the middle of October, 1647. On both occasions intervening events scotched their carefully laid plans.

21. What the mob demanded was the restoration of the old militia committee, the reversal of a vote against a covenant taken by apprentices, and other rather arcane matters. For this, see Kishlansky, *Rise of the New Model Army*, pp. 266–7.

## 8.   FROM CAVALIER TO ROUNDHEAD TYRANNY, 1642–9   *Robert Ashton*

1. J. Rushworth, *Historical Collections*, 7 vols (1692) vol. IV, p. 653.

2. Clarendon, *History*, vol. II, pp. 85–6.

3. Lois G. Schwoerer, *'No Standing Armies!' The Anti-army Ideology in Seventeenth-Century England* (Baltimore, 1974) pp. 38–9. See also pp. 45–6.

4. Rushworth, *Historical Collections*, vol. V, p. 183.

5. [Thomas Povey], *The Moderator expecting sudden peace* (1643) p. 4.

6. *The Cordiall of Mr. David Jenkins or his Reply to H.P. . . . Answered* (1647) p. 19.

7. *The Ordinance and Declaration of the Lords and Commons for the Assessing* (Oxford, 1642) pp. 12–13; Clarendon, *History*, vol. II, p. 427.

8. Clarendon, *History*, vol. II, pp. 247–8. See A. Everitt, *The Community of Kent and the Great Rebellion, 1640–60* (Leicester, 1966) pp. 95–107; T. S. P. Woods, *Prelude to Civil War: Mr. Justice Malet and the Kentish Petitions* (1980) *passim*.

9. Clarendon, *History*, vol. II, pp. 525–6.

10. *CSPD*, 1645–7, p. 11.

11. *To . . . the Lords and Commons . . . the humble Petition of the Knights, Gentry, Clergy and Commonalty of the County of Kent* (1648) (BL E441 (25)) p. 2.

12. For a similar request in the Surrey petition presented on 16 May 1648, see *Old Parliamentary History* (1751–62) vol. xvii, p. 139.

13. On the royal reply see esp. C. C. Weston, 'The Theory of Mixed Monarchy under Charles I and After', *EHR*, lxxv (1966) esp. 426–33.

14. See e.g. *His Majesties Declaration to all his Loving Subjects of August 12, 1642* (Cambridge, 1642) pp. 73–4; 'The Remonstrance of the Commons of England to the House of Commons . . .' (1642), *Somers Tracts*, 2nd coll., ii (1750), 258; *His Majesties Declaration to all his loving Subjects in Answer to a Declaration . . . 3 June 1643* (Oxford, 1643) p. 35.

15. BL Add. MSS 31, 116, fo. 295; BL Harl. MSS, 164, fo. 243. For other examples of the questioning by both Royalists and Parliamentarians of the legality of parliamentary ordinances, see Bodl. Lib., Clarendon MSS, 21, fo. 69; *His Majesties Answer to the xix Propositions* (1642) p. 2: Lawrence Wormock, *Sober Sadnes: or Historical Observations* (Oxford, 1643) pp. 37–8; *Judge Jenkins' Remonstrance to the Lords and Commons* (1648) p. 5; *Somers Tracts*, 2nd coll., ii, 259–60; Clement Walker, 'The Mystery of the Two Juntoes, Presbyterian and Independent' (1648) in *Select Tracts Relating to the Civil Wars in England . . .* ed. F. Maseres (1815) vol. ii, p. 348; 'The Parliamentary Diary of John Boys, 1647–8', ed. D. E. Underdown, *Bulletin of the Institute of Historical Research*, xxxix (1966) 161–2.

16. *Judge Jenkins' Remonstrance*, no pagination. John Lilburne, *The Peoples prerogative and privileges* (1648) pp. 40–1. For similar observations in the Leveller petitions of Mar. and Nov. 1647, see *Leveller Manifestoes of the Puritan Revolution*, ed. D. M. Wolfe (1967) pp. 136–7, 240–1; Walker, 'The Mystery of the Two Juntoes', in Maseres, *Select Tracts*, vol. ii, pp. 338–9.

17. Wolfe, *Leveller Manifestos*, pp. 121, 136.

18. D. E. Underdown, *Somerset in the Civil War and Interregnum* (Newton Abbot, 1973) pp. 135–6.

19. *The Lawes Subversion: or Sir John Maynard's Case truly stated* (1648) (BL E431(2)) p. 6. See also [Nathaniel Ward], *To the High and Honourable Parliament of England . . . the Humble Petitions, Serious Suggestions* (1648) pp. 12–13.

20. *His Majesties Declaration to all his Loving Subjects of August 12, 1642* pp. 70–1.

21. Bodl. Lib., Clarendon MSS 21, fo. 69.

22. On the violation of parliamentary privilege in the matter of the eleven members, see *A Declaration of the Lord Maior Aldermen. . . of London* (1647) pp. 4, 8; *The Petition of Right of the Freeholders and Freemen of the Kingdom of England . . .* (1648) (BL E422 (9)) pp. 9–16, 19; [Ward], *Parliament*, pp. 17, 18.

23. *The Parliament under the Power of the Sword* (1648) p. 4.

24. W. Prynne, 'The Case of the old secured, secluded and now excluded Members, briefly and truly stated' (1660), *Somers Tracts*, 3rd coll., ii (1751) 189–96.

25. *A New Found Stratagem* (1647) pp. 5–6 and *passim*.

26. D. Jenkins, *An Apology for the Army touching* (1647) *passim*, and esp. pp. 2–4, 8,10.

27. *His Majesties Declaration to all his Loving Subjects of August 12, 1642* p. 63; cf. the King's declaration on the parliamentary assessment ordinance of 8 Dec. 1642, *The Ordinance and Declaration of the Lords and Commons for the Assessing* (Oxford, 1642) pp. 13–14; Clarendon, *History*, vol. II, p. 427; for similar remarks on the arbitrariness of the 'twentieth part', see *A letter from a Scholler in Oxfordshire to his Uncle* (Oxford, 1643) p. 17; Wormock, *Sober Sadnes*, pp. 41–2.

28. Everitt, *Community of Kent*, p. 157; A. Hassell Smith, 'Militia Rates and Militia Statutes, 1558–1663', in *The English Commonwealth, 1547–1640* ed. P. Clark, A. G. R. Smith, and N. Tyacke (Leicester, 1979) pp. 107–9.

29. D. Jenkins, *Lex Terrae* (1647) pp. 1–2.

30. [Ward], *Parliament*, p. 17. See also p. 25.

31. *His Majesties Declaration to all his Loving Subjects of August 12, 1642*, pp. 74–5.

32. See R. Ashton, *The City and the Court, 1603–1643* (Cambridge, 1979) pp. 83–98, 101–36, 149–56.

33. Wolfe, *Leveller Manifestoes*, pp. 124, 136–7, 139; *The Leveller Tracts*, ed. W. Haller and G. Davies (Gloucester, Mass., 1964) p. 159. See also the petition of September 1648 against the Treaty of Newport, *Old Parliamentary History*, vol. XVII, p. 457; Dr Robert Brenner points out also that the leaders of the City Independents in the late 1640s and the Commonwealth period were drawn preponderantly from the ranks of domestic rather than overseas traders, with the notable exception of what he calls 'the colonial-interloping complex'. (R. Brenner, 'The Civil War Politics of London's Merchant Community', *Past and Present*, no. 58 (1973) 92, 96–7. On the Commonwealth, see J. E. Farnell, 'The Usurpation of Honest London Householders: Barebone's Parliament' *EHR* LXXXII (1967) 38.

34. *Acts and Ordinances of the Interregnum*, ed. C. H. Firth and R. S. Rait (1911) vol. I, pp. 311–5, 322–7, 571–3.

35. BL Add. MSS 15, 903, fo. 32.

36. *His Majesties Declaration to all his Loving Subjects of August 12, 1642* p. 49.

37. For references to complaints against the Scots in this regard, see BL Add. MSS 37,978, fos 28–28(b), 29(b), 34; Bodl. Lib., Tanner MSS 59, fos 195, 216–6(b), 225, 254, 265, 266, 294, 321, 366–6(b), 387–7(b), 392–5; Tanner MSS 60, fo. 361; Washington D.C., Folger Library, Folger MSS Ga 6, fos 5–7; *Some Papers given by the Commissioners* [of the Parliament of Scotland] (Edinburgh, 1646) pp. 14–15; *Old Parliamentary History*, vol. XIV, pp. 85–9, 145–50.

38. *The Petition of Right of the Free-holders and Free-men of the Kingdom of England humbly presented to the Lords and Commons* (1648) (BL E422(9)) pp. 16–17, also p. 20. See also *Vox Populi: or the Supplication* (1647) *passim; The Earnest and Passionate Petition of divers thousands of Well-affected Knights, Gentlemen, Freeholders, Tradesmen and others* (1648) (BL E425(10)) pp. 2–3.

39. *A Publicke Declaration and Solemne Protestation . . . against the illegall Intollerable . . . Grievance of Free-quarter* (1648) (BL E426(3)) pp. 1–6. See also BL Stowe MSS 361, fos 100–100(b); [Ward], *Parliament*, p. 25.

40. C. Holmes, *The Eastern Association in the English Civil War* (Cambridge, 1974) p. 188.

41. D. M, Wolfe, *Leveller Manifestoes*, pp. 243–7: cf. John Lilburne, *The Peoples Prerogative and Privileges* (1648) pp. 42–4; and Haller and Davies, *Leveller Tracts*, pp. 164, 166.

42. BL Stowe MSS 361, fo. 100.

43. Firth and Rait, *Acts*, vol. I, pp. 953–4; *Old Parliamentary History*, vol. xv, p. 406.

44. For examples of complaints against the operation of Indemnity Ordinances see *The Petition of Right of the Freeholders*, pp. 8–9, 18; Walker, 'The Mystery of the Two Juntoes', in Maseres, *Select Tracts*, vol. II, p. 336.

45. J. S. Morrill, *The Revolt of the Provinces* (1976) p. 76. Yet even these sweeping provisions did not satisfy the soldiers (see ibid., pp. 175–6).

46. *Old Parliamentary History*, vol. XVII, p. 454.

47. See e.g. Bodl. Lib., Tanner MSS 62, fo. 118; Bodl. Lib., Tanner MSS 64, fo. 156; *His Majesties Answer to the xix Propositions* (1642) p. 3; The *Ordinance and Declaration of the Lords and Commons for the Assessing* p. 13; Clarendon, *History*, vol. II, pp. 427, 434, 445; *A Letter from a Scholler in Oxfordshire to his Uncle* (1643) p. 17; *Three Letters: the first from an Officer* (Oxford, 1643) pp. 32–3; Wormock, *Sober Sadnes*, pp. 39–41.

48. *The Lawes Subversion: or Sir John Maynard's Case Truly Stated*, passim, and esp. pp. 7–12. See also P. Gregg, *Free-born John* (1961) pp. 197–8.

49. BL Egerton MSS 2618, fo. 31.

50. *Judge Jenkins Plea* (1648) passim; *Judge Jenkins Remonstrance*, p. 5.

51. John Lilburne, *Peoples Prerogative*, introduction, no pagination.

52. Wolfe, *Leveller Manifestoes*, pp. 156–88, esp. pp. 163–9.

53. *Memorials of the Great Civil War in England*, ed. H. Cary (1842) vol. II, pp. 141–8. For the analogy with Christ as applied to the execution of the King, see R. Ashton, *The English Civil War: Conservatism and Revolution, 1603–1649* (1978) pp. 346–7.

54. James Howell, *A Letter to the Earle of Pembrooke* (1647) (BL E522(5)) p. 11.

55. *The Lawes Subversion: or Sir John Maynard Case Truly Stated*, pp. 13–14.

56. Walker, 'The Mystery of the Two Juntoes' in Maseres, *Select Tracts*, vol. II, p. 338.

57. On the peculiarities of local government in Cheshire, see J. S. Morrill, *Cheshire, 1630–1660* (Oxford, 1974) passim.

58. [Edward Bowles], *Manifest Truths* (1646) p. 51.

59. Bodl. Lib., Tanner MSS 58, fo. 173; see also fos 218–218(b), 230–0(b).

60. Walker, 'The Mystery of the Two Juntoes', in Maseres, *Select Tracts*, vol. II, p. 339. On King, see Edward King, *A Discovery of the Arbitrary, Tyranicall and Illegal Action* (1647); also C. Holmes, 'Colonel King and Lincolnshire Politics, 1642–1646', *Historical Journal*, XVI (1973) 451–84.

61. *The Committee at Stafford, 1643–1645*, ed. D. H. Pennington and I. A. Roots (Manchester, 1957) p. 343.

62. Walker, 'The Mystery of the Two Juntoes', in Maseres, *Select Tracts*, vol. II, pp. 338, 351.

63. Bodl. Lib., Tanner MSS 60, fo. 254. For a no less eloquent denunciation by Dorset men, some of whom, significantly, had themselves been Clubmen, see *The Declaration of the County of Dorset* (1648) (BL E427(26)) esp. pp. 3–6. For a Kentish complaint, see *A Letter from a Gentleman in Kent* (1648) (BL E448(34)) esp. pp. 1–2.

64. *The Earnest and Passionate Petition of divers thousands of Well-affected Knights, Gentlemen, Freeholders, Citizens, Tradesmen and others*, esp. pp. 3–4; *A Publike Declaration and Solemne Protestation . . . against the Illegal, Intollerable . . . Grievance of Free-Quarter* p. 6.

65. See, for example, the army's declaration or remonstrance of 14 June 1647 (Haller and Davies, *The Leveller Tracts*, p. 62). The power given to committees and deputy lieutenants is also questioned in the Heads of the Proposals (*The Constitutional Documents of the Puritan Revolution, 1625–1660*, ed. S. R. Gardiner (Oxford, 1962) p. 325). Deputy lieutenants are also included in these criticisms.

66. Walker, 'Mystery of the Two Juntoes', in Maseres, *Select Tracts*, vol. II, p. 338.

67. King, *Discovery*, pp. 11–20.

68. *The Declaration and Resolution of the Knightes, Gentry and Freeholders of the County of Kent, 29 May, 1648*. (BL E445(10)) pp. 1–3. See also *A Declaration of the Inhabitants of the County of Kent to the Disterbers* (sic) *of the peace* (1648) (BL E443(9)) no foliation.

69. [Howell], *A Letter to the Earle of Pembrooke*, pp. 10–11. For examples of earlier complaints about the incompleteness of Parliament see *His Majesties Declaration to all his Loving Subjects of August 12, 1642*, pp. 76–77; *The Ordinance and Declaration of the Lords and Commons for the Assessing*, p. 14.

70. *The Cordiall of Mr. David Jenkins or his Reply to H.P. . . . Answered*, esp. pp. 6, 16. For Jenkins's arguments, see Jenkins, *Lex Terrae*, p. 11, *The Cordiall of Judge Jenkins* (1647) pp. 9–10, *An Apology for the Army touching*, p. 5.

71. BL Add. MSS 25,277, fos 60–1; *Old Parliamentary History*, vol. III, pp. 87–116; Clarendon; *History*, vol. III, pp. 303–5.

72. *An Apology for the Army touching*, p. 9.

73. *His Majesties Answer to the xix Propositions*, p. 3.

74. *The Cordiall of Mr. David Jenkins . . . Answered*, pp. 19–20.

75. *Puritanism and Liberty*, ed. A. S. P. Woodhouse (1966) pp. 111–12.

76. Maseres, *Select Tracts*, vol. II, p. 349.

77. Bodl. Lib., Tanner MSS 58, fo. 54. See also Jenkins, *The Cordiall of Judge Jenkins*, pp. 4–7; *The Vindication of Judge Jenkins* (1647) pp. 1–2.

78. [Ward], *Parliament*, p. 12.

79. *The Declaration of Many Thousands of the City of Canterbury or County of Kent* (1648) (BL E421(23)) pp. 4,7.

80. *CSPD*, 1648–9, pp. 63–4; *To the Lords and Commons Assembled in Parliament . . . the Humble Petition . . . of the County of Kent* (1648) [BL E441(25)] pp. 2–3; *The Declaration together with the Petition . . . of the County of Hampeshire* (1648) (BL E447(18)); *The Declaration of the County of Dorset* (1648) (BL E447(26)), pp. 3, 4–5; HMC, *7th report* (House of Lords MSS) p. 30: *Old Parliamentary History*, vol. XVII, pp. 139–41.

81. *The Declaration of Col. Poyer and Col. Powel and the Officers and Soldiers under their Command* (1648) (BL E435(9)) pp. 1–6; *Collonell Powell and Col. Poyers Letters to His Highnesse the Prince of Wales* (1648) (BL E436(14)); *The Declaration of the King's Army in South Wales* (1648) (BL E438(13)) p. 6; *The Declaration of Sir Marmaduke Langdale . . . and of the Gentlemen . . . now in Action for His Majesties Service in the Northern Parts* (1648) (BL 446(17)) p. 7.

82. On this see C. C. Weston, 'The Authorship of the *Freeholders Grand Inquest*', *EHR*, XIV (1980) esp. 78–86.

83. Bodl. Lib., Clarendon MSS 31, fo. 86; *A Declaration of the Knights, Gentlemen and Freeholders of the County of Surrey concerning their late Petition* (1648) (BL E433(8)); *CSPD*, 1648–9, pp. 63–4; *Old Parliamentary History*, vol. XVII, pp. 139–41, 169–70: Underdown, *Diary of John Boys*, p. 164.

84. Bodl. Lib., MSS Add. C. 132, fos 70–70(b).

85. C. V. Wedgwood, *The Trial of Charles I* (1964) p. 131.

86. *His Majesties Answer to the xix Propositions*, p. 22.

87. Wedgwood, *Trial of Charles I*, p. 164.

# Notes on Contributors

ROBERT ASHTON has been Professor of English History at the University of East Anglia since 1963. He is a graduate of London University, a former pupil of the late Professor R. H. Tawney. He was a Visiting Fellow of All Souls College, Oxford, in 1973–4. He is the author of *The Crown and the Money Market, 1603–1640* (1960), *James I by His Contemporaries* (1969), *The English Civil War: Conservatism and Revolution, 1603–1649* (1978) and *The City and the Court, 1603–1643* (1979).

ANTHONY FLETCHER is senior lecturer in History at the University of Sheffield. He has published *Tudor Rebellions* (1967), *A County Community in Peace and War: Sussex, 1600–1660* (1975) and *The Outbreak of the English Civil War* (1981).

ROGER HOWELL, JR., Professor of History, Bowdoin College, Brunswick, Maine. Graduate of Bowdoin College and Oxford; formerly president of Bowdoin College, Visiting Professor of History at the University of Maine, and Junior Research Fellow at St John's College, Oxford. His publications include *Newcastle-upon-Tyne and the Puritan Revolution* (1967); *Sir Philip Sidney: The Shepherd Knight* (1968); *Cromwell* (1977); *Monopoly on the Tyne, 1650–58: Papers Relating to Ralph Gardner* (1978).

RONALD HUTTON is a lecturer in History at the University of Bristol. He was formerly an undergraduate in Cambridge and a graduate student in Oxford, where he was also a Fellow of Magdalen College from 1979 to 1981. He is the author of *The Royalist War Effort, 1642–1646* (1981) and of several articles. He is currently working on a book on the Restoration Settlement.

MARK KISHLANSKY received his M.A. and Ph.D. from Brown University where he studied under David Underdown. He is currently Associate Professor of English History at the University of Chicago. His writings include *The Rise of the New Model Army* (Cambridge, 1979) and several articles on political developments during the English Revolution.

JOHN MORRILL is an Oxford-trained historian who migrated to Cambridge via the University of Stirling in 1975. He is now Fellow, Tutor and Director of Studies in History at Selwyn College, Cambridge, and a University Lecturer in History. He has published five monographs, notably *The Revolt of the Provinces* (1976; revised ed. 1980), and a dozen articles. He is just completing a general study of the period 1637–62 for Longman, and has been commissioned to write the later-seventeenth-century volume for the New Oxford History of England.

DONALD PENNINGTON is Fellow and Tutor in Modern History at Balliol College, Oxford, and was formerly Reader in History at Manchester University. He is the author of *Seventeenth-Century Europe* (1970); with D. Brunton, of *Members of the Long Parliament* (1954); with Ivan Roots, *The Committee at Stafford, 1643–45* (1957); and of many articles.

RICHARD TUCK is Fellow and Director of Studies in History at Jesus College, Cambridge, and a University Lecturer in History. He is the author of *Natural Rights Theories* (Cambridge, 1979) and of a number of articles both on seventeenth-century thought and on political philosophy.

# INDEX